Automotive Electrical Systems

**By Chek-Chart,
a Division of
The H. M. Goushā Company**

Ken Layne, CGAM, *Editor*
Sydnie W. Changelon, *Contributing Editor*
Gordon Clark, *Managing Editor*

Harper & Row, Publishers
New York Hagerstown Philadelphia San Francisco London

Acknowledgments

The comments and suggestions of the following educators were invaluable: Karl A. Pape, DeAnza College, Cupertino, Calif.; Don Nilson, Chabot College, Hayward, Calif.;

In producing this series of textbooks for automobile mechanics, Chek-Chart has drawn extensively on the technical and editorial knowledge of the nation's carmakers and suppliers. Automotive design is a technical, fast-changing field, and we gratefully acknowledge the help of the following companies in allowing us to present the most up-to-date information and illustrations possible:

- Allen Testproducts
- American Motors Corporation
- Borg-Warner Corporation
- British Leyland UK Limited
- Caldo Automotive Supply
- Champion Spark Plug Company
- Chrysler Corporation
- Ford Motor Company
- Fram Corporation, A Bendix Company
- General Motors Corporation
    - AC-Delco Division
    - Delco-Remy Division
    - Rochester Products Division
    - Saginaw Steering Gear Division
    - Buick Motor Division
    - Cadillac Motor Car Division
    - Chevrolet Motor Division
    - Oldsmobile Division
    - Pontiac Division
- Marquette Mfg. Co., a division of Applied Power Inc.
- The Prestolite Company, An Eltra Company
- Robert Bosch Corporation
- Sun Electric Corporation
- Volkswagen of America

The authors have made every effort to ensure that the material in this book is as accurate and up-to-date as possible. However, neither Chek-Chart nor Harper & Row nor any related companies can be held responsible for mistakes or omissions, or for changes in procedures or specifications made by the carmakers or suppliers.

At Chek-Chart, editorial contributions were made by Jim Ashborn, Roger L. Fennema (CGAM), and William Grinager. Laura Kenyon and Ray Lyons participated in the production of the book, under the direction of Elmer M. Thompson. Original art and photographs were produced by Jim Geddes, Gordon Agur, Kalton C. Lahue, and F. J. Zienty, and coordinated by Gerald McEwan. Paul E. Sanderson is an educational advisor for the series, and the entire project is under the general direction of Robert J. Mahaffay and Robert M. Bleiweiss.

For Harper & Row, the sponsoring editor is John A. Woods. The production manager is Laura Argento and the designers are James Stockton and Donna Davis.

On The Cover:
The Chrysler Electronic Lean-Burn Ignition System, courtesy of the Chrysler Corporation.

Automotive Electrical Systems, Classroom Manual and Shop Manual Copyright © 1978 by Chek-Chart, a Division of The H. M. Gousha Company.

Library of Congress Cataloging and Publication Data:
Chek-Chart, 1978
  Automotive Electrical Systems
  (Canfield Press/Chek-Chart Automotive Series)
Includes index.
1. Classroom Manual.   2. Shop Manual.
ISBN: 0-06-454000-6
Library of Congress Catalog Card No.: 78-447

Contents

Chapter 5 — A.C. Charging System
On-Car Inspection and Testing 47

Charging System Symptoms
and Possible Causes 47

Charging System Inspection 47

Alternator Testing Overview 48

Testing Specific Alternators 49

Alternator Testing with an Oscilloscope 60

Field Relay and Regulator Service 62

Chapter 6 — Alternator Overhaul 65

Alternator Removal 65

Alternator Bench Tests and Procedures 65

Alternator Overhaul Procedures 69

Delco-Remy 10-SI Alternator
Overhaul Procedure 70

Delco-Remy 10-DN Alternator
Overhaul Procedure 73

Motorcraft Rear-Terminal
Alternator Overhaul Procedure 75

Motorcraft Side-Terminal
Alternator Overhaul Procedure 78

Chrysler Late-Model Standard
Alternator Overhaul Procedure 80

Chrysler Early-Model Alternator
Overhaul Procedure 83

Motorola 37-Ampere Alternator
Overhaul Procedure 84

Alternator Installation 87

PART THREE —
STARTING SYSTEM SERVICE 89

Chapter 7 —
Starting System Testing 90

System Inspection 90

On-Car Testing 91

Cranking Voltage Test 93

Current Draw Test 97

Circuit Resistance Tests 94

Starting Safety Switch Test
and Adjustment 98

Chapter 8 —
Starter Motor Overhaul 100

Starter Motor Removal 100

Starter Motor and
Solenoid Bench Test Procedures 100

Starter Motor Overhaul Procedures 104

Delco-Remy Solenoid-Actuated
Starter Overhaul Procedure 105

Motorcraft Solenoid-Actuated
Starter Overhaul Procedure 107

Motorcraft Movable Pole Shoe
Starter Overhaul Procedure 109

Chrysler Reduction Gear Starter
Overhaul Procedure 111

Chrysler Direct Drive Starter
Overhaul Procedure 114

Starter Motor Installation 116

PART FOUR —
IGNITION SYSTEM SERVICE 117

Chapter 9 —
Breaker-Point Ignition
System Testing 118

Primary Circuit Voltmeter Tests 118

Ballast Resistor Test
and Replacement 121

Coil Tests 123

Condenser Tests 127

Secondary Circuit Inspection 128

Oscilloscope Testing 129

Chapter 10 — Breaker-Point Ignition
Service and Adjustment 138

Installing and
Adjusting Breaker Points 138

Checking and Adjusting Dwell 140

Ignition Timing Tests and Adjustments 143

Cap, Rotor, and Cable Replacement 151

Spark Plug Service 151

Contents

Introduction to Automotive Electrical Systems

Automotive Electrical Systems is part of the Harper & Row/Chek-Chart Automotive Series. The package for each course has two volumes, a *Classroom Manual* and a *Shop Manual*.

Other titles in this series include:
- Automatic Transmissions
- Fuel Systems and Emission Controls
- Engine Performance Diagnosis and Tune-Up
- Heating and Air Conditioning (planned)
- Steering, Suspension, Alignment, Wheels, and Tires (planned).
- Brake Systems (planned)
- Engine Overhaul and Rebuilding (planned)
- Manual Transmissions, Drivelines, and Differentials (planned).

Each book is written to help the instructor teach students to become excellent professional automotive mechanics. The 2-manual texts are the core of a complete learning system that leads a student from basic theories to actual hands-on experience.

The entire series is job-oriented, especially designed for students who intend to work in the car service profession. A student will be able to use the knowledge gained from these books and from the instructor to get and keep a job. Learning the material and techniques in these volumes is a giant leap toward a satisfying, rewarding career.

The books are divided into *Classroom Manuals* and *Shop Manuals* for an improved presentation of the descriptive information and study lessons, along with the practical testing, repair, and overhaul procedures. The manuals are to be used together: the descriptive chapters in the *Classroom Manual* correspond to the application chapters in the *Shop Manual*.

Each book is divided into several parts, and each of these parts is complete by itself. Instructors will find the chapters to be complete, readable, and well thought-out. Students will benefit from the many learning aids included, as well as from the thoroughness of the presentation.

The series was researched and written by the editorial staff of Chek-Chart, and was produced by Harper & Row Publishers. For over 50 years, Chek-Chart has provided car and equipment manufacturers' service specifications to the automotive service field. Chek-Chart's complete, up-to-date automotive data bank was used extensively to prepare this textbook series.

Because of the comprehensive material, the hundreds of high-quality illustrations, and the inclusion of the latest automotive technology, instructors and students alike will find that these books will keep their value over the years. In fact, they will form the core of the master mechanic's professional library.

How
To Use
This Book

Why Are There Two Manuals?

This two-volume text — **Automotive Electrical Systems** — is not like any other textbook you've ever used before. It is actually two books, the *Classroom Manual* and the *Shop Manual*. They should be used together.

The *Classroom Manual* will teach you what you need to know about basic electricity and the electrical systems in a car. The *Shop Manual* will show you how to fix and adjust those systems, and how to repair the electrical parts of a car.

The *Classroom Manual* will be valuable in class and at home, for study and for reference. It has text and pictures that you can use for years to refresh your memory about the basics of automotive electrical systems.

In the *Shop Manual*, you will learn about test procedures, troubleshooting, and overhauling the systems and parts you are studying in the *Classroom Manual*. Use the two manuals together to fully understand how the parts work, and how to fix them when they don't work.

What's In These Manuals?

There are several aids in the *Classroom Manual* that will help you learn more:

1. The text is broken into short bits for easier understanding and review.

2. Each chapter is fully illustrated with drawings and photographs.

3. Key words in the text are printed in **boldface type** and are defined on the same page and in a glossary at the end of the manual.

4. Review questions are included for each chapter. Use these to test your knowledge.

5. A brief summary of every chapter will help you to review for exams.

6. Every few pages you will find short blocks of ''nice to know'' information, in addition to the main text.

7. At the back of the *Classroom Manual* there is a sample test, similar to those given for National Institute for Automotive Service Excellence (NIASE) certification. Use it to help you study and to prepare yourself when you are ready to be certified as an expert in one of several areas of automobile mechanics.

The *Shop Manual* has detailed instructions on overhaul, test, and service procedures. These are easy to understand, and many have step-by-step, photo-illustrated explanations that guide you through the procedures. This is what you'll find in the *Shop Manual*:

1. Helpful information tells you how to use and maintain shop tools and test equipment.
2. Safety precautions are detailed.
3. System diagrams help you locate trouble-spots while you learn to read the diagrams.
4. Tips the professionals use are presented clearly and accurately.
5. A full index will help you quickly find what you need.
6. Test procedures and troubleshooting hints will help you work better and faster.

Where Should I Begin?

If you already know something about a car's basic electrical system and how to repair it, you may find that parts of this book are a helpful review. If you are just starting in car repair, then the subjects covered in these manuals may be all new to you.

Your instructor will design a course to take advantage of what you already know, and what facilities and equipment are available to work with. You may be asked to take certain chapters of these manuals out of order. That's fine. The important thing is to really understand each subject before you move on to the next.

Study the vocabulary words in boldface type. Use the review questions to help you understand the material. While reading in the *Classroom Manual*, refer to your *Shop Manual* to relate the descriptive text to the service procedures. And when you are working on actual car systems and electrical parts, look back to the *Classroom Manual* to keep the basic information fresh in your mind. Working on such a complicated piece of equipment as a modern car isn't always easy. Use the information in the *Classroom Manual*, the procedures of the *Shop Manual*, and the knowledge of your instructor to help you.

The *Shop Manual* is a good book for work, not just a good workbook. Keep it on hand while you're working on equipment. It folds flat on the workbench and under the car, and can withstand quite a bit of rough handling.

When you do test procedures and overhaul equipment, you will also need a source of accurate manufacturers' specifications. Most auto shops have either the carmaker's annual shop service manuals, which lists these specifications, or an independent guide, such as the **Chek-Chart Car Care Guide**. This unique book, which is updated every year, gives you the complete service instructions, electronic ignition troubleshooting tips, and tune-up information that you need to work on specific cars.

PART ONE

Basic Electrical Test Procedures

1

Circuit Tracing, Troubleshooting, and Wiring Repair

Finding the cause of an electrical problem and then repairing that problem can be done in a haphazard way or in a logical, organized manner. The hit-or-miss approach to electrical service is inefficient and inaccurate. Time and effort can be wasted without solving the problem. An organized approach to service is often called troubleshooting. It consists of a step-by-step examination of the problem, isolation of the cause, and repair.

We begin by reviewing automotive wiring diagrams, which can be one of the troubleshooter's most helpful guides. Then, you will be introduced to a 10-step troubleshooting checklist that can guide you through almost any electrical service job. Finally, some common wiring repair procedures will be presented.

In Chapter 2, we will examine the use of common troubleshooting tools. Before troubleshooting any electrical problem, the condition of the battery should be checked. Battery service is detailed in Chapter 3.

TRACING SPECIFIC CIRCUITS

As we learned in Chapter 5 of the *Classroom Manual*, circuit diagrams and system diagrams of an automotive electrical system are used to show you, on paper, what the electrical system of a particular car contains. These diagrams use color coding, circuit numbers, and symbols that you must be able to interpret. Figure 1-1 shows the symbols for some common automotive electrical parts and photographs of the units as they actually appear on the car.

When faced with the system diagram of an entire automobile, it may be difficult at first for you to locate and follow an individual circuit. However, once you get to know how the various automakers design their circuit diagrams, this will be easier. The first step in finding a particular circuit is to check the index to the diagram, if there is one.

Diagrams are usually indexed by grids, figure 1-2. The diagram is marked into equal sections like a street map. Each section is lettered along the top of the diagram and numbered along one side. The diagram's index will list a letter and number for each major part and many connection points, such as the fuse panel and the bulkhead connector. Figure 1-3 shows how to find a part when the letter and number of its grid are known.

If the diagram is not indexed, you must locate a major part by its location in the automobile. Most system diagrams are drawn so that the headlamps are on one side of the diagram and the taillamps are on the opposite side. The front of the car is usually on the left of the diagram, figure 1-4.

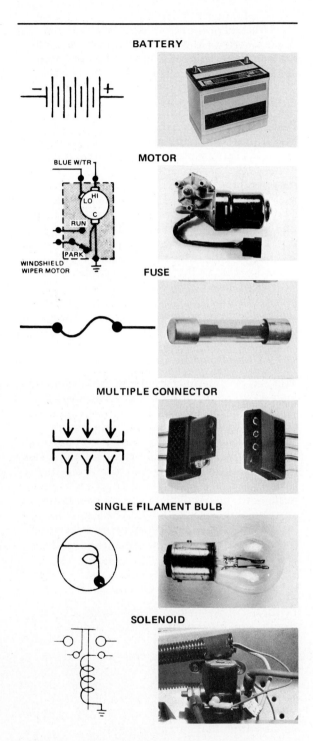

BATTERY

MOTOR

BLUE W/TR

WINDSHIELD
WIPER MOTOR

FUSE

MULTIPLE CONNECTOR

SINGLE FILAMENT BULB

SOLENOID

Figure 1-1. Here are some common automotive diagram symbols and the actual hardware that they represent.

Once you have found a major part of the circuit you are looking for, the rest of the circuit can be traced. Sometimes it is helpful to lay a blank sheet of paper on top of the system diagram and actually draw the individual circuit.

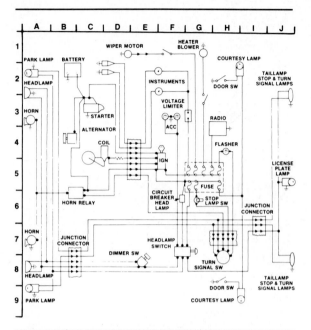

Figure 1-2. This simple system diagram has been divided into grids so that an index can be used.

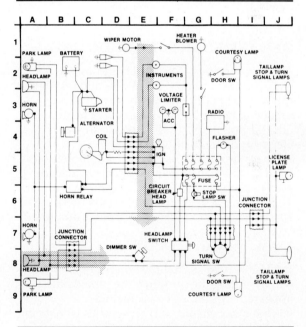

Figure 1-3. To find the dimmer switch, look in grid E8.

Remember, the circuit must include:
- A power source
- All related loads
- A ground connection for each circuit branch.

You need to know how to interpret an electrical diagram and relate it to the automobile in order to troubleshoot an automobile. There is more to troubleshooting, however, than being able to understand the circuit that has failed.

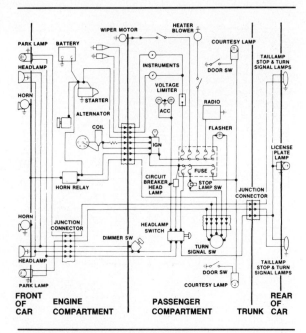

Figure 1-4. When no index is supplied, you must search the area of the diagram that corresponds to the area of the car in which the specific component is installed.

ORGANIZED TROUBLESHOOTING

The most common electrical faults are opens, shorts, and grounds. Test meters and test lights can be used to track down these faults. The following paragraphs explain the general methods that should be used to troubleshoot an electrical circuit malfunction.

The complexity of a modern automobile electrical system demands that you approach any system problem in a logical, organized manner. To help you develop this good habit, here is a 10-step checklist for electrical troubleshooting.

1. Ask The Owner Or Driver

If possible, you should talk to the person who was operating the car when the problem first appeared. Questions to ask include:
• What other circuits and accessories were being used when the problem occurred?
• Were there any sparks, odors, noises, or other unusual signs?
• Has this problem occurred before? If so, what repairs were made?

Many shops have a service writer who talks to the customers and prepares a work order for the mechanic to follow. If you cannot talk to the customer, check the work order for any of this information.

2. Know The System

Review the appropriate chapters in the *Class-*

room Manual or the manufacturer's shop manual to get a general idea of what circuits and loads are involved. This is the time to locate the car's system diagram for reference.

3. Operate The System

Now that you know what the general problem area is and what units are involved, you can begin to examine the automobile. You should make sure that the customer or service writer described the situation accurately and completely. For example, if the service order says "Fix headlamp high beams," you should turn on the high beams and see if they are totally out, glow dimly, or if only one side is not working. At the same time, you can look for related problems that may not have been noticed or mentioned. For example, is the high-beam indicator also completely out? These related symptoms can give you clues to the circuit problem.

4. List The Possible Causes

This can be a mental list, or you can make notes on a slip of paper. It should include any ideas you gained from steps 1 through 3. By looking at the system diagram, you may see other possible causes. For example, if the complaint is that a certain fuse is frequently burnt out, check to see what circuits share that fuse. If the fuse serves the turn signals, the backup lamps, the radio, and the windshield washer pump, then any one of those circuits could be bad. A list of possible causes will help you to organize your thoughts when you begin to actually test the system.

5. Isolate The Problem Circuit

If your list of possible causes includes several circuits, you must narrow the list. In step 4, our sample list of possible causes included the turn signals, the backup lamps, the radio, and the windshield washer pump. To narrow this list, you can turn off all other accessories and operate the suspected circuits one at a time. If you turn on one and the fuse blows, then the trouble will be within that particular circuit.

6. Know The Problem Circuit

Now that you know which circuit is to be investigated, you can study that circuit in detail. The circuit diagram will tell you:
• Where the circuit receives battery current
• What switches control current flow
• What circuit protection is involved
• How the loads operate
• Where the circuit is grounded.
   Understanding the total circuit is necessary if

you are to troubleshoot efficiently.

7. Test Systematically

All d.c. automotive circuits are connected to the battery terminal at one end and to ground at the other. There may be more than one ground path through parallel circuit branches, but the basic pattern remains. Because of this pattern, the most logical way to troubleshoot an automotive circuit is to start at one end and work your way to the other.

These general guidelines will help you when the problem circuit has many components:
• If the fault is in a single unit of a multiple-unit circuit, start the test at that unit.
• If the fault affects all the units in a multiple-unit circuit, start the test at the point where the circuit gets its power.

For example, if the problem is in a lighting circuit, are all the bulbs out? If only one bulb in the circuit will not operate, start testing at the bulb. If all the lights in a circuit do not operate, start testing at the point where the current first enters the circuit.

8. Verify Your Findings

Once the exact trouble spot has been located, be sure of the failure. For example, if the fault has been traced to a switch, remove the switch and test it separately. If it works outside of the circuit, then perhaps a loose connection is to blame. Checking and tightening a terminal connection takes much less time than replacing a part that was never at fault.

9. Repair

Only after you have narrowed the problem down to a specific conductor, terminal, or part should you begin repairs. Much of the *Shop Manual* covers repair procedures for specific electrical parts. Much of troubleshooting requires only the simple procedures for wiring repair that are outlined at the end of this chapter.

10. Test Your Repair

Many times this will be the last step of your troubleshooting procedure. If you operate the problem circuit and the problem is gone, then you have succeeded. Sometimes, a circuit will have more than one problem in it. For example, a lighting circuit could suffer from both a corroded connector and a loose ground wire. If cleaning the connector doesn't solve the problem, you must return to step 7 and test the remainder of the circuit. Testing your repair work can avoid added frustration for you and the customer.

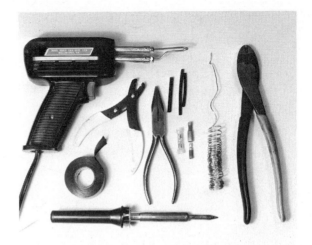

Figure 1-5. These tools will be needed during most wiring repair jobs.

WIRING REPAIR

Most automotive conductors are multistrand copper with plastic insulation, as we learned in Chapter 4 of the *Classroom Manual*. The rest of this chapter presents common repair procedures for this type of wiring. General guidelines for repairing or replacing specialized conductors will be presented throughout the remainder of the book, where they most apply.

Safety

Several steps of conductor repair involve special procedures that you must understand fully before beginning. Read all instructions before attempting a repair job.

You will be using a soldering tool to heat the copper wire, then melting solder (a soft tin-lead compound) onto the hot wire strands. Soldering tools can reach 500° F, so keep them away from your skin, clothing, wiring insulation, and all flammables. The melting solder gives off dangerous fumes. Don't inhale them.

Tools And Supplies

Most wiring repairs can be performed using these few tools, figure 1-5:
• Wire cutting, stripping, and crimping tool. This can be a combination tool or separate units. A knife and pliers will not do the job properly, but can be used in an emergency.
• Assorted styles and sizes of terminals.
• Soldering tool. A soldering gun heats faster than an iron, and often has a smaller tip for delicate jobs.
• Pliers for holding heated metal

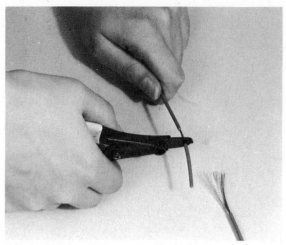

Figure 1-6. Removing insulation with a wire stripping tool.

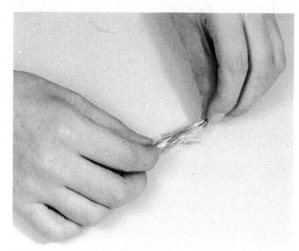

Figure 1-7. Braiding together the bare strands of wire.

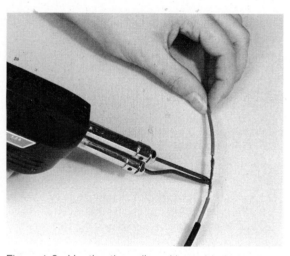

Figure 1-8. Heating the splice with a soldering tool.

Figure 1-9. Applying solder.

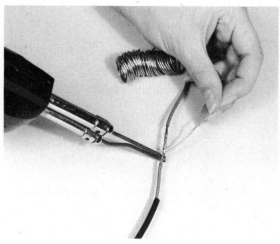

Figure 1-10. A correctly soldered splice.

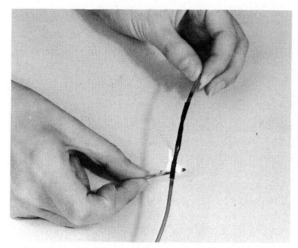

Figure 1-11. Insulating the splice with heat-shrink tubing.

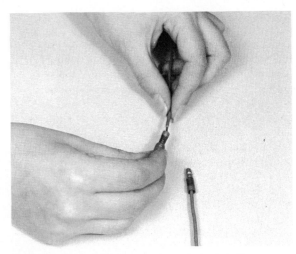

Figure 1-12. Inserting the stripped wire into the terminal barrel.

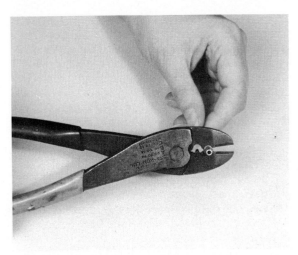

Figure 1-13. Crimping the terminal.

• Resin-core solder. The core material eats away oxidation on metal without leaving corrosion. Don't use acid-core solder, because the acid will promote corrosion.
• Electrician's tape, or heat-shrink tubing and heat source such as matches or a hot-air gun. These insulate the finished job.

Repair Methods

The three most common repair methods are:
• Splicing
• Terminal attachment
• Insulation repair.

Splicing

Connecting two or more wires without using a terminal is called splicing. It is commonly used to insert fusible links or to replace a section of damaged wiring. If you are going to use heat-shrink tubing for insulation, slip a piece over one of the sections of wire before soldering. Proceed as follows:
1. Use the wire stripping tool to remove about 1 inch of insulation from the wire ends to be joined, figure 1-6.
2. Braid the bare strands together and twist, figure 1-7.
3. Hold the broad side of the soldering tool to the bare wires, figure 1-8.
4. Touch the solder strand to the bare wire, not to the soldering tool, figure 1-9.
5. Use only enough solder to flow into the cracks, not a large amount, figure 1-10. Cool thoroughly.

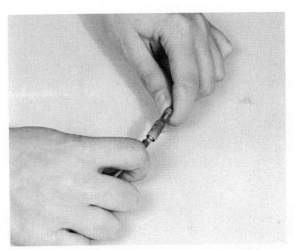

Figure 1-14. Insulating the terminal with the supplied tubing.

6. Wrap with tape or use heat-shrink tubing to insulate. To use heat-shrink tubing, slip a length of tubing over the wire and past the splice area before soldering. After soldering, slip the tubing over the splice. Apply heat using a match or a hot air gun, figure 1-11. The tubing will shrivel tightly over the repaired area.

Connector attachment

Connectors can be attached with solder or simply by crimping, depending on what service conditions they are for. Butt-type connectors can be used for splicing. Attach connectors as follows:

1. Match the terminals to the wire gauge. Most terminals will fit a small range of gauges.
2. Strip the insulation off only enough wire to fit the terminal barrel. Insert the bare wire into the barrel, figure 1-12.
3. Use a crimping tool to squeeze the barrel. If the barrel has a seam, place the seam toward the convex side of the crimping hole, figure 1-13.
4. If needed, solder and cool the barrel.
5. Insulate the barrel with the terminal's tubing, figure 1-14, or with tape or heat-shrink tubing.

Insulation repair

If insulation is damaged but the conductor is not affected, the insulation can be repaired with electrician's tape or heat-shrink tubing. After the repair, secure the wiring away from whatever caused the damage originally. This may be an exposed screw, rough metal edges, or other rough surfaces.

Aluminum wiring repair

Late-model GM products use aluminum wiring in the front body wiring harness. Special repair prodecures for this harness are outlined below. GM recommends the use of a repair kit that includes an assortment of aluminum wires in 6-inch lengths with terminals attached to one end, splice clips, and anticorrosion petroleum jelly.

If a terminal in this harness fails:

1. Cut off about 6 inches of wire connected to the defective terminal.
2. Strip about ¼ inch of insulation from the end of the wire being repaired and from the kit replacement wire.
3. Place wire ends in a splice clip and crimp firmly.
4. Apply protective jelly to splice area and terminal.
5. Wrap splice area with insulating tape.
6. Insert terminal into proper connector hole.

If a wire has been damaged and a section must be replaced:

1. Cut out the damaged section.
2. Strip ¼ inch of insulation from ends of wire on both sides of the damage.
3. Splice in a replacement section as outlined in Steps 3, 4, and 5 above.

2

Electrical Faults and Basic Test Equipment

ELECTRICAL FAULTS

In the *Classroom Manual*, we saw some ways to stop current flow through a circuit, such as switches, relays, and circuit protectors. Sometimes current flow stops when we do not want it to, and sometimes too much current will flow in a circuit. We will now see what can cause some electrical faults and ways to identify and find the problems. We also will learn about the use of meters and other basic test equipment.

The problems which stop or affect current flow fall into two categories:
1. High-resistance faults
2. Low-resistance faults.

High-Resistance Faults

A high-resistance connection, figure 2-1, can be caused by corrosion, a damaged wire, a defective part, or a loose connection. Because of the increase in resistance, the current flow is less than what is needed to properly operate the loads in the circuit.

An open circuit, figure 2-2, results from a broken wire, no contact between connectors, or a defective part. The resistance across an open circuit, or simply, an "open," is infinite, so no current can flow.

Low-Resistance Faults

A shorted circuit, figure 2-3, is the result of an unwanted connection between two conductors. This is often called an unwanted "copper-to-copper" connection. This allows current to bypass all or part of the normal circuit and normal resistance. This is called a short circuit, or simply, a "short."

A grounded circuit, figure 2-4, is the result of an unwanted connection between a conductor and ground. This is also called an unwanted "copper-to-iron" connection. All or part of the normal circuitry and normal resistance is bypassed. This is called, simply, a "ground."

A ground is really a type of short circuit. From the point where the short occurs, the current bypasses all remaining circuit conductors and loads and flows directly to ground. The short circuit path is simply a short to ground. Because automotive electrical systems are single-wire systems using a common chassis ground, most short circuits occur as shorts to ground. It is possible, however, to find a short circuit within a circuit component, such as a short across part of the windings in an alternator rotor or stator. Remember that all grounds are shorts but that not all shorts are grounds.

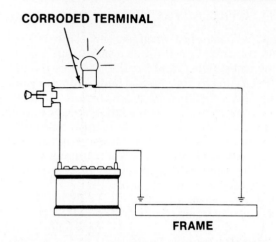

Figure 2-1. A high-resistance connection reduces current flow.

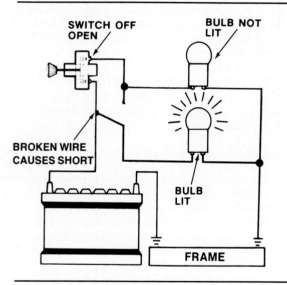

Figure 2-3. A short circuit.

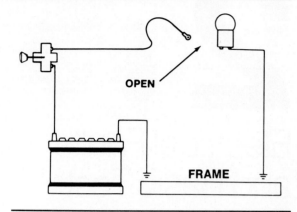

Figure 2-2. An open circuit creates infinite resistance and stops current flow.

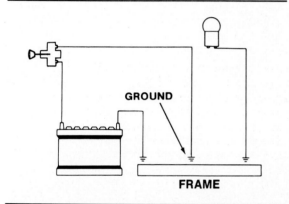

Figure 2-4. A grounded circuit.

METERS AND TEST EQUIPMENT

In order to fix these electrical faults, you must be able to locate and identify the problem. Many good tools exist to help in this search. These tools range from complex, expensive engine analyzers to simple test lamps. In this chapter, we will study the basic operation of these tools, and we will see how they are used to test simple circuits.

Because most automotive systems and test equipment operate on the conventional theory of current flow (+ to −), we will be using that theory throughout this chapter.

Meter Design

Voltage, amperage, and resistance can be measured by three basic test meters:
1. Voltmeter
2. Ammeter
3. Ohmmeter.

These meters all use the same mechanism, called a D'Arsonval movement, to indicate the value of voltage, amperage, or resistance for which they are testing. The D'Arsonval movement, also called a moving coil, is a small coil of fine wire mounted on bearings within the field of a permanent horseshoe magnet, figure 2-5. Fine wire springs, called hair springs, are connected to either end of the coil wire. These hair springs act as conductors to the coil. They return the coil to a base position, and they are used to adjust that base position. When the meter is used, current flows through the coil, and a magnetic field is created. This coil magnetic field interacts with the permanent field of the horseshoe magnet and causes the coil to

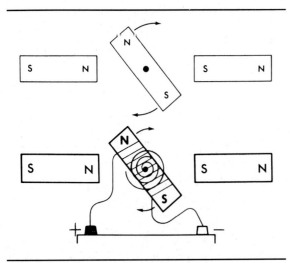

Figure 2-5. Coil motion in a D'Arsonval movement is caused by the interaction of magnetic fields. (Chevrolet)

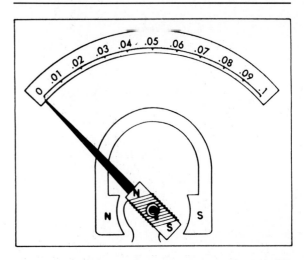

Figure 2-6. This coil movement can be used to display a value reading on a scale.

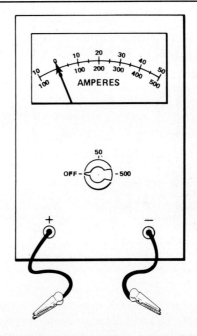

Figure 2-7. A typical ammeter.

rotate in one direction or the other, figure 2-5. The direction of rotation is controlled by the direction of current flow. A pointer, connected to the coil, indicates the value of voltage, amperage, or resistance on the meter dial, figure 2-6. The meter is calibrated, or adjusted for accuracy, by the manufacturer. In addition, some meters have adjustment screws that allow the user to recalibrate the meter before using it.

Test meters have two leads — long pieces of wire with a connector on the ends — to make contact with the circuitry being tested. The connectors are usually either small spring-loaded clips, called alligator clips, or long thin shafts, called probes. Probes are held against the test point; alligator clips require a larger contact surface for attachment. The leads may be permanently connected to the meter, or they may plug into different sockets in the meter for different uses.

When measuring voltage or amperage in a circuit, the polarity of the test meter and the leads must correspond to the polarity of the circuit being tested. One lead is usually colored red, for positive (+), and should be used on the part of the circuit or component being tested that is nearer to the greatest positive voltage. This is usually the battery positive terminal, except for some charging system tests when it is the alternator or generator output terminal. The other lead is usually colored black or white, for negative (−), and should be connected to the test point nearer to the greatest negative voltage. We will learn more about test lead connections shortly.

AMMETER

An ammeter, figure 2-7, measures the amount of current flowing in a circuit and can also be used to test circuit continuity. This could be done simply by allowing the circuit current to flow through the D'Arsonval movement. However, the D'Arsonval coil is very small, with

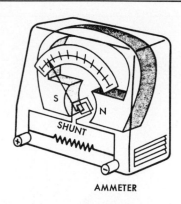

Figure 2-8. A shunt resistor is placed in parallel with the ammeter coil. (Delco-Remy)

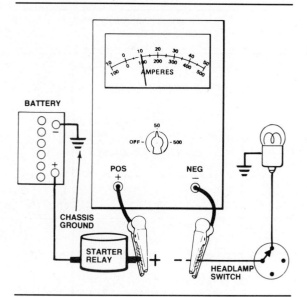

Figure 2-10. The polarity of ammeter leads must be observed, or the meter could be damaged.

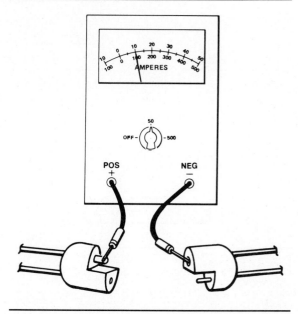

Figure 2-9. An ammeter must be connected in series with the circuit being tested.

little current capacity. Too much current flow through the coil will damage the test meter.

To avoid this excessive current flow, ammeters have a resistor wired in parallel, or shunt, with the coil, figure 2-8. The resistance of the shunt resistor is very low. It actually acts as a low-resistance internal conductor in parallel with the meter movement. Therefore, the meter coil has to measure only a small part of the current flow to determine the total current flow. Many meters have a knob or switch that moves shunt resistors of different values into parallel with the coil. This changes the proportion of current flow through the coil and creates different ranges of amperage values which the meter can safely measure.

Ammeter Use

Ohm's Law tells us that current flow is equal at all points in a series circuit or within any single branch of a parallel circuit. An ammeter can be used to measure current flow and to test circuit continuity.

An ammeter is always connected in series with the circuit or object to be tested, figure 2-9. Because the ammeter's internal circuitry has the large shunt resistor in parallel with the meter movement, the total resistance of the meter is very low and does not affect test measurements. This low resistance also means that if an ammeter is connected in parallel with, or across, a circuit, it will draw too much current and destroy the internal movement.

Ammeter polarity
The ammeter positive (+) lead is usually colored red. This lead must be connected into the circuit at the test point nearest the positive voltage potential, figure 2-10. Current flow must *enter* this positive lead.

The ammeter negative (−) lead is usually colored black or white. This lead must be connected into the circuit at the test point nearest to the negative voltage potential, or ground. Current flow must *exit* this negative lead.

If the ammeter's polarity is not maintained, the meter movement could be damaged. The meter would give inaccurate readings and might even be ruined.

Ammeter scales
Many ammeters have more than one amperage scale on the dial and a range selector switch,

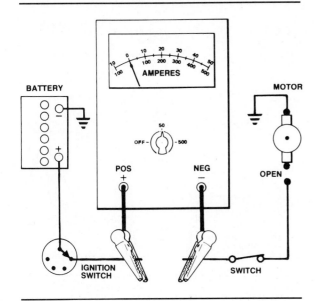

Figure 2-11. This ammeter reading of zero indicates that the circuit is open at some point.

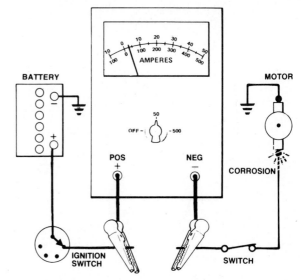

Figure 2-12. A lower than normal ammeter reading indicates a high-resistance fault in the circuit.

figure 2-7. Before beginning any test, set the selector switch to the range above the maximum expected current draw. For example:

1. Set the range selector to the highest amperage scale.
2. Connect the ammeter in series with the circuit or component being tested.
3. If the current reading is below the full-scale reading of the next lowest range, switch to that range for a more precise reading.

If the meter is set on a scale that is below the current draw of the circuit or part, the meter may be damaged by too much current flow.

Ammeter Tests

Compare the current flow reading given by the ammeter with the manufacturer's specifications for the circuit being tested, or use Ohm's Law to calculate the proper amount of current flow for a particular circuit.

• If the ammeter shows *no current flow*, figure 2-11, the circuit is *open* at some point. This indicates that there is no continuity.

• If the ammeter shows *less current flow than is normal*, figure 2-12, the circuit is complete but contains *too much resistance*. This can be caused by improper or defective components or by loose or corroded connections.

• If the *current flow is greater than normal*, figure 2-13, some of the circuit's normal resistance has been bypassed by a *short* or a *ground*.

For example, many manufacturers provide current draw specifications for their ignition coils. To test the coil with an ammeter, figure 2-14:

1. With the ignition switch off, disconnect the

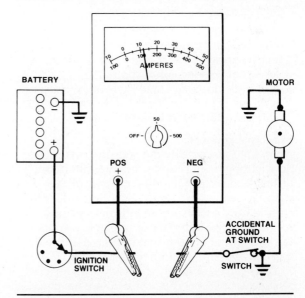

Figure 2-13. A higher than normal ammeter reading indicates a low-resistance fault in the circuit.

coil primary positive wire from the coil cap.
2. Connect the ammeter positive (+) lead to the primary positive (+) wire.
3. Connect the ammeter negative (−) lead to the primary positive (+) terminal on the coil cap.
4. Turn the ignition switch on and, depending on the manufacturer's test instructions, either start the engine or close the ignition points.
5. Compare the ammeter reading to the coil current draw specifications.

   a. No current draw indicates an open (no continuity) primary circuit. The ignition system would not operate at all in this case.

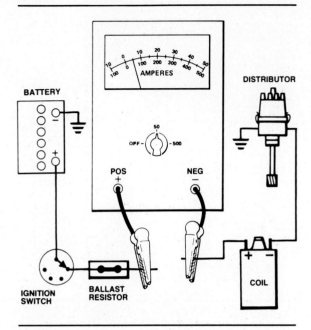

Figure 2-14. Testing an ignition coil with an ammeter.

b. A low amperage reading indicates a discharged battery, high resistance in the primary wiring or the primary coil winding, or loose or corroded connections.

c. A high amperage reading usually indicates a shorted or incorrect coil for the car, or a shorted or incorrect ballast resistor.

Inductive ammeter
An inductive ammeter can measure current flow without being connected into the circuit. Its test lead is a clip that fits over one of the circuit's conductors, figure 2-15. Remember that current flow creates a magnetic field around the conductor. The inductive ammeter measures the strength of the conductor's magnetic field and converts it to an amperage reading.

Tests can be performed quickly with an inductive ammeter because you do not have to disconnect any of the circuit parts to insert test probes. However, the inductive clip must be placed over the conductor in the correct direction, figure 2-15, so that current flows through the clip in the proper direction. This maintains the correct ammeter polarity. Most inductive ammeter clips are large enough to fit over battery cables and, therefore, may not fit into cramped test spaces.

VOLTMETER

A voltmeter, figure 2-16, can be used to:
• Measure the source voltage of a circuit
• Measure the voltage drop caused by a load
• Check for circuit continuity
• Measure the voltage at any point in the circuit.

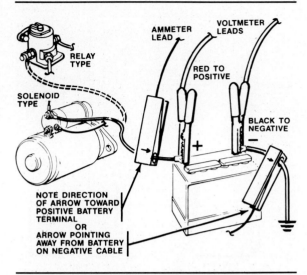

Figure 2-15. These inductive ammeter clips are measuring current flow from the battery into the starting circuit.

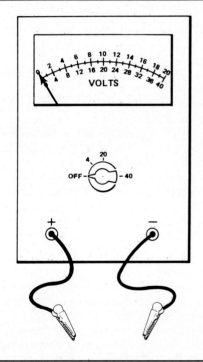

Figure 2-16.. A typical voltmeter.

A voltmeter is normally connected in parallel with a circuit or across (parallel with) a voltage source. Therefore, to protect the D'Arsonval movement from too much current flow, a resistor is wired in series with the coil, figure 2-17. Because the value of this resistor is known, the coil current flow is governed by the amount of voltage in the circuit. The high internal resistance of a voltmeter means that it will draw very little current from a circuit. This makes it safe to connect the meter in parallel or across a circuit

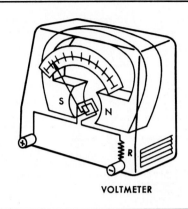

Figure 2-17. A resistor is placed in series with the voltmeter coil. (Delco-Remy)

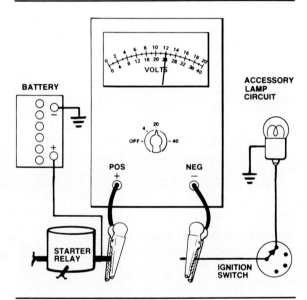

Figure 2-19. Here, the voltmeter is in series with the circuit to check circuit continuity.

or component. The small amount of current drawn by the voltmeter is not enough to significantly affect the circuit voltage drop.

Some voltmeters have a switch that connects resistors of various values into series with the meter movement. This creates ranges of voltage levels that the meter can safely measure.

Voltmeter Use

We know that voltage is impressed equally on all branches of a parallel circuit. We also know that the sum of the voltage drops across all the loads in a branch or a series equals the source voltage. To measure voltage or voltage drop, the voltmeter is connected in parallel with the circuit or part, figure 2-18. When checking for circuit continuity, the voltmeter can be connected in series with portions of the circuit, figure 2-19.

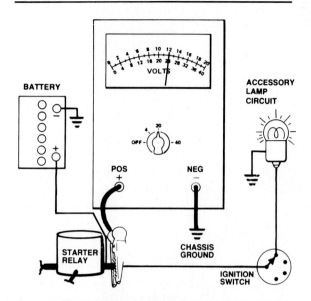

Figure 2-18. A voltmeter can be connected in parallel with a circuit to measure available voltage.

Voltmeter polarity

Like an ammeter, a voltmeter usually has a red positive (+) lead and a black or white negative (−) lead. Whether the meter is connected in series or in parallel, the polarity of the test leads must be maintained. The red positive lead is connected to the test point nearest the positive voltage potential, and the black or white negative lead is connected to the test point nearest to the negative voltage potential.

Voltmeter scales

Most voltmeters have more than one voltage scale on the dial and a range selector switch, figures 2-18 and 2-19. A typical voltmeter will have a 2- to 4-volt low-range scale, a 16- to 20-volt mid-range scale, and a 32- to 40-volt high-range scale. Before beginning any voltage test, set the selector switch to the range above the maximum system voltage. For example:
1. Set the range selector to the highest scale.
2. Connect the voltmeter in parallel with the circuit or part to be tested, figure 2-18.
3. If the voltage reading is below 20 volts, switch to the 20-volt scale for a clearer reading.
4. If the voltage is below 4 volts, switch to the 4-volt scale for a clearer reading.

If the meter is set on a 2-volt or a 4-volt scale and connected in parallel with 12 volts, the meter movement may be damaged.

Available Voltage Tests

The voltage available within a circuit can be measured with current flowing through the circuit or with no current flowing through the circuit. When there is current flow, the voltmeter reading will show the voltage drop

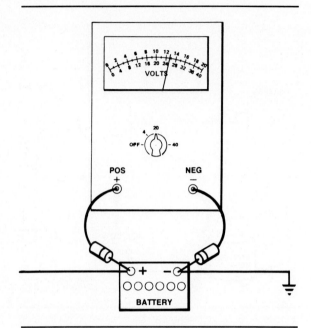

Figure 2-20. A voltmeter connected in parallel with the battery will measure actual battery voltage.

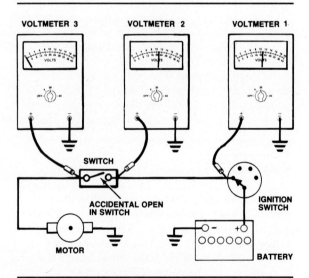

Figure 2-22. When no current is flowing in the circuit, a few no-load voltage tests will pinpoint the problem.

caused by circuit loads. This is because the available voltage decreases when a load comes between the test point and the battery positive terminal. When there is no current flow, the available voltage should be about 12 volts at all test points above ground in a circuit, assuming that the circuitry is in good condition. This is usually called open-circuit or no-load voltage.

Available voltage at source
The available voltage source for all d.c. automotive circuits is the battery. Battery voltage is checked by connecting the voltmeter positive

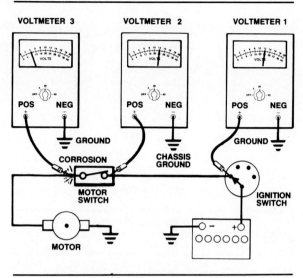

Figure 2-21. These available voltage tests will pinpoint the area of high resistance.

(+) lead to the battery positive (+) terminal and the negative (−) lead to the battery negative (−) terminal, figure 2-20. This measures the battery's no-load, or open-circuit, voltage.

To test available voltage under load, turn on a circuit (headlamps, starter, air conditioning, etc.) and note the voltmeter reading. The voltage will be slightly lower than open-circuit voltage, depending on the condition of the battery and the current draw of the circuit.

Available voltage at points in a circuit
When available voltage is checked with current flowing in the circuit, high-resistance faults can be detected. The positive voltmeter lead is connected to the test point and the negative lead is grounded. For example, if an accessory motor is not turning fast enough to do its job, an available voltage test can pinpoint the fault. Figure 2-21 shows that the circuitry is at fault, not the motor. A corroded switch connection has reduced the voltage available to the motor so that the motor cannot run properly.

When no current is flowing, an available voltage test can pinpoint an open in the circuit. Figure 2-22 shows a circuit being tested for available voltage.
• Voltmeters 1 and 2 show that system voltage is available at those test points.
• Voltmeter 3 reads zero voltage, indicating that the circuit is open at some point between voltmeter 2 and voltmeter 3.

Voltage drop tests
Voltage drop is the amount of voltage that an electrical load uses to do its work. Voltage drop can also result from a high-resistance connection. Remember that *the sum of the voltage drops around a circuit equals the source voltage*.

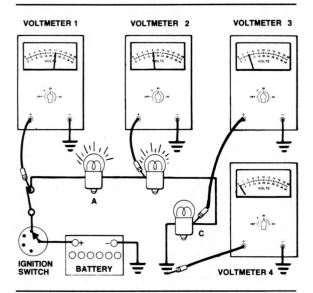

Figure 2-23. Voltage drops can be computed from a series of available voltage readings.

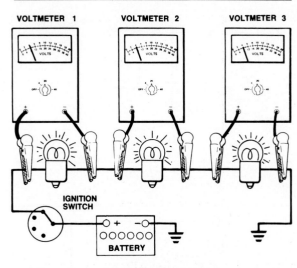

Figure 2-24. Voltage drops can be measured directly by connecting a voltmeter across the load.

Voltage drop tests can tell you if the load is using too much voltage to do its work. This could mean that the load's resistance is too high, or that current flow is too high. If not enough voltage is being used, then some of the load's resistance may have been bypassed by a short or a ground. Conductors usually have no significant voltage drop, but corrosion and loose connections can create a drop and not allow enough voltage to be applied to the rest of the circuit.

Voltage drop tests are made while current is flowing through the circuit. This means that the normal operating conditions (heat, vibration, etc.) are affecting the circuit. Voltage drop tests are especially useful for pinpointing faults that occur during these operating conditions, but that may not occur without current flow through the circuit.

Voltage drops can be computed indirectly, or they can be measured directly.

Computed voltage drop
By doing the available voltage test described earlier, you can compute the voltage drops of any part of a circuit. Figure 2-23 shows a circuit being tested for available voltage. Voltage drops can be computed by comparing the voltage available on one side of a load to the voltage available on the other side of the load. For example:
• Voltmeter 1 reads 12 volts, while voltmeter 2 reads 8 volts. The voltage drop across bulb A is 4 volts (12 − 8 = 4).
• Voltmeter 3 reads 4 volts, so the voltage drop across bulb B is 4 volts (8 − 4 = 4).
• Voltmeter 4 reads zero volts. The voltage drop across bulb C is 4 volts (4 − 0 = 4).

By computing the voltage drop across loads while you do an available voltage test, you can detect bad conditions such as the corroded switch in figure 2-21.

Direct voltage drop
Voltage drop does not have to be computed from two voltmeter readings. In some cases, it can be measured directly, figure 2-24. The voltmeter positive lead (+) is placed on the side of the load nearest the battery positive terminal. The negative (−) lead is placed on the side of the load nearest to ground. The voltmeter will show the voltage drop across the load. Figure 2-24 shows the voltage drop readings for an entire circuit. You can see that the voltage drops add up to the source voltage.

A single voltage drop test can be useful if you know what a normal drop should be. For example, the voltage drop across the ignition breaker points can be measured as follows:
1. Connect the positive voltmeter lead to the primary wire connection at the breaker points, figure 2-25.
2. Be sure the breaker points are closed.
3. Turn the ignition on.
4. Turn the voltmeter to the lowest range and note the reading.
5. The normal voltage drop across the points is 0.1 volt.
6. If the voltage drop exceeds 0.2 volt, the points are probably burned, corroded, bent, or loose.

Whether you measure a voltage drop directly across a load, figure 2-24, or compute it by measuring between ground and both sides of a load, figure 2-23, usually depends on which way is easier to connect your voltmeter for a particular circuit.

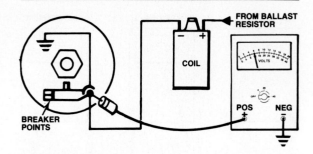

Figure 2-25. Measuring voltage drop across the ignition breaker points.

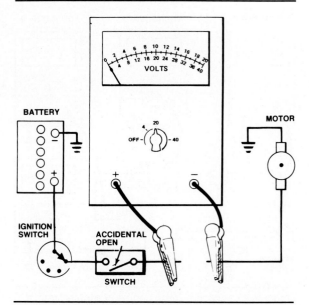

Figure 2-26. To test continuity to this motor, the voltmeter is connected in series with the circuit.

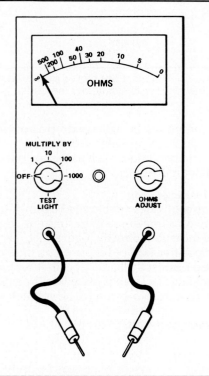

Figure 2-27. A typical ohmmeter.

Continuity Testing

Continuity testing is very similar to no-load voltage testing. Each will tell you if system voltage is being applied to a part of the circuit. During a no-load voltage test, the voltmeter is connected in parallel with the circuit, figure 2-22. Make a continuity test as follows, figure 2-26:

1. Disconnect the circuit leads at the test point.
2. Connect the voltmeter positive (+) lead to the circuit lead nearer to the battery positive terminal (voltage source).
3. Connect the voltmeter negative (−) lead to the other side of the test point. This places the voltmeter in series.

4. Close the switch and note the voltmeter reading.
   a. If the voltmeter reads system voltage, the circuit is complete.
   b. If the voltmeter reads zero voltage, the circuit is open.

OHMMETER

An ohmmeter, figure 2-27, measures the resistance in ohms of a load or conductor. It is constructed and used somewhat differently than a ammeter and a voltmeter. It uses a D'Arsonval movement, but also has a separate power source and a resistor connected in series with the coil, figure 2-28.

When the ohmmeter leads are connected to the device being tested, current from the meter's power source flows through the device and back to the meter. Because the source voltage and the meter's internal resistance are known, the current flow through the coil is determined by the resistance of the device being tested. Current flow through the meter coil is shown on the meter scale as a resistance measurement.

The ohmmeter is used to check the resistance of a load or conductor while there is *no* system voltage applied to the circuit. Ohmmeters can be battery-powered or they can plug into commercial alternating current. In either case, any current flow from an outside source will damage the meter. Before testing a part with an ohmmeter, remove the part from the circuit or be sure that the circuit is open.

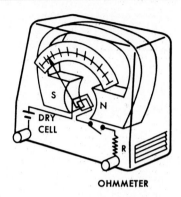

Figure 2-28. A resistor and a dry cell battery are placed in series with the ohmmeter coil. (Delco-Remy)

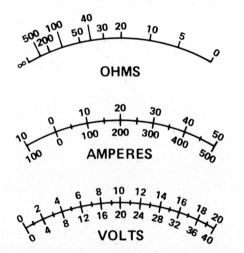

Figure 2-30. The ohmmeter scale is the reverse of the ammeter and voltmeter scales.

Ohmmeter Use

Because the ohmmeter does not use system voltage, the meter leads have no polarity. Either lead can be connected to any test point. An ohmmeter must be adjusted, or calibrated, before use.

Calibrating the ohmmeter
If there are batteries in an ohmmeter, they will weaken with age and change with temperature. The voltage applied to a.c.-powered ohmmeters also can vary. An ohmmeter must be calibrated before each use. To calibrate the meter, connect the two test leads together, figure 2-29. The meter should read zero resistance. If it does not, move the calibration knob until the needle indicates zero ohms. The meter will now give accurate test measurements.

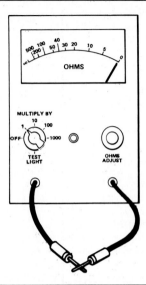

Figure 2-29. An ohmmeter is calibrated by touching the leads together and adjusting the needle to read zero.

Ohmmeter scale
Just as with an ammeter and voltmeter, the ohmmeter internal circuitry reacts to current flow to move the needle. The ammeter and voltmeter scales show increasing values from left to right as current flow through the meter increases. The ohmmeter must show *decreasing* resistance readings in ohms as current flow through the meter increases. The ohmmeter scale is marked opposite to an ammeter or voltmeter scale, figure 2-30. The ohmmeter reads infinite resistance (no current flow) where the ammeter and the voltmeter read zero.

Like ammeters and voltmeters, ohmmeters often have several scales on the dial. When using an ohmmeter, begin testing on the *lowest* scale and switch to the highest scale that gives the most precise reading.

Ohmmeter tests
The ohmmeter is connected across the item to be tested, figure 2-31. This looks similar to the parallel connection used with a voltmeter, but because there is no system voltage applied to the ohmmeter it is not truly a parallel circuit branch. The ohmmeter's self-contained voltage creates current flow through a circuit consisting of the meter movement and the load being tested. That is, the ohmmeter provides a complete series circuit.

Ohmmeter measurements can pinpoint a high-resistance or a low-resistance fault.
● If a conductor or load has a high resistance or is open, the ohmmeter will measure high or infinite resistance.

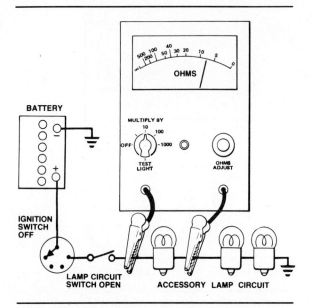

Figure 2-31. No outside current must flow through an object being tested with an ohmmeter.

• If a load has a short or ground that bypasses some of its normal resistance, the ohmmeter will indicate low resistance.

An ohmmeter is commonly used to check alternator diodes, figure 2-32:
1. Connect one ohmmeter test lead to the diode lead and the other ohmmeter test lead to the diode base. Observe the ohmmeter reading.
2. Reverse the ohmmeter test leads so that the test lead that touched the diode base in step 1 now touches the diode lead, and the test lead that touched the diode lead in step 1 now touches the diode base. Observe the ohmmeter reading.
3. Compare the two meter readings.
   a. If the diode has very high or infinite resistance in one direction and very low resistance in the other direction, the diode is good.
   b. If the diode has high resistance in both directions, it is bad.
   c. If the diode has low resistance in both directions, it is bad.
The ohmmeter can also be used to check the ignition coil primary winding. Manufacturers often provide a resistance specification for their ignition coils. To test this:
1. Either remove the two coil primary wires from their terminals on the coil cap, or make sure that the ignition switch is off.
2. Connect one ohmmeter lead to each coil primary terminal on the coil cap. Observe the ohmmeter reading.
3. Compare the reading to the manufacturer's specification.
   a. If there is an infinite resistance, the coil

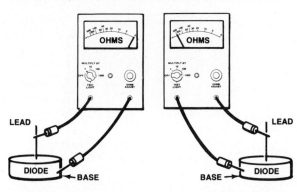

Figure 2-32. Ohmmeters are commonly used to test diodes.

primary winding is open.
b. If the resistance is lower than specified, the coil primary winding is shorted.

Ohmmeter and Voltmeter Comparison

Resistance can be measured directly with an ohmmeter, or it can be computed from voltage-drop measurements made with a voltmeter. Resistance faults in wiring and connections often result in the generation of heat, which further increases the operating circuit resistance. In these cases, the fault may not show up readily when the circuit is shut off or the component is removed for testing. Therefore, voltage drop tests are often the best way to find a resistance problem in an operating circuit. Other advantages to voltage drop tests are:
• Meter reading is often easier and faster because small increases in wiring resistance show up as sharp increases in readable voltage drop.
• A complete circuit can be tested quickly because a voltmeter can be moved from point to point in a circuit while the circuit is operating.

An ohmmeter, however, has definite advantages for other test situations. They are particularly useful for:
• Measurement of major load parts that have specific resistance values within the usable range of the meter
• Measurement of high resistance items, such as spark plug cables and electronic ignition pickup coils
• Testing the internal parts of items, like alternators, which require disassembly to get at the test points
• Bench testing new or used parts like switches, circuit breakers, and relays before assembly or installation.

MULTIMETERS

Various test meters can be built into a single

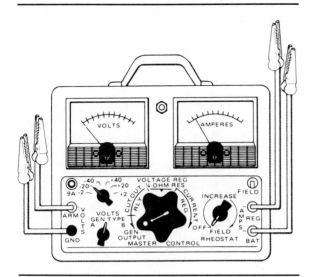

Figure 2-33. Multimeters, such as this, are used for most automotive testing.

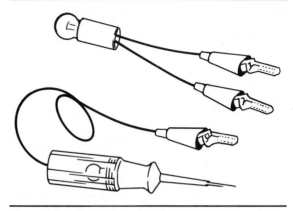

Figure 2-34. Typical 12-volt test lamps.

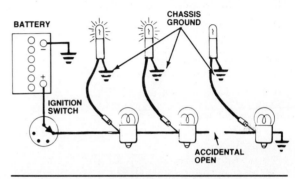

Figure 2-35. This voltage-seeking test with a 12-volt probe lamp is similar to a voltmeter's available voltage test.

console, figure 2-33. These are often called volt-amp testers, battery-starter testers, or multimeters. The individual meters all operate the same, no matter how they are constructed. These multimeters may also contain fixed-value resistors and variable-resistance carbon piles for making specific tests. We will learn more about their use in later chapters.

SIMPLE TEST DEVICES

Although test meters are needed when an accurate value must be known, there are three other test devices which can be used quickly and easily to answer certain questions about a circuit or a load. These devices are:
1. 12-volt test lamp
2. Self-powered test lamp
3. Jumper wire.
In the following paragraphs, we will see how these simple tools operate and how to use them to test electrical components.

12-Volt Test Lamp

The 12-volt test lamp is available in different designs. Two common types are shown in figure 2-34. The bulb in the test lamp works on a 12-volt current, so the tester can be used to check circuits and components while electrical current is flowing through them. The two checks which the 12-volt test lamp can make are called voltage-seeking and ground-seeking.

The voltage-seeking test, like the available-voltage test, indicates whether or not voltage is available to the circuit at a particular point. This test could be used in a lighting circuit, figure 2-35:

1. Connect one test lamp lead to a known chassis ground.
2. Touch the other test lamp lead to various parts of the circuit.
3. If the lamp lights at one test point but not at the next, the circuit is open between these two points.

The ground-seeking test indicates whether or not a conductor, switch, or load is grounded. This test could be used in a warning lamp circuit that has a grounding switch. For example, the oil pressure warning lamp in figure 2-36 should light when the ignition switch is on the Accessory or On position with the engine not running. If it does not:
1. Disconnect the wire from the grounding switch.
2. Connect one test lamp lead to the wire and touch the other test lamp lead to the engine block, position A. If the test lamp and the warning lamp light, the problem may be at the grounding switch.
3. Keep one test lamp lead connected to the wire and touch the other test lamp lead to the grounding switch, position B. If the test lamp and the warning lamp do not light, the grounding switch is defective.

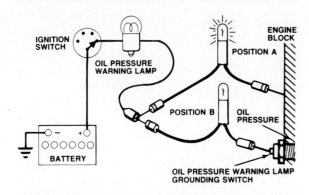

Figure 2-36. This ground-seeking test with a 12-volt probe lamp shows that the oil pressure warning lamp grounding switch is defective.

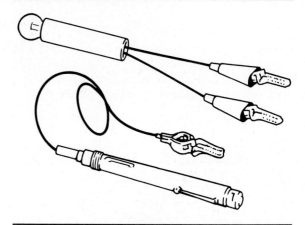

Figure 2-37. Typical self-powered test lamps.

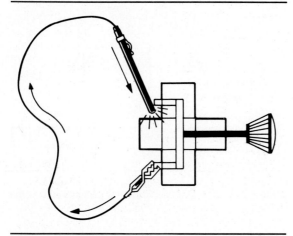

Figure 2-38. Testing a switch with a self-powered test lamp.

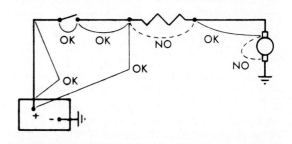

Figure 2-39. Some proper and improper connections with a jumper wire. (Chevrolet)

Self-Powered Test Lamp

The self-powered test lamp, figure 2-37, is often called a continuity lamp. It can be used to test for complete circuits or for a connection between two points in a circuit. Like many ohmmeters, the self-powered test lamp draws current from its own dry cell battery. Items being tested with the lamp must be disconnected from any other voltage source. To test for continuity in a circuit or part of a circuit, connect the test lamp leads to either end of the conductor or device, figure 2-38. If the lamp lights, the circuit is complete, or there is continuity through the component. These test lamps cannot be used to check high-resistance components, such as suppression-type ignition cables, because the low voltage of the lamp's battery cannot overcome the resistance of the cables.

Jumper Wire

A jumper wire is a length of wire with an alligator clip or a probe on each end. Although it

is not a true test instrument, it can be used to bypass switches, connectors, and other non-resistive components. It must *never* be used to bypass an item that has resistance, or in a way that would ground a hot lead. This would reduce circuit resistance, allowing excessive current flow which could damage loads and conductors, or even start an electrical fire. Many jumper wires include an inline fuse or circuit breaker to protect the circuit. Figure 2-39 illustrates some proper and improper jumper wire connections. When the jumper wire is properly used, figure 2-40, it can indicate whether a component such as the switch is faulty. To make this test:
1. Turn all switches on.
2. If the lamps do not light, bypass the lamp switch with a jumper wire.
3. If the lamps then light, the lamp switch is defective.

OSCILLOSCOPE

An oscilloscope is a sophisticated electronic test instrument that shows the changing voltage levels in an electrical system over a period of time. In this section, we will discuss the operation of the oscilloscope. Later chapters explain its use.

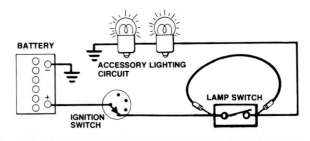

Figure 2-40. If the lamps light only when the switch is bypassed with a jumper wire, there is a problem with the switch.

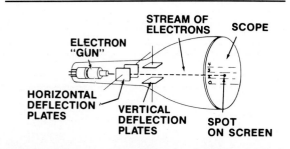

Figure 2-42. The electron gun traces a pattern of light on the inside of the cathode ray tube screen. (Marquette)

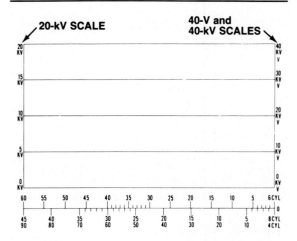

Figure 2-41. This oscilloscope screen has kilovolt scales on both sides and a low-voltage scale on the right side.

The oscilloscope, or scope, has a screen, much like a television screen, which displays a line of light called a trace. The trace indicates the voltage levels over a period of time during the electrical system's operation. The automotive oscilloscope screen is marked with various scales, figure 2-41, which show the values of various positions of the trace. The vertical sides of the screen illustrated are marked in kilovolts (abbreviated kV, meaning thousands of volts). Just as many voltmeter scales are marked with several voltage ranges, most oscilloscope screens have different voltage ranges marked on each side.

Some scopes also have a low-voltage scale on one or both sides of the screen, figure 2-41. The kV scales are used to measure voltage in the secondary circuit of the ignition system. The low-voltage scales can be used to measure voltage in the ignition primary circuit and the charging system. Using a switch on the oscilloscope console, you can select the range that will give you the most legible voltage reading for the test being performed. On the screen shown in figure 2-41, the zero-voltage line is at the bottom. Some scopes have the zero line above the bottom so that both positive and negative voltage can be shown.

The distance across the screen represents time. In figure 2-41, no periods of time are shown in milliseconds or microseconds. In-

stead, time measurements across the bottom of the screen are given in terms of degrees of ignition distributor rotation. This is used to measure ignition dwell.

Cathode Ray Tube

The oscilloscope screen is the front of a cathode ray tube. As we said, this is the same kind of device as the picture tube in your television set. Although a cathode ray tube is a complex electronic device, its operation can be explained in simple terms.

A cathode ray tube, figure 2-42, has an electron gun which shoots a high-speed stream of electrons. The inside of the oscilloscope screen is specially coated so that it glows at the spot where the electron stream hits it. The stream is controlled by two pairs of electrically charged plates. Depending upon the type of charge present upon the plates (+ or −), they will either attract or repel the negatively charged electron stream, causing it to bend, or deflect.

One set of plates bends the stream up and down to change the height of the trace. These are called the vertical deflection plates. They are controlled by the voltage present in the system being tested. The higher the voltage, the higher the stream is deflected, making the light appear farther up the voltage scale on the screen.

The second set of plates bends the stream from side to side so that the light travels across the screen from left to right. These are called the horizontal deflection plates. They are controlled by the speed of the engine being tested. The faster the engine runs, the faster the light will travel across the screen. At high engine speeds, the light travels so quickly that the trace appears

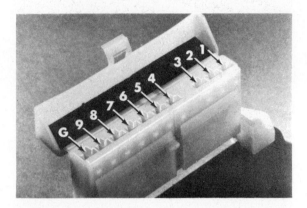

Figure 2-43. The General Motors diagnostic connector allows several circuits to be tested from a single point on the car. (Chevrolet)

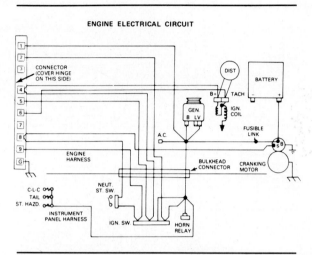

Figure 2-44. Diagnostic connector installation on Chevettes and Acadians. (Chevrolet)

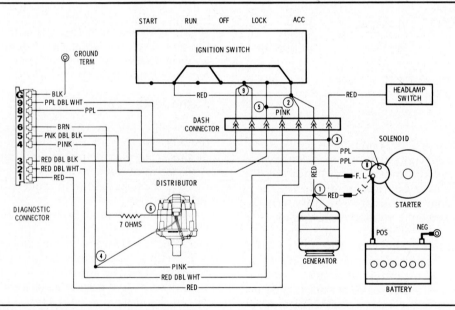

Figure 2-45. Diagnostic connector installation on full size cars. (Oldsmobile)

as a solid line. Our eyes cannot see the single dots of light on the screen, but instead see the trace as a line of light across the entire screen. The internal circuitry of the oscilloscope controls the electron stream so that we see only the left-to-right movement line of the trace. The returning right-to-left line travels even faster, and we do not see it at all.

GENERAL MOTORS DIAGNOSTIC CONNECTORS

Chevrolet Chevettes, Pontiac Acadians, and 1977 and later full-size GM cars (except Cadillacs) have diagnostic connectors that allow you to test several electrical circuits from a single

point on the car. These connectors, figure 2-43, are mounted on the firewall or fender panel and have 10 terminals, numbered 1 through 9 and G for ground. Each terminal is connected in parallel with a voltage test point in the electrical system, as follows:
1. Battery voltage at the wire from the alternator BAT terminal to the starter BAT terminal
2. Battery voltage at the ignition switch BAT terminal
3. Applied voltage at the headlamp switch feed (This terminal is not used on Chevettes and Acadians.)
4. Applied voltage at the distributor BAT or B+ distributor terminal
5. Applied voltage at the ignition switch IGN 1

terminal
6. Voltage at the distributor TACH terminal, used as a tachometer connection
7. Blank, not used
8. Cranking voltage at the starter solenoid S terminal
9. Cranking voltage at the ignition switch START terminal.

Figure 2-44 shows the diagnostic connector wiring to the electrical system on Chevettes and Acadians. Figure 2-45 shows the installation on full-size GM cars. Many test equipment companies make special testers, figure 2-46, that plug into the connector. These have the advantage of fast hookup and test time, but you can make the same tests at the connector, using only your voltmeter.

By connecting the voltmeter negative (−) lead to the G (ground) terminal and the positive (+) lead to the other terminals in turn, you can make seven or eight voltage tests from a single point on the car. You may need jumper wires to connect some voltmeters to the connector.

Tests using the GM diagnostic connector are covered in later chapters in this *Shop Manual* that deal with the systems and circuits to be serviced. Chevettes, Acadians, and full-size GM cars with air conditioning have a second connector to test the air conditioning electrical circuits. Chrysler Corporation's Omni and Horizon models, introduced in 1978, have similar diagnostic connectors, but the circuit connections are slightly different from GM systems.

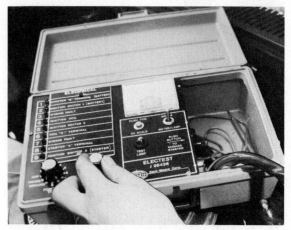

Figure 2-46. This special tester plugs into the diagnostic connector to test seven or eight different circuits. (Chevrolet)

3

Battery Service

A dead battery can cause problems in all areas of a car's electrical system. A quick check of the battery should be the first step before any other troubleshooting. If the battery is not in good shape, service or replace it before testing any other circuits. This chapter has information on battery safety, servicing, and replacement.

BATTERY SAFETY

A battery should be treated with respect. The acid of the battery electrolyte can damage the car's paint or corrode metal parts if spilled. The acid can also cause severe burns if it contacts your skin. Wear safety glasses to protect your eyes when servicing a battery.

If electrolyte contacts your skin, rinse it with water, then cover it with a solution of baking soda and water. If electrolyte contacts your eyes, flood them with water for 5 minutes, then with a mild solution of baking soda and water. Do not rub them. Call a doctor immediately.

Even when a battery is standing idle, it gives off a slight amount of hydrogen gas, which is highly explosive. Follow these safety precautions to avoid a battery explosion:
• Keep sparks, open flame, and cigarettes away from batteries at all times.
• Operate charging equipment in a well-ventilated area.
• Do not short across the battery terminals.
• Do not connect or disconnect battery charger leads to battery terminals while the charger is turned on.

Electrical burns caused by arcing between a battery terminal and a ring or wristwatch is another hazard. To avoid this, remove rings and watches before servicing a battery.

Batteries are heavy and can be awkward to handle. If a battery is dropped, electrolyte may be spilled or the case may be damaged. Always use a battery carrier or lifting strap, figure 3-1, to make battery handling easier and safer.

The electrolyte in a fully charged battery will not freeze until temperatures drop to −60° to −90° F. But, electrolyte in a partially charged or discharged battery can freeze at temperatures at 5 degrees above zero and warmer. Winter temperatures in many areas are cold enough to freeze a weak battery.

Before charging or boost-starting a dead battery in winter, check the electrolyte in the cells for signs of freezing. If ice or slush can be seen, or if the electrolyte level *cannot* be seen, allow the battery to thaw at room temperature before charging. Passing current through a frozen battery can cause it to rupture or explode.

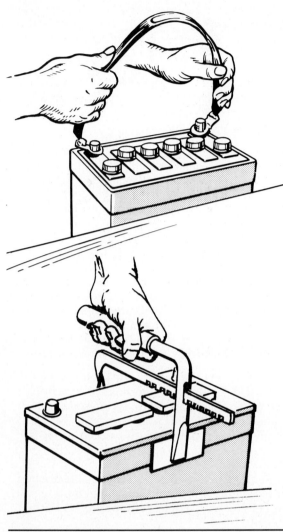

Figure 3-1. Battery carriers are designed to handle a battery without danger to the battery or the mechanic.

INSPECTION, CLEANING, AND REPLACEMENT

Inspection, cleaning, and replacement of a few parts are often the only services a battery needs. These simple jobs can be done with the following tools, figure 3-2:
- Baking soda or ammonia solution
- Cleaning brushes
- Connector pliers or wrenches
- Connector puller
- Battery carrier or strap
- Connector and terminal cleaning tool
- Connector spreader
- Protective coating (spray or jelly).

Battery Inspection

Complete battery inspection includes the following points:

Figure 3-2. These are some of the tools and supplies you will need to service a battery.

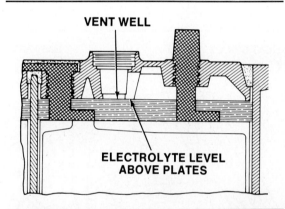

Figure 3-3. Electrolyte should completely cover the battery plates.

1. Check the battery electrolyte level, figure 3-3. It should be above the tops of the plates or at the indicated level within the cells. Add water to raise the electrolyte level. Distilled water or a good grade of mineral-free drinking water should be used. Do not overfill.
2. Inspect the battery case and cover for dirt or grease that could cause a voltage leak to ground.
3. Inspect the battery terminals, cable connectors, and metal parts of the holddown and tray for acid corrosion.
4. Inspect the battery for cracks, loose terminal posts, and other physical damage, figure 3-4. A battery with any of this type of damage should be replaced.
5. Check for missing or damaged cell caps. Replace any that are broken or missing.
6. Inspect the cables for broken or corroded wires, worn insulation, and loose or damaged connectors, figure 3-5. Replace bad parts.

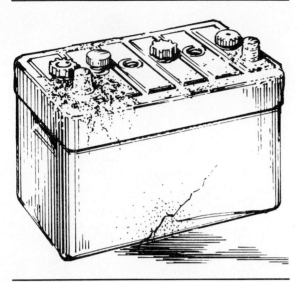

Figure 3-4. A battery that is obviously damaged should be replaced.

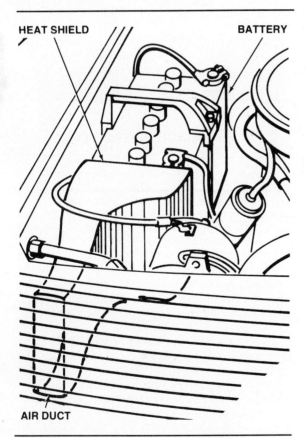

HEAT SHIELD   BATTERY

AIR DUCT

Figure 3-6. Be sure that battery heat shields are properly installed.

7. Check all cable connections for looseness and dirt.
8. Inspect the tray and holddown for looseness, damage, and missing parts.

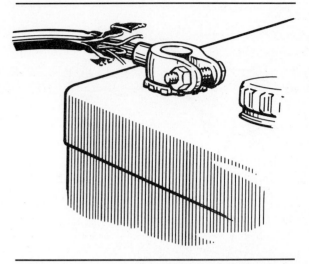

Figure 3-5. Damaged cables will reduce a battery's power output.

9. Ensure that heat shields are properly placed on batteries that need them, figure 3-6.

Battery Cleaning

Begin cleaning the battery and cables by neutralizing acid corrosion on terminals, connectors, and other metal parts with baking soda and water or an ammonia solution, figure 3-7. Be careful to keep corrosion off painted surfaces and rubber parts. *Do not let the soda solution enter the battery*.

Remove heavy corrosion with a stiff-bristled brush, figure 3-8. Avoid splashing. Remove dirt and grease with a detergent solution or with solvent.

After corrosion and dirt are removed, rinse the battery and cable connections with fresh water. Dry with a clean cloth or low-pressure compressed air. If battery terminals and cable connectors are badly corroded, the cables should be removed from the battery for thorough cleaning. *Begin by removing the ground cable first*. Use a cable puller to remove a cable that is stuck on a post, figure 3-9. Do not pry it off with a screwdriver or hit it with a hammer.

Use a connector-spreading tool to open the cable connector and ream the inside. Neutralize acid corrosion on the cable connectors with a baking soda solution. A combination wire brush with internal and external bristles, figure 3-10, is a handy tool for cleaning battery posts and the inside of cable connectors. Be sure the posts and connectors are completely clean for good electrical contact when replaced.

Battery Replacement

Before installing a battery, review the safety

Figure 3-7. A solution of baking soda and water will clean most corrosion off a battery.

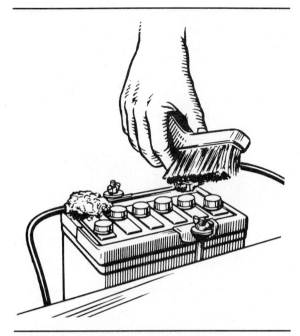

Figure 3-8. A stiff-bristled brush will remove excessive corrosion.

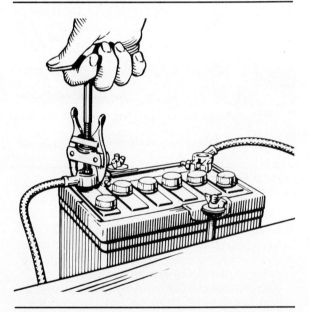

Figure 3-9. Battery connector pullers will remove the cable without damaging the battery post.

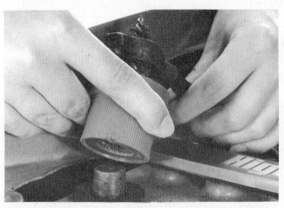

Figure 3-10. This 2-piece brush cleans both battery posts and cable connectors.

precautions listed earlier in this chapter. Handle batteries only with a lifting strap or battery carrier. To avoid electrical burns, remove rings and wristwatches before removing or installing a battery.

Before removing the old battery, mark the cable that is connected to the positive (+) terminal. Most 12-volt electrical systems on domestic vehicles are negative-ground systems. In these systems, the positive terminal is connected to the starter relay or motor. Some imported cars

and some older vehicles with 6-volt systems have positive-ground electrical systems. To avoid reversing the battery polarity during installation, mark the positive cable.

On top-terminal batteries, the positive post is larger than the negative post. Many side-terminal batteries have different-sized connectors for the positive and negative terminals.

Remove the ground cable from the battery first; then remove the insulated (hot) cable. Use the correct size wrench for clamp-type connectors, figure 3-11, or pliers for spring-type connectors, figure 3-12. Use a cable puller to remove clamp-type connectors that are stuck on battery posts.

Loosen and remove the battery holddown and any heat shields that require removal. Lift the battery from the tray with a carrier or strap. Inspect and clean the battery tray and both

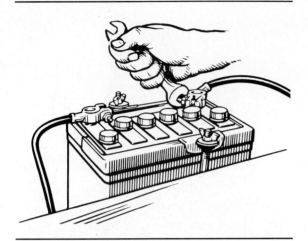

Figure 3-11. Use the proper tool to loosen bolt-type connectors.

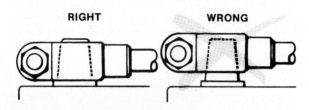

Figure 3-13. The connector must be firmly seated on the battery post.

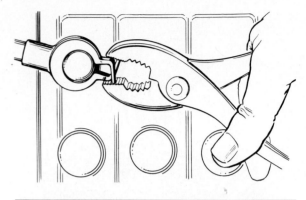

Figure 3-12. A pair of pliers will spread this type of connector.

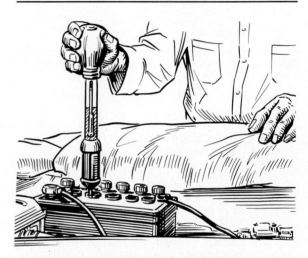

Figure 3-14. Draw enough electrolyte into the hydrometer to float the indicator.

cables. If new cables are needed, install them now.

Install the new battery in the tray and secure the holddown and all heat shield parts. If necessary, spread clamp-type connectors with a spreading tool to fit them onto the posts. Never hammer a connector onto a battery post.

Connect the insulated (hot) cable to the battery first; then connect the ground cable. Clamp-type connectors shoud be flush with or slightly below the tops of the posts, figure 3-13. To help prevent corrosion, apply a light coat of anticorrosion compound to the terminals and connectors after installation

BATTERY TESTING

The state of charge and the capacity of a battery may be tested by several different methods. The most common are described below.

Specific Gravity Test

A hydrometer is used to measure the specific gravity of a battery's electrolyte. This test is usually enough to determine a battery's state of charge, but cannot be used on sealed-top, maintenance-free batteries.

If the electrolyte level is too low to take a

sample, water must be added to each cell. The battery must then be charged for 5 or 10 minutes at a low charging rate, about 5 amps, to mix the water with the electrolyte before testing.

Remove the cell caps and put the hydrometer into either end cell. Draw enough electrolyte into the hydrometer to float the indicator without it touching the sides or top of the tube, figure 3-14. If the hydrometer has a built-in thermometer, draw electrolyte into the hydrometer several times to stabilize the temperature.

Hold the hydrometer at eye level and read the specific gravity on the indicator, figure 3-15. After reading, return the electrolyte to the cell from which it was drawn. Take specific gravity readings from all cells.

The specific gravity of a fully charged battery should be between 1.260 and 1.280, with electrolyte temperature at 80° F. The following table indicates the relationship between specific gravity and state of charge.

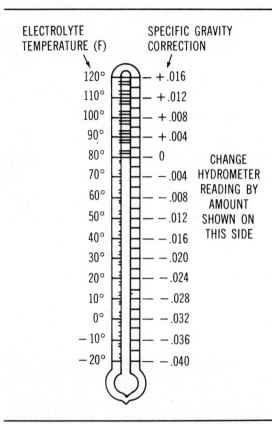

Figure 3-15. Many hydrometers have a correction table printed on the side.

Specific Gravity	State of Charge
1.260-1.280	100%
1.230-1.250	75%
1.200-1.220	50%
1.170-1.190	25%
1.140-1.160	Very little useful capacity
1.110-1.130	Discharged

If the electrolyte temperature is above or below 80° F, the specific gravity reading must be corrected by adding 4 points (.004) for each 10° above 80° F or subtracting 4 points for every 10° below 80° F. For example:
• The indicator reading is 1.230, and the temperature reading is 10° F. The specific gravity must be corrected for a variation of 70°. That means that 28 points (.004 × 7 = .028) must be subtracted from the indicator reading of 1.230. The true corrected reading is 1.202.
• The indicator reading is 1.235, and the temperature reading is 120° F. Since the temperature reading is 40° above the standard of 80° F, 16 points (.004 × 4 = .016) must be added to the indicator reading of 1.235. The true corrected reading is 1.251.

A battery should be recharged when the specific gravity drops below 1.230. A specific-

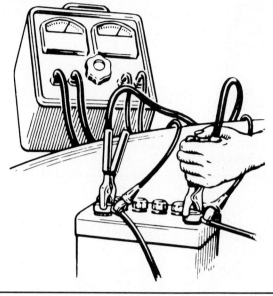

Figure 3-16. Hooking up a battery-starter tester.

gravity variation of more than 50 points (.050) between cells indicates a bad battery that should be replaced.

Capacity (Load) Test

A capacity test, or load test, determines how a battery will work under load. It indicates the battery's ability to furnish starting current and still maintain enough voltage to operate the ignition system. This test should be made only if the battery is at least ½ to ¾ charged. A test instrument called a battery-starter tester is used. It consists of an ammeter, a voltmeter, and either a fixed resistor or a variable resistance carbon pile. The carbon pile is used to imitate the current draw of the starting system.

The test can be made with the battery in or out of the car. Electrolyte temperature should be about 80° F. Some testers have a temperature compensation feature for testing at other temperatures, because a cold battery will show a considerably lower capacity than a warm battery.
1. With the tester control off, connect the positive (+) voltmeter lead and the positive (+) ammeter lead to the battery positive (+) terminal.
2. Connect the voltmeter negative (−) lead and the ammeter negative (−) lead to the battery negative (−) terminal.
3. Be sure that the leads at each terminal do not touch each other, figure 3-16. Special adapters may be needed to connect the tester to a side-terminal battery, figure 3-17.
4. Refer to the battery maker's specifications to

Figure 3-17. You may need adapters to test side-terminal batteries.

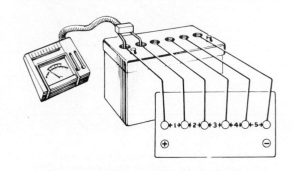

Figure 3-19. Test sites for the cadmium probes.

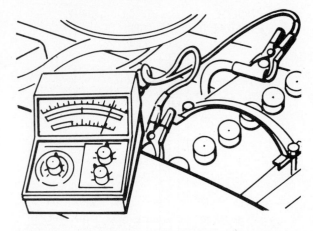

Figure 3-18. Electronic battery testers have only two cables to connect to the battery.

find the ampere-hour rating of the battery being tested.
5. Turn the tester control knob to draw battery current at a rate equal to three times the battery's ampere-hour rating. For example, if the battery is rated at 80 ampere-hours, current draw is adjusted to 240 amperes (80 × 3 = 240).
6. If the ampere-hour rating is unknown, you can estimate the test current as follows:
   a. If the battery is used with a V-8 engine, set the current draw as follows: large V-8, 225 to 300 amps; small V-8, 175 to 250 amps.
   b. If the battery is used with a 4- or 6-cylinder engine, set the current draw at 170 amperes.
7. Maintain this current draw load for 15 seconds while watching the voltmeter. Turn the control knob off after exactly 15 seconds.
8. Voltage should not fall below 9.6 volts for a 12-volt battery or 4.8 volts for a 6-volt battery. If the voltage falls below these limits, the battery is weak and should be replaced.

Alternative capacity test
If a battery starter tester is not available, the starter motor can be used as a battery loading device for a capacity test.
1. Lift the coil secondary lead from the center tower of the distributor cap and ground it with a jumper wire.
2. Connect a voltmeter to the battery terminals, checking for proper polarity.
3. Crank the engine continuously for 15 seconds

and watch the voltmeter reading at the end of the period.
4. If the voltmeter reading is 9.6 volts or higher for a 12-volt battery or 4.8 volts for a 6-volt battery, the battery and starting circuit are in good condition. If the voltage reading drops below these figures, the battery may be in poor condition or the starting circuit may be drawing too much current.

Electronic battery tester
Some battery testers rely on solid-state circuitry to measure the battery's kilowatts, voltage, and condition. The condition reading is usually a good-bad judgment based on the battery maker's rating for ampere-hours, wattage, or cold-cranking performance. This type of tester does not use a carbon pile to load the battery, so the battery is not discharged during testing. To use an electronic battery tester, figure 3-18:
1. Attach the positive (+) tester lead to the positive (+) battery terminal and the negative (−) tester lead to the negative (−) battery terminal.
2. To measure kilowatts, set the selector switch to the kilowatt position and read the kilowatt scale.
3. To measure voltage, set the selector switch to the voltage position and read the voltage scale.
4. Measure battery condition as follows:
   a. Set the selector switch to the battery condition position.
   b. Set the temperature switch to the estimated temperature of the battery in degrees Fahrenheit.
   c. Set the battery rating switch to the maker's rating in ampere-hours, watts, or cold-cranking performance. If these ratings are not known, you can estimate the ampere hour

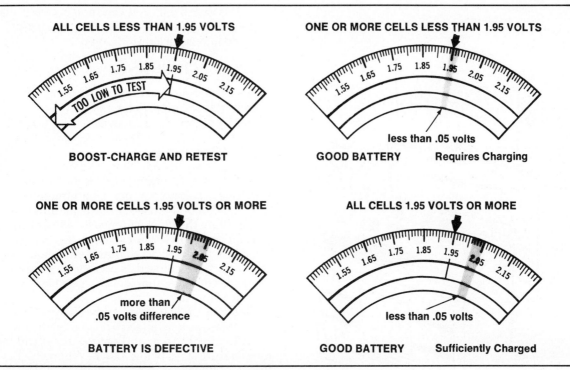

ALL CELLS LESS THAN 1.95 VOLTS

TOO LOW TO TEST

BOOST-CHARGE AND RETEST

ONE OR MORE CELLS LESS THAN 1.95 VOLTS

less than .05 volts

GOOD BATTERY   Requires Charging

ONE OR MORE CELLS 1.95 VOLTS OR MORE

more than
.05 volts difference

BATTERY IS DEFECTIVE

ALL CELLS 1.95 VOLTS OR MORE

less than .05 volts

GOOD BATTERY   Sufficiently Charged

Figure 3-20. Compare your cadmium probe test readings to these standards.

rating as explained under the Load Test instructions.

d. The battery condition scale will indicate whether the battery is good or bad.

Three-Minute Charge Test

To see if a discharged battery can be recharged or whether it is too badly sulphated to accept a charge, do a 3-minute charge test. This test should *not* be made on maintenance-free batteries, because the test results will not be accurate. A fast battery charger is used to pass a high charging current through the battery for three minutes. If the battery is not badly sulfated, the high current will knock the sulfate deposits off the plates. If the battery is too badly sulfated to accept a fast charge, the sulfate will not be knocked off and high voltage will be measured across the battery terminals.

If the battery is to be tested in the car, disconnect both battery cables to avoid damaging the alternator and electrical system. If high voltage is recorded early in the test, *stop the test*. High internal resistance due to sulfation or poor internal connections will develop heat that can boil the electrolyte. Here is how to do the 3-minute charge test:

1. Connect the charger leads to the battery, with the positive (+) lead to the positive (+) terminal and the negative (−) lead to the negative (−) terminal.

2. Connect a voltmeter across the battery, + to + and − to −.

3. Turn the charger on and adjust it for the highest charging rate but not exceeding 40 amperes for a 12-volt battery or 75 amperes for a 6-volt battery. If the charger has a timer, set it for three minutes.

4. After 3 minutes, read the voltmeter. If it is not more than 15.5 volts for a 12-volt battery or 7.75 volts for a 6-volt battery, the battery can be safely recharged at the maker's suggested charging rate.

5. If the voltage reading is more than the values given in step 4, the battery is bad and should be replaced.

Cadmium Probe Test

The cadmium probe test measures the voltage level of each battery cell. It cannot be done on sealed, maintenance-free batteries. The tester has two probes made of cadmium. When placed in the battery's electrolyte, the cadmium reacts like a battery plate. If there is too much variation between the lowest and the highest cell readings, the battery is defective and must be replaced.

Perform a cadmium probe test as follows:

1. Put the positive (+) test probe into the end cell nearest the positive (+) terminal, and the negative (−) test probe into the next cell, figure 3-19. Record the meter reading.

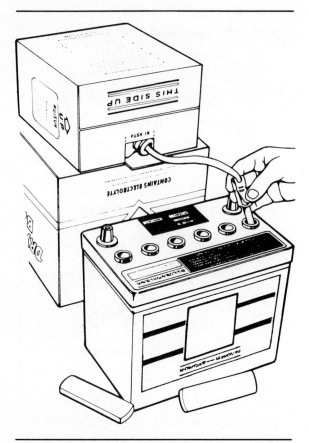

Figure 3-21. Dry-charged batteries must be filled with packaged electrolyte.

2. Move the positive (+) probe into the second cell from the positive (+) terminal and the negative (−) probe to the next cell. Record the meter reading. Repeat this procedure for the remaining cells.

3. To measure the voltage of the end cells, figure 3-20, put the positive (+) probe on the positive (+) battery terminal and the negative (−) probe into the nearest cell. Record the meter reading. Put the negative (−) probe on the negative (−) battery terminal and the positive (+) probe into the nearest cell. Record the meter reading. Add these two readings, observing their positive and negative values, to get the end cell voltage.

4. Compare all meter readings, figure 3-20.

   a. If all cells read less than 1.95 volts, the battery is too discharged to test. Boost-charge it and retest.

   b. If one or more cells are 1.95 volts or more and there is more than a 0.1 volt variation between the lowest and the highest reading, the battery is defective.

   c. If one or more cells are less than 1.95 volts and there is less than a 0.05 volt variation between the lowest and the highest reading, the battery is good but requires charging.

   d. If all cells are 1.95 volts or more and there

is less than a 0.05 volt variation between the lowest and the highest reading, the battery is good and sufficiently charged.

BATTERY CHARGING

Battery charging means applying a charging current rate in amperes for a period of time in hours. For example, a 20-ampere charging rate for 3 hours would be a 60-ampere-hour charging input to the battery.

Batteries are usually charged at rates from 3 to 50 amperes. Charging rates at the low end of this scale are slow charging. Charging rates at the high end of the scale are fast charging. Fast chargers are the most widely used kind of charging equipment in service stations and garages. Most fast chargers can charge at either a fast or a slow rate. Many motorists own slow chargers, or trickle chargers, that will charge a battery only at a slow rate.

Generally, any battery can be charged at any current rate as long as electrolyte gassing and spewing do not occur and as long as electrolyte temperature stays below 125° F. When you have the time, however, the best charging is at a slow rate of about 5 to 15 amperes.

Whether charging at a slow or a fast rate, begin by checking the electrolyte level. If should be about ¼-inch above the separators in each cell. Charging with the electrolyte below the separators may damage the battery. Charging with the electrolyte level too high may cause the electrolyte to overflow because of the heat of charging. The proper electrolyte level is important for fast charging. Leave the cell caps in place during charging, *but be sure the vent holes are open*. Place a damp cloth over the battery while it is charging.

Be sure also that the a.c. power line to which the charger is attached is delivering full power. Do not connect the charger to a heavily loaded circuit. An a.c. voltage drop of 20 percent can reduce the charger's output by 35 to 40 percent. If an extension cord is necessary, use a number-14 or larger heavy-duty cord not over 25 feet long. The charger power cord and the extension cord should both be the 3-wire type so the charger case can be grounded. Special adapters may be required to connect the charger to a side-terminal battery.

Whether fast or slow charging, remember:
• Charge in a well-ventilated area away from sparks and open flame.
• *Be sure the charger is off* before connecting or disconnecting cables at the battery.
• Never try to charge a frozen battery.
• Wear eye protection.

If you are charging the battery while it is in the car:

1. Disconnect both battery cables to avoid damage to the alternator or other electrical parts.
2. Connect the charger cables to the battery, checking for correct polarity (+ to + and − to −).
3. Turn on the charger and set it for the desired rate.
4. Check the specific gravity and electrolyte temperature periodically during charging. Stop charging *immediately* if the temperature rises above 125° F.
5. Check the voltage across the battery terminals with a voltmeter or a battery tester. If voltage is more than 15.5 volts for a 12-volt battery or 7.5 volts for a 6-volt battery, lower the charging rate until the voltage drops below these maximum values.
6. The battery is fully charged when all cells are gassing freely and specific gravity does not increase for three continuous hours. The fully charged specific gravity should be 1.260 to 1.280, corrected for electrolyte temperature, unless otherwise specified by the battery maker. If the specific gravity stays below the maximum value for three hours, the battery is not in good condition and will not provide the best performance.
7. When charging a sealed, maintenance-free battery, follow the maker's specifications for charging rate and time. If the battery has a state-of-charge indicator, charge until the indicator shows a full charge. In any case, do not exceed the maker's rate or time specifications.
8. After charging, wash and dry the battery top to remove any acid from electrolyte gassing. Check the electrolyte level and add mineral-free or distilled water if necessary to bring all cells up to the level marks.
9. Replace the battery if removed. *Connect the insulated cable first, then the ground cable.*

Fast Charging Precautions

Fast charging a battery delivers a higher charging rate for a short period of time. Follow the charger maker's instructions for charging rate and length of time, according to the battery's specific gravity and capacity or ampere-hour rating. Also, follow these specific precautions for fast charging:

• *Never* fast charge a battery that has failed a 3-minute charge test.
• *Never* fast charge a battery that is sulfated or that has plate or separator damage.
• Watch electrolyte temperature closely and *stop charging* if the temperature rises above 125° F.

    Whenever possible, follow a fast charge with a period of slow charging to fully charge the battery. Most battery chargers have a gradually decreasing charge rate as the battery comes to a

DANGER: POISON
CAUSES SEVERE BURNS
ACID PACKAGE
CONTAINS SULFURIC ACID
 AVOID CONTACT WITH THE SKIN OR EYES
ANTIDOTES
EXTERNAL: Flood with water, then cover with moistened sodium bicarbonate. If eyes are involved, wash first with water then with 1 per cent solution of freshly prepared sodium bicarbonate. Call physician immediately.

INTERNAL: Do not use emetics, stomach pump, carbonates or bicarbonates. Give at least 20 to 30 cc (2/3 to 1 ounce) of milk of magnesia or preferably aluminum hydroxide gel diluted with water. If these alkalies are not available, the white of eggs (2 or 3) well beaten may be used. Give large quantities of water. Prevent collapse. Call physician immediately.

FLUSH THE PLASTIC LINER WITH WATER WHEN EMPTY

KEEP OUT OF REACH OF CHILDREN

Figure 3-22. The electrolyte package label instructions must be read and obeyed. (Atlas)

full charge. This protects the battery from overcharging.

ACTIVATING DRY-CHARGED BATTERIES

To ensure the best possible service, activate a dry-charged battery just before you install it in a car. To avoid damage from spilled acid, do not activate the battery after it is in a car.

1. Fill each battery cell to the top of the separators with the packaged electrolyte, figure 3-21. Be sure to read and follow the precautions listed on the electrolyte package, figure 3-22.
2. After filling, charge a 12-volt battery at 30 to 40 amperes or a 6-volt battery at 60 to 70 amperes until the electrolyte temperature is about 80° F and specific gravity is above 1.250.
3. After charging, check the electrolyte level. If it is low, add enough electrolyte to bring the level up to the indicated marks in each cell. After that, when servicing the battery, add only mineral-free or distilled water to maintain the electrolyte level.

4. When the battery is properly filled and charged, destroy any extra electrolyte by neutralizing it with baking soda and pouring it down a floor drain or utility sink. Be careful with this to avoid acid burns.

JUMP STARTING WITH CABLES

It is often necessary to jump-start a car with a dead battery by using a booster battery and jumper cables. Follow this procedure to avoid damage to the charging system and to prevent any sparks that might cause a battery explosion:
1. Set the hand brake, turn off accessories and the ignition switch, and place the gearshift lever in Neutral or Park.
2. Attach one end of the first cable to the terminal of the discharged battery that is connected to the starter switch or the solenoid. Note whether this is the positive or negative terminal. *Do not connect to the grounded terminal first*.

3. Connect the other end of the same cable to the corresponding terminal post on the booster battery: + to +, or − to −.
4. Connect the first end of the other cable to the remaining terminal of the booster battery. Connect the opposite end of this cable to a good ground on the *engine block* of the disabled car, as far from the battery as possible. The alternator mounting bracket is usually a convenient place for this.
5. Turn on the ignition and starter of the disabled car. If it doesn't start immediately and if the booster battery is in another car, start the engine of the other car to avoid excessive drain on the booster battery. Be sure that the cars are not touching each other.
6. After the disabled car is started, remove the cable connection to the engine block *first*. Then remove the other end of that cable from the booster battery.
7. Finally, remove the other cable by disconnecting it at the booster battery first.

PART TWO

Charging System Service

4

D.C. Charging System On-Car Inspection and Testing

Several quick, simple checks of a d.c. charging system will tell you if parts must be removed from the system for repair or if they can be adjusted on the car. This chapter presents troubleshooting tips, visual checks of the system condition, and step-by-step instructions for testing the d.c. charging system with a voltmeter and ammeter.

Whenever you work with the charging system, remember these basic safety rules:
• Keep hands, hair, jewelry, and clothing away from belts and pulleys.
• Always turn the ignition switch off except during an actual test procedure.
• Disconnect the battery ground cable before removing any electrical parts from the car.

CHARGING SYSTEM CONDITIONS AND POSSIBLE CAUSES

Several conditions can indicate a charging system failure:
• A discharged battery
• Unusual indicator lamp or meter behavior
• Noisy generator
• Burned regulator points
• Chattering cutout relay.

If the dashboard ammeter or voltmeter needle flutters or stays on the discharge side of the gauge, or if the warning lamp flickers or stays on, the generator output is less than normal. This could be caused by:
• Broken or loose drive belt
• Defective or incorrectly set regulator
• Too much charging circuit resistance in either the insulated or the ground circuit
• Defective generator.

Noises from the generator can be caused by:
• Defective armature shaft bearings
• High insulation on the commutator
• Out-of-round commutator
• Defective brushes.

Burned regulator points are usually caused by shorts in the generator field windings.

A chattering cutout relay can be caused by:
• Wrong generator polarity
• Wrong battery installation
• Wrong cutout relay setting.

The rest of this chapter has test procedures to help you isolate these causes.

CHARGING SYSTEM INSPECTION

1. Check the battery's electrolyte level and state of charge, as explained in Chapter 3. Fast electrolyte loss with no sign of leakage can mean that the battery is being overcharged. An undercharged battery can be caused by generator or regulator failure. If the battery is defective, the charging system may not be at fault. Charging

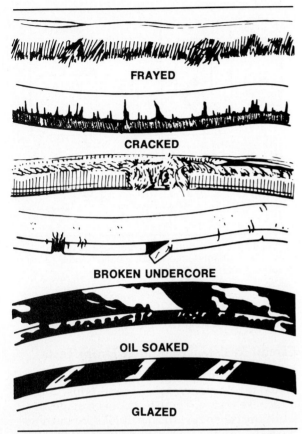

Figure 4-1. Many kinds of damage can make a drive belt operate inefficiently.

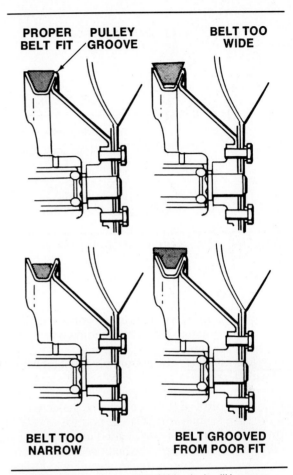

Figure 4-2. The wrong size of drive belt will hamper charging system operation.

Figure 4-3. This belt tension gauge can be used when the manufacturer's specification is known.

system voltage and amperage tests should be made with a fully charged battery.

2. Inspect the charging system wiring for broken or damaged wires or loose connections. Repair any damage.

3. Check the generator and regulator mounting for loose or missing bolts. Replace any that are needed.

4. Inspect the generator drive belt for fraying or cracking, figure 4-1, or looseness. A damaged or loose belt should be replaced or adjusted, because it will not drive the generator properly.

Drive Belt Installation

When installing a new belt, check the carmaker's specifications for the correct replacement. A correctly installed belt should ride on the sides of the pulley, not the bottom, figure 4-2. The top of the belt should be flush with, or not more than 1/16 inch above, the top of the pulley grooves.

Belt tension specifications are given in pounds and are different for new and used belts on the same installation. New-belt tension specifications apply only to replacement belts when first installed. A belt will stretch after the first 10 to 15 minutes of operation. It is then considered

a used belt and should be adjusted to used-belt specifications.

The best way to check belt tension is with a strand tension gauge. There are many types of tension gauges available, but all are used similarly. One type has a belt hook attached to a spring-loaded plunger and a dial indicator registering in pounds, figure 4-3. The plunger is depressed to engage the hook under the belt,

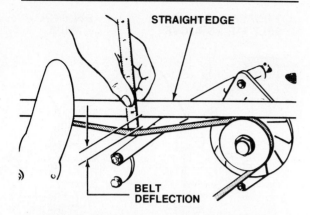

Figure 4-4. If the specification for belt tension is not known or a tension gauge is unavailable, press on the belt with a ruler. The belt should not deflect more than ½ inch.

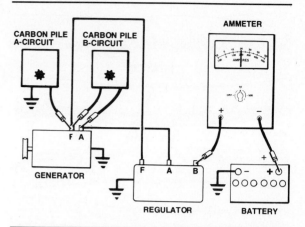

Figure 4-5. Before performing any voltage drop tests, make these meter hookups and maintain a steady 20 ampere generator output.

then released. The pounds of tension are read on the dial. Take two or more readings, moving the belt each time.

A less accurate, but reasonably reliable, belt tension test is to depress the belt on the longest section midway between two pulleys with your thumb, figure 4-4. If the belt can be deflected more than ½ inch with 20 to 22 pounds of pressure (about the force needed to replace a crimp-type bottle cap), the belt needs retensioning. Placing a straightedge from pulley to pulley helps to measure deflection.

SYSTEM TESTS WITH A VOLT-AMP TESTER

For most of the in-car charging system tests you will do, you will concentrate on checking the general system condition, the generator's output, and the regulator's performance. To do these tests, you will need the following items:
• Voltmeter and ammeter (or volt-amp multimeter)
• Field rheostat
• Variable-resistance carbon pile
• Fixed ¼-ohm resistor
• Jumper wire
• Assorted screwdrivers
• Feeler gauges.
The field rheostat, carbon pile, and ¼-ohm resistor are built into some volt-amp testers.

A field rheostat and a carbon pile are both variable resistors, but a rheostat is more accurate than a carbon pile. The rheostat can be used in many of the tests where we show a carbon pile connected to a regulator. *Do not connect a rheostat across the battery* to simulate a load. The rheostat's resistance is not great enough for this job, and a carbon pile must be used.

All of the test connections shown in this chapter are for negative-ground systems.

Circuit Resistance (Voltage Drop) Tests

Charging circuit voltage drop tests can help you to find poor grounds, loose connections, and undersize wiring. These tests can be made while the car engine warms up. Before starting the tests, use the ammeter and the carbon pile or field rheostat to make the following connections, figure 4-5:
1. With the ignition switch off, disconnect the lead from the battery terminal at the regulator. Connect the ammeter positive lead to the regulator terminal and the ammeter *negative* lead to the battery lead. This may appear to be reversed ammeter polarity, but it is not. Remember that charging current from the generator will be flowing *from* the regulator *to* the battery positive terminal, and current flow must enter the ammeter positive lead.
2. On an A-circuit generator, connect the carbon pile or field rheostat between the field terminal at the generator and the grounded regulator base.
3. On a B-circuit generator, connect the carbon pile or field rheostat between the armature terminal and the field terminal at the generator.
4. Run the engine at 1,500 rpm and adjust the carbon pile so that the ammeter registers 20 amperes output.

Insulated circuit voltage drop tests
1. Battery-to-armature voltage drop — place the voltmeter positive (+) lead on the armature terminal at the generator and the voltmeter negative (−) lead on the battery positive terminal, figure 4-6. This hookup measures the voltage drop of the entire battery-to-armature insulated circuit. The drop should not exceed the manufacturer's specifications, usually less than 0.8

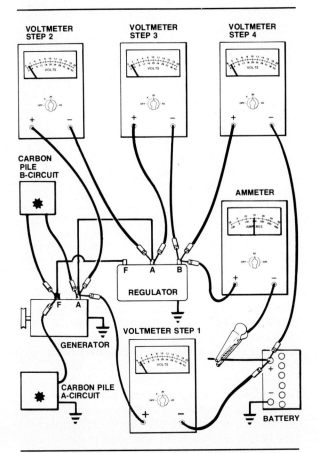

Figure 4-6. The voltmeter connections for wiring voltage drop tests.

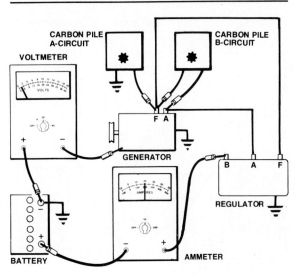

Figure 4-7. The ground circuit voltage drop test.

volt. If it does, perform the individual voltage drop tests described in steps 2, 3, and 4.

2. Armature-lead voltage drop — place the voltmeter positive (+) lead on the armature terminal at the generator and the voltmeter negative (−) lead on the armature terminal at the regulator. The drop should not exceed 0.2 volt.

3. Cutout-points voltage drop — place the voltmeter positive lead (+) on the armature terminal at the regulator and the voltmeter negative (−) lead on the battery terminal at the regulator. The drop should not exceed 0.2 volt.

4. Battery-to-regulator-lead voltage drop — place the voltmeter positive (+) lead on the battery terminal at the regulator and the voltmeter negative (−) lead on the battery positive (+) terminal. The drop should not exceed 0.4 volt.

5. Repair or replace any loose connectors or damaged wiring found during the voltage drop test.

Ground circuit voltage drop tests

1. Generator-to-battery voltage drop — place the voltmeter positive (+) lead on the battery negative (−) terminal and the voltmeter nega-

tive (−) lead on the generator frame, figure 4-7. The drop should not exceed 0.1 volt.

2. Engine-block-to-body voltage drop — turn off the car engine and turn on all lights and accessories. Place the voltmeter positive (+) lead on the engine block and the voltmeter negative (−) lead on the fender wall or frame near the battery. The drop should not exceed 0.1 volt.

3. Repair or replace any loose connectors or damaged wiring found during the voltage drop test.

Current Output Test

Manufacturers specify the amperage output of their generators at a certain temperature, engine speed, and battery voltage. These ratings may be stamped on the generator or listed in the manufacturer's literature. Other independent publishers often list test specifications for popular models. If the specifications are unknown, use the general values listed in these testing guidelines.

The test meter hookup during a current output test lets the generator operate with unregulated field current. The test should be done as quickly as possible to avoid overheating the generator. Because of the field circuit differences between A-circuit and B-circuit generators, the test equipment is hooked up differently for each circuit.

Use the ammeter, the voltmeter, the carbon pile, and the jumper wire to make the following connections, figure 4-8:

1. Connect the carbon pile across the battery terminals. Do not use a field rheostat.

2. Disconnect the lead from the battery terminal at the regulator. Connect the ammeter positive

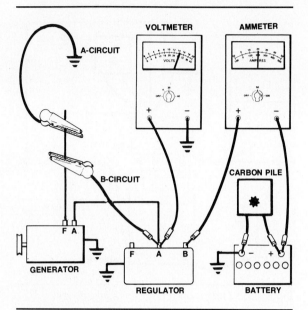

Figure 4-8. Test meter hookups for a generator current output test.

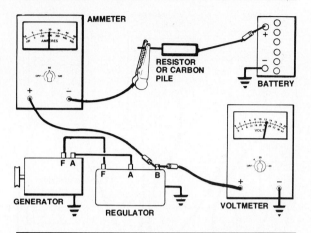

Figure 4-9. Test meter hookups for testing the voltage limiter.

(+) lead to the regulator terminal and the ammeter negative (−) lead to the battery lead.
3. Connect the voltmeter positive (+) lead to the armature terminal at the regulator and the voltmeter negative (−) lead to ground.
4. For an A-circuit generator, disconnect the lead from the field terminal at the regulator. Use the jumper wire to ground the lead.
5. For a B-circuit generator, disconnect the lead from the field terminal at the regulator. Use the jumper wire to connect the field lead to the armature terminal at the regulator.
6. Start the engine and adjust the carbon pile so that the voltmeter reads 14 to 15 volts. Check the manufacturer's specifications.
7. Gradually increase the engine speed to 1,600 rpm. The ammeter reading should be at least the specified output.
8. If no amperage output is registered but the voltmeter reads 15 volts, the cutout relay is not closing. The relay should be tested and adjusted.
9. If the generator's amperage output is below specifications the unit should be removed from the car for disassembly and testing.

REGULATOR TESTS AND ADJUSTMENTS

Regulator tests and adjustments should be done in the following order:
1. Run voltage limiter until it warms up; check and adjust.
2. Check cutout relay.
3. Run current limiter until it warms up; check and adjust.

Manufacturer's test specifications usually include the outside operating temperature of the regulator and the proper engine speed. The temperature should be measured as close as possible to the regulator without touching the thermometer to any metal surfaces. If this specification is not known or cannot be measured, operate the generator at a 10-ampere output for 30 minutes to warm up the regulator temperature before testing. If the specified engine speed for testing is not known, use the general values given in these testing guidelines.

Voltage Limiter Test and Adjustment

To test the voltage limiter, connect the voltmeter, the ammeter, and either the ¼-ohm resistor or the carbon pile as follows, figure 4-9:
1. Disconnect the lead from the battery terminal at the regulator. Connect the ammeter positive (+) lead to the terminal and the ammeter negative (−) lead to the resistor or the carbon pile. Connect the other side of the resistor or the carbon pile to the battery lead. The carbon pile or resistor acts like a charged battery to allow accurate voltage limiter testing.
2. Connect the voltmeter positive (+) lead to the battery terminal at the regulator and the voltmeter negative (−) lead to ground.
3. For a single-contact voltage limiter, run the engine at 1,500 rpm. If you are using a carbon pile, adjust the pile until the ammeter measures 10 amperes of charging current or as specified by the manufacturer. The voltmeter reading is the limiter's operating voltage. If it is not within specifications, the limiter must be adjusted.
4. For a double-contact voltage limiter:
     a. Run the engine at 2,000 rpm. If you are using a carbon pile, adjust the pile until the ammeter measures 10 amperes of charging

Figure 4-10. The voltage limiter air gap is adjusted with a nut. (Delco-Remy)

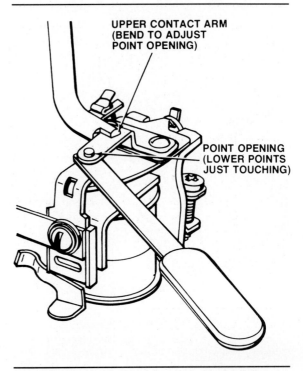

Figure 4-11. On a 2-contact voltage regulator, the point gap is adjusted by bending the contact arm. (Delco-Remy)

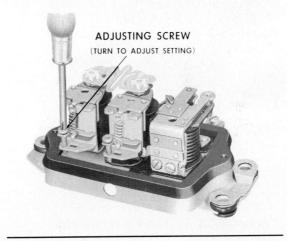

Figure 4-12. The voltage setting of the voltage limiter can be adjusted with a screw to change the armature spring tension. (Delco-Remy)

current. The voltmeter reading is the grounding contact setting.

b. Reduce the engine speed until the voltmeter needle jumps. The voltmeter reading then is the resistor contact setting.

5. For a double-contact voltage limiter, compare the two readings taken in step 4 to the manufacturer's specifications:

a. If the resistor contact reading is within specifications and there is less than 0.3 volt difference between the two readings, the voltage limiter is operating correctly.

b. If the difference between the two readings is greater than 0.3 volt, adjust the unit.

c. If the resistor contact reading is not within specifications, adjust the unit.

d. If the voltmeter needle did not jump when the contacts switched but the readings are within specifications, the unit is operating properly.

The adjustments of a voltage limiter are:
• Air gap
• Point gap (two-contact limiters)
• Voltage control setting.

To adjust the voltage limiter:

1. Leave the test hookups in place.

2. Turn off the ignition switch and remove the regulator cover.

3. Check the armature-to-coil air gap and adjust it if necessary. Adjustment is made with a nut on many units, figure 4-10.

4. On a 2-contact limiter, check and adjust the point gap, figure 4-11, by bending the contact arm.

5. Start the engine and run it at the test speed.

6. Adjust the voltage control setting by changing the armature spring tension until the voltmeter reading is the same as specifications.

a. Some units are adjusted with a screw, figure 4-12

b. Some units are adjusted by bending the adjustment arm, figure 4-13

c. For an accurate adjustment with either method, make the final setting an *increase* in spring tension.

7. Turn off the ignition switch and replace the regulator cover.

8. Start the engine and run it at the test speed.

9. Retest the voltage control setting and repeat the adjustment procedure if necessary.

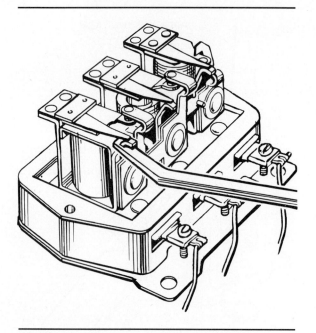

Figure 4-13. The voltage setting of the voltage limiter can be changed by bending an adjustment arm.

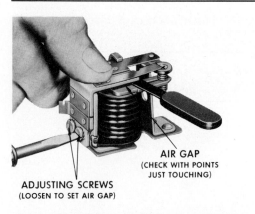

ADJUSTING SCREWS
(LOOSEN TO SET AIR GAP)

AIR GAP
(CHECK WITH POINTS
JUST TOUCHING)

Figure 4-15. The cutout relay air gap is adjusted with 2 adjusting screws. (Delco-Remy)

Cutout Relay Test and Adjustment

To test the cutout relay, connect the ammeter, the voltmeter, and the carbon pile or field rheostat as follows, figure 4-14:

1. Disconnect the lead from the battery terminal at the regulator. Connect the ammeter positive (+) lead to the terminal and the ammeter negative (−) lead to the battery lead.
2. Connect the voltmeter positive (+) lead to the armature terminal at the regulator and the voltmeter negative (−) lead to the ground.
3. Disconnect the lead from the field terminal at the regulator. Connect the carbon pile in series between the field terminal at the regulator and the field terminal at the generator. Set the carbon pile at its greatest resistance.

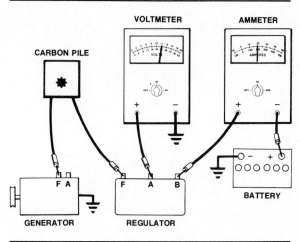

Figure 4-14. Test meter hookup for testing the cutout relay.

4. Run the engine at 1,500 rpm. Decrease the carbon pile's resistance to build the generator's voltage output until the cutout relay points close. The highest voltmeter reading before the points close is the relay's closing voltage.
5. Adjust the carbon pile until the ammeter reads 10 to 15 amperes, then use the carbon pile to reduce the amperage slowly. The lowest amperage reading before the contacts open is the relay's discharge amperage setting.
6. If the readings are not within specifications, adjust the unit.

The cutout relay's adjustments are:
• Point closing voltage
• Point gap
• Air gap.

To adjust the cutout relay:
1. Leave the test hookups in place.
2. Turn off the ignition switch and remove the regulator cover.
3. Disconnect the regulator from the battery.
4. Check the armature-to-coil air gap and adjust it if necessary. Adjustment is made with a screw on some units, figure 4-15.
5. Check the point gap and adjust it if necessary by bending the armature, figure 4-16.
6. Reconnect the regulator and run the engine at the test speed.
7. Adjust the point closing voltage by changing the armature spring tension until the voltmeter reading is the same as specifications. Adjustment is made with a screw, on some units, figure 4-17. Others are adjusted by bending the spring hanger. For an accurate adjustment, make the final setting an *increase* in spring tension.

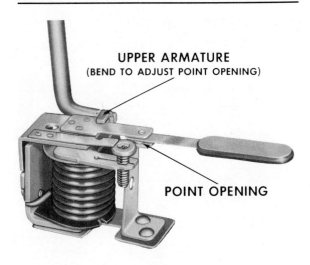

Figure 4-16. The cutout relay point gap is set by bending the armature. (Delco-Remy)

Figure 4-17. The cutout relay's closing voltage can be adjusted with a screw. (Delco-Remy)

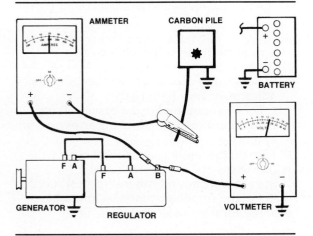

Figure 4-18. Test meter hookup for testing the current limiter.

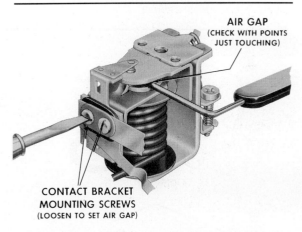

Figure 4-19. The current limiter's air gap is set by moving the armature bracket. (Delco-Remy)

8. Turn off the ignition switch and replace the regulator cover.
9. Start the engine and run it at the test speed.
10. Retest the point closing voltage and repeat the adjustment procedure if necessary.

Current Limiter Test and Adjustment

To test the current limiter, connect the ammeter, the voltmeter, and the carbon pile as follows, figure 4-18:
1. Disconnect the lead from the battery terminal at the regulator and connect the ammeter positive (+) lead to the terminal. Connect the ammeter negative (−) lead to the carbon pile, and connect the other side of the carbon pile to ground.
2. Connect the voltmeter positive (+) lead to the battery terminal at the regulator and the voltmeter negative (−) lead to ground.

3. Run the engine at 1,500 rpm and adjust the carbon pile to get the highest amperage reading possible.
4. The highest amperage reading is the setting of the current limiter. If it is not within specifications, adjust the unit.
5. If a carbon pile is not used, the starting system can be used as a load:
   a. Remove the secondary coil lead from the distributor cap and ground it.
   b. Crank the engine for 15 seconds.
   c. Replace the coil lead and run the engine at 1,500 rpm with the headlamps and other accessories on. The amperage reading is the current limiter setting.
   The current limiter's adjustments are:
● Air gap
● Amperage control setting.

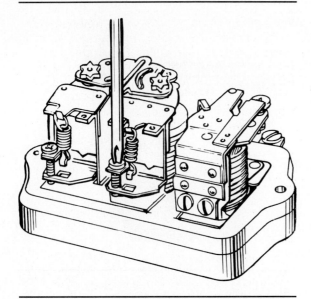

Figure 4-20. The current limiter's amperage setting can be adjusted with a screw.

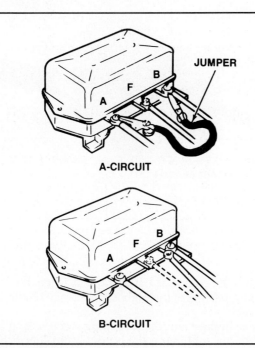

A-CIRCUIT

B-CIRCUIT

Figure 4-22. Generators must be polarized after any service is done.

To adjust the current limiter:
1. Leave the test hookups in place.
2. Turn off the ignition switch and remove the regulator cover.
3. Check the armature-to-coil air gap and adjust it if necessary. Adjustment is made with a screw on some units, figure 4-19.
4. Start the engine and run it at the test speed.
5. Adjust the amperage control setting by changing the armature spring tension until the ammeter reading is the same as the specifications.

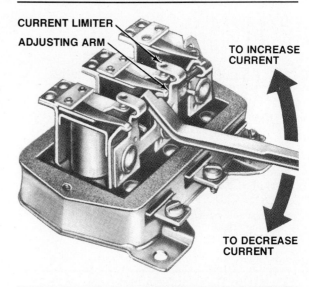

Figure 4-21. The current limiter's amperage setting can be changed by bending an adjusting arm. (Ford)

a. Some units are adjusted with a screw, figure 4-20.
b. Some units are adjusted by bending the adjustment arm, figure 4-21
c. For an accurate adjustment with either method, make the final setting an *increase* in spring tension.
6. Turn off the ignition switch and replace the regulator cover.
7. Start the engine and run it at the test speed.
8. Retest the amperage control setting and repeat the adjustment steps if necessary.

POLARIZING A GENERATOR

Whenever a generator or a generator regulator is tested, repaired, or replaced, the generator must be polarized to make sure that the field pole pieces have the correct polarity. If this is not done, the generator may be damaged and the regulator contacts burned. Also, if generator polarity is reversed, the battery will be discharged.
   The method for polarizing a generator depends on whether the field is grounded through the regulator (A-circuit) or grounded internally (B-circuit), figure 4-22:
● To polarize an A-circuit generator, momentarily connect a jumper wire between the armature terminal at the regulator and the battery terminal at the regulator.
● To polarize a B-circuit generator, disconnect the lead from the field terminal at the regulator and momentarily touch it to the battery terminal at the regulator.

5

A.C. Charging System On – Car Inspection and Testing

Inspecting and testing the a.c. charging system on the car will help you to pinpoint problems. If the problem is with the alternator or with a solid-state regulator, the unit must be removed from the car for service or replacement. Off-the-car repairs for alternators are detailed in Chapter 6.

When working with the charging system, remember these safety precautions:
• Keep hands, hair, jewelry, and clothing away from moving parts. Remove any jewelry when servicing the battery.
• Keep the ignition switch off at all times except during actual test procedures.
• Disconnect the battery ground cable before removing any leads from the alternator.
• Remember that the output terminal at the alternator has voltage present all the time while system connections are still in place.
• Never polarize an alternator.
• Make sure you connect up the right terminals when you install a battery.
• Disconnect the battery cables before charging the battery.
• Never operate an alternator without an external load connected to the unit.
• Keep the carbon pile set at open at all times except during test procedures.

CHARGING SYSTEM SYMPTOMS AND POSSIBLE CAUSES

Some common warning signs of charging system failures are:
• Ammeter, voltmeter, or warning lamp indications
• Low battery state of charge
• Alternator noise.

These symptoms, their possible causes, and cures are outlined in figure 5-1. The rest of this chapter explains how to test a.c. charging systems with common test equipment and pinpoint these causes.

CHARGING SYSTEM INSPECTION

1. Check the battery's electrolyte level and state of charge as explained in Chapter 3. If the battery is worn out, the charging system may not be at fault.
2. Inspect the alternator drive belt as explained in Chapter 4. If you must adjust the belt, be careful not to pry against the alternator's thin aluminum housing.
3. Inspect all system wiring and connections. Be sure to inspect fusible links for fusing, and make sure multiple plug connectors are latched correctly.
4. Check the alternator and regulator mountings for loose or missing bolts. Replace or tighten as needed.

SYMPTOMS	POSSIBLE CAUSE	CURE
• The meter needle flutters • Warning lamp flickers	1. Loose connections in system wiring 2. Loose or worn brushes 3. Oxidized regulator points	1. Repair system wiring 2. Disassemble and test alternator 3. Replace regulator
• Ammeter needle reads discharge • Voltmeter needle shows low system voltage • Warning lamp stays on • Battery is discharged	1. Faulty alternator drive belt 2. Corroded battery cables 3. Loose system wiring 4. Defective field relay 5. Defective battery 6. Wrong battery in car 7. Alternator output low	1. Check and adjust belt 2. Replace battery cables 3. Repair system wiring 4. Replace field relay 5. Replace battery 6. Replace battery 7. Test and repair alternator
• Ammeter needle reads charge • Voltmeter needle shows high system voltage • Battery is overcharged	1. Loose system wiring 2. Poor regulator ground 3. Burned regulator points 4. Incorrect regulator setting 5. Defective regulator	1. Repair system wiring 2. Tighten regulator ground 3. Replace regulator 4. Adjust regulator 5. Replace regulator
• Warning lamp stays on when ignition switch is off	1. Shorted positive diode	1. Disassemble and test alternator
• Alternator makes squealing noise	1. Loose or damaged drive belt 2. Worn or defective rotor shaft bearing 3. Defective stator 4. Loose or misaligned pulley	1. Adjust or replace drive belt 2. Disassemble and inspect alternator 3. Disassemble and test alternator 4. Adjust pulley
• Alternator makes whining noise	1. Shorted diode	1. Disassemble and test alternator

Figure 5-1. Alternator charging system troubleshooting table.

ALTERNATOR TESTING OVERVIEW

On-car alternator charging system tests are all about the same, regardless of the car being tested. The main differences are the meter test points and the specifications. The next few paragraphs are general descriptions of the most common of these on-car tests.

Then, we will discuss the procedures for doing these tests for individual carmakers. Not all carmakers require all of these tests, and some suggest even more. These will be covered in detail. If the directions tell you to remove the alternator for more testing, check Chapter 6 for full instructions for removing, disassembling, and testing it. If the directions tell you to adjust the voltage regulator, follow the steps listed at the end of this chapter.

During the tests, you will have to refer to the manufacturer's specifications for the model you are testing. These specifications are vital to your work. They are the only tool that will tell you where the system is bad.

Specifications can be found in the manufacturer's shop manual or in books prepared by independent publishers. Before you begin any test, find the correct specifications. Keep a copy handy while you work, so that you can quickly refer to it.

Circuit Resistance Testing

This is a voltage drop test of the charging system. The tests are usually done with the engine running at 1,500 to 1,800 rpm and the alternator producing a specific amperage. The first measurement is taken from the battery positive terminal to the battery (output) terminal at the alternator. If the voltage drop is high, then test the connections within the circuit to pinpoint the area of resistance.

A voltage drop test of the ground circuit is made from the alternator frame to the battery grounded terminal. A voltage drop test of the field circuit is made at the regulator. Any loose or corroded connections or damaged wiring must be replaced before the rest of the charging system tests are made, or you will not get accurate test results.

Current Output Testing

Current output tests are made in two stages. Some carmakers suggest doing only one stage or the other. First, a carbon pile is connected across the battery, a voltmeter is connected between the battery positive terminal and ground, and an ammeter is connected between the battery positive terminal and the battery terminal at the alternator. The engine is run at the test speed, and the carbon pile is adjusted either to keep a steady 15-volt level or to get the greatest possible ammeter reading. Compare the ammeter reading to your specifications.

Second, if the ammeter reading does not meet specifications, bypass the voltage regulator. With a remotely mounted regulator, do this

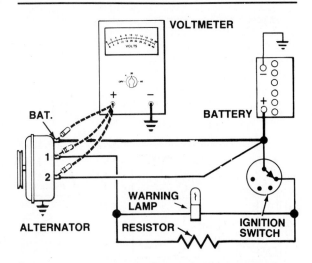

Figure 5-2. Delco-Remy 10-SI circuit resistance test.

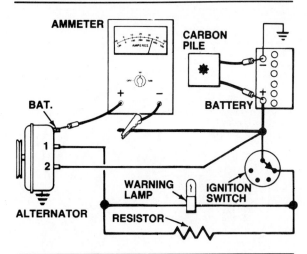

Figure 5-3. Delco-Remy 10-SI current output test with voltage regulator in circuit.

with a jumper wire. With an integral regulator, there are several methods to bypass it. With either type, bypassing the regulator connects the field winding to full battery voltage. Run the engine at the test speed and adjust the carbon pile. Compare the ammeter reading to specifications. If it meets specifications, then the voltage regulator may be faulty. If it still does not meet specifications, remove the alternator for further testing.

Voltage Output

The voltage output test is similar to the current output test. It is recommended by some manufacturers to avoid possible damage to an electronic ignition system during a current output test. Run the engine at fast idle, and use either the headlamps or a carbon pile to load the battery. If battery voltage measured at the positive battery terminal is below 13 volts, bypass the regulator and do the test again. If the battery voltage then increases to about 16 volts, the regulator may be faulty. If the battery voltage remains low, remove the alternator for further testing.

Field Current Draw

This test is made with the engine off. Often, the carmakers tell you to bypass the regulator or the warning lamp circuit, or both. Connect an ammeter between either the battery positive terminal and the field, or between the field and ground. When you turn on the ignition switch *without* starting the engine, or bypass the ignition switch and warning lamp with a jumper wire, the ammeter will measure the field current draw. If it is not within specifications, remove

the alternator for further testing. If it is within specifications, turn the alternator pulley by hand. If the ammeter reading fluctuates, the brushes and sliprings may need servicing.

Voltage Regulator Test

The regulated voltage can be checked with a voltmeter connected either between the alternator output terminal and ground or between the battery positive terminal and ground. Bring the regulator to operating temperature by running the engine at fast idle with a load on the battery for 10 to 15 minutes. The voltmeter reading at this point is the setting of the normally closed, or series, contacts of an electromechanical regulator.

Then, reduce the load and increase the engine rpm. This voltmeter reading is the setting of the normally open, or grounding, contacts of an electromechanical regulator, or the setting of a solid-state regulator. If the readings do not meet specifications, adjust or replace the regulator.

TESTING SPECIFIC ALTERNATORS

Delco-Remy 10-SI

Delco recommends that you do a circuit resistance test and a current output test on the 10-SI alternator series.

Circuit resistance test
1. Refer to figure 5-2.
2. Turn the ignition switch on.
3. Connect the voltmeter negative (−) lead to ground.

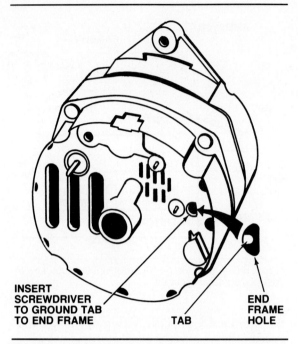

Figure 5-4. To bypass the 10-SI's voltage regulator, use a screwdriver to ground the tab in the end frame hole.

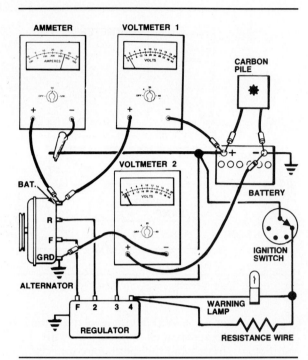

Figure 5-5. Delco-Remy 10-DN circuit resistance test.

4. Touch the voltmeter positive (+) lead to:
   a. The battery terminal at the alternator
   b. The number 1 terminal at the alternator
   c. The number 2 terminal at the alternator.
5. A zero-voltage reading at any of the test points indicates an open in the circuit between the test point and the battery positive (+) terminal. Check and repair any opens.
6. If voltage is present at the number 2 terminal and the battery is constantly overcharged, remove the alternator for further testing of the field circuit.

Current output test
1. Refer to figure 5-3.
2. Disconnect the battery ground cable.
3. Disconnect the wire from the battery terminal at the alternator.
4. Connect the ammeter positive (+) lead to the alternator terminal; connect the ammeter negative (−) lead to the wire.
5. Reconnect the battery ground cable.
6. Connect the carbon pile across the battery terminals.
7. Run the engine at moderate speed with all of the accessories operating.
8. Adjust the carbon pile to obtain the maximum possible ammeter reading.
9. Compare the ammeter reading to specifications:
   a. If the reading is within 10 percent of specifications, both the alternator and the regulator are operating properly.

   b. If the reading is not within 10 percent of specifications, go to step 10.
10. Insert one inch of a screwdriver blade into the test hole on the back of the alternator, figure 5-4. This bypasses the regulator and grounds the alternator field winding.
11. Compare the ammeter reading to specifications:
   a. If the reading is within 10 percent of specifications, remove the alternator for further testing of the regulator and field winding.
   b. If the reading is not within 10 percent of specifications, remove the alternator for further testing of the rectifier, the diode trio, and the stator.

Delco-Remy 10-DN

Delco recommends that a circuit resistance test, a current output test, a field current draw test, and a voltage regulator test be made on the 10-DN alternator series.

Circuit resistance test
1. Refer to figure 5-5.
2. Disconnect the wire from the battery terminal at the alternator.
3. Connect the ammeter positive (+) lead to the alternator terminal; connect the ammeter negative (−) lead to the wire.
4. Connect the carbon pile across the battery terminals.
5. Connect the voltmeter positive (+) lead to the

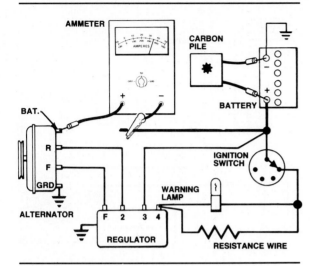

Figure 5-6. Delco-Remy 10-DN current output test with voltage regulator in circuit.

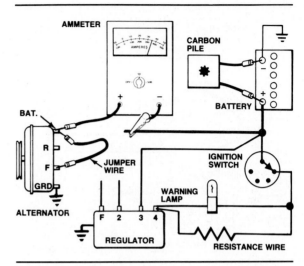

Figure 5-7. Delco-Remy 10-DN current output test with voltage regulator bypassed.

battery terminal at the alternator; connect the voltmeter negative (−) lead to the battery positive (+) terminal.

6. Run the engine at 1,000 rpm.

7. Adjust the carbon pile so that the ammeter measures 20 amperes of charging current.

8. Watch the voltmeter reading:
   a. If the reading is 0.3 volt or less, the insulated circuit is in good condition; go to step 11.
   b. If the reading exceeds 0.3 volt, go to step 9.

9. Touch the voltmeter positive (+) lead to all of the circuit connections in turn to pinpoint the area of resistance.

10. Repair or replace any loose or corroded connections or damaged wiring before doing the rest of the tests.

11. Connect the voltmeter positive (+) lead to the battery negative (−) terminal; connect the voltmeter negative (−) lead to the ground terminal at the alternator.

12. Observe the voltmeter reading:
   a. If the reading is 0.1 volt or less, the circuit's ground connections are good.
   b. If the reading is more than 0.1 volt, go to step 13.

13. Check the circuit's ground connections. Repair or replace any loose or corroded connections or damaged wiring before doing the rest of the tests.

Current output test

1. Refer to figure 5-6.

2. Disconnect the battery ground cable.

3. Disconnect the wire from the battery terminal at the alternator.

4. Connect the ammeter positive (+) lead to the alternator terminal; connect the ammeter negative (−) lead to the wire.

5. Reconnect the battery ground cable.

6. Connect the carbon pile across the battery terminals.

7. Run the engine at fast idle.

8. Adjust the carbon pile to get the highest ammeter reading.

9. Compare the ammeter reading to specifications:
   a. If the reading is within 10 percent of specifications, both the alternator and the regulator are operating properly.
   b. If the reading is not within 10 percent of specifications, go to step 10.

10. Turn the ignition switch off (leave the carbon pile on the battery).

11. Refer to figure 5-7.

12. Unplug the connector from the field terminals at the alternator.

13. Connect a jumper wire from the field F-terminal at the alternator to the battery terminal at the alternator.

14. Run the engine at fast idle and adjust the carbon pile to get the highest ammeter reading.

15. Compare the ammeter reading to specifications:
   a. If the reading is within 10 percent of specifications, the alternator is operating properly but the regulator must be tested.
   b. If the reading is not within 10 percent of specifications, remove the alternator for further testing.

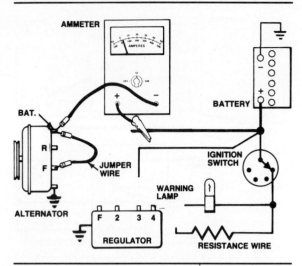

Figure 5-8. Delco-Remy 10-DN field current draw test.

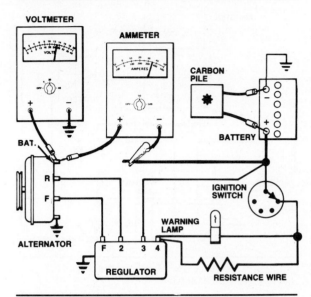

Figure 5-9. Delco-Remy electromechanical voltage regulator test.

Field current draw test
1. Refer to figure 5-8.
2. Disconnect the battery ground cable.
3. Disconnect the wire from the battery terminal at the alternator.
4. Connect the ammeter positive (+) lead to the wire; connect the ammeter negative (−) lead to the alternator terminal. (During this test, field current will flow *from* the battery *to* the alternator.)
5. Unplug the connector from the regulator.
6. Reconnect the battery ground cable.
7. Unplug the connector from the field terminals at the alternator.
8. Connect a jumper wire between the field F-terminal at the alternator and the battery terminal at the alternator.
9. Compare the ammeter reading to specifications:
   a. If the reading matches specifications, the alternator field circuit is in good condition.
   b. If the reading does not match specifications, remove the alternator for further testing.

Electromechanical voltage limiter test
1. Refer to figure 5-9.
2. Disconnect the battery ground cable.
3. Disconnect the wire from the battery terminal at the alternator.
4. Connect the ammeter positive (+) lead to the alternator terminal; connect the ammeter negative (−) lead to the wire.
5. Reconnect the battery ground cable.
6. Connect the voltmeter positive (+) lead to the battery terminal at the alternator; connect the voltmeter negative (−) lead to ground.
7. Connect the carbon pile across the battery terminals.

8. Bring the regulator to operating temperature by running the engine at 1,500 rpm for 15 minutes with the parking lights on; then turn the lights off.
9. Cycle the regulator by dropping the engine speed to idle then returning to 1,500 rpm.
10. Adjust the carbon pile to maintain 10 amperes of charging current.
11. Bring the engine speed to 2,000 rpm.
12. The voltmeter reading is the setting of the normally open (shorting) contacts; compare it to specifications:
   a. If the reading is within specifications and the battery has not been discharging rapidly, go to step 13.
   b. If the reading is not within specifications *or* the battery has been discharging, adjust the voltage regulator upper contact setting.
13. Turn on the parking lights.
14. Decrease the engine speed from 2,000 rpm until the voltmeter reading drops by a few tenths of a volt.
15. The voltmeter reading is the setting of the normally closed (series) contacts; compare it to specifications:
   a. If the reading is within specifications, the voltage regulator is operating properly.
   b. If the reading is not within specifications, adjust the voltage regulator air gap.

Motorcraft

Ford recommends that a regulator circuit test, a voltage output test, a regulator test, and a diode test be made on all of its alternators, regardless of the regulator style.

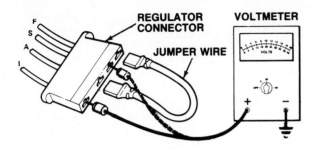

Figure 5-10. Motorcraft regulator circuit test (circuit with warning lamp).

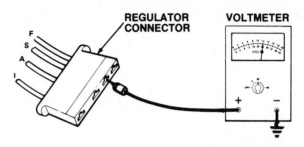

Figure 5-11. Motorcraft regulator circuit test (circuit with ammeter).

Regulator circuit test (indicator lamp circuit)
1. Refer to figure 5-10
2. With the ignition switch off, unplug the connector from the regulator.
3. Connect a jumper wire between the A-terminal and the F-terminal of the connector.
4. Run the engine at idle.
5. Connect the voltmeter positive (+) lead to the S-terminal of the connector; connect the voltmeter negative (−) lead to ground.
6. Note the voltmeter reading.
7. Move the voltmeter positive (+) lead to the I-terminal of the connector.
8. Note the voltmeter reading.
9. Compare the two voltmeter readings taken in steps 6 and 8:
   a. If the S-terminal reading is about 6 volts and the I-terminal reading is about 13 volts, the regulator circuit is all right.
   b. If either reading is zero voltage, repair the wiring to that terminal and repeat the test.
   c. If these readings are within specifications but the voltage output test is not, then replace the regulator and repeat the voltage output test.

Regulator circuit test (ammeter circuit)
1. Refer to figure 5-11.
2. With the ignition switch off, unplug the connector from the regulator.
3. Connect the voltmeter positive (+) lead to the S-terminal at the connector; connect the voltmeter negative (−) lead to ground.
4. *Do not start the engine.* Turn the ignition switch on.
5. Watch the voltmeter reading:
   a. If the reading is at or near battery voltage, the regulator circuit is all right.
   b. If the reading is zero voltage, repair the wiring from the ignition switch to the S-terminal at the connector. Test for voltage output.

Voltage output and regulator test
1. Refer to figure 5-12.
2. With the ignition switch off, connect the

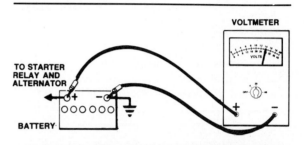

Figure 5-12. Motorcraft voltage output and regulator test with regulator in circuit.

voltmeter positive (+) lead to the battery positive (+) terminal; connect the voltmeter negative (−) lead to the battery negative (−) terminal.
3. Note the voltmeter reading (battery voltage).
4. Run the engine at 1,500 rpm.
5. Note the voltmeter reading (charging voltage without a load).
6. Turn on the high-speed blower motor and the high-beam headlamps.
7. Increase the engine speed to 2,000 rpm.
8. Note the voltmeter reading (charging voltage with a load).
9. Compare the three voltmeter readings:
   a. If the step 5 reading was 1 to 2 volts more than the step 3 reading, and the step 8 reading was 0.5 volt more than the step 5 reading, then the regulator and the alternator are operating properly.
   b. If the step 5 reading was more than 2 volts above the step 3 reading, go to step 10.
   c. If the step 8 reading was not 0.5 volt more than the step 5 reading, go to step 13.
10. Check the alternator and the regulator ground connections and repeat the test.
11. If the step 10 retest still shows too much charging voltage without a load:
   a. Turn the ignition switch off.
   b. Unplug the connector from the regulator.
   c. Start the engine and repeat the test.
12. Compare the voltmeter readings to specifications:

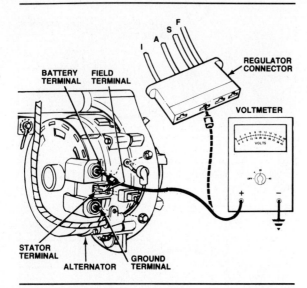

Figure 5-13. Motorcraft voltage test of circuit wiring.

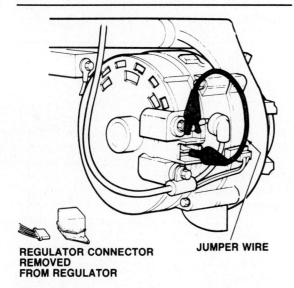

Figure 5-15. Motorcraft voltage output test with field windings connected to full battery voltage.

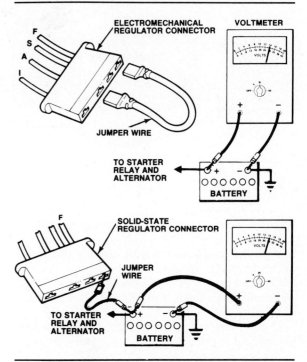

Figure 5-14. Motorcraft voltage output test with regulator bypassed.

   a. If the retest was within specifications, replace the regulator and repeat the test.
   b. If the step 11 retest was not within specifications, check for a short in the wiring between the alternator and the regulator. Repair if necessary.
   c. If a short was found and repaired, replace the regulator and repeat the test.
13. If the charging voltage with a load (step 8) was not 0.5 volt more than the charging voltage without a load (step 5):
   a. Refer to figure 5-13.
   b. Connect the voltmeter negative (−) lead to ground.
   c. Touch the voltmeter positive (+) lead to

the battery terminal at the alternator and to the A-terminal at the regulator connector.
   d. If either reading is zero voltage, repair the wiring between the test point and the battery positive terminal and repeat the test.
14. If the step 13 retest still does not meet specifications:
   a. Refer to figure 5-14.
   b. Turn the ignition switch off.
   c. Unplug the connector from the regulator.
   d. With an electromechanical voltage regulator, connect a jumper wire between the A-terminal and the F-terminal at the connector.
   e. With a remotely mounted solid-state voltage regulator, connect a jumper wire between the battery positive (+) terminal and the F-terminal at the connector.
   f. If the jumper wire sparks and heats, go to step 17.
   g. Repeat the test.
15. If the step 14 readings are still not within specifications:
   a. Refer to figure 5-15.
   b. Remove the jumper wire but leave the connector unplugged.
   c. Connect the jumper wire between the field terminal at the alternator and the battery terminal at the alternator.
   d. Repeat the test.
16. Compare the voltmeter readings to specifications:

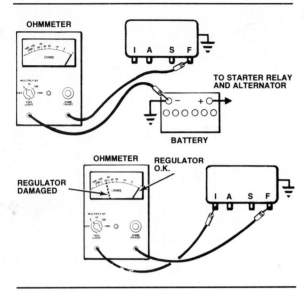

Figure 5-16. Motorcraft regulator test using ohmmeter.

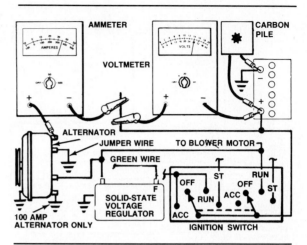

Figure 5-17. Testing circuit resistance of Chrysler with solid-state regulator.

a. If the readings are within specifications, repair the wiring between the alternator and the regulator and repeat the test.

b. If the readings are still not within specifications, remove the alternator for further testing.

17. If the jumper wire in step 14 sparks and heats:

a. Refer to figure 5-16.

b. With the regulator plug disconnected, connect an ohmmeter between the F-terminal at the regulator and the battery negative (−) terminal. The reading should be between 4 and 250 ohms.

c. Connect the ohmmeter between the I-terminal at the regulator and the F-terminal at the regulator. The reading should be zero ohms.

d. If either reading does not meet specifications, replace the regulator and repeat the test.

Chrysler With Transistorized Regulator

Chrysler alternators with transistorized regulators should be given a circuit resistance test, a current output test, a field current draw test, and a voltage regulator test.

Circuit resistance test

1. Refer to figure 5-17.
2. Disconnect the battery ground cable.
3. Disconnect the wire from the battery terminal at the alternator.
4. Connect the ammeter positive (+) lead to the alternator terminal; connect the ammeter negative (−) lead to the wire.
5. Connect the voltmeter positive (+) lead to the wire from the battery terminal at the alternator;

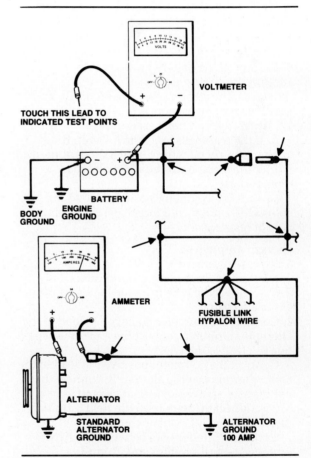

Figure 5-18. Additional test points for circuit resistance test of Chrysler with solid-state regulator.

connect the voltmeter negative (−) lead to the battery positive (+) terminal.

6. Disconnect the wire from the regulator-to-field terminal at the alternator; insulate the wire.

7. Connect a jumper wire between the regulator-to-field terminal and ground.

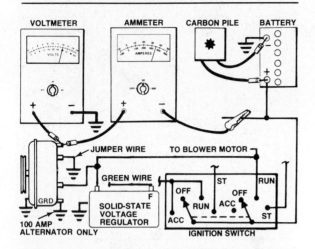

Figure 5-19. Current output test of Chrysler with solid-state regulator.

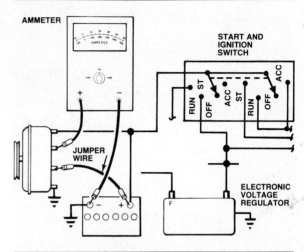

Figure 5-20. Field current draw test of Chrysler solid-state regulator.

8. Connect a carbon pile across the battery terminals.
9. Reconnect the battery ground cable.
10. Run the engine at idle.
11. Adjust the carbon pile to maintain 20 amperes of charging current.
12. Watch the voltmeter reading:
   a. If the reading is less than 0.7 volt, the charging circuit wiring is in good condition.
   b. If the reading exceeds 0.7 volt, go to step 13.
13. Touch the voltmeter positive lead to the connectors shown in figure 5-18 to pinpoint the area of resistance.

Current output test
1. Refer to figure 5-19.
2. Disconnect the battery ground cable.
3. Disconnect the wire from the battery terminal at the alternator.
4. Connect the ammeter positive (+) lead to the alternator terminal; connect the ammeter negative (−) lead to the wire.
5. Connect the voltmeter positive (+) lead to the battery terminal at the alternator; connect the voltmeter negative (−) lead to ground.
6. Disconnect the wire from the field terminal at the alternator and insulate the wire.
7. Connect a jumper wire between the field terminal at the alternator and ground.
8. Reconnect the battery ground cable.
9. Connect the carbon pile across the battery.
10. Run the engine at idle.
11. Adjust the carbon pile and engine speed to these levels:
• Standard alternator: 1,250 rpm, 15 volts
• 100-ampere alternator: 900 rpm, 13 volts
12. Compare the ammeter reading to specifications:

   a. If the reading is within specifications, the alternator and the regulator are operating properly.
   b. If the reading is not within specifications, remove the alternator for further testing.

Field current draw test
1. Refer to figure 5-20.
2. Disconnect the battery ground cable.
3. Disconnect the wires from both field terminals at the alternator.
4. Connect a jumper wire between one field terminal at the alternator and the battery positive (+) terminal.
5. Connect the ammeter positive (+) lead to the second field terminal at the alternator; connect the ammeter negative (−) lead to the battery negative (−) terminal.
6. Reconnect the battery ground cable.
7. Slowly rotate the alternator pulley by hand.
8. Compare the ammeter reading to specifications:
   a. If the reading is within specifications, the alternator field circuit is in good condition.
   b. If the reading is not within specifications, remove the alternator for further testing.

Voltage regulator test (transistorized regulator)
1. Refer to figure 5-21.
2. Connect the voltmeter positive (+) lead to the battery positive (+) terminal; connect the voltmeter negative (−) lead to ground.
3. Run the engine at 1,250 rpm with all accessories off.
4. Compare the voltmeter reading to specifications:
   a. If the reading is within specifications, the regulator is operating properly.
   b. If the reading is not within specifications,

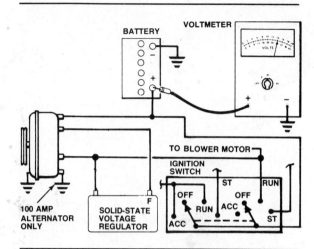

Figure 5-21. Testing Chrysler solid-state regulator.

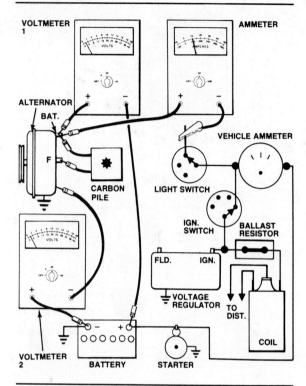

Figure 5-22. Testing circuit resistance of Chrysler with electromechanical regulator.

or if the reading fluctuates, go to step 5.
5. Check the voltage regulator ground and re-peat the test.
6. Turn the ignition switch off.
7. Unplug the connector from the regulator and check the connector for bent or distorted termi-nals. Repair if necessary.
8. Leave the regulator connector unplugged. *Do not start the engine.* Turn the ignition switch on.
9. Touch the voltmeter positive (+) lead to both of the regulator connector terminals.
   a. If either reading is zero voltage, check the charging circuit wiring and the alternator field circuit for faults. Repair if necessary.
   b. If battery voltage is present at both termi-nals, replace the regulator and repeat the test.

Chrysler With Electromechanical Regulator

Chrysler alternators with an electromechanical voltage regulator should be given a circuit resis-tance test, a field circuit resistance test, a current output test, a field current draw test, and a voltage regulator test.

Circuit resistance test
1. Refer to figure 5-22.
2. Disconnect the battery ground cable.
3. Disconnect the wire from the battery terminal at the alternator.
4. Connect the ammeter positive (+) lead to the alternator terminal; connect the ammeter nega-tive (−) lead to the wire.
5. Disconnect the wire from the field terminal at the alternator and insulate the wire.
6. Connect the carbon pile or field rheostat between the field terminal at the alternator and the battery terminal at the alternator.

7. Connect the voltmeter positive (+) lead to the battery terminal at the alternator; connect the voltmeter negative (−) lead to the battery posi-tive (+) terminal.
8. Reconnect the battery ground cable.
9. Turn on the headlamp high beams and the high-speed blower motor.
10. Start the engine and run it at 1,250 rpm.
11. Adjust the carbon pile or rheostat to main-tain 10 amperes of charging current.
12. Compare the voltmeter reading to specifications:
   a. If the reading is 0.3 volt or less, the circuit is in good condition.
   b. If the reading is more than 0.3 volt, check, clean, and tighten the connections within the circuit and repeat the test.
13. Connect the voltmeter positive (+) lead to the battery negative (−) terminal; connect the voltmeter negative (−) lead to the alternator frame.
14. Compare the voltmeter reading to specifications:
   a. If the reading is 0.3 volt or less, the ground circuit is in good condition.
   b. If the reading is more than 0.3 volt, check the ground connections within the charging circuit.

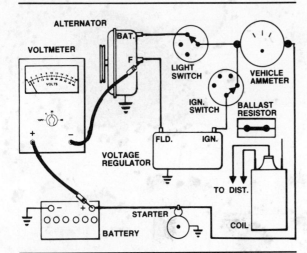

Figure 5-23. Field circuit test of Chrysler with electromechanical regulator.

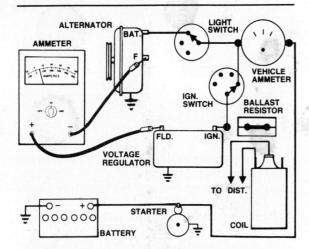

Figure 5-25. Testing field current draw of Chrysler with electromechanical regulator.

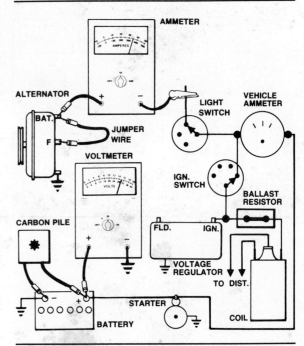

Figure 5-24. Testing current output of Chrysler with electromechanical regulator.

Field circuit resistance test
1. Refer to figure 5-23.
2. With the ignition switch off, disconnect the leads from both ends of the ignition ballast resistor.
3. Connect the voltmeter positive (+) lead to the battery positive (+) terminal; connect the voltmeter negative (−) lead to the field terminal at the regulator.
4. Turn the ignition switch on and observe the voltmeter reading:
    a. If the reading is 0.55 volt or less, the field circuit is in good condition.
    b. If the voltmeter reading is more than 0.55 volt, check, clean, and tighten the connections within the field circuit and repeat the test.

Current output test
1. Refer to figure 5-24.

2. Disconnect the battery ground cable.
3. Disconnect the wire from the battery terminal at the alternator.
4. Connect the ammeter positive (+) lead to the alternator terminal; connect the ammeter negative (−) lead to the wire.
5. Disconnect the wire from the field terminal at the alternator and insulate the wire.
6. Connect a jumper wire between the field terminal at the alternator and the battery terminal at the alternator.
7. Connect the voltmeter positive (+) lead to the battery positive (+) terminal. Connect the voltmeter negative (−) lead to ground.
8. Reconnect the battery ground cable.
9. Connect the carbon pile across the battery terminals.
10. Turn on the headlamp high beams and the high-speed blower motor.
11. Start the engine and run it at 1,250 rpm.
12. Adjust the carbon pile so that the voltmeter reads 15 volts.
13. Compare the ammeter reading to specifications:
    a. If the reading is within 5 amperes of specifications, the alternator is operating properly.
    b. If the reading is not within 5 amperes of specifications, remove the alternator for further testing.

Field current draw test
1. Refer to figure 5-25.
2. Disconnect the battery ground cable.

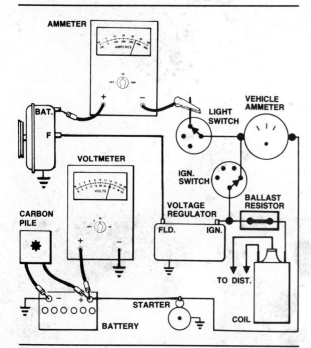

Figure 5-26. Testing Chrysler electromechanical regulator.

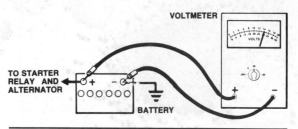

Figure 5-27. Motorola voltage output test with regulator in circuit.

3. Disconnect the leads from both sides of the ignition ballast resistor.

4. Disconnect the wire from the field terminal at the alternator.

5. Connect the ammeter positive (+) lead to the wire; connect the ammeter negative (−) lead to the alternator field terminal.

6. Reconnect the battery ground cable.

7. *Do not start the engine*; turn the ignition switch on.

8. Compare the ammeter reading to specifications:

　　a. If the reading is within specifications, then the alternator field circuit is in good condition.

　　b. If the reading is not within specifications, remove the alternator for further testing.

Electromechanical voltage regulator test

1. Refer to figure 5-26.

2. Disconnect the battery ground cable.

3. Disconnect the wire from the battery terminal at the alternator.

4. Connect the ammeter positive (+) lead to the alternator terminal; connect the ammeter negative (−) lead to the wire.

5. Reconnect the battery ground cable.

6. Connect the carbon pile across the battery terminals.

7. Connect the voltmeter positive (+) lead to the battery positive (+) terminal; connect the voltmeter negative (−) lead to ground.

8. Start the engine and run it at 1,250 rpm.

9. Adjust the carbon pile to maintain 15 amperes

of charging current .

10. After 15 minutes, cycle the regulator by dropping the engine speed to idle and then returning to 1,250 rpm.

11. The voltmeter reading is the setting of the normally closed (series) contacts; compare it to specifications:

　　a. If the reading is within specifications, go to step 12.

　　b. If the reading is not within specifications, adjust the voltage regulator spring tension.

12. Increase the engine speed to 2,200 rpm.

13. If necessary, adjust the carbon pile to maintain 5 amperes of charging current.

14. Cycle the regulator by dropping the engine speed to idle and then returning to 2,200 rpm.

15. The voltmeter reading is the setting of the normally open (grounding) contacts; compare it to the reading taken in step 11:

　　a. If the reading increase between step 11 and step 15 is more than 0.2 volt and less than 0.7 volt, the voltage regulator is good.

　　b. If the reading increase is not within specifications, adjust the regulator normally open contact point gap.

Motorola

The Motorola alternator used by AMC should be given a voltage output test, a field current draw test, and a diode trio test.

Voltage output test

1. Refer to figure 5-27.

2. With the ignition switch off, connect the voltmeter positive (+) lead to the battery positive (+) terminal; connect the voltmeter negative (−) lead to the battery negative (−) terminal.

3. Start the engine and turn on the headlamp low beams.

4. Run the engine at 1,000 rpm for 2 minutes while watching the voltmeter reading:

　　a. If the reading remains above 13 volts, the alternator and the regulator are good.

　　b. If the reading does not remain above 13 volts, go to step 5.

5. Turn the ignition switch off.

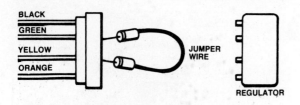

Figure 5-28. Bypassing Motorola regulator.

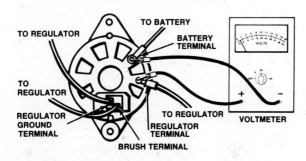

Figure 5-30. Testing the Motorola diode trio.

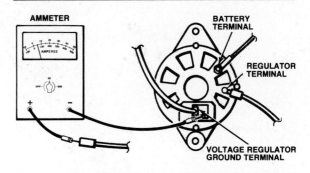

Figure 5-29. Testing Motorola field current draw.

6. Unplug the connector from the voltage regulator.
7. Connect a jumper wire between the regulator plug terminals of the yellow and the green wires, figure 5-28. This bypasses the voltage regulator and connects the field winding directly to battery voltage.
8. Start the engine and run it at idle.
9. Slowly increase the engine speed while watching the voltmeter reading; *do not exceed 16 volts*:
   a. If the reading approaches 16 volts, the alternator is in good condition, but the voltage regulator is bad.
   b. If the reading does not approach 16 volts, the alternator must be removed for further testing.

Field current draw test
1. Refer to figure 5-29.
2. With the ignition switch off, unplug the connector from the voltage regulator.
3. Disconnect the wire from the insulated brush terminal at the alternator.
4. Connect the ammeter positive (+) lead to the wire; connect the ammeter negative (−) lead to the terminal.
5. *Do not start the engine*; turn the ignition switch on.
6. Compare the ammeter reading to specifications:
   a. If the reading is within specifications, the alternator field circuit is in good condition.
   b. If the reading is not within specifications, remove the alternator for further testing.
7. Turn the rotor slowly by hand. If the reading fluctuates, the alternator must be removed for further testing.

Diode trio test
1. Refer to figure 5-30.
2. Start the engine and run it at idle.
3. Connect the voltmeter between the output terminal at the alternator and the regulator terminal at the alternator. If no voltage drop registers, switch the voltmeter leads.
4. Turn on the headlamp low beams and the high speed blower motor for 2 minutes, then turn them off.
5. Watch the voltmeter reading:
   a. If the reading is 0 to 0.2 volt, the diode trio is operating properly.
   b. If the reading is greater than 0.2 volt, remove the alternator for further testing.
   c. If the reading fluctuates, remove the alternator for further testing.

ALTERNATOR SYSTEM TESTING WITH AN OSCILLOSCOPE

Although the oscilloscope is most often used to give the voltage levels of the ignition system, it also can be used to check the alternator voltage output and condition.

Oscilloscope Connections

Many oscilloscopes have an inductive pickup lead that is clamped around either the alternator output wire or the battery positive (+) terminal, figure 5-31. Certain testers may require that the headlamps or some other load be applied.

Voltage Patterns And Diagnosis

The voltage trace shown on the oscilloscope screen is a result of the alternator's rectification process, figure 5-32. A normal trace will be a smooth, rippled line. If any of the diodes or the stator windings are bad, it will affect the trace.

By studying the change in the trace, you can find what is wrong with the alternator. In general, a shorted diode will have a greater effect on the trace than will an open diode. This is because a shorted diode not only reduces the

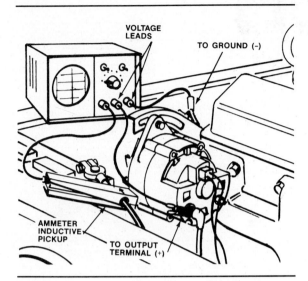

Figure 5-31. Alternator oscilloscope connections.

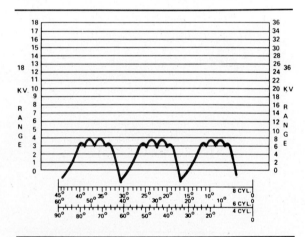

Figure 5-33. An open diode will cause this trace, in which one pulse is missing and the adjacent pulses are compressed.

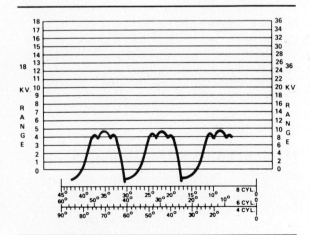

Figure 5-34. If two diodes in the same phase are open, two full pulses will be missing.

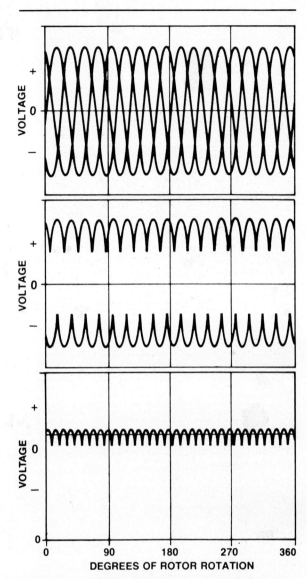

Figure 5-32. The alternator's full-wave rectification causes the rippled oscilloscope trace. (Bosch)

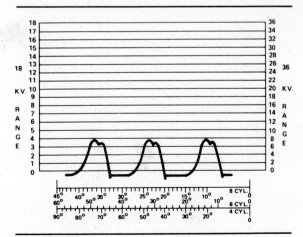

Figure 5-35. When two diodes of the same polarity are open, two output phases will be affected.

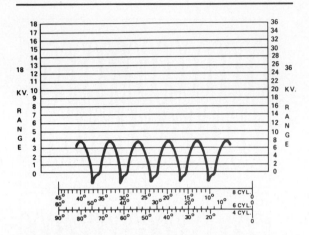

Figure 5-36.   This trace is caused by one open positive diode and one open negative diode in different phases.

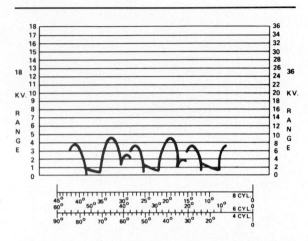

Figure 5-37.   One shorted diode will have a great effect upon the trace.

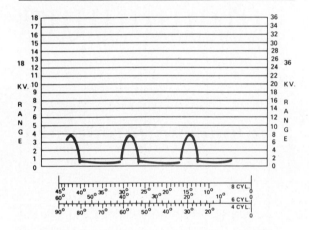

Figure 5-38.   When two diodes of the same polarity are shorted, only one phase can produce voltage output.

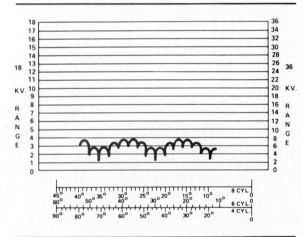

Figure 5-39.   This trace shows that none of the diodes have failed, but one diode is offering high resistance to current flow.

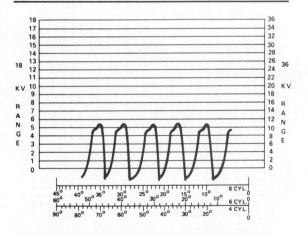

Figure 5-40.   The trace caused by shorted stator windings is very similar to that caused by shorted diodes.

output of its own phase, but it also affects the output of the following phase. The short allows current to flow back through the stator and oppose the next phase's flow.

Figures 5-33 through 5-40 show typical faulty alternator traces and explain the faults.

FIELD RELAY AND REGULATOR SERVICE

Most of the solid-state voltage regulators used with late-model alternators cannot be serviced or adjusted. The earlier electromechanical regulators and field relays can be adjusted. Because these units are similar from manufacturer to manufacturer, we will give general steps that can be applied to many different systems.

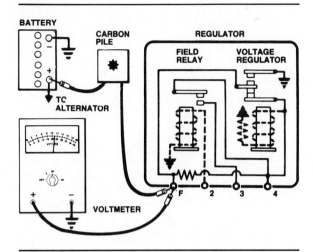

Figure 5-41. Testing the field relay closing voltage.

Figure 5-42. Adjusting the field relay closing voltage. (Delco-Remy)

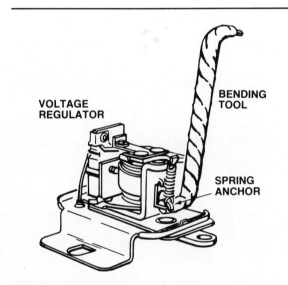

Figure 5-43. Bending the spring anchor to adjust the voltage regulator's spring tension. (Chrysler)

Field Relay Tests And Adjustments

The only test for most field relays is the point closing voltage:
1. Refer to figure 5-41.
2. Unplug the connector from the regulator, or from the field relay if it is a separate unit.
3. Set the carbon pile or field rheostat at maximum resistance (open) and connect it between the battery positive (+) terminal and the field relay coil.
4. Connect the voltmeter positive (+) lead to the field relay coil terminal; connect the voltmeter negative (−) lead to ground.
5. Adjust the carbon pile or rheostat until the field relay points close.

6. Compare the voltmeter reading to specifications:
    a. If the reading is within specifications, the relay is operating properly.
    b. If the reading is not within specifications, go to step 7.
7. Adjust the armature spring tension by bending the armature bracket, figure 5-42, until the points close at the proper voltage setting.

Voltage Regulator Adjustments

Three adjustments can be made on most electromechanical voltage regulators:
• Normally closed (series) contact voltage setting
• Normally open (grounding) contact point gap or voltage setting
• Armature-to-coil air gap.
    To adjust the normally closed contact voltage setting:
1. Leave the test equipment hooked up as it was for a voltage regulator test.
2. Turn off the ignition switch and remove the regulator cover.
3. Run the engine at the specified test speed and charging current.
4. Adjust the regulator spring tension until the voltmeter reading is within specifications:
    a. Some units are adjusted by bending the spring anchor, figure 5-43.
    b. Some units are adjusted with a screw, figure 5-44.
5. Always make the final adjustment an *increase* in spring tension.
6. Turn the ignition switch off and replace the regulator cover.
7. Repeat the voltage regulator test.

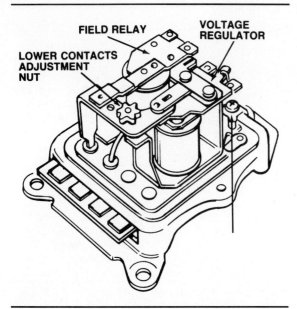

Figure 5-44. This voltage regulator has an adjustment screw for spring tension and an adjustment nut for the lower contact points.

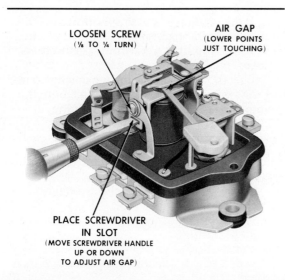

Figure 5-46. The voltage regulator air gap is adjusted by loosening a screw and moving the armature bracket. (Delco-Remy)

There are two different test procedures to adjust the normally open contact points. One method has the engine running and the adjustment made according to the voltmeter reading. The other method has the engine off and the adjustment made according to a feeler gauge in the point gap.

To adjust the normally open contact points with the engine running:
1. Turn off the ignition switch and remove the regulator cover.
2. Run the engine at the specified test speed and charging current.

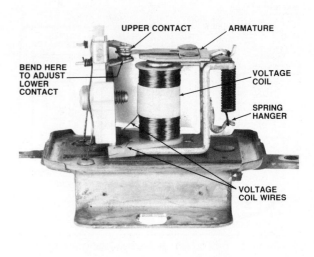

Figure 5-45. The lower contact point gap can be adjusted by bending the stationary bracket. (Chrysler)

3. Adjust the contact bracket until the voltmeter reading is within specifications:
   a. Some units are adjusted with a nylon nut on top of the armature, figure 5-44.
   b. Some units are adjusted by bending the contact arm, figure 5-45.
4. Turn off the ignition switch and replace the regulator cover.
5. Repeat the voltage regulator test.
   To adjust the normally open contact points with a feeler gauge:
1. Turn off the ignition switch and remove the regulator cover.
2. Place the proper size feeler gauge in the contact point gap.
3. If necessary, adjust the contact arm to create the proper point gap.
4. Replace the regulator cover.
5. Repeat the voltage regulator test.
   If the regulator voltage settings are correct but the regulator tests are not within specifications, adjust the regulator armature-to-coil air gap:
1. Turn off the ignition switch and remove the regulator cover.
2. Place the proper size feeler gauge in the armture-to-coil air gap, figure 5-46.
3. If necessary, loosen the adjusting screw and move the armature bracket to create the proper air gap.
4. Replace the regulator cover.
5. Repeat the voltage regulator test.
6. If the voltage regulator test results are erratic or if the unit cannot be adjusted to specifications, replace the new regulator.

6

Alternator Overhaul

This chapter has removal, disassembly, testing, repair, and installation instructions for Delco-Remy, Motorcraft, Chrysler, and Motorola alternators. Alternator removal, bench testing, and installation procedures are given as general instructions that will help you do these jobs on most domestic cars and light trucks. Overhaul procedures are given as photographic sequences for seven specific alternator models.

ALTERNATOR REMOVAL

You may have to remove, or loosen and relocate, other engine-driven accessories, such as an air injection pump or air conditioning compressor, to remove the alternator. It may help to tag all nuts, bolts, and washers removed from the alternator and other parts. You also may want to tag all drive belts removed from other engine accessories during alternator service. Observe all electrical safety precautions and shop safety regulations during alternator service. Remove the alternator as follows:

1. Disconnect the battery ground cable.
2. Identify and carefully disconnect all leads from the alternator. Some are held by nuts on terminal studs. Others are plug-in connections. Be sure to release any clips or springs holding the plugs in the alternator. You may want to tag the leads for identification at reinstallation.
3. Loosen the adjusting bolt securing the alternator to the alternator support bracket, figure 6-1.
4. Loosen bolts securing the power steering pump, air pump, or any other unit that interferes with alternator removal.
5. Move other units away from the alternator. You may have to loosen or disconnect some hoses.
6. Loosen the lower mounting bolt and push the alternator toward the engine until the drive belt, or belts, can be removed from the alternator pulley.
7. Remove the belt, or belts, from the pulley and let it hang on its engine drive pulley. Make sure all belts are clear of the alternator.
8. Remove the mounting bolt and the adjusting bolt and remove the alternator.

ALTERNATOR BENCH TEST PROCEDURES

Alternators built by different manufacturers can be tested for rotor continuity, rotor ground, stator continuity, stator ground, capacitor continuity, and rectifier continuity in a similar manner. Standard procedures also apply to the removal and installation of single diodes that are pressed into heat sinks and end frames.

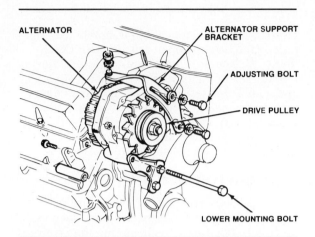

Figure 6-1. Disconnect the ground cable and all leads before removing all bolts securing an alternator to the engine. (Chevrolet)

Figure 6-2. Test rotor continuity by touching one test lamp lead to each slip ring.

Figure 6-3. Test for a grounded rotor winding by touching one test lamp lead to one slip ring. Touch the other test lead to the rotor shaft.

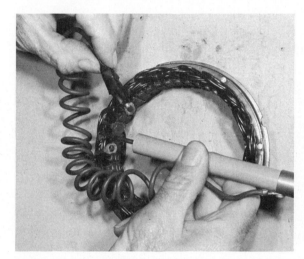

Figure 6-4. Test stator continuity by touching one test lamp lead to the neutral junction. Touch the other test lead to each of three stator leads.

The following general tests should be made on the alternators covered in the overhaul procedures later in this chapter. These tests can be made at several convenient points during the disassembly and reassembly sequences. Read these test instructions before overhauling an alternator and refer to them whenever you need to during the overhaul sequence.

Continuity and ground tests can be made with a self-powered test lamp or with an ohmmeter. High resistance or an open circuit is indicated when an ohmeter gives a very high or an infinite reading or when the test lamp does not light. Continuity is indicated when the test lamp lights or the ohmmeter reads low or zero resistance.

Rotor Continuity

Test the continuity of a rotor winding by touching one test lamp lead to each slipring, figure 6-2. The rotor winding is good if the lamp lights.

Rotor Ground

Test for a grounded rotor winding by touching one test lamp lead to a slipring and the other test lead to the rotor shaft, figure 6-3. If the lamp lights, the rotor winding is grounded.

Stator Continuity

Test stator continuity by touching one test lamp lead to one stator lead or to the neutral junction. Touch the other test lead to each remaining stator lead, in turn, figure 6-4. The stator is

Figure 6-5. Test stator ground by touching one test lamp lead to the stator frame. Touch the other test lead to each of three stator terminals.

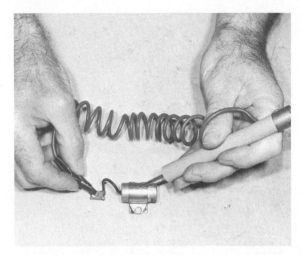

Figure 6-6. Test for a shorted capacitor by touching one test lamp lead to the capacitor case. Touch the other test lead to the capacitor terminal. Reverse the test leads.

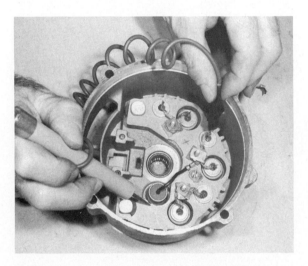

Figure 6-7. Test the continuity of individual diodes by touching one test lamp lead to the lead of the diode. Touch the other test lead to the heat sink for that diode.

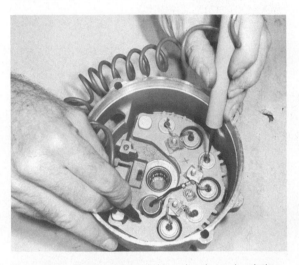

Figure 6-8. Reverse the test lamp leads to check the continuity of an individual diode.

open if the lamp does not light at any point.

Stator Ground

Test the stator for grounded windings by touching one test lamp lead to the stator frame. Touch the other test lead to each stator lead, figure 6-5. The stator windings are grounded if the lamp lights at any point.

Shorted Capacitor

Test capacitor continuity by touching one test lamp lead to the capacitor lead and the other test lead to the capacitor case, figure 6-6. The capacitor is shorted if the lamp lights.

If an ohmmeter is used, it should show infinite resistance. A capacitor cannot be tested

for an open circuit without the use of a capacitor tester.

Diode and Rectifier Assembly Test and Replacement

Test individual alternator diodes as follows:
1. Touch one test lamp lead to the diode lead and the other to the diode heat sink, figure 6-7. The heat sink for some diodes is the alternator end frame on some models.
2. Reverse the test leads, figure 6-8. The diode is bad if the lamp lights in both directions or if it does not light at all. The diode is good if the lamp lights in one direction and not in the other.

When an ohmmeter is used, it should show low resistance in one direction and very high or infinite resistance in the other. Special diode

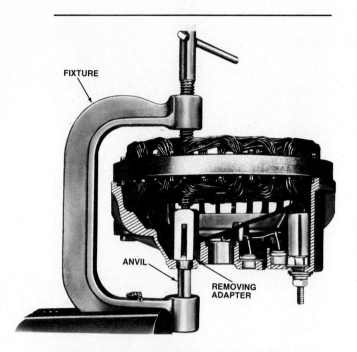

FIXTURE

ANVIL

REMOVING
ADAPTER

Figure 6-9. Diode removal. (Chrysler)

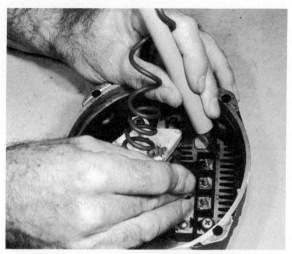

Figure 6-10. Test the rectifier in a Delco-Remy 10-SI alternator by touching one test lamp lead to the base of each diode. Touch the other test lead to the grounded heat sink.

Figure 6-12. Repeat steps 1 and 2 between each diode and the insulated heat sink.

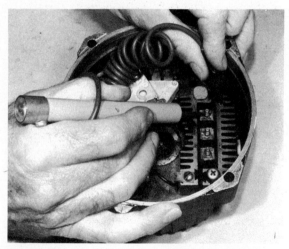

Figure 6-11. Reverse the test leads for each diode in the rectifier.

testers are also available for these tests. When using a diode tester, follow the manufacturer's directions.

A bad single diode can be replaced by pressing it out of its heat sink with special tools. A diode press is a metal sleeve, or removing adapter, with the same inside diameter as the outside diameter of the diode. The sleeve is placed over the large end of the diode, and the diode is pressed out with a shop press or a special fixture that looks like a C-clamp, figure 6-9.

Test the rectifier of a Delco-Remy 10-SI al-

ternator as follows:
1. Touch one test lamp lead to the base of a diode terminal. Do not touch the lead to the terminal stud. Touch the other test lead to the outer (grounded) heat sink, figure 6-10.
2. Reverse the test leads for each diode terminal base and the outer (grounded) heat sink, figure 6-11.
3. The lamp should light in one direction but not the other for each diode. Replace the rectifier with a new one if the lamp lights in both directions, or not at all, for any diode.
4. Repeat steps 1 and 2, using the inner (insulated) heat sink and the base of each diode, figure 6-12. Replace the entire rectifier with a

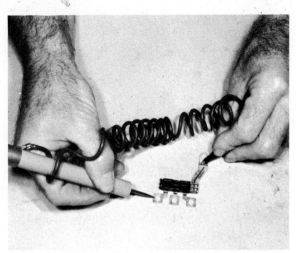

Figure 6-13. Test a field diode, or diode trio, by touching one test lamp lead to the solitary terminal and the other test lead to each of three diode terminals, in turn.

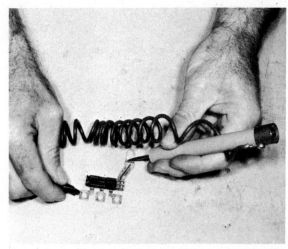

Figure 6-14. Reverse the test leads for each of three terminals in the diode trio.

new one if the test lamp lights in both directions or not at all for any diode.

Some 10-SI alternators have diodes with round, rather than square, bases. Test these rectifiers as we just described, except, touch one test lamp lead to the diode terminals, not to the diode bases.

Test a diode trio, or field diode assembly, as follows:

1. Touch one test lamp lead to the solitary terminal of the diode trio. Touch the other test lead to each of the three remaining terminals, in turn, figure 6-13.

2. Reverse the test leads, and repeat step 1 for each terminal, in turn, figure 6-14. If the test lamp lights in both directions, or it fails to light in one direction for any terminal, the diode trio is not good.

ALTERNATOR OVERHAUL PROCEDURES

The following pages contain photographic procedures for the disassembly, overhaul, and reassembly of seven common domestic alternators:

• Delco-Remy Model 10-SI — 1970 and later model with integral solid-state regulator; used by GM

• Delco-Remy Model 10-DN — 1963-69 model, used with remote electromechanical regulator; used by GM and AMC

• Motorcraft rear-terminal alternator — Used by Ford and AMC with remote solid-state and electromechanical regulators

• Motorcraft side-terminal alternator — Used by Ford and AMC with remote electromechanical regulators

• Chrysler late-model standard-duty alternator — 1972 and later model, used with remote solid-state regulator

• Chrysler early-model standard-duty alternator — 1960-71 model, used with remote electromechanical regulator

• Motorola 37-ampere alternator — Used on some AMC cars with transistorized regulators.

Chapter 8 of your *Classroom Manual* contains descriptive information and additional drawings of these alternators. You may find it helpful to refer to the *Classroom Manual*, also, when overhauling an alternator. Before starting any overhaul, be sure you read and understand the test procedures in the preceding section of this chapter. Make the tests at convenient points during the overhaul sequence. Read through the step-by-step procedure for the specific alternator that you will be overhauling before you begin work.

All soldering and unsoldering of electrical parts should be done with a medium-hot soldering iron (approximiately 100 watts). Use only rosin-core solder.

DELCO-REMY 10-SI ALTERNATOR OVERHAUL PROCEDURE

1. Draw chalk mark across both end frames and remove four through-bolts that secure frames. Separate end frames.

2. Remove three nuts attaching stator leads to rectifier. Remove stator.

3. Test stator for opens and grounds with self-powered test lamp or ohmmeter.

4. This is also convenient time to test rotor for opens and grounds with test lamp or ohmmeter.

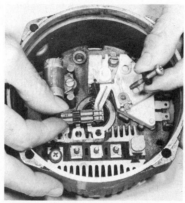

5. Remove screw holding diode trio to brush holder. Remove diode trio and test it for opens and shorts.

6. Rectifier can be tested with test lamp or ohmmeter while still in end frame.

7. Disconnect capacitor lead from rectifier. Remove screw from capacitor bracket and remove capacitor from end frame.

8. Remove nut, washer, and insulator from BAT terminal on rear of end frame. Then remove BAT terminal. Remove ground screw and rectifier.

9. Remove two screws holding brush holder and regulator. *Be sure* to note position of insulators and insulating sleeves for reassembly.

DELCO-REMY 10-SI ALTERNATOR OVERHAUL PROCEDURE

10. Remove brush holder and regulator. Separate brush holder from regulator and inspect brushes for wear. Replace brushes in matched pairs if necessary.

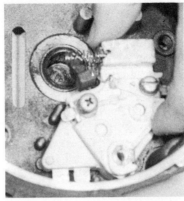

11. Install regulator and brush holder. Replace insulating sleeves and washers if needed. *Be sure* insulating sleeves and washers are correctly installed on two screws.

12. Position brushes and springs in brush holder. Insert drill bit or toothpick through rear of end frame to hold brushes above sliprings when rotor is reinstalled.

13. Install rectifier. When rectifier is in place, insert BAT terminal through rectifier and end frame. Install ground screw.

14. Install nut and insulating washer on BAT terminal on rear of end frame.

15. Attach capacitor lead to rectifier and install capacitor mounting screw through bracket.

16. Install diode trio. This screw must have insulating sleeve. Other three diode trio leads fit over rectifier terminals.

17. Install stator, placing three leads over rectifier terminals. Align notches in stator frame with bolt holes in end frame.

18. To replace parts in drive end frame, *carefully* clamp rotor in vise. Then remove shaft nut, washer, pulley, and fan.

DELCO-REMY 10-SI ALTERNATOR OVERHAUL PROCEDURE

19. Remove collar from shaft behind fan. Then separate rotor and shaft from end frame.

20. If drive end frame bearing is to be replaced, remove three screws holding bearing retainer. Then remove retainer plate.

21. Support bearing hub of end frame on suitable fixture and *carefully* drive or press bearing from end frame.

22. To install bearing, tap in carefully with block and hammer or press in with collar over outer race. Old bearing can be relubricated. Do not overfill with grease.

23. Replace bearing retainer if felt seal is hardened or worn. Install three retaining screws.

24. Assemble rotor and shaft into end frame. Install collar on shaft.

25. Attach fan, pulley, washer, and nut. *Carefully* hold rotor in vise; torque shaft nut to 50 ± 10 foot-pounds.

26. Align chalk marks on end frames and assemble end frames.

27. Remove drill bit or toothpick holding brushes away from sliprings. Install and tighten four through-bolts. Overhaul is complete.

DELCO-REMY 10-DN ALTERNATOR OVERHAUL PROCEDURE

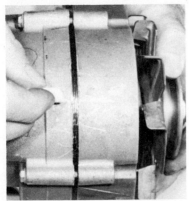

1. Draw chalk mark across both end frames before starting disassembly.

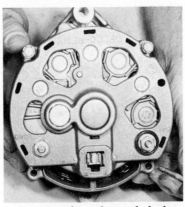

2. Remove four through-bolts securing end frames. Separate end frames.

3. Remove three nuts attaching stator leads to diode terminals in rear end frame. Remove stator.

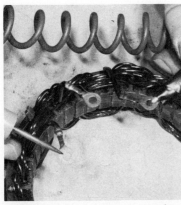

4. Test stator continuity with test-lamp as shown here. Test ground from frame to stator leads.

5. Remove two screws securing brush holder to rear end frame. Remove brush holder. Inspect brushes and replace as pair if worn.

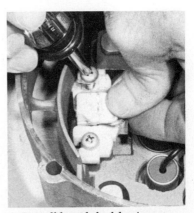

6. Install brush holder in rear end frame with two screws and washers. Be sure brush holder strap fits over diode terminal.

7. Insert drill bit or toothpick through brush holder and rear end frame, to keep brushes retracted in holder.

8. Test rotor for ground with test-lamp lead on rotor shaft and other lead on slipring, as shown here. Test rotor continuity with test lead to each slipring.

9. Test diode continuity with test-lamp lead to diode lead and other test lead to diode heat sink. Then reverse test leads.

DELCO-REMY 10-DN ALTERNATOR OVERHAUL PROCEDURE

10. Position stator in rear end frame with stator leads and brush holder lead on three diode studs. Secure leads with three nuts.

11. To replace parts in drive end frame, *carefully* clamp rotor in vise. Then remove shaft nut, washer, pulley, and fan.

12. Remove collar from shaft behind fan. Then separate rotor and shaft from end frame.

13. If drive end frame bearing is to be replaced, remove three screws holding bearing retainer. Then remove retainer plate.

14. Support bearing hub of end frame on suitable fixture and *carefully* drive or press bearing from end frame.

15. To install bearing, tap in carefully with block and hammer or press in with collar that just fits over outer race. Old bearing can be relubricated. Do not overfill with grease.

16. Replace bearing retainer if felt seal is hardened or worn. Install three retaining screws.

17. Position front end frame, collar, fan, pulley, and washer on shaft. *Carefully* hold rotor in vise; torque shaft nut to 50 ± 10 foot-pounds.

18. Align chalk marks on end frames and assemble end frames. Remove drill bit or toothpick holding brushes away from sliprings. Install and tighten through-bolts.

MOTORCRAFT REAR-TERMINAL ALTERNATOR OVERHAUL PROCEDURE

1. Draw chalk mark across both end frames and remove three through-bolts securing frames.

2. Separate drive end frame and rotor from rear end frame and stator-rectifier assembly. Brushes and springs will pop from brush holder.

3. Remove integral regulator, if present. Remove nuts, washers, and insulators from rear end frame terminals. Tag all fasteners.

4. Separate rear end frame from stator and rectifier assembly.

5. Remove insulators from large BAT terminal (top) and smaller STA terminal (bottom). Remove capacitor. No BAT insulator is used with integral regulator.

6. Unsolder stator leads from printed circuit board terminals. Remove STA terminal from rectifier. Separate stator from rectifier.

7. Remove two screws securing brush holder to rear end frame. Ground brush is attached to one screw. Remove brush holder.

8. Remove brush holder and springs. Note position of insulated brush, insulator, and FLD terminal in end frame. Reinstall the same way.

9. Remove insulated brush, insulator, and FLD terminal. Inspect brushes. Replace both if worn. Replace brush holder if broken.

MOTORCRAFT REAR-TERMINAL ALTERNATOR OVERHAUL PROCEDURE

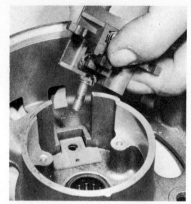

10. Install brush holder and insulated brush like this. Be sure insulator is in place and that brush lead does not touch end frame.

11. Install ground brush and two screws. Insert drill bit or toothpick through end frame and brush holder to hold brushes.

12. Test rectifier by touching one test lamp lead to BAT terminal, other lead to each of three stator winding terminals.

13. Reverse test leads and repeat step 12. Lamp should light at all three positions in one direction, not in the other.

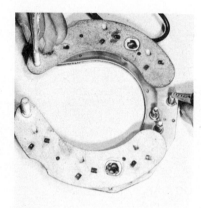

14. Repeat steps 12 and 13 from GRD terminal to all three stator leads. Replace rectifier if it fails any part of tests.

15. Put neutral lead and insulator on STA terminal and install in rectifier. Solder other stator leads to rectifier.

16. Test capacitor and install on BAT and ground terminals. Install insulating washer on BAT terminal.

17. Assemble end frame to stator-rectifier assembly. Be sure all insulators are properly installed. Install nuts, washers, and insulators outside end frame.

18. Test rotor for opens and grounds (as shown here) before reassembling alternator.

MOTORCRAFT REAR-TERMINAL ALTERNATOR OVERHAUL PROCEDURE

19. If drive end frame parts are to be removed, *carefully* hold rotor in vise and remove nut, washer, pulley, fan, and collar.

20. Separate rotor from end frame. Note spacer on shaft. Reinstall in same direction. Leave it on shaft unless replacing it.

21. If front bearing is to be replaced, remove bearing retainer.

22. After old bearing is removed, fit new one into end frame hub.

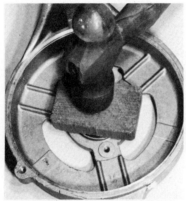
23. *Carefully* tap bearing into place with wooden block and hammer.

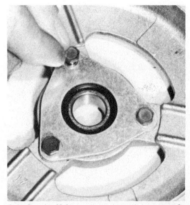
24. Install bearing retainer and tighten three screws carefully.

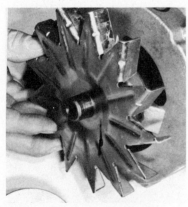
25. Install collar, fan, pulley, and washer. Then carefully hold rotor in vise and tighten nut on rotor shaft.

26. Align chalk marks and assemble drive end frame and rotor with rear end frame and stator-rectifier assembly.

27. Install through-bolts and tighten carefully. Remove drill bit or toothpick holding brushes away from slirings.

MOTORCRAFT SIDE-TERMINAL ALTERNATOR OVERHAUL PROCEDURE

1. Mark on end frames and remove through-bolts. Separate end frames.

2. Unsolder stator leads from rectifier and remove stator from end frame.

3. Unsolder brush holder lead from rectifier. Remove screws securing brush holder and remove brush holder with brushes.

4. Remove nuts from BAT and GRD terminals outside rear end frame. Remove insulator from BAT terminal.

5. Disconnect capacitor lead from rectifier and remove rectifier. Be sure rectifier insulators in end frame are reinstalled later.

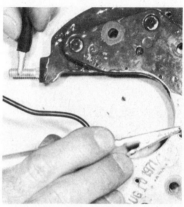

6. Test rectifier by touching one test lamp lead to BAT terminal, other lead to each of three stator winding terminals.

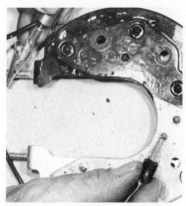

7. Reverse test leads and repeat step 6. Lamp should light at all three positions in one direction, not in the other.

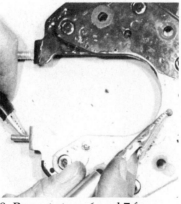

8. Repeat steps 6 and 7 from GRD terminal to all three stator leads. Replace rectifier if it fails any tests.

9. Inspect brushes and replace if worn. Install brush holder with two screws. Insert drill bit or toothpick to hold brushes in place.

MOTORCRAFT SIDE-TERMINAL ALTERNATOR OVERHAUL PROCEDURE

10. Install capacitor. Be sure two insulators are on bosses inside rear end frame.

11. Place rectifier inside end frame with insulating washer on BAT terminal. Secure rectifier to end frame with four screws.

12. Place insulating washer on ouside of BAT terminal. Attach nuts to BAT and GRD terminals.

13. Attach capacitor lead to rectifier with screw. Solder brush holder lead to rectifier.

14. Test stator for opens or shorts (shown here) with test lamp or ohmmeter before reassembly. Replace defective stator.

15. Place stator in rear end frame and solder stator leads to three stator terminals on rectifier.

16. Test rotor for grounds and opens (shown here) before reassembling alternator. Drive end frame service is similar to rear-terminal alternators.

17. Align marks on end frames and assemble drive end frame and rotor to rear end frame and stator-rectifier assembly.

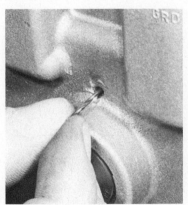

18. Install and tighten four through-bolts. Remove drill bit or toothpick holding brushes away from sliprings.

CHRYSLER LATE-MODEL STANDARD ALTERNATOR OVERHAUL PROCEDURE

1. Remove two screws, washers, and brush holders from rear end frame.

2. Draw chalk mark across both end frames and remove three through-bolts securing frames. Separate end frames.

3. Remove three nuts securing stator leads to rectifier terminals. Remove stator.

4. Test stator for ground (shown here) and for continuity with test lamp or ohmmeter.

5. To test positive rectifier, touch one test lamp lead to rectifier heat sink. Touch other lead to strap at base of each diode, in turn.

6. Reverse leads. Lamp should light in one direction for each diode, not in other. Replace rectifier if lamp does not light at all or lights in both directions.

7. To test negative rectifier, touch one test lamp lead to rectifier heat sink. Touch other lead to strap at base of each diode, in turn.

8. Reverse leads. Lamp should light in one direction for each diode, not in other. Replace rectifier if lamp does not light or lights in both directions.

9. Remove nut holding capacitor to insulated stud. Remove capacitor. Remove nut from BAT terminal and remove positive rectifier.

CHRYSLER LATE-MODEL STANDARD ALTERNATOR OVERHAUL PROCEDURE

10. Remove four screws securing negative rectifier to end frame. Remove rectifier.

11. If rear bearing is to be replaced, carefully press or drive it from end frame. Install new bearing from outside of end frame.

12. Install mica insulating washer between rectifier and end frame. Install BAT terminal and insulator from outside end frame.

13. Be sure mica insulating washer is on other mounting stud. Then install positive rectifier.

14. Test capacitor for opens and shorts, then install. Secure capacitor and positive rectifier with two nuts to BAT terminal and stud.

15. Install negative rectifier and secure with four screws through top of end frame.

16. Align stator with through-bolt holes. Fit stator dowels into holes in end frame and secure stator leads to rectifier terminals.

17. Test rotor for continuity (shown here) and for ground with test lamp or ohmmeter. Sliprings on Chrysler rotors are at right angles.

18. To disassemble drive end frame, pulley must be removed with *special* puller. *Carefully* clamp end frame in vise and attach puller to pulley hub.

CHRYSLER LATE-MODEL STANDARD ALTERNATOR OVERHAUL PROCEDURE

19. You may need impact wrench to remove pulley with puller. Hold puller with vise grips, *securely*.

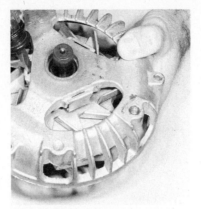

20. Use screwdriver to release three tabs for front bearing grease retainer.

21. If rotor does not separate from front end frame, tap carefully with soft mallet.

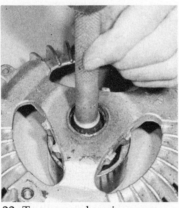

22. To remove bearing, support end frame hub and carefully press or drive bearing from end frame.

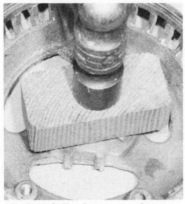

23. Carefully drive new bearing into end frame with block of wood and hammer. Assemble rotor with end frame. Then latch grease retainer tabs to end frame.

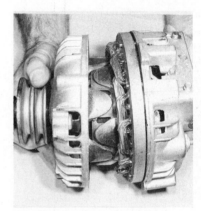

24. New pulley must be installed on shaft with press. Align dowels on stator with holes in end frame and assemble. Secure with three through-bolts.

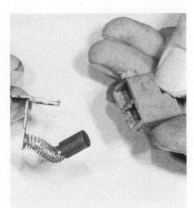

25. Inspect brushes for wear and replace if necessary. Replace as matched pair. Install brushes and springs in brush holders.

26. Install brush holders with brushes on rear end frame. Be sure insulators are between brush holders and screw heads.

27. Be sure BAT terminal and insulator are secure in end frame. Install insulating washer and nut. Overhaul is complete

CHRYSLER EARLY-MODEL ALTERNATOR OVERHAUL PROCEDURE

1. Remove two brush holders. Draw chalk marks across end frames. Remove three through-bolts, and separate end frames.

2. Remove nuts and washers holding BAT terminal and diode heat sink to rear end frame. Remove heat sink, terminal, and stator.

3. Cut or unsolder stator and capacitor leads. Tag leads and remove stator. At reassembly, solder stator leads to diodes and capacitor.

4. To remove defective front bearing or rotor, remove pulley with puller as shown here.

5. Remove bearing retainer. Press or drive out bearing. Press in new bearing. Install bearing retainer.

6. Carefully install front end frame and pulley on shaft with arbor press.

7. Secure BAT terminal and positive heat sink to rear end frame with insulating washers and nuts. Align front and rear end frames with chalk marks.

8. Assemble end frames and secure with three through-bolts.

9. Install brushes and springs in brush holders and attach brush holders with insulating washers, lockwashers, and screws.

MOTOROLA 37-AMPERE ALTERNATOR OVERHAUL PROCEDURE

1. Remove two screws securing brush cover. Remove cover and brush holder. Disconnect capacitor from output terminal. Remove capacitor.

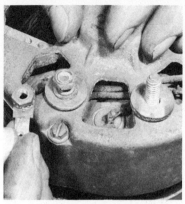

2. Remove regulator terminal, terminal nut, and insulating washer. Remove 7-volt a.c. terminal, if present. Tag fasteners and insulators.

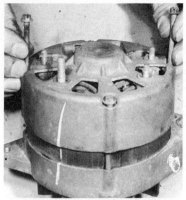

3. Remove all terminal nuts. Draw chalk mark across both end frames and stator. Remove four through-bolts securing end frames.

4. Gently pry end frames from stator by inserting two screwdrivers in stator notches. Be careful not to gouge stator.

5. Lift off rear end frame, which covers stator and rectifier assembly. Rear bearing comes out with rotor.

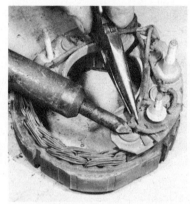

6. Unsolder three stator leads and three field diode leads from diodes in positive rectifier. Tag leads if desired.

7. Unsolder three stator leads from diodes in negative rectifier. Remove positive and negative rectifiers from stator.

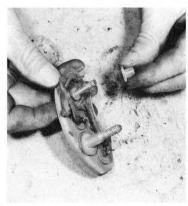

8. Remove insulators from regulator terminal on positive rectifier.

9. Unsolder three leads of field diode trio from positive rectifier. This is early model with plate-type diode trio.

MOTOROLA 37-AMPERE ALTERNATOR OVERHAUL PROCEDURE

10. Remove nut securing diode trio and regulator terminal to positive rectifier. In newer models, remove potted diode trio and regulator terminal.

11. Test positive rectifier by touching test lamp lead to output terminal. Touch other lead to each diode lead, in turn. Note if lamp lights; reverse test leads.

12. Test negative rectifier by touching one test lamp lead to heat sink and other lead to each diode lead, in turn. Note if lamp lights; reverse test leads.

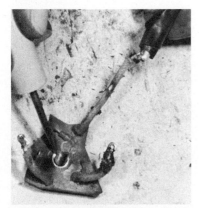

13. Test field diode by touching test lamp lead to metal plate or to threaded stud. Touch other test lead to each diode lead, in turn. Note if lamp lights; reverse test leads.

14. Install field diode to positive rectifier with insulator and nut.

15. Solder field diode leads to positive rectifier diodes.

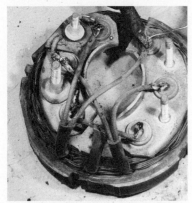

16. Solder positive and negative rectifiers to stator leads.

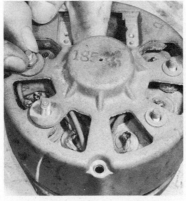

17. Secure rectifiers and stator to rear end frame with insulators and nuts. Install capacitor, regulator terminal, and 7-volt a.c. terminal, if present.

18. To service rotor or front end frame, remove nut, lockwasher, pulley, fan, key, and spacer. Tap rotor shaft to separate.

MOTOROLA 37-AMPERE ALTERNATOR OVERHAUL PROCEDURE

19. Remove snapring securing front bearing in front end frame. Remove snapring from its groove and leave hanging on shaft.

20. Tap rotor from end frame. If bearing is lodged in end frame, *carefully* drive it out with socket and mallet.

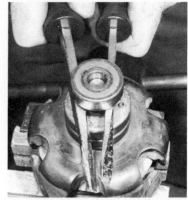

21. If front bearing is lodged on rotor shaft, pry bearing off shaft with two screwdrivers.

22. Press new front bearing into front end frame with 1⅛-inch socket and mallet. Install snapring in front end frame to hold bearing.

23. Tap rotor shaft to seat in front bearing inside front end frame. Install rear bearing on rotor shaft with mallet and deep socket.

24. Install spacer, key, fan, pulley, and lockwasher with nut.

25. Install stator and rectifier in rear end frame. Align both end frames with chalk marks and assemble. Install through-bolts.

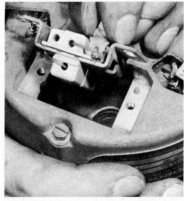

26. Inspect brushes for wear. Replace worn brushes. Install brushes and springs in brush holder and place in rear end frame.

27. Place brush cover over brush holder in rear end frame. Secure brush cover to rear end frame with two screws.

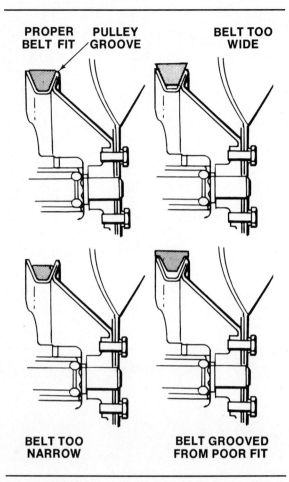

PROPER BELT FIT — PULLEY GROOVE — BELT TOO WIDE

BELT TOO NARROW — BELT GROOVED FROM POOR FIT

Figure 6-15. A properly installed drive belt should be flush with, or not more than 1/16'' above the top of the pulley grooves.

ALTERNATOR INSTALLATION

Spin the shaft of the assembled alternator by hand to be sure the rotor and pulley do not bind. Make sure the brushes contact the slip-rings without binding. Be sure the rotor or fan blades do not snag the stator windings.

Before installing the alternator, inspect the drive belt for wear or damage. Belts that are cracked, broken, glazed, or oil soaked should be replaced. For maximum pulling power, a properly adjusted belt should ride on the sides of the pulley, not on the bottom, figure 6-15. Look at the bottom surface of the pulley. If it is bright and shiny, the belt is bottoming and not gripping the sidewalls.

When installing new belts, it is important that the correct belt, or belts, be used. Check the manufacturer's specifications for the correct belt application. When multiple belts are used to drive one unit, they should be replaced in matched sets. Unmatched belts, even though of the same size, can place more stress on one belt than on the other.

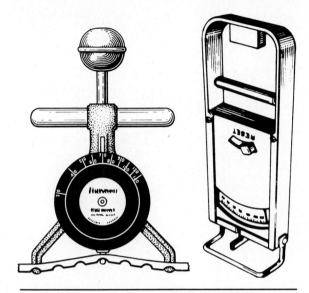

Figure 6-16. Typical belt strand tension gauges.

In addition to being in good condition, all drive belts must be in proper adjustment. Correct belt tension is necessary for satisfactory operation of all belt-driven components. All car manufacturers specify proper belt tension adjustments for both new and used belts.

Specifications for tensioning new and used belts are different. New belt tension specifications apply *only* to replacement belts when first installed. New drive belts will stretch after the first 10 to 15 minutes of operation. Therefore, once a new belt has been tensioned and run, it is considered a used belt and should be adjusted to used belt specifications. In either case, there are several ways to check a belt for proper tension.

The most widely recommended method of checking belt tension is with a strand tension gauge, figure 6-16. There are many commercial tension testers available, but all are used similarly.

One type has a belt hook attached to a spring-loaded plunger and a dial indicator registering in pounds. The plunger is depressed to engage the hook under the belt, then released. When using the gauge on a notched belt, the hook should be placed in a notch of the belt. The pounds of tension are read on the dial and compared to the manufacturer's specifications. Always take two or more readings, moving the belt each time.

Make sure the lower mounting bolt is tightened before the adjusting bolt is tightened for the last time during installation. This prevents binding of the alternator bearings, rotor, shaft,

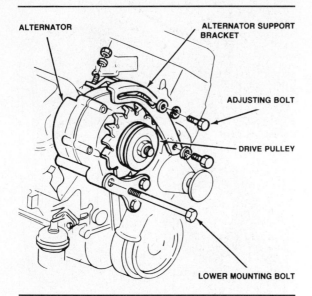

Figure 6-17. Install the alternator on the engine mounting brackets. Loosely secure the alternator with the lower mounting bolt and the adjusting bolt. (Chevrolet)

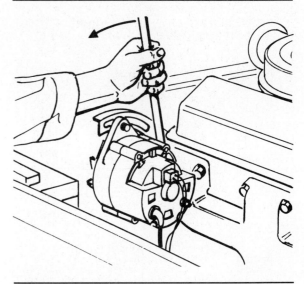

Figure 6-18. Adjust belt tension by carefully prying the alternator away from the engine with a hammer handle or pry bar.

mounting bracket, or adjusting bolt. Install an alternator as follows:

1. Put the alternator on the engine and the alternator mounting brackets. Loosely secure the alternator with the lower mounting bolt and the adjusting bolt, figure 6-17.
2. Attach all belts to the alternator pulleys and pull the alternator away from the engine by hand just enough to keep light tension on the belts.
3. Tighten the lowering mounting bolt and the adjusting bolt enough to hold the alternator in position under light belt tension.
4. Reposition or reinstall the air pump, air conditioning compressor, power steering pump, and any other unit that may have been loosened or removed to aid alternator removal.
5. Gently pry the alternator away from the engine with a wooden hammer handle or a pry bar to adjust the final belt tension, figure 6-18. Do not pry against thin-walled sections of the alternator. Tighten the adjusting bolt and the lower mounting bolt.
6. Use a belt tension gauge to check the tension of all belts on the alternator pulley, figure 6-19. Loosen the mounting and adjusting bolts and readjust, if necessary.
7. Check the belt tension on all other engine accessories that were loosened to install the alternator. Tighten the mounting and adjusting bolts on these accessories. Repeat the belt adjustment and tension checks until all belts are adjusted to specifications.

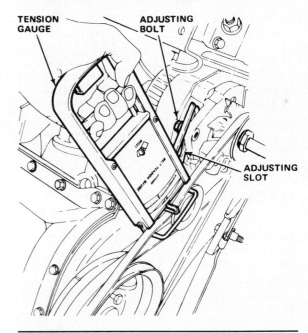

Figure 6-19. Check belt tension with a belt tension gauge. Adjust belt tension to the manufacturer's specifications. (AMC)

8. Identify all tagged leads and attach them to their appropriate alternator terminals or plug sockets.
9. Connect the ground cable to the battery.
10. Test the alternator by running the engine. Check for noise or vibration from the alternator.
11. Test the alternator current output and voltage as explained in Chapter 5 of this manual.

PART THREE

Starting System Service

7
Starting System Testing

This chapter has instructions for the on-car testing of starting systems. Figure 7-1 will help you pinpoint the problem in a particular system. Remember, many electrical system problems can be caused by the battery. Test the battery as explained in Chapter 3 before beginning these starting system tests. When these test procedures direct you to remove the starter motor for further testing, refer to Chapter 8 for step-by-step instructions.

SYSTEM INSPECTION

Many problems within the starting system can be found with nothing more than a simple inspection. Inspection areas include the:
1. Battery
2. Ignition switch
3. Starting safety switch, if present
4. Magnetic switch or switches
5. Starter motor.
   At the battery, check for:
- Loose or corroded terminals
- Loose or corroded ground cable connections
- Frayed cables
- Damaged insulation.
   Check the ignition switch for:
- Loose mounting
- Sticking contacts
- Damaged wiring
- Loose connections.
   If the system has a starting safety switch, check for:
- Poor adjustment
- Loose mounting
- Loose or damaged wiring (electrical switch).

Figure 7-2 will help you find the starting safety switch on the particular car you are testing.
   Check any magnetic switches for:
- Loose mounting
- Loose connections
- Damaged wiring.

All GM cars have a solenoid mounted on or enclosed within the starter housing. All Ford cars have a starter relay mounted on a fender panel, and some also have a solenoid at the starter. All Chrysler cars have a starter relay mounted on a fender panel or the firewall and a solenoid at the starter. All AMC cars have a starter relay mounted on a fender panel.
   Inspect the starter motor for:
- Loose mounting
- Poor pinion adjustment
- Loose wiring and connections
- Damaged wiring and connections.

SYMPTOMS	POSSIBLE CAUSE	CURE
• Starter will not crank engine	1. Battery discharged 2. Open in control circuit 3. Defective starter relay or solenoid	1. Recharge or replace. 2. Test control circuit for continuity; repair. 3. Repair or replace.
• Starter spins but will not crank engine	1. Starter drive defective	1. Repair or replace.
• Starter cranks engine slowly	1. Battery charge low 2. Excessive resistance in starting system 3. Defective starter 4. Problem in engine	1. Recharge or replace. 2. Perform voltage drop tests; repair or replace as necessary. 3. Repair or replace.

Figure 7-1. Starting system troubleshooting chart.

MANUFACTURER		AUTOMATIC TRANSMISSION		MANUAL TRANSMISSION	
		column shift	floor shift	column shift	floor shift
GENERAL MOTORS	full-size	mechanical on column	electrical on floor	electrical on column	clutch switch
	all others	electrical on column	electrical on floor	electrical on column	clutch switch
FORD	full-size	mechanical on column	electrical on floor	N/A	N/A
	all others	mechanical on column	electrical on transmission	N/A	N/A
CHRYSLER		electrical on transmission	electrical on transmission	clutch switch	clutch switch
AMERICAN MOTORS		electrical on transmission	electrical on transmission	N/A	N/A

Figure 7-2. The types and locations of starting safety switches used by major manufacturers (N/A indicates that no safety switch is used in a particular system).

ON-CAR TESTING

The tests detailed in this chapter can be made using:
- A voltmeter
- An ammeter
- A variable-resistance carbon pile
- Jumper wires
- A remote starter switch.

All of these units, except for the remote starter switch and jumper wires, may be contained within a single tester. These are often called battery-starter testers.

A remote starter switch is a hand-held, push-button switch with two leads, figure 7-3. The leads can be connected to various system parts so that the button controls current flow through the system. The remote starter switch is often used to bypass the ignition switch so that you can control the starting system from under the hood, rather than from the driver's seat.

Figure 7-3. A remote starter button is a handy tool when working on the starting system.

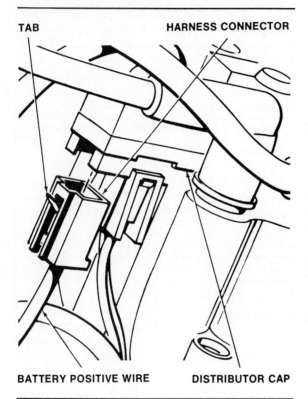

TAB   HARNESS CONNECTOR

BATTERY POSITIVE WIRE   DISTRIBUTOR CAP

Figure 7-5. To disable the Delco-Remy HEI system, unplug the outermost harness connector from the distributor cap.

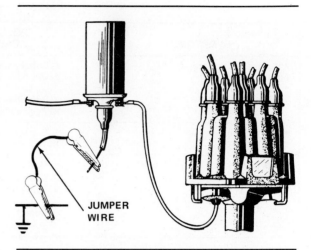

JUMPER WIRE

Figure 7-4. If the ignition system must be disabled, remove the secondary lead from the distributor center tower and ground the lead.

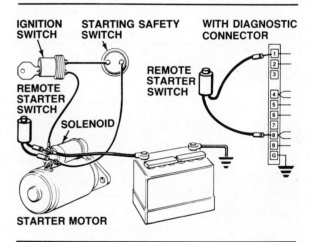

IGNITION SWITCH   STARTING SAFETY SWITCH   WITH DIAGNOSTIC CONNECTOR

REMOTE STARTER SWITCH

REMOTE STARTER SWITCH

SOLENOID

STARTER MOTOR

Figure 7-6. Bypassing the ignition system of a GM car.

Almost all starting system tests must be made while the starter motor is cranking the engine. The engine must not start and run during the test, or the readings will be inaccurate.

To keep the engine from starting, you can bypass the ignition switch with the remote starter switch. The switch will allow current to flow to the starting system but not to the ignition system. On vehicles with the ignition starting bypass in the ignition switch or the starter relay, you must disable the ignition as described below.

If the remote starter switch is not available, or if you must do the test while current flows through the ignition switch, disable the ignition system. On most systems, do this by removing the secondary lead from the center of the distributor cap and grounding the lead, figure 7-4. On Delco-Remy HEI systems, remove the outermost harness connector from the distributor cap, figure 7-5.

Before testing the starting system, be sure the transmission is in Park or Neutral (a remote starter switch bypasses the starting safety switch). Set the parking brake and block the wheels.

Do not crank the starter motor for more than 30 seconds at a time, or it could overheat. Allow two minutes between tests for the motor to cool.

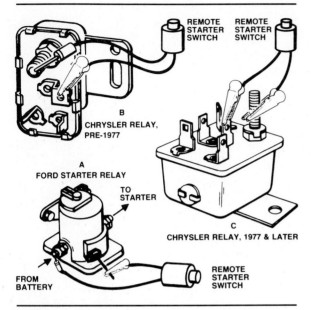

Figure 7-7. Bypassing the ignition system of Ford, AMC, and Chrysler cars.

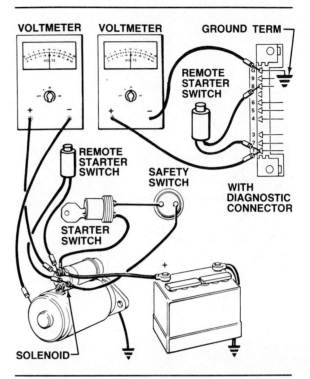

Figure 7-8. Measuring cranking voltage on a GM car.

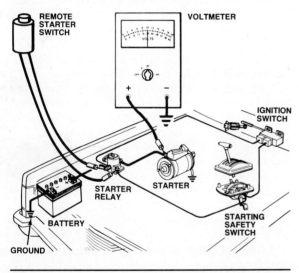

Figure 7-9. Measuring cranking voltage of a Ford or AMC car. (Ford)

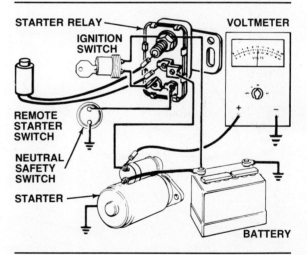

Figure 7-10. Measuring the cranking voltage of a Chrysler car. (Chrysler)

CRANKING VOLTAGE TEST

1. Bypass the ignition switch with the remote starter switch:

    a. On GM cars, figure 7-6, the switch can be connected between the ignition switch terminal and the starting safety switch terminal on the starter solenoid. If the car has a diagnostic connector, the remote starter switch can be connected between terminals 1 and 8.

    b. On Ford, Chrysler, and AMC cars, figure 7-7, connect the switch leads between the battery terminal at the starter relay and the terminal illustrated.

2. Connect the voltmeter negative (−) lead to ground; connect the voltmeter positive (+) lead to the test point indicated below:

    a. For GM cars, refer to figure 7-8.
    b. For Ford and AMC cars, refer to figure 7-9.
    c. For Chrysler cars, refer to figure 7-10.

3. While cranking the engine, watch the voltmeter reading.

4. Compare the voltmeter reading to the specifications:

    a. If the reading is within the specifications, usually about 9 volts or more, but the motor

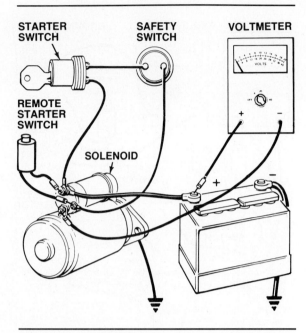

Figure 7-11. Testing the resistance of the starting system insulated circuit.

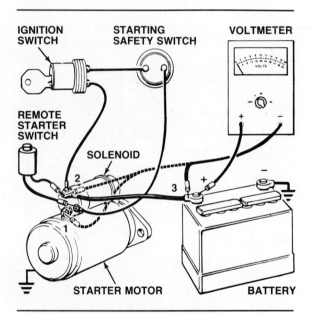

Figure 7-13. Testing the resistance between specific points of the GM starting system insulated circuit.

still cranks poorly, the motor must be removed for further testing. Refer to Chapter 8.
b. If the reading is below specifications with a fully charged battery, test the circuit resistance to pinpoint the area of high resistance. This reaction can also be caused by heavy overloading of the starter by the engine due to seizing, dragging, or preignition.

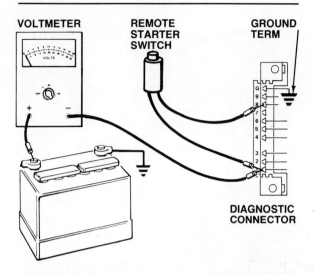

Figure 7-12. Using the GM diagnostic connector to test the resistance of the starting system insulated circuit. (GM)

CIRCUIT RESISTANCE TESTS

Insulated Circuit Test

1. Bypass the ignition switch with the remote starter switch (refer to figures 7-6 and 7-7).
2. Connect the voltmeter positive (+) lead to the battery positive (+) terminal. Connect the meter lead to the post or terminal nut, not to the cable. If you connect to the cable, you will miss a possible area of high resistance in the cable-to-post connection. Then, connect the voltmeter negative (−) lead to the terminal at the starter, figure 7-11. For GM diagnostic connectors, refer to figure 7-12.
3. While cranking the engine, watch the voltmeter reading.
4. Compare the voltmeter reading to the specifications:
    a. If the reading is within the specifications, usually 0.2 to 0.6 volt, go to the ground resistance test.
    b. If the reading is above the specifications, go to step 5.
5. Move the voltmeter negative (−) lead to the test points indicated below to pinpoint the high resistance. Make each test in the order indicated. Take all voltmeter readings while cranking the engine:
    a. For GM cars, refer to figure 7-13.
    b. For Ford and AMC cars, refer to figure 7-14.
    c. For Chrysler cars, refer to figure 7-15.
6. Repair or replace any damaged wiring or faulty connections.

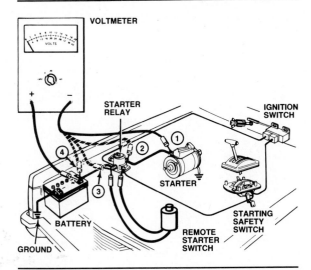

Figure 7-14. Testing the resistance between specific points of the Ford and AMC starting system insulated circuit. (Ford)

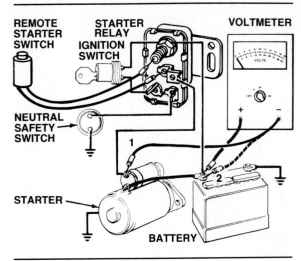

Figure 7-15. Testing the resistance between specific points of the Chrysler starting system insulated circuit. (Chrysler)

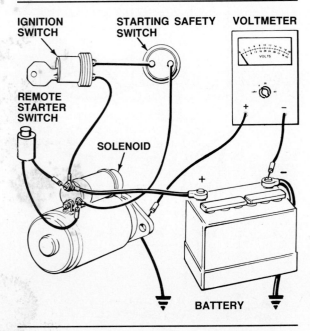

Figure 7-16. Testing the resistance of the ground circuit.

Ground Circuit Test

1. Bypass the ignition switch with the remote starter switch (refer to figures 7-6 and 7-7).
2. Connect the voltmeter positive (+) lead to the starter housing; connect the voltmeter negative (−) lead to the battery negative (−) terminal, figure 7-16. Connect the negative lead to the battery post or terminal nut, *not* to the cable, or you will miss any resistance in the cable-to-post connection.

3. While cranking the engine, watch the voltmeter reading.
4. Compare the voltmeter reading to the specifications:
    a. If the reading is within specifications, usually 0.1 to 0.3 volt, go to the control circuit resistance test.
    b. If the reading is above specifications, go to step 5.
5. Tighten the system ground connections, inspect the battery ground cable, and repeat the test. Replace the battery ground cable, if necessary.

Control Circuit Test

1. Disable the ignition system (refer to figures 7-4 and 7-5).
2. Connect the voltmeter positive (+) lead to the battery positive (+) terminal; connect the voltmeter negative (−) lead to the switch terminal at the relay or solenoid:
    a. For GM cars, refer to figure 7-17.
    b. For Ford and AMC cars, refer to figure 7-18.
    c. For Chrysler cars, refer to figure 7-19.
3. While cranking the engine *with the ignition switch*, watch the voltmeter reading.
4. Compare the voltmeter reading to the specifications:
    a. If the reading is within specifications, usually about 2.5 volts, the control circuit is in good condition.
    b. If the reading is above specifications, go to step 5.

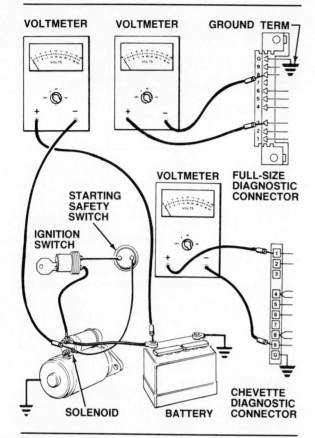

Figure 7-17. Testing the resistance of the GM starting system control circuit.

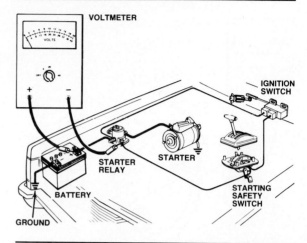

Figure 7-18. Testing the resistance of the Ford or AMC starting system control circuit. (Ford)

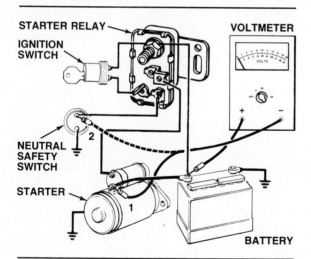

Figure 7-19. Testing the resistance of the Chrysler starting system control circuit. (Chrysler)

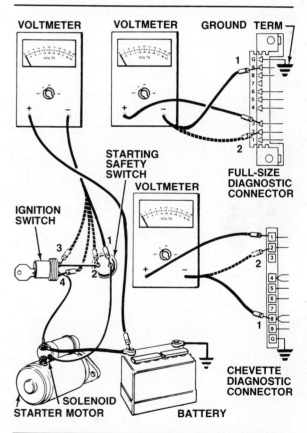

Figure 7-20. Testing the resistance between specific points of the GM starting system control circuit. (GM)

5. Touch the voltmeter positive (+) lead to the test points shown in the drawings to pinpoint the area of high resistance. Take all voltmeter readings while cranking the engine *with the ignition switch*:

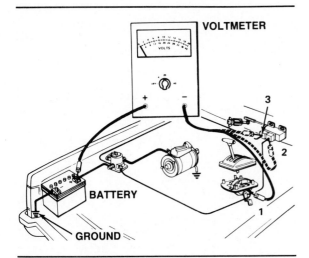

Figure 7-21. Testing the resistance between specific points of a Ford or AMC starting system control circuit. (Ford)

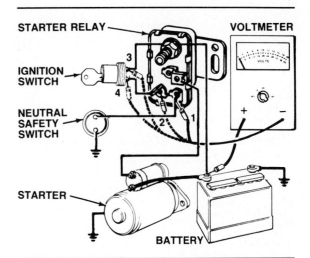

Figure 7-22. Testing the resistance between specific points in the Chrysler starting system control circuit. (Chrysler)

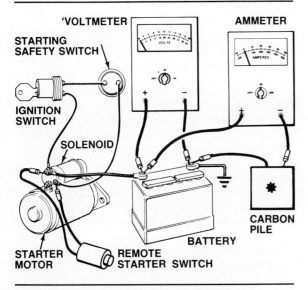

Figure 7-23. The test meter hookup for a starter current draw test.

a. For GM·cars, refer to figure 7-20.
b. For Ford and AMC cars, refer to figure 7-21.
c. For Chrysler cars, refer to figure 7-22.
6. Repair or replace any damaged wiring or faulty connections.

CURRENT DRAW TEST

1. Bypass the ignition switch with the remote starter switch (refer to figures 7-7 and 7-8).
2. Refer to figure 7-23 for test connections.
3. Connect the voltmeter positive (+) lead to the battery positive (+) terminal; connect the volt-

meter negative (−) lead to the battery negative (−) terminal.
4. Set the carbon pile to its maximum resistance (open).
5. Connect the ammeter positive (+) lead to the battery positive (+) terminal; connect the ammeter negative (−) lead to one lead of the carbon pile.
6. Connect the other lead of the carbon pile to the battery negative (−) terminal.
7. While cranking the engine, watch the voltmeter reading.
8. With the starter motor *off*, adjust the carbon pile until the voltmeter reading matches the reading taken in step 7.
9. Watch the ammeter reading and set the carbon pile back to open.
10. Compare the ammeter reading to the manufacturer's specifications. The table below summarizes the most probable causes of current draw that is too low or too high. If you suspect too much resistance, test the starting system resistance as explained earlier. If the problem is in the starter motor, it will have to be removed for further service. Refer to Chapter 8 for instructions.

PROBLEM	PROBABLE CAUSE
Current draw too high	Short in starter
	Starter or engine binding
Current draw too low	Excessive resistance in starting system
	Battery undercharged or defective

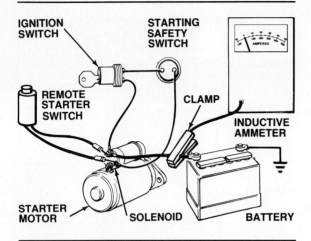

Figure 7-24. Testing the starter current draw with an inductive ammeter.

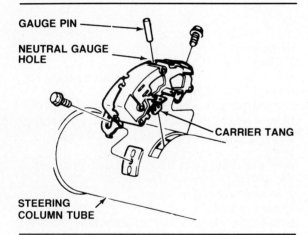

Figure 7-26. Using a gauge pin to adjust a starting safety switch. (Buick)

Current Draw Test With Inductive Ammeter

1. Bypass the ignition switch with the remote starter switch (refer to figures 7-7 and 7-8).
2. Refer to figure 7-24 for test connections.
3. Connect the ammeter inductive pickup to the battery positive (+) cable. Be sure the arrow on the inductive pickup is pointing in the right direction as specified on the ammeter.
4. Crank the engine for 15 seconds while watching the ammeter reading.
5. Compare the ammeter reading to the specifications. Use the current draw test we just discussed to interpret the readings.

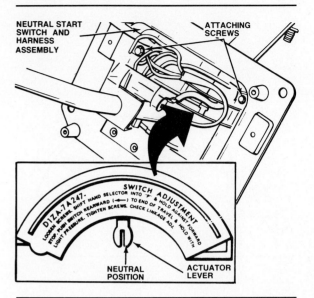

Figure 7-25. Adjusting the Ford floor-mounted starting safety switch. (Ford)

STARTING SAFETY SWITCH REPLACEMENT AND ADJUSTMENT

A bad starting safety switch must be replaced, but sometimes a simple adjustment will cure the problem. The following paragraphs present general instructions for replacing and adjusting various types of electrical starting safety switches. Mechanical blocking devices, as used by GM, should not need servicing during normal use.

Clutch-operated switches cannot be adjusted. To replace the switch, screw or bolt a new unit into the mounting holes of the original switch.

The automatic transmission safety switch used by Chrysler and AMC is threaded into the transmission housing. If a known-good switch is not operating correctly when installed, the transmission internal gear levers must be adjusted.

To adjust the floor-mounted switch on large Ford cars, figure 7-25:
1. Remove the shift lever handle.
2. Remove the dial housing.
3. Remove the pointer backup shield.
4. Loosen the two screws that hold the switch to the shift lever housing.

5. Hold the shift lever against the forward stop of the Park position.

6. Move the switch rearward to the end of its travel.

7. Tighten the two attaching screws.

8. Check that the engine will start only when the shift lever is in Park or Neutral; readjust the switch if necessary.

9. Reinstall the pointer backup shield, the dial housing, and the shift lever handle.

The other electrical switches used by Ford and GM have special alignment holes. To adjust these switches:

1. Disconnect the battery ground cable.

2. Loosen the switch attaching screws.

3. Move the switch until the two alignment holes match.

4. Check the hole alignment with a gauge pin of the size specified by the manufacturer, figure 7-26.

5. Tighten the switch attaching screws.

6. Reconnect the battery ground cable.

7. Check that the engine will start only when the shift lever is in Park or Neutral; readjust the switch if necessary.

Chapter

8

Starter Motor Overhaul

This chapter contains removal, disassembly, testing, repair, and installation instructions for Delco-Remy, Motorcraft, and Chrysler starter motors. Starter motor removal, bench testing, and installation procedures are presented as general instructions to help you do these jobs on most domestic cars and light trucks. Overhaul procedures are presented as photographic sequences for five specific starter motor models.

STARTER MOTOR REMOVAL

You may have to remove, loosen, or relocate heat shields, support brackets, or exhaust pipes to remove the starter motor. It may help to tag nuts, bolts, and washers removed from the starter motor and from other parts. It may also help to tag all wires disconnected from the starter motor. Observe all electrical safety precautions and shop safety regulations during removal of the starter motor. Remove the starter motor as follows:

1. Disconnect the battery ground cable.
2. Raise the car high enough to gain easy access to the starter motor. Support the car on safety stands or a hoist.
3. If necessary, turn the front wheels and disconnect the tie rods for easy access to the starter motor. On some cars, you may have to remove the front wheel nearest the starter motor.
4. Loosen or remove exhaust pipes and other components that interfere with starter motor removal.
5. Disconnect all wires from the starter motor or solenoid, figure 8-1. You may want to tag the wires and fasteners removed from the solenoid or motor.
6. Remove bolts securing heat shields and support brackets to the starter motor. Remove the heat shields and brackets.
7. Remove all mounting bolts and shims, if used, securing the starter motor to the engine. Remove the starter motor.

STARTER MOTOR AND SOLENOID BENCH TEST PROCEDURES

All starter motors listed in this chapter can be given the same standard no-load test, the same armature growler tests for shorts and opens, and the same tests for grounded or open field circuits.

All solenoids on the motors covered in this chapter can be tested for continuity in the same way.

Starter No-Load Test

The no-load test can be used to locate open or shorted windings, worn bushings, a bent armature shaft, and other problems with the arma-

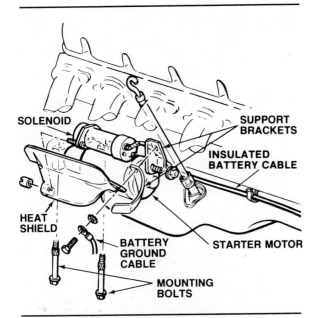

Figure 8-1. Disconnect all wires and remove heat shields and brackets before removing the starter motor from the engine. (Chevrolet)

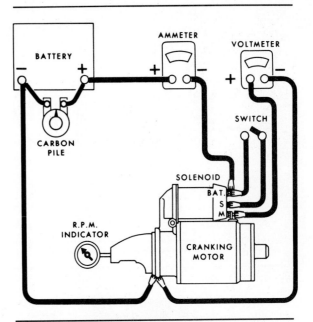

Figure 8-2. No-load test connections for solenoid-actuated starters. (Delco-Remy)

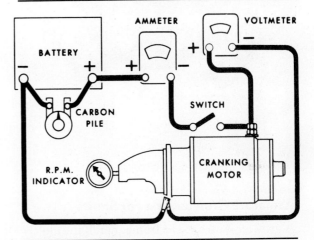

Figure 8-3. No-load test connections for movable pole shoe starters. (Delco-Remy)

ture and fields. You will need the starter motor maker's specifications for current draw and motor speed for the particular motor you are testing.

The no-load test is made with the starter on the workbench. The starter should be clamped in a vise or similar fixture. Begin the test by connecting a voltmeter, an ammeter, and a switch to a fully charged battery and to the starter. Make connections for solenoid-actuated starters as shown in figure 8-2 and for movable pole shoe starters as shown in figure 8-3. If the solenoid motor terminal is not exposed, connect the voltmeter to the solenoid battery terminal. The carbon pile is optional if you want to regulate battery voltage exactly during the test. Connect an rpm indicator to the pinion shaft to measure motor speed.

Close the switch and note the current draw and motor speed. Compare them to the manufacturer's specifications. Interpret test results as explained in the following paragraphs.

A low no-load speed and high current draw can be caused by bearings that are tight, dirty, or worn. A bent armature shaft or loose field pole screws can also cause the armature to drag and result in a low no-load speed and high current draw.

A low no-load speed and low current draw can be caused by an open field winding, high resistance due to poor connections, broken or weak brush springs, worn brushes, high mica on the commutator, a shorted armature, a grounded armature, or a grounded field.

A high no-load speed and high current draw can be caused by shorted fields or by an open shunt field on some starters.

If the starter motor fails to operate under high current draw, the insulated terminal or the fields may be grounded. The shaft bearings may also be frozen.

If the starter motor fails to operate with no current draw, there could be an open field circuit, an open armature coil, broken or weak brush springs, worn brushes, or high mica on the commutator.

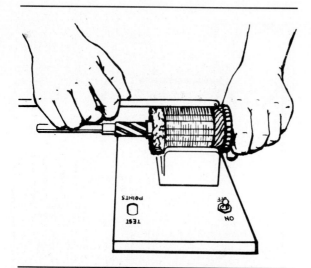

Figure 8-4. Growler test for armature shorts.

Figure 8-5. Armature ground test.

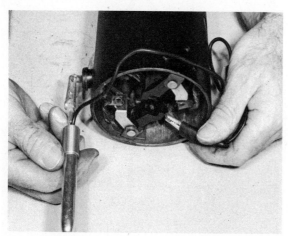

Figure 8-6. Field coil open circuit test.

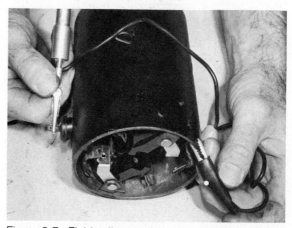

Figure 8-7. Field coil ground test.

Armature Growler Test For Shorts

A growler is an a.c. electromagnet. If the alternating current in the growler is 60-cycle, the current reverses direction 120 times every second. The magnetic field in the electromagnet therefore changes direction 120 times every second. If a starter motor armature is placed in a growler, changing magnetism puts a changing magnetic force on the armature. This causes a growling noise. Test for shorts as follows:
1. Place the armature on the growler and hold a hacksaw blade flat against the length of the armature core, figure 8-4. Start the growler.
2. Slowly rotate the armature while holding the hacksaw blade against each section of the armature core.
3. If the saw blade jumps or vibrates over any section of the core when the armature is rotated, the armature is shorted.

Armature Test for Grounded Windings

Place one lead of a 110-volt test lamp or a self-powered test lamp, figure 8-5, on the armature core or shaft. Place the other test lead on the commutator. If the lamp lights, the armature is grounded.

You also can test for grounded windings with an ohmmeter. Place one ohmmeter lead on the commutator and the other lead on the shaft. The ohmmeter should show infinite resistance. If the ohmmeter indicates continuity or low resistance, the armature windings are grounded to the shaft.

Field Coil Tests

Test the field coils for open circuits or grounded windings with a 110-volt test lamp or a self-powered test lamp. Most starter motors have two insulated brushes and two ground brushes.

Field coil test for open circuits
Touch one test lamp lead to the insulated brush and the other test lead to the field coil ground lead, figure 8-6. The lamp should light. The coils are open if the lamp does not light. Repeat the test with the other insulated brush, if present.

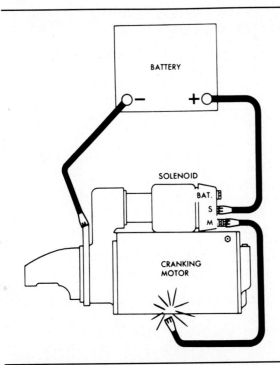

Figure 8-8. Circuit to check pinion clearance. (Chevrolet)

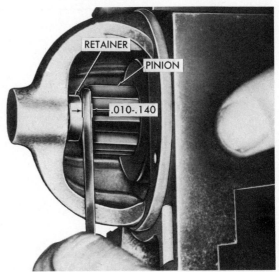

Figure 8-9. Use a feeler gauge to check pinion clearance. (Delco-Remy)

Field coil test for grounded windings

Disconnect the field ground leads. Touch one test lamp lead to the field insulated lead or solenoid connector and the other test lead to the grounded brush or frame, figure 8-7.

The test lamp should not light. The field coils are grounded if the lamp lights.

Delco-Remy Pinion Clearance Test

Test the drive pinion clearance on Delco-Remy starters with the starter motor assembled. Pinion clearance cannot be adjusted on motors with an enclosed shift fork, but it must be correct to avoid a damaged pinion, a stripped flywheel, or a burned out starter motor.

To test pinion clearance:
1. Disconnect the field coil connector from the solenoid motor terminal. Insulate the connector.
2. Connect a battery from the solenoid switch terminal to the solenoid frame, figure 8-8. Make sure the battery is the same voltage as the solenoid and motor.
3. Quickly touch a jumper wire from the solenoid motor terminal to the motor frame. The pinion should snap into position and stay there until the battery is disconnected. This test also proves the continuity of the solenoid.
4. Push the pinion back toward the commutator to eliminate slack or end play on the pinion.

5. Measure the distance between the pinion and the pinion stop with a feeler gauge, figure 8-9. Clearance should be 0.010″ to 0.140″.
6. Disconnect the battery.

If the pinion clearance is not within specified limits, check the shift fork, the pivot pin, and the starter drive for improper installation or wear. Replace the shift fork and pin or the drive if worn.

Brush Replacement

Brushes are some of the most often replaced items in any electric motor. As a general rule, any brush should be replaced when it has worn to one-half of its original length. For a starter motor brush, this is usually ¼ to ⅜ of an inch. As a brush wears, spring tension on it decreases. This can cause the brush to bounce on the commutator and to arc, which reduces the efficiency of the motor. Brushes should also be replaced if they are cracked, chipped, or otherwise damaged.

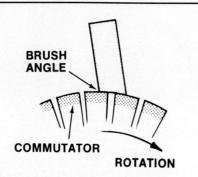

Figure 8-10. The brush angle and contour must match the commutator for proper motor operation.

When you install new brushes, match the contour of the brush face with the curve of the commutator, figure 8-10. If the brush angle is reversed, surface contact with the commutator is reduced. This will cause arcing between the commutator segments, premature brush and commutator wear, and loss of motor efficiency. Always check the brush angle and be sure it is not reversed when reinstalling or replacing brushes.

STARTER MOTOR OVERHAUL PROCEDURES

The following pages contain photographic procedures for disassembly, overhaul, and reassembly of five common domestic starter motors:
• Delco-Remy solenoid-actuated starter — Used by GM, it has a solenoid to engage the pinion and close the contact points.
• Motorcraft solenoid-actuated starter — Used by Ford, and similar to the Delco-Remy starter.
• Motorcraft movable pole shoe (positive-engagement) starter — Uses a pole shoe in place of a solenoid; used by Ford and AMC.
• Chrysler direct drive starter — Used on 6-cylinder engines, it has a direct drive solenoid actuator.
• Chrysler reduction drive model — Engaged by a solenoid, it uses a reduction gear along with the starter drive.

Chapter 11 of your *Classroom Manual* contains descriptions and more drawings of these starter motors. You may find it helpful to refer to the *Classroom Manual*, also, when overhauling a starter motor. Before starting any overhaul, be sure you read and understand the test procedures in the preceding section of this chapter. Make the tests at convenient points during the overhaul sequence. Read through the step-by-step procedure for the specific starter motor that you will be overhauling before you begin work.

All soldering and unsoldering of starter motor components should be done with a medium- to high-heat soldering iron (approximately 100 to 300 watts) with a fairly large tip. Use only rosin-core solder.

DELCO-REMY SOLENOID-ACTUATED STARTER OVERHAUL PROCEDURE

1. Disconnect field coil connector from solenoid motor terminal.

2. Remove two through-bolts and commutator end frame.

3. Remove field frame from drive housing and solenoid. On many motors, you can remove solenoid by removing two screws and turning to unlatch from field frame.

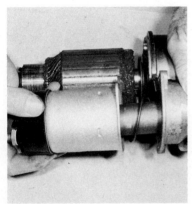

4. Remove two screws and remove solenoid from drive housing. Spring will pop out as solenoid is removed.

5. Solenoid plunger is attached to shift fork. Tilt shift fork and remove armature and drive assembly from drive housing.

6. Remove snapring securing pivot pin in drive housing. Remove pivot pin, then shift fork and plunger.

7. Remove worn commutator end frame bushing with puller. Install new bushing with wooden block and hammer. Replace drive end bushing in same way.

8. Remove thrust collar from end of shaft. Use deep socket and hammer to drive pinion stop collar toward pinion on shaft to expose snapring.

9. Remove snapring from shaft grove. Then slide starter drive and pinion stop collar off shaft.

DELCO-REMY SOLENOID-ACTUATED STARTER OVERHAUL PROCEDURE

10. Replace brushes if worn to one-half original length. Remove screws holding brushes and leads. Replace leads by disconnecting from ground or field connectors.

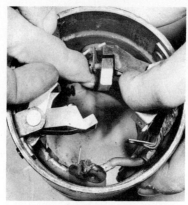

11. Attach leads and new brushes to holders with screws. Broken holders and springs are replaced by pulling pins at base of holders.

12. Apply silicone lubricant to drive end of shaft. Slide starter drive and collar onto shaft with cupped side of collar toward end of shaft.

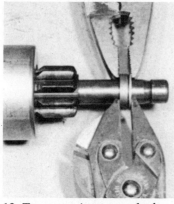

13. Tap snapring onto shaft and slide into groove. Place thrust collar on shaft with flange toward end. Use two pliers to squeeze collars together over snapring.

14. Install shift fork and plunger in drive end housing. Insert pivot pin and secure with snapring, if used. Some pivot pins are tapped in.

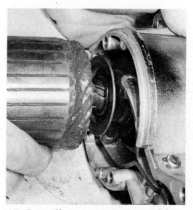

15. Install armature assembly into drive housing. Engage shift fork with collar on drive.

16. Place solenoid spring on plunger and install solenoid on drive housing. Secure with two screws.

17. Install field frame over armature. Hold all four brushes away from commutator. Work slowly; do not force. Do not bend brush holders or nick brushes.

18. Place thrust washer on end of shaft. Install end frame. Secure with through-bolts. Attach motor connector to solenoid motor terminal.

MOTORCRAFT SOLENOID-ACTUATED STARTER OVERHAUL PROCEDURE

1. Disconnect field coil connector from solenoid motor terminal. Notice that solenoid battery and switch terminals are linked.

2. Remove two screws securing solenoid. Remove solenoid. Spring will pop out.

3. Loosen screw and remove brush cover. Hold each brush spring away from brush with hook. Pull each brush from its holder.

4. Remove two through-bolts and commutator end frame. Remove worn end frame bushing with puller. Drive in new bushing.

5. Separate field frame and armature from drive housing.

6. Remove shift fork and solenoid plunger from drive housing. Small seal fits in housing above shift fork pivot pin.

7. Remove thrust washer and stopring retainer from end of shaft.

8. Drive stopring out of groove in shaft and discard it. Ring may break when removed. Then slide starter drive off shaft.

9. Remove ground brush retaining screws. Remove brushes. Replace brushes if worn to one-half original length.

MOTORCRAFT SOLENOID-ACTUATED STARTER OVERHAUL PROCEDURE

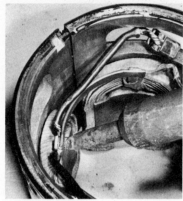

10. To remove insulated brushes, unsolder leads from field coils or cut leads as close to field coil connection as possible.

11. Test field coils. Install ground brush leads with screws. Crimp insulated brush lead clips to field coil connection. Then solder connection.

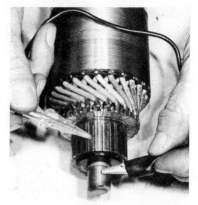

12. Test armature for shorts (shown here) and opens. Lubricate shaft with Lubriplate before installing starter drive and commutator end frame.

13. Install starter drive and position stopring in groove on shaft.

14. Support shaft as shown and tap new stopring into groove. Install stopring retainer and thrust washer on shaft after stopring is in place.

15. Install shift fork and plunger. Be sure seal fits above pivot pin in drive housing. Align field frame with drive housing. Assemble frame, armature and housing.

16. Replace commutator end frame if insulators under insulated brush holders are broken. Install end frame and secure with two through-bolts.

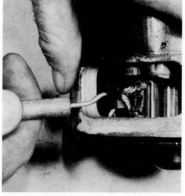

17. Pull springs away from brush holders and insert brushes in holders. Place springs on brushes. Be sure insulated leads do not touch frame. Install cover band.

18. Place solenoid spring on plunger. Install solenoid and secure to drive housing with two screws. Attach field connector to solenoid motor terminal.

MOTORCRAFT MOVABLE POLE SHOE STARTER OVERHAUL PROCEDURE

1. Ford calls it the ''Positive Engagement'' starter. Remove brush cover band and pole shoe cover.

2. Hold each brush spring away from brush with hook. Pull each brush from its holder.

3. Remove two through-bolts and commutator end frame. Remove worn end frame bushing with puller. Drive in new bushing.

4. Separate drive end housing from field frame and armature. Plunger return spring will pop out of housing. Don't lose it.

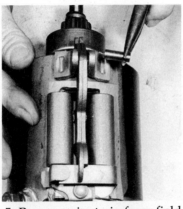

5. Remove pivot pin from field frame and pole shoe plunger. Then remove pole shoe plunger and shift fork assembly.

6. Separate armature from field frame. Test armature and field coils for opens and shorts before reassembly.

7. Remove thrust washer and stopring retainer from end of shaft.

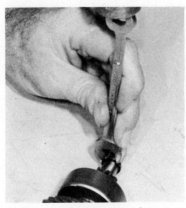

8. Drive stopring out of groove in shaft, as shown. Discard ring; it may break when removed. Then slide starter drive off shaft.

9. Remove ground brush retaining screws. Remove brushes. Replace brushes if worn to one-half original length.

MOTORCRAFT MOVABLE POLE SHOE STARTER OVERHAUL PROCEDURE

10. To remove insulated brushes, unsolder leads from field coils or cut leads as close to field coil connections as possible.

11. Lubricate shaft with Lubriplate and install starter drive on armature. Install new stopring into groove.

12. Install stopring retainer and thrust washer on end of shaft. Install armature and drive assembly into field frame.

13. Install plunger and shift fork on starter frame. Install pivot pin. Be sure shift fork engages starter drive properly.

14. Place plunger return spring on plunger as shown.

15. Fill drive housing bearing ¼ full of grease. Assemble drive housing to field frame. Plunger spring seats in hole at top of drive housing.

16. Place fiber thrust washer on end of shaft, if used. (No washer is used with molded commutator.) Install commutator end frame and two through-bolts.

17. Pull springs away from brush holders and insert brushes in holders. Place springs on brushes. Be sure insulated leads do not touch frame.

18. Install pole shoe cover, gasket, and brush cover band. Secure with screw.

CHRYSLER REDUCTION GEAR STARTER OVERHAUL PROCEDURE

1. Remove two through-bolts and front end frame. Remove armature; note thrust washers on both ends of shaft.

2. Remove worn front end frame bushing with puller. Install new bushing with driver or with wooden block and hammer.

3. Pull field frame far enough from drive end housing to expose field terminal screw. Remove screw and field frame.

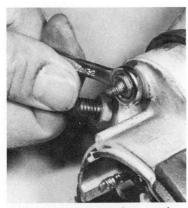

4. Remove nut, washer, and insulating washer from solenoid terminal. Then unsolder solenoid pull-in coil lead from brush terminal.

5. Unwind solenoid pull-in coil lead from brush terminal. Remove brush holder from housing. Some brush holders have more screws to remove.

6. Remove solenoid contact and plunger shaft from solenoid. Tanged washer that fits over shaft hole below solenoid has already been removed.

7. Remove solenoid winding and return spring from drive end housing. Plunger core stays in end housing with shift fork.

8. Remove battery terminal nut from brush holder. Remove brush holder.

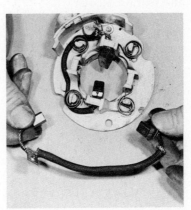

9. Inspect brushes for wear and damaged leads. Replace damaged brushes. Replace all brushes if any are worn to one-half original length.

CHRYSLER REDUCTION GEAR STARTER OVERHAUL PROCEDURE

10. Pry off dust cover. Then use punch or screwdriver to remove snapring holding driven gear to pinion shaft. *Caution*: snapring is under tension and will pop off.

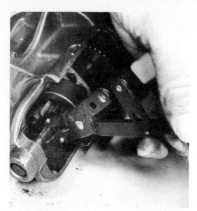

11. Remove C-clip or snapring between pinion and end of drive housing.

12. Tap pinion gear toward driven gear with punch and hammer.

13. Remove shaft from gear end of housing. Remove pinion, clutch, retainer, washers, and two shift fork actuators from other end. Remove gear and friction washer.

14. Pull shift lever toward rear end of housing and remove solenoid plunger core.

15. Remove pivot pin and shift fork. Use pliers or punch and hammer to remove pin.

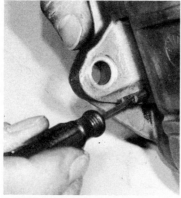

16. Begin reassembly by installing shift fork and pivot pin as removed in step 15. Bend one side of pin after installation.

17. Place driven gear and friction washer in position. Install shaft through front of housing. Install pinion assembly from other end. Engage shift fork with actuators.

18. Friction washer must be on shoulder of shaft splines before driven gear is secured to shaft. Install driven gear snapring.

CHRYSLER REDUCTION GEAR STARTER OVERHAUL PROCEDURE

19. Install pinion shaft C-clip or snapring. Tap pinion shaft into drive end bushing with soft mallet.

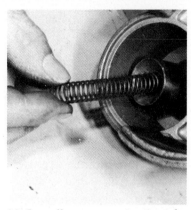

20. Install return spring in solenoid plunger core.

21. Assemble battery terminal to brush holder. Install contact plunger in solenoid. Place solenoid on brush holder. Some models are secured with screws.

22. Secure solenoid terminal with insulating washer and nut. Wrap pull-in coil lead around ground brush terminal and solder.

23. Assemble solenoid and brush holder with drive end housing. Some models are attached with screws.

24. Install brushes in slots. Place brush springs away from brushes with screwdriver.

25. Install thrust washer with tangs against brushes. Place springs on brushes. Washer holds brushes from commutator when armature is installed.

26. Test field coils before assembling field frame. Align field frame with end housing and connect field lead to brush terminal with screw.

27. Test armature before assembling. Be sure thrust washers are on both ends of shaft and install armature. Finally, install end frame and two through-bolts.

CHRYSLER DIRECT DRIVE STARTER OVERHAUL PROCEDURE

1. This is early-model starter. Later ones are similar. Remove brush cover strap and through-bolts. Lift springs and remove brushes before removing end frame.

2. Remove commutator end frame. Then remove thrust washer from end of shaft.

3. Remove worn commutator end frame bushing with puller. Install new bushing with bushing driver or with wooden block and hammer.

4. Remove cotter pin and clevis pin securing shift fork to solenoid. Then remove field frame and solenoid from armature.

5. Disconnect field coil strap and screws securing solenoid to field frame. Remove solenoid.

6. To replace worn ground brushes, unscrew brush leads from field frame.

7. To replace worn field brushes, unsolder brush leads from field coil leads. Solder new brushes in place.

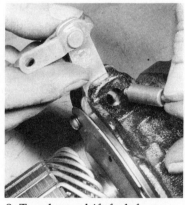

8. To release shift fork from end frame, remove rubber boot, pivot pin retainer, and pivot pin.

9. Remove two screws securing armature plate to drive end frame. Remove armature, starter drive, and shift fork from end frame.

CHRYSLER DIRECT DRIVE STARTER OVERHAUL PROCEDURE

10. Drive stop retainer from snapring on armature shaft. Use 11/16-inch socket and mallet. Remove snapring, stop retainer, and starter drive.

11. To reassemble, place armature plate and starter drive on shaft. Install stop retainer, snapring, and thrust washer. Press together with two pliers.

12. Place shift fork on starter drive. Slide armature and shift fork into end frame. Install shift fork pivot and pivot retainer.

13. Attach solenoid to field frame. Connect field coil strap to solenoid motor terminal. Be sure insulators are in place.

14. Replace rubber boot. Attach armature plate to end frame with screws. Slide armature and drive end frame into field frame. Do not snag brushes.

15. Connect solenoid plunger to shift fork clevis with clevis pin and cotter pin.

16. Slide field frame and end frame completely together. Do not snag brushes on armature. Place thrust washer on end of shaft.

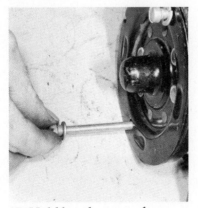

17. Hold brushes out of way and install commutator end frame. Secure with two through-bolts.

18. Hold brush springs away from brush holders. Install brushes in holders and place springs on brushes. Install brush cover strap.

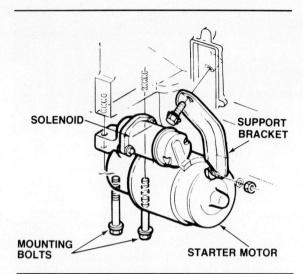

SOLENOID

SUPPORT
BRACKET

MOUNTING
BOLTS

STARTER MOTOR

Figure 8-11. Install a starter motor by securing the motor and any support brackets to the engine with bolts. Connect all terminal leads to the motor or solenoid. (Chevrolet)

STARTER MOTOR INSTALLATION

To install a starter motor:
1. If they are used, attach the support brackets to the starter motor. Heat shields may be installed before or after the motor, depending on the motor and engine installation in the car.
2. Install the starter motor and the support brackets to the engine with shims, if needed, and bolts, figure 8-11. If the starter motor pinion does not engage the engine flywheel completely, add shims to the upper or outer mounting position. If the starter motor pinion chatters and fails to disengage, add shims to the lower or inner mounting position.
3. Connect all of the terminal leads to the motor or solenoid.
4. Connect the ground cable to the negative battery post.
5. Connect any parts such as exhaust pipes, tie rods, or wheels that may have been removed to gain access to the starter motor. Lower the car to the ground.

PART FOUR

Ignition System Service

9

Breaker-Point Ignition System Testing

This chapter gives you detailed instructions for on-car testing of breaker-point ignition systems. The test equipment ranges from simple meters to an oscilloscope, the visual voltmeter that was introduced in Chapter 2. On-car adjusting and servicing is covered in Chapter 10, and Chapter 11 presents step-by-step instructions for off-car distributor service. Later chapters will explain testing and servicing procedures for the electronic ignition systems used by major manufacturers. Figure 9-1 will help you pinpoint the problem in a particular ignition system.

To avoid hurting yourself or the ignition system, follow these precautions during ignition system tests:
• Turn the ignition switch off, or disconnect the battery ground cable, before disconnecting any ignition system wiring.
• Do not touch any exposed connections while the engine is cranking or running.

PRIMARY CIRCUIT VOLTMETER TESTS

Primary circuit voltage has a directly proportional effect on secondary circuit voltage. A 1-volt loss in the primary circuit can reduce secondary circuit voltage by as much as 10,000 volts. Voltage losses in the primary circuit can be caused by too much circuit resistance or too little source voltage. A series of voltmeter tests can pinpoint any excessive voltage drops in the primary circuit.

High resistance can be caused by:
• Loose, corroded, or damaged wiring connections
• An incorrect or defective ballast resistor
• An incorrect or defective coil, points, or condenser.

Low voltage can be caused by:
• Excessive starter motor current draw
• Low charging voltage
• A discharged battery.

Make the following series of voltage-drop and available-voltage tests in the order given. Faults found during these tests could make the car run poorly or fail to start. Be sure that the battery is the correct capacity and that it is fully charged before beginning the tests. Battery testing is explained in Chapter 3 of this *Shop Manual*.

Unless instructed otherwise, do all primary circuit voltmeter tests with the ignition system disabled:
1. Remove the secondary ignition cable from the center tower of the distributor cap.
2. Connect a jumper wire between the cable and a good engine ground.

To check the battery voltage while cranking:
1. Refer to figure 9-2.
2. Connect the voltmeter positive (+) lead to the

CONDITION	CAUSE	CURE
• Engine cranks normally, will not start and run	1. Open primary circuit (breaker-point or solid-state)	1. Check connections, coil, breaker points, pickup coil, module, ignition switch.
	2. Coil grounded	2. Replace coil.
	3. Points not opening	3. Adjust.
	4. Points burned	4. Replace.
	5. Poor timing	5. Adjust timing.
	6. Defective condenser	6. Replace.
	7. Secondary voltage leak	7. Check coil top, distributor cap and rotor, and leads.
	8. Spark plugs fouled	8. Clean and adjust or replace.
	9. Problem in fuel system	
	10. Problem with engine	
• Engine runs, one cylinder misses	1. Defective spark plug	1. Clean and adjust or replace.
	2. Distributor cap or spark plug cable	2. Replace.
	3. Problem with engine	
• Engine runs, different cylinders miss	1. Points dirty, worn, out of adjustment	1. Replace or adjust.
	2. Condenser defective	2. Replace.
	3. Advance units defective	3. Repair or replace.
	4. Defective secondary wiring or insulation	4. Replace as necessary.
	5. Weak coil	5. Replace.
	6. Poor circuit connections	6. Clean and tighten.
	7. Defective spark plugs	7. Clean and adjust or replace.
	8. Problem in fuel system	
	9. Problem with engine	
• Loss of engine power	1. Poor timing	1. Check and adjust.
	2. Defective advance units	2. Repair or replace.
	3. Wrong fuel	3. Use correct fuel.
	4. Wrong engine oil	4. Use correct oil.
• Engine backfires	1. Poor timing	1. Check and adjust.
	2. Ignition crossfire	2. Check secondary insulation and routing of plug wires.
	3. Wrong spark plug heat range	3. Use correct plugs.
	4. Problem with fuel system	
	5. Problem with engine	
• Engine knocks, pings	1. Poor timing	1. Check and adjust.
	2. Defective advance units	2. Repair or replace.
	3. Points out of adjustment	3. Adjust.
	4. Wrong heat range spark plugs	4. Use correct plugs.
	5. Wrong fuel	5. Use correct fuel.
• Contact points burned or oxidized	1. Resistance in condenser circuit	1. Clean and tighten condenser connections; replace if necessary.
	2. High system voltage	2. Check charging system.
	3. Excessive dwell angle	3. Adjust points.
	4. Weak spring tension	4. Adjust or replace.
	5. Oil vapors in distributor from faulty PCV system or overlubricated distributor	5. Check PCV system; remove excess lubricant from distributor.

Figure 9-1. Ignition system troubleshooting chart.

battery positive (+) terminal, *not* to the cable connector. Connect the voltmeter negative (−) lead to ground.
3. While cranking the engine, watch the voltmeter reading:
    a. If the reading is 9 volts or more, the battery is in good condition.

b. If the reading is less than 9 volts, go to step 4.
4. To find the cause of the battery voltage drop:
    a. Check the voltage drop across the battery ground cable as explained in the next test.
    b. Test the starter motor for too much current draw as explained in Chapter 7.
    c. Test the charging system for correct charg-

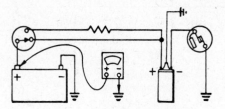

Figure 9-2. Testing battery voltage while cranking.

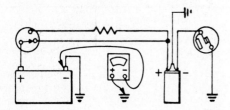

Figure 9-3. Testing the voltage drop across the battery ground cable.

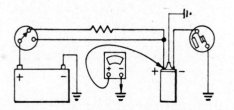

Figure 9-4. Testing available voltage at the coil.

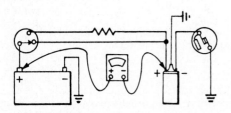

Figure 9-5. Testing the voltage drop across the ignition resistor bypass circuit.

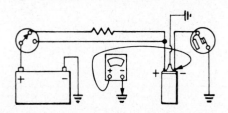

Figure 9-6. Testing the voltage drop across the breaker points.

ing voltage as explained in Chapters 4 and 5.

To test the voltage drop across the battery ground cable while cranking:
1. Refer to figure 9-3.
2. Connect the voltmeter positive (+) lead to ground; connect the voltmeter negative (−) lead to the battery negative (−) terminal, *not* to the cable connector.
3. While cranking the engine, observe the voltmeter reading:
  a. If the reading is 0.2 volt or less, the battery ground connection and cable are in good condition.
  b. If the reading exceeds 0.2 volt, go to step 4.
4. Clean and tighten the battery ground connection and the battery negative terminal connection. Repeat the test. Replace the ground cable if necessary.

To test the available voltage at the coil:
1. Refer to figure 9-4.
2. Connect the voltmeter positive (+) lead to coil positive (+), or battery, terminal; connect the voltmeter negative (−) lead to ground.
3. Bump the engine with the starter motor until the breaker points are closed.

4. With the ignition switch on, note the voltmeter reading. It should be 5 to 7 volts (one-half battery voltage).
5. Bump the engine with the starter motor until the breaker points are open.
6. With the ignition switch on, note the voltmeter reading. It should be about 12 volts (battery voltage).
7. If either voltmeter reading is not within the specifications:
  a. Check the primary ballast resistor circuit connections. Repair or replace any loose or damaged connections.
  b. Test the ballast resistor as explained in this chapter, and replace it if necessary.
  c. Test the coil, as explained in this chapter, and replace it if necessary.
  d. Repeat the test.

To test the voltage drop across the ignition resistor bypass circuit:
1. Refer to figure 9-5.
2. Connect the voltmeter positive (+) lead to the battery positive (+) terminal; connect the voltmeter negative (−) lead to the coil positive (+), or battery, terminal.
3. While cranking the engine, watch the voltmeter reading:
  a. If the reading is less than 0.5 volt, the bypass circuit is in good condition.
  b. If the reading is more than 0.5 volt, go to step 4.
4. To find the area of too much resistance:
  a. Check the resistor bypass circuit connections. Repair or replace any loose or damaged connections.
  b. Repeat the test.

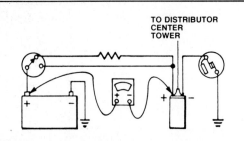

TO DISTRIBUTOR
CENTER
TOWER

Figure 9-7. Testing the voltage drop across the ignition resistor with the engine running.

To measure the voltage drop across the breaker points:
1. Refer to figure 9-6.
2. Connect the voltmeter positive (+) lead to the coil negative (−), or distributor, terminal; connect the voltmeter negative (−) lead to ground.
3. Bump the engine with the starter motor until the breaker points are closed.
4. With the ignition switch on, watch the voltmeter reading:
   a. If the reading is less than 0.2 volt, the breaker points are in good condition.
   b. If the reading is more than 0.2 volt, go to step 5.
5. Inspect the breaker points for:
   a. Loose wiring connections
   b. Poor ground connection
   c. Poor alignment
   d. Burned, pitted, or oxidized contacts
   e. Excessive wear.
6. Adjust or replace the breaker points if necessary and repeat the test.
   To test the voltage drop across the ballast resistor circuit with the engine running:
1. Refer to figure 9-7.
2. Return the grounded secondary ignition cable to the center tower of the distributor cap.
3. Connect the voltmeter positive (+) lead to the battery positive (+) terminal; connect the voltmeter negative (−) lead to the coil positive (+), or battery, terminal.
4. Run the engine at 1,500 rpm and observe the voltmeter reading.
5. Compare the voltmeter reading to the manufacturer's specifications (usually 1.5 to 3.5 volts):
   a. If the reading is within specifications, the ballast resistor circuit is in good condition.
   b. If the reading is not within specifications, go to step 6.
6. Check the resistor circuit:
   a. Repair or replace any loose or damaged connections.
   b. Test the ballast resistor, as explained in this chapter, and replace it if necessary.
   c. Test the coil, as explained in this chapter, and replace it if necessary.
   d. Repeat the test.

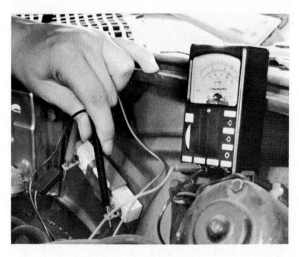

Figure 9-8. Testing the Chrysler ceramic resistor.

BALLAST RESISTOR TEST AND REPLACEMENT

The ignition ballast resistor can be measured directly with an ohmmeter. The most common problem with the resistor is high, or infinite, resistance caused by an internal open. Whether the resistor is a length of special wire or a ceramic unit, the manufacturer will specify the exact amount of resistance that should be present.

Ballast Resistor Testing

Some ballast resistors, like Chrysler's, which are separate resistors in a ceramic block, can be tested easily with an ohmmeter, figure 9-8. To measure the resistance directly with an ohmmeter:
1. Be sure the ignition switch is off or disconnect the battery ground cable.
2. Disconnect the ignition wiring connectors from the resistor.
3. Connect the ohmmeter leads to the resistor terminals, figure 9-8, and note the meter reading.
4. Compare the reading to the manufacturer's specifications:
   a. If the reading is within specifications, the ballast resistor is good.
   b. If the reading is not within specifications, replace the resistor.
   Ballast resistors that are lengths of resistance wire within the car wiring harness often are not easily tested with an ohmmeter. This is particularly true when one end of the wire is attached to the ignition switch in the driver's compartment and the other end of the wire is attached to the ignition coil in the engine compartment. In these cases, the resistance wire should be tested by the voltage-drop method explained in the previous section.

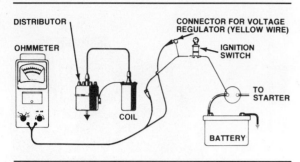

Figure 9-9. Testing the AMC resistance wire.

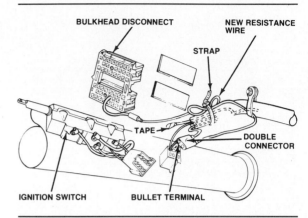

Figure 9-10. Replacing the Ford resistance wire. (Ford)

The resistance wires on some AMC cars are connected from the voltage regulator to the coil. Because both test points are within the engine compartment, you can check the resistance with an ohmmeter as shown in figure 9-9.

Ballast Resistor Replacement

General Motors and American Motors
To replace a GM or an AMC resistance wire:
1. Locate both ends of the resistance wire in the engine compartment wiring harness.
2. Cut the old resistance wire about a half inch from the points at which it is spliced into the wiring harness:
    a. If possible, remove the old resistance wire and discard it.
    b. If the old wire is hard to remove, insulate both cut ends and leave it in the harness.
3. Crimp butt connectors onto the cut wire ends that remain in the harness.
4. Cut a length of resistance wire as specified by the manufacturer.
5. Insert the ends of the new resistance wire into the butt connectors and crimp them.
6. Insulate the wiring harness at the points where the connectors have been installed.
7. Tape or clip the new resistance wire to the outside of the wiring harness so that the wire does not dangle.
8. Reconnect the battery ground cable.
9. Start and run the engine. If the engine will start but will not run, check the connections at either end of the new resistance wire.

An alternate method of replacing the original resistance wire on these cars is to install a ceramic resistor of the manufacturer's specified value and connect it to bypass the original resistance wire with low-resistance primary wire.

Ford
To replace a Ford resistance wire:
1. Refer to figure 9-10.
2. Disconnect the battery ground cable.
3. Remove the multiple-plug connector from the ignition switch.
4. Refer to the system diagram of the specific

model you are working on:
    a. One terminal of the connector will have two wires entering it.
    b. One of these wires, usually colored either pink or red with a stripe, is the resistance wire.
    c. The other wire, usually colored red with a stripe, is connected to an accessory circuit.
5. Cut the bad resistor wire about 1 inch from the connector. Insulate the cut end that stays at the connector.
6. Cut the other wire about 2 inches from the connector.
7. Crimp or solder bullet connectors onto both cut wire ends.
8. Insert the bullet connectors into opposite sides of a female double connector.
9. Cut a length of resistance wire as specified by the manufacturer.
10. Crimp or solder bullet connectors onto both ends of the new resistance wire.
11. Insert one end of the new resistance wire into the female double connector.
12. Route and tape the new resistance wire along the main wiring harness to the bulkhead disconnect.
13. Unplug the bulkhead disconnect and locate the red-with-stripe wire that is connected to the old, defective resistance wire.
14. Cut the red-with-stripe wire about 1 inch from the bulkhead disconnect.
15. Crimp or solder a bullet connector onto the cut wire end that remains in the bulkhead disconnect; insulate the other cut end.
16. Plug the remaining end of the new resistance wire into the bullet connector on the red-with-stripe wire.
17. Reassemble the connectors that were unplugged at the ignition switch and the bulkhead disconnect.
18. Reconnect the battery ground cable.
19. Start and run the engine. If the engine will start but not run, check the connections at either end of the new resistance wire.

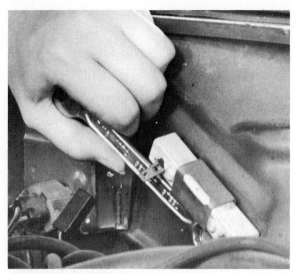

Figure 9-11. Replacing the Chrysler ceramic resistor.

Chrysler

To replace a Chrysler ballast resistor:
1. Refer to figure 9-11.
2. Disconnect the battery ground cable.
3. Unplug the leads from both ends of the ballast resistor.
4. Unbolt the resistor from the car body; install a new resistor in the original mounting holes.
5. Plug the leads into both ends of the new resistor.
6. Reconnect the battery ground cable.
7. Start and run the engine. If the engine will start but not run, check the connections at both ends of the new resistor.

COIL TESTS

The resistance, current draw, and polarity of the ignition coil can be tested with an ohmmeter, an ammeter, and a voltmeter. Special coil testers are also available; we will explain their use. Later in this chapter, we will give instructions for checking coil output and polarity with an oscilloscope.

A coil should be tested at its normal operating temperature because coil resistance changes directly with temperature. Before testing a coil, make these preliminary checks:
1. Be sure the coil is mounted securely and that all connections are clean and tight.
2. Check for a cracked or burned coil tower.
3. Check for a dented or cracked housing.
4. Check for oil leakage.

Winding Resistance Test

To measure the resistance of the primary and secondary windings:
1. Refer to figure 9-12.
2. Disconnect the battery ground cable or remove the coil from the car.

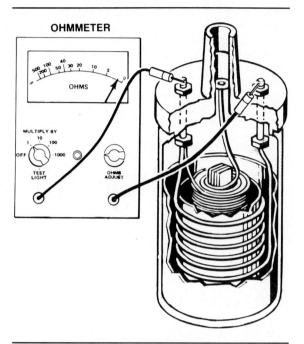

Figure 9-12. Testing the resistance of the coil primary windings.

3. Set the ohmmeter on a low scale.
4. Measure the primary winding resistance:
   a. Connect one ohmmeter lead to the coil positive (+), or battery, primary terminal.
   b. Connect the other ohmmeter lead to the coil negative (−), or distributor, primary terminal.
5. Compare the ohmmeter reading to the manufacturer's specifications for primary winding resistance:
   a. If the reading is within the specifications, go to step 6.
   b. If the reading is not within the specifications, replace the coil.
6. Disconnect the ohmmeter leads.
7. Set the meter on the highest scale.
8. Refer to figure 9-13.
9. Measure the secondary winding resistance:
   a. Connect one ohmmeter lead to the coil tower secondary terminal.
   b. Touch the second ohmmeter lead to one primary terminal and note the reading.
   c. Then move the second ohmmeter lead to the other coil primary terminal and note the reading.
10. Compare the lowest ohmmeter reading from step 9 to the manufacturer's specifications for secondary resistance:
   a. If the reading is within specifications, go to step 11.
   b. If the reading is not within specifications, replace the coil.

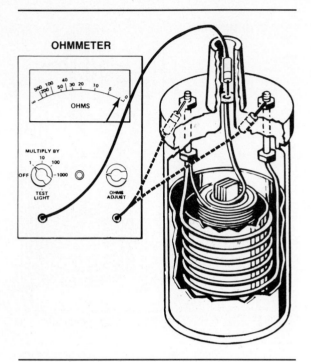

Figure 9-13. Testing the resistance of the coil secondary winding.

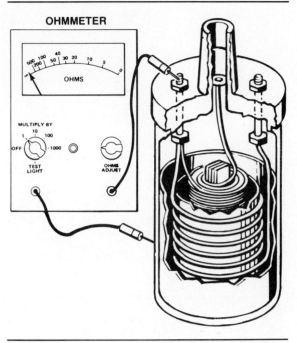

Figure 9-14. Testing the coil for shorted windings.

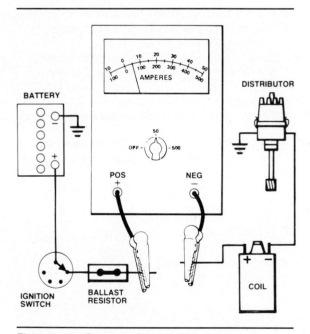

Figure 9-15. Checking the coil current draw.

11. Disconnect the ohmmeter leads.
12. Refer to figure 9-14.
13. Set the ohmmeter on the lowest scale.
14. Test the coil for shorted windings:
   a. Connect one ohmmeter lead to either primary terminal.
   b. Touch the other ohmmeter lead to the metal case of the coil; watch the meter reading.

15. The meter should indicate infinite resistance. Any reading other than infinite resistance means that the coil windings are shorted to the case and the coil must be replaced.

Current Draw Test

Many manufacturers give current-draw specifications for their ignition coils. To test the coil with an ammeter:
1. Refer to figure 9-15.
2. Be sure the ignition switch is off.
3. Disconnect the coil positive (+) primary wire from the coil.
4. Connect the ammeter positive (+) lead to the positive (+) primary wire; connect the ammeter negative (−) lead to the positive (+) primary terminal at the coil.
5. Turn the ignition switch on and, depending on the manufacturer's test instructions, either start the engine or close the ignition breaker points.
6. Compare the ammeter reading to the manufacturer's specifications:
   a. No current draw means an open in the primary circuit. The ignition system would not operate at all in this case.
   b. If the reading is less than the specifications, go to step 7.
   c. If the reading is more than the specifications, go to step 8.
7. Low coil current draw can be caused by:
   a. A discharged battery
   b. High resistance in the primary wiring or

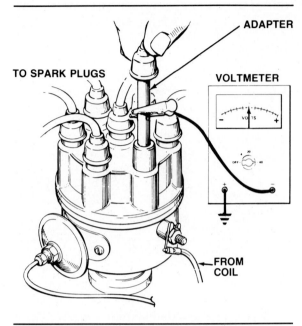

Figure 9-16. Using a positive and negative reading voltmeter to check the coil polarity.

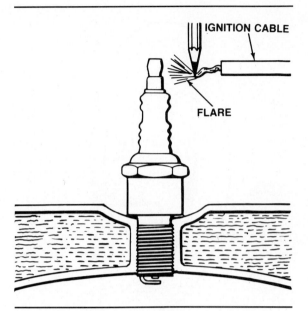

Figure 9-17. Visually checking the coil polarity.

the coil primary winding
c. Loose or corroded connections.
8. High coil current draw can be caused by:
a. A shorted coil or ballast resistor
b. The incorrect coil or ballast resistor for the car.

Polarity Test

If the coil polarity is reversed, the engine will start and run, but the required voltage will be increased by 20 to 40 percent. This can cause misfiring under some operating conditions. If coil polarity cannot be determined from the markings at the coil primary terminals, polarity can be checked with a voltmeter or with a visual test.

The voltmeter used in this test should have a negative as well as a positive scale; that is, the zero voltage position should be in the center of the scale or above the left hand side of the scale. If the voltmeter does not have this feature, it could be damaged during the test.

Later in this chapter, you will learn to test coil polarity using an oscilloscope.

Voltmeter polarity test
To test the coil polarity with a voltmeter:
1. Refer to figure 9-16.
2. Connect an adapter with an exposed terminal into any spark plug cable, either at the plug or at the distributor cap.
3. Start and idle the engine.
4. Set the voltmeter on the highest scale.
5. Connect the voltmeter positive (+) lead to an

engine ground; momentarily touch the voltmeter negative (−) lead to the adapter terminal.
6. Note the direction in which the voltmeter needle moves:
a. If the needle moves toward the positive scale, the coil polarity is correct.
b. If the needle moves toward the negative scale, the coil polarity is reversed; go to step 7.
7. Reversed coil polarity can be caused by:
a. Reversed primary circuit connections at the coil
b. Reversed cable connections at the battery (this would damage the alternator and other solid-state parts).

Visual polarity test
To test the coil polarity visually:
1. Refer to figure 9-17.
2. Remove the cable from any spark plug.
3. Hold a pencil tip between the cable terminal and the spark plug electrode.
4. Crank the engine briefly with the starter motor.
5. Observe the spark at the exposed plug electrode:
a. If the spark flares between the pencil tip and the spark plug, as shown in figure 9-17, the coil polarity is correct.
b. If the spark flares between the pencil tip and the cable, the coil polarity is reversed.

Using A Coil Tester

Not all coil problems can be detected through the tests presented so far. A coil might not fail until it is put under normal operating conditions. On the other hand, a problem that

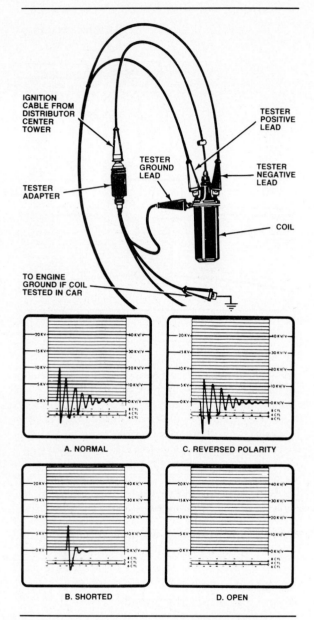

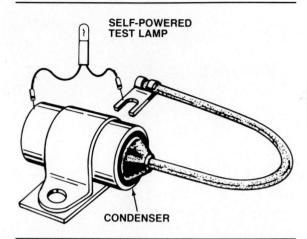

Figure 9-19. Testing the condenser insulation with a self-powered test lamp.

Figure 9-18. Connections and test patterns for a typical coil tester. (Sun)

seems to be the fault of the ignition coil can often be caused by some other part of the car's electrical system.

Special coil testers isolate the coil from the rest of the electrical system and test it separately, under normal operating conditions. The coil tester may be a single piece of equipment, or it may be built into the console of an oscilloscope. Most coil testers include an ohmmeter for measuring the resistance of the windings and a cathode-ray tube for viewing the coil's voltage output trace. If the tester is built into a larger oscilloscope console, the coil trace will be shown on the large central oscilloscope screen. Separate coil testers have small cathode-ray

tubes that display only the coil trace.

The coil can be tested while it is installed in the car, or it can be removed from the car and placed in a special holder at the tester. To test the coil while it is installed in the car:
1. Refer to figure 9-18.
2. Disconnect both primary leads from the coil primary terminals.
3. Disconnect the secondary ignition cable from the center tower of the distributor cap.
4. Connect the tester's volt-ohm test leads to the coil primary terminals (observe tester lead polarity, if marked).
5. Connect the tester's ground lead to the coil case or to an engine block ground.
6. Connect the tester's secondary adapter lead to the secondary ignition cable (this can be a series connection, as shown, or an inductive pickup clamp).
7. Set tester control for breaker-point or transistorized ignition, depending on test vehicle.
8. Following tester manufacturer's instructions, adjust tester control until the coil trace on the oscilloscope screen extends to 20-30 kV.
9. Compare the coil trace to figure 9-18, position A:
   a. A good coil will produce a series of gradually smaller waves, with the first wave reaching to 20-30 kV. The first wave of the trace will extend up rather than down.
   b. A coil with shorted windings will produce only one or two waves, with the first wave not reaching the coil's rated output, figure 9-18, position B.
   c. If the tester leads on the coil primary terminals are reversed, the first wave of the coil trace will extend down rather than up, position C. Reverse the leads and repeat the test.
   d. A coil with an internal open will not produce a trace, position D.

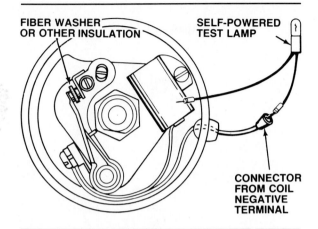

Figure 9-20. If the condenser cannot be removed or disconnected from the distributor, the points can be blocked open and the primary lead from the coil used as a test point.

e. If the trace height reaches 20 to 30 kV but the trace is unstable or wavers, the coil's internal insulation is breaking down under normal operating conditions. The coil should be replaced.

CONDENSER TESTS

Although many mechanics automatically replace the condenser at every tune-up, a condenser can be tested for:
• Series resistance (the condition of the internal connections)
• Capacity
• Insulation condition.

Condenser Testing With A Self-Powered Test Lamp

Insulation condition can be quickly tested with a self-powered test lamp:
1. Refer to figure 9-19.
2. Disconnect the condenser lead from the distributor. If this is not possible, such as with a Uniset points and condenser assembly:
   a. Refer to figure 9-20.
   b. Block the breaker points open with an insulator such as a fiber washer or match stick.
   c. Disconnect the lead from the coil negative (−) primary terminal. Use this lead as the test point.
3. Connect one test lamp lead to the condenser lead; connect the other test lamp lead to the condenser case.
4. Observe the test lamp:
   a. If the lamp does not light, the condenser is probably in good condition.
   b. If the test lamp lights, the condenser insulation has failed. Replace the condenser.

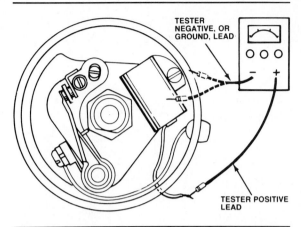

Figure 9-21. Hookups for a typical condenser tester.

This test gives a simple good-or-bad result that may not reveal an intermittent problem. The condenser may have a break in the lead that only fails when it is moist, or the insulation may leak voltage only when it gets hot. Special condenser testers are available that can often detect these conditions.

Using A Condenser Tester

Condenser testers are often combined with the coil testers described previously, or they may be built into oscilloscope consoles. The meter uses a.c. and d.c. to test the condenser's resistance, insulation, and capacity. Most meter scales measure resistance and insulation as either good or bad. Condenser capacity is shown on a scale in microfarads.

The condenser can be tested while it is installed in the distributor, or it can be removed for testing. If a condenser tests "bad" in the car but "good" when out of the car, the problem lies in some other part of the primary circuit. To test a condenser while it is installed in the distributor:
1. Refer to figure 9-21. Be sure the points are open.
2. Set the tester control knob to the condenser testing position.
3. Disconnect the condenser lead from the distributor.
4. Connect one tester lead to the condenser lead; connect the other tester lead to the grounded distributor housing.
5. Following the tester manufacturer's instructions, set the tester to the series resistance position.
6. Watch the meter scale:
   a. If the needle is in the good range, go to step 7.
   b. If the needle is in the bad range, go to step 8.

Figure 9-22. Ignition cables should be removed carefully to avoid damaging the fragile TVRS cable.

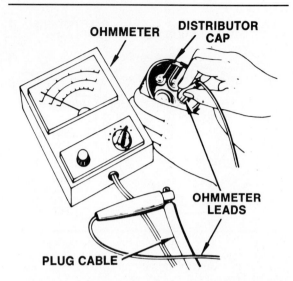

Figure 9-23. When testing the resistance of an ignition cable, one ohmmeter lead should be connected to the terminal *inside* the distributor cap.

7. Wiggle the condenser lead. If the meter needle does not move, go to step 9. If the meter needle moves:
    a. If the test is being made at the coil negative lead, there is a poor connection between the test point and the condenser case.
    b. If the test is being made at the condenser lead, the lead is in poor condition. Replace the condenser.
8. Move the grounded tester lead to the condenser case. If the meter now reads good, the condenser is not well grounded. If the meter still reads bad, replace the condenser.
9. Set the tester to the leakage test position.
10. With one tester lead at the condenser lead and the other tester lead at the condenser case, watch the meter scale:
    a. If the needle is in the good range, the condenser insulation is good. Go to step 11.
    b. If the needle is in the bad range, the condenser insulation is bad. Replace the condenser.
11. Set the tester to the capacity test position (microfarads).
12. Compare the meter reading to the manufacturer's specifications:
    a. If the reading is within specifications, the condenser is the proper rating.
    b. If the reading is not within specifications, replace the condenser.

SECONDARY CIRCUIT INSPECTION

The secondary circuit has to withstand very high voltage during normal operation. The circuit parts must be in good condition or the system will not work properly. Many secondary circuit problems can be found through a visual inspection and a few ohmmeter tests. A more thorough test of the secondary circuit is made during the oscilloscope testing, described later in this chapter.

When you are working with the secondary circuit, some precautions are necessary to protect both you and the circuit parts:
● Remember that secondary ignition cables carry very high voltage. The voltage can arc across an air gap, so do not bring an exposed cable end near your body while the engine is cranking or running.
● Handle ignition cables carefully. Pulling or kinking cables can cause internal damage that is hard to detect. The correct way to remove an ignition cable and boot is shown in figure 9-22. Grasp the boot, not the cable. Twist the boot in both directions to relieve any suction seal. Lift the boot straight off the spark plug terminal or distributor cap tower.

Visual Inspection

Instructions are given in Chapter 10 for servicing or replacing any damaged parts found during this inspection.
1. Check all ignition cables and boots for cracked, burned, or brittle insulation. Be sure all cable connections are secure and well insulated.
2. Inspect the distributor cap for:
    a. A sticking or worn carbon button
    b. Cracks
    c. Carbon tracks from arcing current
    d. Burned or corroded terminals inside the cap
    e. Corrosion inside the cap towers.
3. Inspect the rotor for:
    a. A bent or broken contact strip

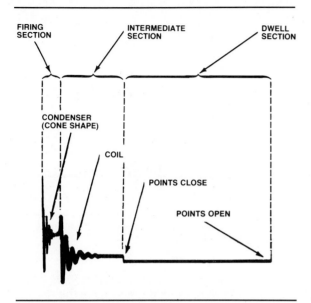

Figure 9-24. A superimposed pattern (this is a primary circuit pattern) traces all of the cylinders, one upon the other. (Marquette)

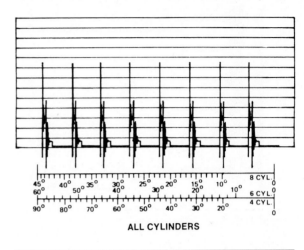

Figure 9-25. A parade pattern shows the individual cylinder traces one after the other in firing order.

b. A burned or eroded tip
c. A cracked or broken positioning lug
d. Carbon tracks or cracks on the body.

Ohmmeter Tests

We have already presented instructions for testing the resistance of the coil secondary winding. Ignition cables should also be checked for resistance. TVRS cables should measure about 4,000 ohms per foot. A completely open cable that shows infinite resistance when tested is a very serious — and not uncommon — problem. Test cable resistance as follows:
1. Refer to figure 9-23.
2. Remove the distributor cap from the housing.
3. Remove the spark plug cable being tested from the spark plug.
4. Connect the ohmmeter lead to the cable at the spark plug terminal. Connect the other ohmmeter lead to the corresponding terminal *inside* the distributor cap.
5. Observe the ohmmeter reading:
    a. If the reading is within specifications, the cable is in good condition.
    b. If the reading is not within specifications, check the cable connections and repeat the test. Replace the cable if necessary.

OSCILLOSCOPE TESTING

We examined the oscilloscope and its basic operation in Chapter 2 of this *Shop Manual*. We know that the ignition system consists of a low-voltage primary circuit and a high-voltage secondary circuit. Voltage varies within these circuits during operation. An oscilloscope displays voltage changes during a period of time, so it is an ideal instrument for testing ignition system operation.

Oscilloscope Connections

All oscilloscope manufacturers provide instructions for the use of their equipment. Although color codes and connector types vary, there are some basic similarities. Because each instrument is measuring the same electrical events, such as spark plug firing and dwell, the instrument test lead connections are similar. Oscilloscopes require connections to:
1. The engine ground path
2. The high-voltage ignition cable that leads from the coil secondary terminal to the distributor
3. The primary wire that leads from the coil primary winding to the distributor
4. The No. 1 spark plug cable.
    The ground connection is necessary for all circuits to be complete. The connection to the coil-distributor ignition cable measures secondary circuit voltage. The connection to the coil-distributor primary wire measures primary circuit voltage. The No. 1 spark plug connection acts as a trigger, so that the oscilloscope can tell when all the engine spark plugs have fired and the cycle is beginning again.

Oscilloscope Patterns

The voltage traces on the oscilloscope screen are called patterns. Most scopes will display three different patterns for both the primary and secondary circuits. This makes a total of six patterns available for your selection. Each pattern

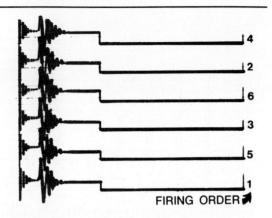

Figure 9-26. The raster pattern (this is a primary circuit pattern) shows the individual cylinder traces stacked one above the other in firing order. (Marquette)

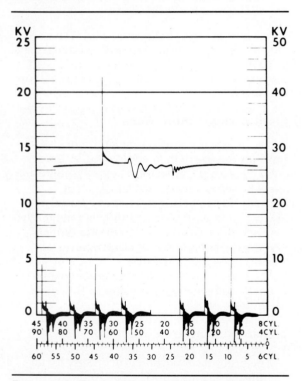

Figure 9-28. The trace for cylinder number 6 (fifth cylinder in the firing order) has been removed from the parade pattern, shifted, expanded, and displayed at the top of the screen for individual examination. (Sun)

is best used to isolate and identify particular kinds of faults. The three basic patterns are:
1. Superimposed pattern — The voltage traces for all cylinders are superimposed upon each other to form a single pattern, figure 9-24.
2. Parade pattern — The voltage traces for all cylinders are displayed one after the other from left to right in firing order sequence, figure 9-25.
3. Stacked, or raster, pattern — The voltage traces for all cylinders are stacked one above the

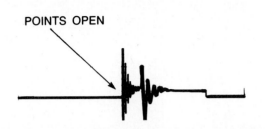

Figure 9-27. This primary superimposed pattern is shifted to the right. (Marquette)

other in firing order sequence, figure 9-26.

Many late-model scopes also have the capabilities to shift patterns on the screen or to enlarge part of a pattern or a complete pattern for a single cylinder. These features enable you to get a close look at a particular phase of ignition operation for accurate troubleshooting. For example, figure 9-27 shows the same primary superimposed pattern as figure 9-24. In figure 9-27, however, the pattern is shifted to the right. This allows closer comparison of the points-open signal and the condenser oscillations. Some scopes also have the capability to remove the trace for a single cylinder from a superimposed, parade, or raster pattern and expand it for examination and comparison with other cylinders, figure 9-28.

To introduce you to oscilloscope operation, we will show examples of superimposed, parade, and raster patterns for the primary and the secondary circuit. Our examples will be patterns for breaker-point ignitions. Solid-state electronic ignitions have patterns that differ in several details. They are generally similar to breaker-point patterns. We will see these in Chapter 11.

Normal Primary Circuit Patterns

Figure 9-24 is a primary circuit superimposed pattern. A primary circuit pattern can be divided into three sections:
1. Firing section
2. Intermediate section
3. Dwell section.

The positive and negative voltage waves, or oscillations, in the firing section occur as the breaker points open the primary circuit and high-voltage current flows in the secondary circuit to arc across the spark plug air gap. Because the primary circuit is open, current does not flow normally, but it does not stop entirely. It

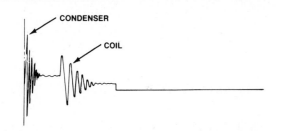

Figure 9-29. In a normal primary pattern, there should be at least five distinct coil oscillations. (Allen)

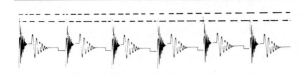

Figure 9-31. When the primary trace is in a parade pattern, the height of the condenser oscillations should not vary greatly from cylinder to cylinder. (Allen)

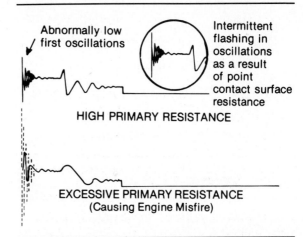

Figure 9-30. Both of these abnormal primary patterns show resistance problems in the primary circuit. (Allen)

oscillates through the condenser and the coil, and that action is the oscillations seen in the firing section of the primary pattern.

The intermediate section lasts from the time the spark plug arc is extinguished to the time the breaker points close again. The shorter oscillations in the intermediate section are caused by current flow back and forth between the coil and the condenser. The oscillations shown here in the firing and the intermediate sections are characteristic of a good coil and condenser.

The dwell section begins with a sharp, but short drop in voltage as the points close and primary current flow resumes. This sharp drop is called the points-close signal. The dwell section continues as an almost flat line until the points open again. This represents low-voltage current flow through the primary circuit, building the coil magnetic field. The dwell section ends with the points-open signal at the far right, which leads immediately into a sharp voltage rise as the pattern begins again at the left.

Figure 9-25 shows a primary circuit parade pattern. The individual traces for each cylinder are much smaller, which means that fewer details are seen. However, it is easy to compare voltage levels for each cylinder because the pattern uses the zero-voltage line as a base. Although most scopes will display a parade pattern for primary circuit operation, a parade pattern for the secondary circuit is more useful for ignition testing.

Figure 9-26 shows a primary circuit raster pattern. Because the individual cylinder traces are stacked one above the other, this pattern is useful for comparing time periods for the firing,

intermediate, and dwell sections for each cylinder. For example, a variation in the length of the dwell period among the cylinders can indicate a mechanical defect in the distributor. Actual voltage levels cannot be compared in the raster pattern because the traces do not use the zero-voltage line as a base.

Primary Circuit Abnormalities

Each section of the primary circuit pattern is caused by the operation of a different circuit part. If the part is defective or not adjusted properly, the pattern will be different. You can compare the changed pattern to a normal pattern and determine why the change occurred. This will tell you which circuit part is faulty, and how to fix the problem. The following paragraphs describe some common faults that can be pinpointed by examining the primary circuit pattern.

Firing section

1. The primary superimposed pattern in figure 9-29 shows normal coil and condenser oscillations. The condenser oscillations should start high and taper off as shown. There should be at least 5 distinct coil oscillations, with the first being the largest.
2. In the top pattern of figure 9-30, the condenser oscillations are shortened, or low, and they do not last through the firing section. The condenser's resistance may be too great, or the condenser circuit may have loose connections.
3. In the bottom pattern of figure 9-30, the condenser oscillations (dotted line) are very large. Excessive resistance has made the engine misfire.
4. In figure 9-31, the primary circuit pattern is shown in parade display. The first oscillations

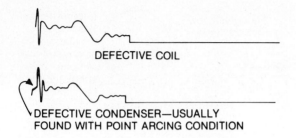

DEFECTIVE COIL

DEFECTIVE CONDENSER—USUALLY
FOUND WITH POINT ARCING CONDITION

Figure 9-32. A defective coil or a defective condenser
can cause a similar pattern. (Allen)

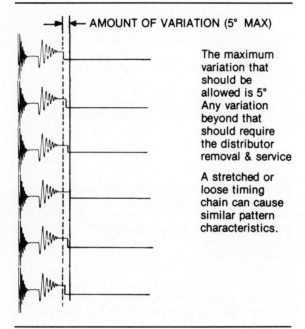

AMOUNT OF VARIATION (5° MAX)

The maximum variation that should be allowed is 5° Any variation beyond that should require the distributor removal & service

A stretched or loose timing chain can cause similar pattern characteristics.

Figure 9-34. The dwell periods of the individual
cylinders should not vary more than 4 to 6 degrees.
(Allen)

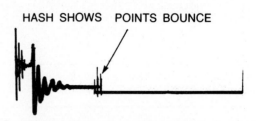

HASH SHOWS   POINTS BOUNCE

Figure 9-33. The hash marks at the points-close
signal indicate bouncing, pitted, or misaligned points
or a loose breaker plate. (Marquette)

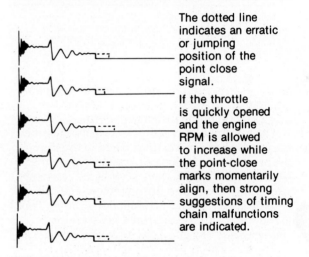

The dotted line indicates an erratic or jumping position of the point close signal.

If the throttle is quickly opened and the engine RPM is allowed to increase while the point-close marks momentarily align, then strong suggestions of timing chain malfunctions are indicated.

Figure 9-35. A similar dwell variation can be caused
by a loose timing chain. (Allen)

in the firing section should all be about the same height:
    a. If the heights all vary at idle to low engine speed, the breaker points may be badly seated, misaligned, or have high resistance.
    b. If the heights all vary at medium to high engine speed, the points may be floating because of low spring tension.
    c. If only one cylinder shows a different height, the distributor cam may be worn or dirty.

Intermediate section
1. In figure 9-32, there are fewer than 5 distinct coil oscillations. The coil primary winding may be defective. Figure 9-32 also shows a similar pattern that can be caused by a defective condenser. This is often caused by high resistance in the condenser and accompanied by point arcing.

2. In figure 9-33, the points-close signal is not a clean break but has some hash marks above and below the break. This means the points are bouncing, pitted, or misaligned. It can also mean a loose breaker plate.

Dwell section
1. In figure 9-34, the primary circuit is shown in raster display. If the dwell sections of the various cylinders vary by more than 4 to 6 degrees, the distributor is mechanically worn. The problem could be a worn cam, worn bushings, or a bent shaft. The dwell period can be measured on the degree scale at the bottom of the scope screen. A similar abnormal pattern can be caused by a loose timing chain, figure 9-35.
2. In figure 9-36, the spot of light at the points-open signal in the primary superimposed pattern indicates point arcing. Look for a bad condenser, defective points, high charging voltage, or a shorted ballast resistor.

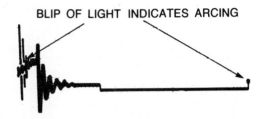

BLIP OF LIGHT INDICATES ARCING

Figure 9-36. The spot of light at the points-open signal indicates arcing. (Marquette)

BRIGHT SLOPING LINES AT POINTS OPEN

Figure 9-37. The sloping line in this shifted pattern also indicates point arcing. (Marquette)

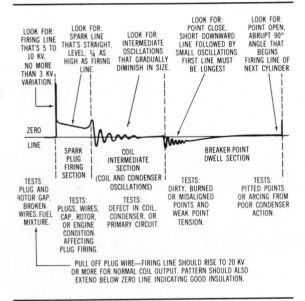

Figure 9-38. This is a normal secondary superimposed pattern, showing the firing, intermediate, and dwell sections. (Sun)

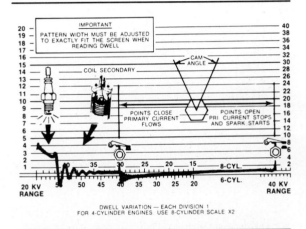

Figure 9-39. This secondary pattern shows the parts of the system that create the pattern.

3. By shifting the primary superimposed pattern, figure 9-37, the bright sloping line at the points-open signal can be seen more clearly. This is another indication of arcing points.

Normal Secondary Circuit Patterns

Figure 9-38 is a secondary circuit superimposed pattern. This pattern is also divided into the firing section, the intermediate section, and the dwell section. Secondary circuit voltages are much higher than primary circuit voltages. The kV scales are used to read the voltage levels in this pattern. Figure 9-39 shows the secondary superimposed pattern in relation to the ignition system parts that create the different sections of the pattern.

The firing section of the secondary super-imposed pattern begins with a straight vertical line that indicates the amount of voltage required to create an arc across the spark plug air gap. This is called the firing line, or voltage spike. As soon as the arc is established, less voltage is required to maintain it. The horizontal line following the voltage spike represents continued current flow across the spark plug gap. This is called the spark line and is about one-quarter the height of the voltage spike.

The intermediate section begins when the spark plug arc is extinguished. The remaining voltage is dissipated as oscillations between the coil and the condenser. This series of oscillations starts at the beginning of the intermediate section and gradually diminishes.

As in the primary pattern, the dwell section of the secondary pattern begins with a points-close signal. The small series of oscillations after the points-close signal is caused by the buildup of current in the coil primary winding, which induces a low voltage in the coil secondary winding. The shape of these oscillations is affected by the breaker points. Once the primary

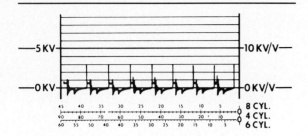

Figure 9-40. Typical secondary circuit parade pattern. (Sun)

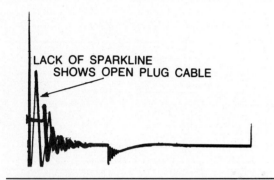

Figure 9-42. These large oscillations with no spark line are caused by an open in one spark plug circuit. (Marquette)

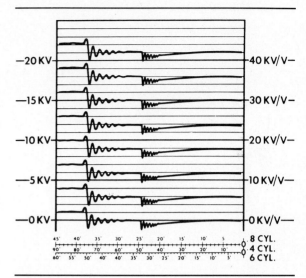

Figure 9-41. Typical secondary circuit raster pattern. (Sun)

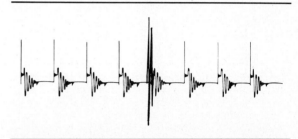

Figure 9-43. The open-circuit firing line for cylinder number 6 indicates the coil's maximum available (open-circuit) voltage. (Allen)

current flow has reached full strength, the dwell section continues as a straight line at zero voltage until the points open at the far right. The pattern then begins again at the left.

Figure 9-40 is a secondary circuit parade pattern. The individual cylinder traces are smaller than in a superimposed pattern, but the individual firing voltages and the other sections of the traces can be compared. The parade and the superimposed patterns can be displayed on either of the kilovolt scales for accurate viewing of any section of the pattern.

Figure 9-41 is a secondary circuit raster pattern. As with the primary circuit raster pattern, the secondary raster pattern is useful in comparing time periods of the pattern sections for each cylinder.

Secondary Circuit Abnormalities

Variations in the secondary circuit pattern, like those in the primary circuit pattern, can indicate if parts are faulty or not properly adjusted. The following paragraphs describe some common problems in the secondary circuit that can be detected by examining an oscilloscope trace. All traces shown are superimposed, unless the problem can be seen more clearly in a parade, raster, or expanded pattern.

Firing section

1. Figure 9-42 shows a large coil oscillation for one cylinder, with little or no spark line. A disconnected or open spark plug cable will cause this. Use the secondary raster display to isolate the faulty plug circuit.

2. In figure 9-43, the secondary circuit parade pattern shows an open-circuit condition where one spark plug is not firing. This, too, can be caused by an open or disconnected plug cable or other open between the distributor rotor and the spark plug. This pattern can be created deliberately to check the coil's maximum voltage output.

   a. Disconnect one spark plug cable from the plug or the distributor cap, preferably from the cylinder opposite the number-1 cylinder in the firing order. (If you disconnect the cable from the plug, hold it away from ground.)

   b. The coil's maximum voltage output (available voltage) is the highest voltage peak on the screen. For a well-tuned ignition system, the available voltage should be 60 percent higher than the firing voltages for the other

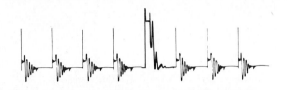

Figure 9-44. If this trace appears when a spark plug cable is deliberately disconnected, then the high voltage is leaking away through poor insulation. (Allen)

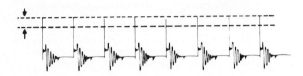

Figure 9-46. The secondary trace firing spikes should not vary greatly from cylinder to cylinder. (Allen)

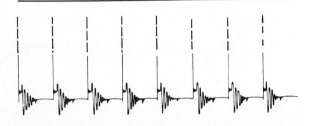

Figure 9-48. Checking the required voltage during sudden acceleration. (Allen)

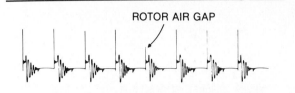

ROTOR AIR GAP

Figure 9-45. The voltage required to jump the rotor air gap can be measured by deliberately grounding a spark plug cable. (Allen)

Cylinders	High	Low	Fluctuating
One/More	Open Plug wire, wide plug gap	Fouled Plug, shorted wire low compression	Fuel Mixture
All Cylinders	Lean fuel mixture car-Carburetor air leak worn plugs.	Rich fuel mixture	Extreme lean mixture, equipped with EGR, sticky valves
All cylinders on same intake runner	Intake manifold leak Unbalanced carburetor		

Figure 9-47. Diagnosis table for firing spike variations. (Allen)

cylinders.

c. Available voltage while cranking can be checked in the same way, by observing the highest voltage peak while the engine is being cranked.

3. In figure 9-44, the spark plug cable has been disconnected deliberately, but a parade pattern shows a short spark line still exists. This indicates that the high voltage is causing a current leak to ground somewhere, usually through the insulation of the ignition cable, the distributor cap, or the rotor. Carbon tracks will often show where this has happened.

4. In figure 9-45, a parade pattern is used while the rotor air gap is being checked:

a. Ground one end of a heavy jumper wire. Insert the other end into a spark plug tower at the distributor.

b. The voltage spike at the grounded cylinder is the voltage required to jump the rotor air gap. If it is greater than the manufacturer's specifications, the cap and rotor should be replaced.

5. In figure 9-46, the firing lines (voltage spikes) for all cylinders are compared in a parade pattern. There should not be more than a 20-percent difference between the highest and the

lowest spike. If there is, refer to the table in figure 9-47 to diagnose the problem. If you cannot tell whether the problem is fuel related or in the electrical system, perform this test:

a. Slowly cover the carburetor air intake.

b. If the spikes go down and engine speed decreases, the problem is fuel related.

c. If the spikes go down and the engine speed remains the same, the plug gaps may be too large.

d. If a single spike remains the same height, the cable to that plug may be damaged.

6. In figure 9-48, a parade pattern is used while the required voltage during sudden acceleration is being tested:

a. Observe the plug firing voltage at 1,000 rpm.

b. Quickly open and close the throttle for a momentary load on the engine.

c. The peak height of the spikes should not exceed 75 percent of the available voltage measured in step 2.

d. If coil output is within specifications but this test is not, regap or replace the spark plugs.

7. In figure 9-49, one spark line is higher and shorter than the rest. This indicates high resistance in the circuit between the distributor cap and spark plug. A damaged or loose cable or a wide plug gap may be at fault.

8. In figure 9-50, one spark line is lower and longer than the rest. This indicates low resist-

Figure 9-49. A high, short spark line is caused by excessive resistance in one cylinder's circuit. (Marquette)

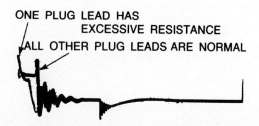

Figure 9-51. A sloping spark line indicates high resistance other than an open circuit in one spark plug circuit. (Marquette)

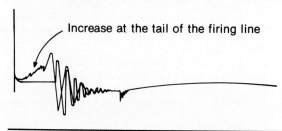

Figure 9-53. A spark line that slopes up toward the end of firing is caused by variations in the air-fuel mixture. (Allen)

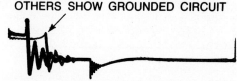

Figure 9-50. A long, low spark line is caused by a grounded, or low-resistance, circuit. (Marquette)

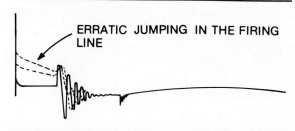

Figure 9-52. An erratic firing line is usually caused by variations in the air-fuel mixture. (Allen)

Figure 9-54. In this trace, the coil and condenser oscillations are gone, but the dwell buildup is normal. (Allen)

ance in the circuit between the distributor cap and spark plug. Carbon tracks in the distributor, poor cable insulation, or a fouled spark plug may be to blame.

9. In figure 9-51, the spark line for one cylinder starts higher than the others and angles downward more sharply. This indicates high resistance other than an open circuit. Look for corrosion on the cable terminals and in the distributor cap.

10. In figure 9-52, the spark line of one cylinder jumps erratically. If the fuel mixture in this cylinder is erratic because of a sticking or worn valve, the mixture will offer varying amounts of resistance to the spark. This will change the spark line from one firing to the next. This trace could also be caused by air leaks or carburetor problems.

11. In figure 9-53, the spark line of one cylinder slopes up rather than down. If this occurs at high engine speed, a valve may be sticking open. This would cause a leaner mixture at the end of combustion and greater resistance to the spark. This trace could be caused by air leaks or carburetor problems.

Intermediate section
1. In figure 9-54, the coil and condenser oscillations are not present, but the dwell section is normal. This indicates a faulty condenser or condenser circuit.

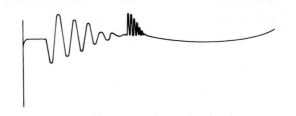

Figure 9-55. This pattern appears upside down because of reversed coil polarity. (Allen)

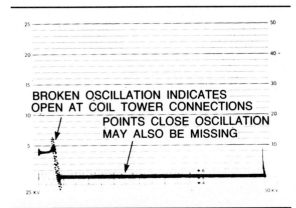

Figure 9-57. This trace shows a reduced coil oscillation and no points-close oscillations. (Marquette)

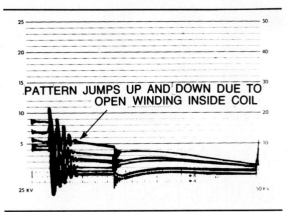

Figure 9-56. A jumping, erratic pattern is caused by an intermittent open in the coil secondary winding. (Marquette)

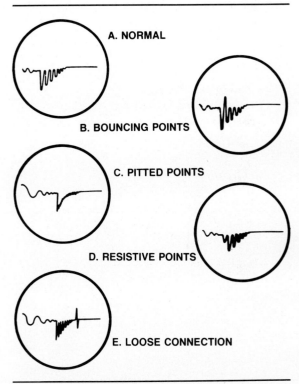

Figure 9-58. Points-close signal comparison. (Allen)

2. In figure 9-55, the secondary circuit pattern is displayed upside-down. This means that the coil polarity is reversed, usually because of reversed primary connections at the coil cap.

3. In figure 9-56, the entire pattern is jumping on the screen. This can be caused by an intermittent open in the coil secondary winding.

4. In figure 9-57, the coil oscillations are reduced and the points-close signal is missing. This can be caused by a problem in the secondary circuit between the coil and the distributor cap.

Dwell section

1. A secondary raster display can be used like the primary raster display in figure 9-34 to check the dwell variation between cylinders. If the dwell varies by more than 4 to 6 degrees, it indicates mechanical wear in the distributor. If the periods do not vary, the dwell can be checked against the manufacturer's specifications. The degree scale at the bottom of the screen is used to measure dwell.

2. A close examination of the points-close signal in a secondary superimposed pattern can reveal other ignition system problems. When the points close, a buildup of primary coil current causes a slight voltage in the secondary circuit. At the points-close signal, there should be at least three downward oscillations, all below the dwell line, and the first should be the longest. Figure 9-58 shows a normal points close-signal and some abnormal patterns and their causes.

a. Figure 9-58, position B, shows a second oscillation that is longer than the first and extending above the dwell line. This indicates bouncing points.

b. Figure 9-58, position C, shows the oscillation is reduced to one jagged buildup. This indicates pitted points.

c. Figure 9-58, position D, shows oscillations that are shorter than normal, and the first is shorter than the rest. This indicates resistive points.

d. Figure 9-58, position E, shows a spike in the dwell line that can be caused by a loose primary connection, which acts as a false trigger signal.

10

Breaker-Point Ignition Service And Adjustment

The tests described in Chapter 9 will show you if any wires or parts of the ignition system need further inspection or servicing. Different parts of the system are serviced differently — by cleaning, adjustment, or replacement. Many of these jobs can be done with the distributor installed in the car. If the distributor must be removed for further service, refer to the distributor removal and overhaul instructions presented in Chapter 11. On-car service may include:
• Installing and adjusting breaker points
• Checking and adjusting dwell
• Checking and adjusting initial timing, timing advance, and timing control systems
• Servicing the secondary circuit, including spark plug service.

INSTALLING AND ADJUSTING BREAKER POINTS

When breaker points become burned or pitted, they should be replaced. It is very difficult to clean and file used points when they are installed in the distributor, but it can be done in an emergency. Most breaker points have a special hardened contact surface. When this is filed away, the points will wear out very rapidly. It is generally much more efficient to simply replace the old point set with a new set.

Breaker point assemblies are usually held to the distributor breaker plate, figure 10-1, by either:
• Two screws
• One screw and a positioning pin.
Replacement ignition points for most distributors come as preassembled sets. The point alignment and spring tension have been set at the factory. Preassembled point sets may not always require alignment, but they should always be checked, and aligned if necessary, when installed. Dwell adjustment is sometimes the only adjustment required for preassembled points.

Replacement points that come as a 2-piece set need alignment and spring tension adjustment as well as dwell adjustment. Spring tension can be measured with several types of spring scales made for this purpose, figure 10-2. Check the manufacturer's specification for proper tension. Do not let the scale arm rub against the distributor housing when checking spring tension, or the reading will be inaccurate. Spring tension is generally adjusted by moving a long notch in the end of the spring back and forth on the spring retainer, figure 10-3.

Point alignment can be adjusted with a special tool, figure 10-4. Never bend the movable contact arm. Bend the stationary contact support to correct the alignment.

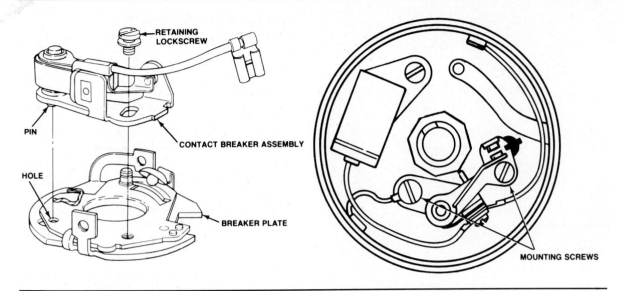

Figure 10-1. Methods of attaching the point assembly to the distributor breaker plate.

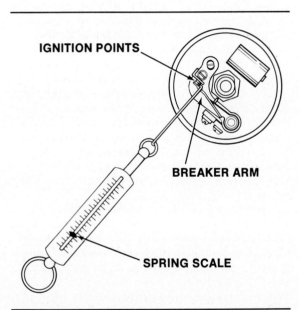

Figure 10-2. Testing the spring tension of the breaker point movable arm.

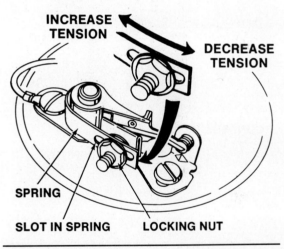

Figure 10-3. Adjusting the movable arm spring tension.

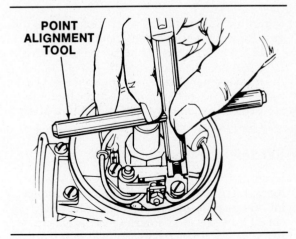

Figure 10-4. The stationary contact point bracket can be bent to correct the point alignment.

New, properly aligned breaker points can be set with a feeler gauge:
1. Refer to figure 10-5.
2. Remove the distributor cap and rotor.
3. Connect a remote starter switch and bump the engine with the starter motor until the breaker point rubbing block is *exactly* on a high point of the cam.
4. Check the manufacturer's specification for proper point gap.
5. Slide the clean, specified feeler gauge between the points. Adjust the gap by shifting the position of the point assembly. A slight drag should be felt as the gauge is drawn between the points, but the point arm *should not move*.

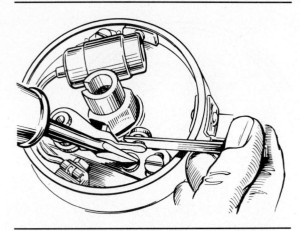

Figure 10-5. Measuring and adjusting the point gap with a feeler gauge.

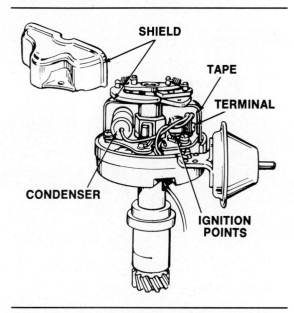

Figure 10-7. Some Delco-Remy distributors have this RFI shield around the points and the condenser.

6. Tighten the holddown screw and recheck the gap. Repeat the adjustment if necessary.

Do not try to set used breaker points with a feeler gauge. The uneven point surface makes the measurement inaccurate, figure 10-6. Used points *must* be set using a tach-dwell meter or an oscilloscope, following the procedure given later in this chapter.

RFI Shield

From 1970 through 1973, Delco-Remy V-8 breaker-point distributors had radiofrequency interference shields (RFI shields). The RFI shield prevents radio interference signals from being picked up by the windshield radio antenna.

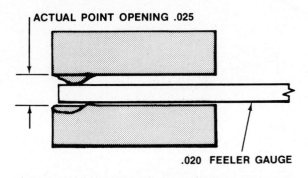

Figure 10-6. Used points should not be set with a feeler gauge. The uneven surface will give an inaccurate reading.

It is important that, after installing new points, there is enough space between the point connector and the shield, figure 10-7. If the connector touches the shield, the primary circuit will be shorted. A piece of insulating tape is stuck inside the shield in the connector area. When installing a new condenser, place it so that the condenser lead end is flush with its mounting bracket to take the slack out of the lead. Then tighten the bracket holddown.

The two halves of the shield and the distributor rotor must be removed when servicing or replacing the points. The halves of the shield are different, so they cannot be installed improperly. Be sure the condenser and primary leads are not caught under the edge of the shield before tightening the two shield retaining screws.

Beginning in 1974, a 1-piece assembly of points and condenser called a Uniset is used. Distributors with the Uniset do not have an RFI shield because the Uniset eliminates radio interference signals. The Uniset can be installed in pre-1974 distributors with no modifications. When this is done, the RFI shield may be discarded.

CHECKING AND ADJUSTING DWELL

The dwell angle of new points can be checked by measuring the point gap with a feeler gauge, as described earlier. A more accurate way to measure dwell, especially with used points, is to use an electronic tester such as an oscilloscope or a tach-dwell meter.

Oscilloscope Test

We have already seen that the dwell section of an oscilloscope trace can be measured against a degree scale at the bottom of the screen, figure 10-8. On some scopes, the primary superimposed pattern can be seen during cranking,

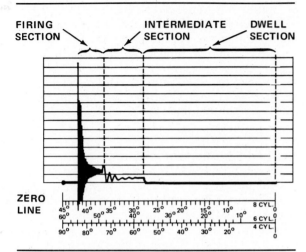

Figure 10-8. This primary superimposed pattern from an 8-cylinder engine shows a dwell angle of 28 degrees.

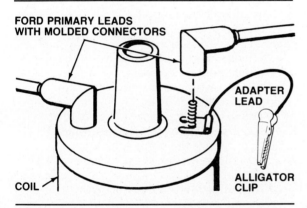

Figure 10-10. You may need an adapter such as this to hook a tach-dwell meter to a Ford coil on a breaker-point ignition system.

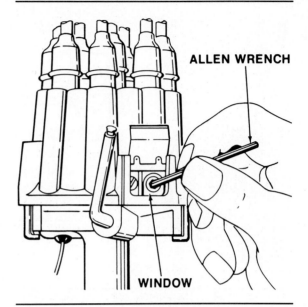

Figure 10-9. This Delco-Remy distributor has points that can be adjusted through a window in the distributor cap while the engine is running.

even when the distributor cap and rotor are removed. The point assembly can be shifted until the trace dwell section matches the manufacturer's specification.

Delco-Remy V-6 and V-8 distributors have a window in the distributor cap, figure 10-9, so that the points can be adjusted while the engine is running. A primary or a secondary trace can be displayed while adjusting the dwell on these models. If the distributor has an RFI shield, the shield must be removed before servicing and replaced after servicing.

Once dwell is adjusted, the oscilloscope also can be used to check for a dwell variation from cylinder to cylinder as explained in Chapter 9. The raster pattern is most useful for this test.

Tach-Dwell Meter Test

A tach-dwell meter will measure either rpm or dwell angle. The meter usually has only two test leads:
• The positive test lead connects to one of the coil primary terminals (terminal specified by the tester manufacturer). Ford coils will need an adapter, figure 10-10.
• The negative test lead connects to an engine ground. Meters that have other test functions built in may have two additional leads to connect to the battery terminals, or they may run on a.c.

The tach-dwell meter's electronic circuitry translates the interruptions of primary current flow into either rpm or dwell angle measurements. Two different scales are printed on the meter face. The choice of scale is controlled by a knob on the meter. Another knob or switch must be set to the number of cylinders in the engine being tested.

Most tach-dwell meters will show a dwell angle reading that is the *average* of all the individual cylinder's dwell angles. This does not alert you to variations in dwell from cylinder to cylinder, as an oscilloscope can. Only a few console-type dwell meters are able to single out the dwell angle of an individual cylinder. However, no on-car adjustment can correct such variations — the distributor must be removed and overhauled to correct the problem. An average dwell reading is accurate enough for most on-car servicing.

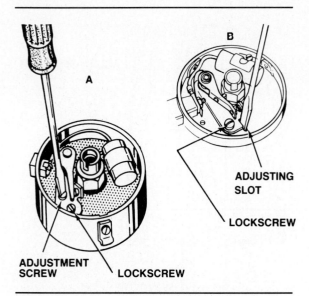

Figure 10-11. The point set in position A is adjusted by turning the eccentric adjustment screw; the point set in position B is adjusted by moving the assembly with a screwdriver set in a slotted hole in the breaker plate.

Dwell Adjustment Procedures

These general procedures can be used with either a scope or a tach-dwell meter. Different procedures are used for internal-adjustment than for external-adjustment (Delco-Remy) distributors.

Internal-adjustment distributors

1. Connect the test leads according to meter instructions.
   a. For an oscilloscope test, select the primary superimposed pattern.
   b. For a tach-dwell meter test, select the dwell position and the correct number of cylinders.
2. Remove the distributor cap and rotor.
3. Connect a remote starter switch.
4. Turn the ignition key to On.
5. While observing the scope screen or meter dial, crank the engine with the remote starter switch.
6. Compare the dwell measurement to the manufacturer's specifications:
   a. If the measurement is within specifications, no adjustment is necessary.
   b. If the measurement is not within specifications, go to step 7.
7. Adjust the point assembly, figure 10-11, until the dwell is within specifications:
   a. Some point sets have an adjustment screw, position A.
   b. Some point sets have a slotted hole for a screwdriver, position B.

8. Tighten the point holddown screw.
9. Recheck the dwell measurement. If it does not remain within specifications after the lockscrew is tightened, repeat the adjustment.
10. Disconnect the remote start switch.
11. Replace the distributor cap and rotor.
12. Start and idle the engine. Compare the dwell measurement to specifications. Repeat the adjustment if necessary.

External-adjustment distributors

1. Connect test leads according to the tester instructions:
   a. For an oscilloscope test, select either the primary or the secondary superimposed pattern.
   b. For a tach-dwell meter, select the dwell position and the proper number of cylinders.
2. If the distributor has an RFI shield, remove the shield and reassemble the distributor rotor and cap.
3. Start and idle the engine.
4. Compare the dwell measurement to the manufacturer's specifications:
   a. If the measurement is within specifications, no adjustment is necessary.
   b. If the measurement is not within specifications, go to step 5.
5. To adjust the points, refer to figure 10-9.
6. While observing the tester, use an allen wrench to change the point adjustment:
   a. Turn the screw clockwise to increase the dwell.
   b. Turn the screw counterclockwise to decrease the dwell.
7. When the dwell is within specifications, remove the wrench and close the distributor cap window. The point adjustment is self-locking.
8. Reinstall the RFI shield, if removed in step 2.

Dwell Angle Variation

Most manufacturers allow a small amount of average dwell variation as engine speed changes. That is, the dwell specification may be 29° to 32°, plus or minus 3° at 2,000 rpm. When you adjust the dwell angle while the engine is cranking, you would set it somewhere between 29° and 32°, say at 30°. Then, use the tachometer setting of the tach-dwell meter to adjust engine speed to 2,000 rpm. Switch to the dwell meter setting and observe the reading. The reading should be within 3° of your 30° dwell setting — from 27° to 33°. If it is not, the distributor is mechanically worn and must be removed for further service. Generally, the allowable dwell variation is less for center-pivot breaker plates (Delco-Remy) than it is for side-pivot breaker plates (Chrysler, Motorcraft). In fact, with a side-pivot breaker plate, the dwell will always

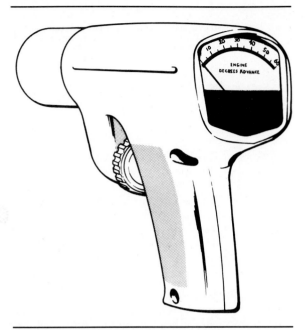

Figure 10-12. This adjustable timing light can be set so that it will flash at a time other than the firing of No. 1 spark plug. The amount of advance or retard is shown on the meter scale.

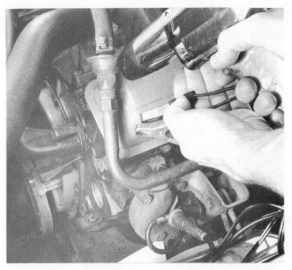

Figure 10-13. The timing light is hooked to the battery terminals and to the No. 1 cylinder spark plug cable (some lights work on a.c. rather than the car's battery).

decrease slightly as the vacuum advance increases. Check the carmaker's specifications for allowable average dwell variation and the engine speed at which it should be tested.

IGNITION TIMING TESTS AND ADJUSTMENTS

Ignition timing can be adjusted statically, with the engine off, or dynamically, with the engine running. Static timing is usually set only when a distributor is being reinstalled in an engine. Final adjustment of the timing is usually made, using a stroboscopic timing light, with the engine running. A few carmakers, however, provide only static timing specifications. Static timing procedures are explained in Chapters 11 and 13. Timing is usually set in relation to number 1 cylinder. International Harvester V-8 engines are a notable exception. They are timed from the number 8 cylinder.

Using A Timing Light

Dynamic timing is done with a stroboscopic timing light triggered by voltage from the number 1 spark plug cable. The light can be attached to an oscilloscope console or it can be a separate piece of equipment. It can draw current from the car battery or it can run on a.c.

Simple timing lights can do nothing more than flash when the number 1 spark plug fires. They can be used to adjust initial timing and to

make simple tests of the advance mechanisms. However, to make precise tests of the advance mechanisms and of timing control systems, an adjustable timing light must be used.

An adjustable timing light contains additional solid-state circuitry. You can set the light to flash at a different time than when the number 1 spark plug fires. For example, you may have the light hooked up to an engine that has an initial timing of top dead center. The adjustable timing light is set to flash when the number 1 spark plug fires. When it flashes, the timing marks are lined up at top dead center. Then, you set the adjustable timing light for 5° on the light's meter, figure 10-12. The light will start to flash at a different time, and the timing marks will be lined up at 5°. The actual timing of the engine has not been changed — just the time of the light's flashing has changed. The adjustable timing light can be used to test advance mechanisms and timing control systems, as we will see.

To hook up either kind of timing light:
1. Refer to figure 10-13.
2. Connect the timing light lead to the number 1 spark plug cable, either at the plug or at the distributor cap. You may need an adapter to do this, figure 10-14. *Never puncture a spark plug cable or boot with a sharp probe to connect a timing light*. Many late-model timing lights have an inductive pickup that clamps around the plug cable.
3. Hook up the timing light to its power source — either the car battery or an a.c.-powered console.

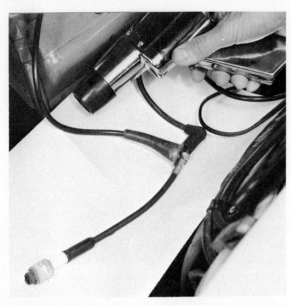

Figure 10-14. Do not puncture the spark plug cable; use an adapter such as this if necessary.

Initial Timing Test And Adjustment

Dwell must be correct and the engine must be at its normal operating temperature before timing is adjusted. Check the carmaker's instructions about disconnecting distributor vacuum lines. The timing is set on most engines with the distributor vacuum lines disconnected and plugged, figure 10-15. However, some manufacturers specify that the vacuum advance line be connected. On dual-diaphragm distributors, the manifold vacuum line that provides spark retard must usually be disconnected and plugged. Note the position of vacuum lines before disconnecting them so that you can re-install them correctly.

If a thermostatically controlled air cleaner is removed, plug the air cleaner vacuum line. It is not necessary to disconnect Chrysler distributor solenoids. Engines with retard solenoids must be running at slow idle so that the idle adjusting screw contacts the carburetor solenoid and energizes the distributor solenoid to retard the timing.

Locate the timing marks on the engine and crankshaft pulley or balancer. Wipe the marks clean and mark them with chalk or paint.

The timing marks on many late-model engines are hard to find or see. They are often hidden behind a maze of belts and engine accessories. If you cannot reach the timing marks to clean them by hand, spray them with carburetor and choke cleaning spray to make them easier to see. Timing marks on some engines, particularly in vans, must be viewed from the bottom of the engine.

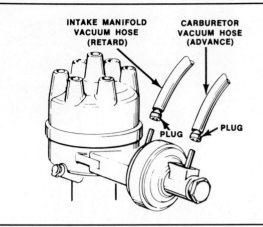

Figure 10-15. Most cars are timed with the distributor vacuum lines disconnected and plugged.

Check the tune-up specifications for the exact timing setting and engine speed for that model. On late-model engines, the timing setting is given on an engine tune-up data decal in the engine compartment. This is the specification that should be followed.

To adjust the initial timing:
1. Connect a tachometer and a timing light.
2. Start the engine and run it *at the specified speed*. Many late-model engines are timed at speeds above or below the normal slow-idle speed.
3. Aim the flashing timing light at the timing marks and observe their position, figure 10-16. If adjustment is necessary:
   a. Loosen the distributor holddown bolt with a distributor wrench or with a ratchet, extension, and U-joint socket.
   b. To advance the timing, rotate the distributor *against* rotor rotation.
   c. To retard the timing, rotate the distributor *with* rotor rotation.
   d. Tighten the holddown bolt and recheck the timing.
4. After timing adjustment, reconnect all vacuum lines and readjust the idle speed if necessary. If idle speed is readjusted, recheck the timing afterward.

Advance Mechanism Tests

Dwell, initial timing, and idle speed should be adjusted before spark advance is tested. If the engine has a timing control system that affects vacuum advance for emission control, this should be checked after the centrifugal and vacuum systems have been tested.

Distributor advance specifications, called advance curves, are essential for precise testing. Curves are listed for each distributor by the manufacturer's part number. Therefore, before you can test a distributor, you must know its

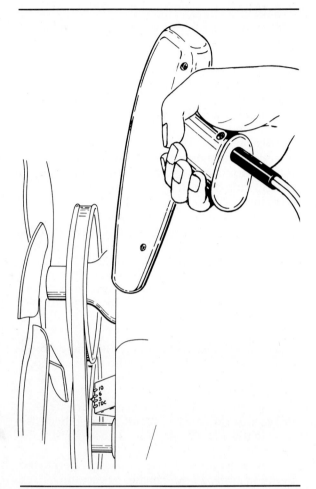

Figure 10-16. Aim the timing light at the timing marks and observe their position as the light flashes.

part number. You will find the part number on the side of the distributor housing. Distributor advance specifications may be given in engine speed and engine degrees or in distributor speed and distributor degrees. If the specifications are listed in distributor speed and degrees, they must be multiplied by two for use when testing the distributor in the engine.

When the distributor is tested in the engine, rather than in a distributor tester, the engine's initial timing setting must be known. The specified degrees of advance must be added to the initial timing setting. Degrees of retard must be subtracted from the initial timing setting when you are reading the timing setting from the engine timing marks. If an advance mechanism is not working properly, the distributor must be removed from the engine for further service.

Timing advance tests with an adjustable timing light
1. Connect a tachometer and an adjustable timing light to the engine.
2. Start and idle the engine; verify the initial

timing setting.
3. Accelerate the engine to 2,500 rpm or to the speed specified for checking total advance.
4. While observing the timing marks, adjust the timing light advance meter until the timing marks are aligned at the step 2 initial timing setting.
5. Read the degrees of total advance recorded on the timing light meter and compare to specifications:
    a. If the reading is within specifications, you may wish to test the individual advance devices anyway.
    b. If the reading is not within the specification, you must test the individual advance devices to determine which is at fault.
    To test the individual advance mechanisms:
1. With the engine at idle, disconnect and plug the distributor vacuum lines.
2. Accelerate the engine to the specified test speed.
3. While observing the timing marks, adjust the advance meter control to align the marks at the initial timing setting.
4. Read the degrees of advance recorded on the timing light meter. This is the *centrifugal advance only*; compare it to specifications:
    a. If the reading is within specifications, go to step 5.
    b. If the reading is not within specifications, the centrifugal advance mechanism must be adjusted or replaced.
5. While still at the specified test speed, unplug and reconnect the vacuum advance line to the distributor vacuum unit.

NOTE: This cannot be done if the car has a speed- or transmission-controlled spark system that denies vacuum advance. In this case, you must test the vacuum advance mechanism by using a hand-operated vacuum pump (as explained in following paragraphs), or by connecting a manifold vacuum line to the distributor advance diaphragm.

6. Again observe the timing marks and adjust the advance meter until the marks are aligned at the initial timing setting.
7. Subtract the centrifugal advance reading of step 4 from the new reading. The result is the amount of vacuum advance; compare it to specifications:
    a. If the reading is within specifications, the vacuum advance unit is working correctly.
    b. If the reading is not within specifications, the vacuum advance unit must be adjusted or replaced.
    Some post-1970 cars with spark timing control emission systems do not provide vacuum advance with the vehicle stationary and the transmission in Neutral. To test such a car, the vehicle must either be raised on a hoist and

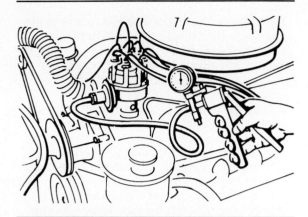

Figure 10-17. Using a hand vacuum pump to check the condition of the vacuum advance unit.

operated in gear at specified speeds, or the vacuum control devices must be bypassed. Vacuum switches and valves can often be bypassed by connecting a hose directly from the carburetor spark port or from a manifold vacuum port to the distributor vacuum unit. Vacuum advance units can also be checked with a vacuum hand pump, as we will soon see.

Distributor advance specifications may be given at several different test speeds. If so, perform the tests at all given speeds to ensure precise control of ignition timing.

If the distributor being tested has a dual-diaphragm vacuum advance unit, check the vacuum retard:

1. Disconnect and plug both vacuum hoses at the distributor, figure 10-15.
2. Run the engine at idle.
3. While observing the timing marks with an adjustable timing light, connect the manifold vacuum hose to the inner (distributor side) vacuum chamber.
4. Timing should immediately retard from the initial setting. Check the amount of retard with the timing light advance meter; compare it to specifications:
   a. If the reading is within specifications, the vacuum retard is operating correctly.
   b. If the reading is not within specifications, the vacuum unit must be replaced.

Timing advance tests without an adjustable timing light
If an adjustable timing light is not available, a nonadjustable timing light can be used to check the general operation of the centrifugal advance, vacuum advance, and vacuum retard mechanisms. Exact degrees cannot be measured.

1. Connect a tachometer and timing light to the engine.

2. Start and idle the engine.
3. Disconnect and plug the distributor vacuum lines.
4. Accelerate the engine to 2,000 or 2,500 rpm while observing the timing marks. The marks should advance smoothly and steadily, indicating that the centrifugal advance is working.
5. While holding the engine speed above idle, unplug and connect the vacuum advance line to the distributor.
6. The timing marks should advance an additional amount and engine speed should increase, indicating that the vacuum advance is working.
7. To check the vacuum retard on dual-diaphragm units, return the engine speed to idle.
8. Unplug and connect the manifold vacuum line to the retard vacuum chamber. Timing should retard about 6 to 12 degrees (or as specified by the carmaker), and engine speed should decrease.

Vacuum advance test with vacuum hand pump
A hand-operated vacuum pump can be used to test the precise vacuum advance curve of a distributor.

1. Disconnect and plug the vacuum line from the vacuum advance unit and connect the tester hose to the advance unit (use an adapter if required), figure 10-17.
2. Close the pump release valve and operate the pump to apply 15 to 20 inches of vacuum.
3. Watch the gauge for at least 10 seconds. If the reading drops, the diaphragm is leaking and the advance unit must be replaced.
4. Using an adjustable timing light, check the centrifugal spark advance at the specified test rpm points. Leave the vacuum line to the advance diaphragm disconnected and plugged.
5. Record the centrifugal advance setting at 1,000 rpm or other engine speed specified for testing the vacuum advance unit.
6. With the engine at the test speed, apply vacuum to the advance diaphragm with the hand pump. Apply the amount of vacuum specified for that test speed.
7. Record the total advance at each test point. Subtract the reading from the centrifugal advance recorded in step 5. The difference is the amount of vacuum advance. If the reading does not meet the specifications at any test point, the vacuum unit must be adjusted or replaced.

Spark Timing Emission Control System Tests

The centrifugal and vacuum advance tests described earlier check the advance mechanisms in the distributor. They do not test the additional spark timing control systems used as part of emission control systems. The various switches, solenoids, and valves in these systems can be tested by the following methods. Because many of the systems exist in different forms from car model to model, you must have the exact specifications for the car you are testing.

You can make a quick overall test of system operation by driving or operating the car and checking for vacuum advance cutoff at low speed or in the low gears and then for vacuum advance at higher speeds or in high gear. Most spark timing control systems include one or more of the following parts:
- A vacuum solenoid
- A transmission-controlled, or speed-controlled switch
- A thermostatic vacuum switch
- A delaying or reversing relay
- A spark delay valve.

Systems with spark delay valves usually do not have a transmission or speed switch or a vacuum solenoid. Specific systems may also have additional valves and switches. Regardless of how the system is wired and plumbed together, you can test its overall operation by checking for vacuum at the distributor at certain times and for absence of vacuum at other times. You will need a timing light or a vacuum gauge, or both, for this test. Check the system as follows:

1. Connect the timing light to the ignition if the car is to be tested in the shop.
2. If you are going to drive the car to test it, connect a vacuum gauge to the vacuum solenoid with a long hose and route the gauge to the driver's compartment. Be careful not to pinch the hose.
3. Operate the car as follows:
   a. For transmission-controlled systems with manual transmissions, start the engine and shift the transmission through all gear ranges.
   b. For speed-controlled systems and for transmission-conrolled systems with automatic transmissions, raise the car on a hoist and run it through the required speed or gear ranges.
   c. For all front-wheel-drive cars, drive the car on the road through the required speed or gear ranges.

NOTE: Operating the car on a hoist, on a dynamometer, or on the road is necessary for most systems with automatic transmissions because the transmission switch is actuated by high-gear hydraulic pressure, which is not available until the transmission actually upshifts into high gear. Some systems with automatic transmissions also provide vacuum advance in reverse. You can test for this by placing the transmission in reverse while stationary on the shop floor.

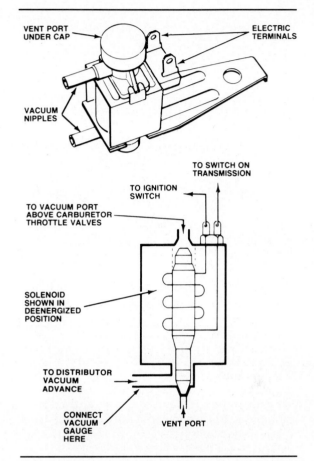

Figure 10-18. A vacuum solenoid test diagram (bottom) and a typical solenoid (top).

Front-wheel-drive cars should not be tested in operation on a hoist because of the danger involved in working around the engine compartment while the wheels are turning.

4. With the spark timing control system in operation, check the operation of the vacuum solenoid by one of the following methods. You may need the help of an assistant:
   a. Watch the engine timing marks with the timing light. Advance should increase when vacuum is applied (high gear or cruising speed) and decrease when it is cut off (low gears or lower speeds).
   b. Watch the vacuum gauge connected to the distributor port of the solenoid, figure 10-18. The gauge should show no vacuum in low gears or at low speed, and it should show a reading in high gear or at cruising speed.

If these tests show that the solenoid is applying vacuum to the distributor at the correct speed or gear ranges, the system is working properly. If the vacuum is not applied properly, and you have tested the vacuum advance unit, do the following tests.

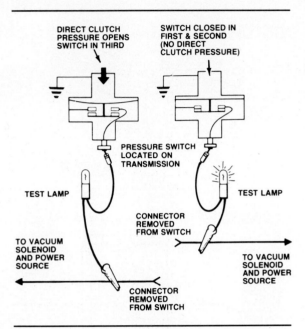

Figure 10-19. Testing a normally closed TCS switch.

Vacuum solenoid test

A vacuum solenoid can be tested for proper air-vacuum flow and for internal leaks around the plunger. Replace a solenoid if it does not pass this test sequence:

1. Disconnect the hoses and electrical connectors from the solenoid.
2. Connect a hose to the distributor vacuum port on the solenoid and blow air through it. Air should come out of the:

   a. Carburetor vacuum port, if the solenoid must be energized to deny vacuum.
   b. Vent port, if the solenoid must be deenergized to deny vacuum.

3. Connect a jumper wire from one solenoid electrical terminal to ground.
4. Connect a second jumper wire from the other solenoid terminal to the battery positive terminal.
5. Again blow air through the hose. Air should now come out of the:

   a. Vent port, if the solenoid must be energized to deny vacuum.
   b. Carburetor vacuum port, if the solenoid must be deenergized to deny vacuum.

6. Blocking the airflow through the appropriate port while still blowing into the hose should block all airflow. If not, the solenoid has internal leakage.

To test a vacuum solenoid for correct plunger operation:

1. Disconnect the 2-wire connector from the vacuum solenoid.
2. Connect a jumper wire from one solenoid terminal to ground.
3. Connect a second jumper wire to the other

solenoid terminal. Touch this lead to the battery positive terminal momentarily.
4. A click should be heard every time the circuit opens and closes. Repeat several times. The plunger should operate promptly each time. If it does not, replace the solenoid.

Transmission switch tests

The TCS systems of GM, AMC, and some 1972 Chrysler models and the TRS systems of Ford use transmission-operated switches to actuate a solenoid that controls vacuum spark advance. Most transmission switches are *normally closed* in low and intermediate gears to *energize* the solenoid and *deny* vacuum advance. The switches on some systems, however, (mostly Chevrolet) are *normally open* in low and intermediate gears to leave the solenoid *deenergized* yet still *deny* vacuum advance. To further complicate the picture, some systems use a *normally closed* switch to activate a *reversing relay* that *deenergizes* the solenoid to deny vacuum advance in low gear.

To test the operation of a transmission control switch:

1. Connect a voltmeter or test lamp in series with the switch feed wire, figure 10-19. The test lamp should have an 1893 bulb or equivalent. This bulb draws only 0.8 ampere. If the test lamp has a bulb that draws more current than this, the transmission control switch contacts could be damaged.
2. With the ignition switch on, operate the transmission through all gear ranges.
3. The lamp will go on and off, or the voltmeter will show a reading, as the switch closes and opens.
4. Some automatic-transmission systems in which the switch is operated by high clutch pressure may not operate unless the car is lifted on a hoist and driven through the gear ranges.
5. Some switches can be adjusted.

Thermostatic vacuum switch test

Thermostatic vacuum switches come in a variety of shapes, sizes, and names. TVS devices are also called PVS, CTO, TIC, and TVV units. Thermostatic switches are activated by engine coolant or by air temperature. The vacuum switch may be opened or closed by high or low temperatures, depending upon its use and the system design. Therefore, the manufacturer's specifications and test procedures must be followed to interpret the results correctly.

Coolant-controlled switches should be tested with the engine cold, at normal operating temperature, and in some cases, at high temperature. When the test procedure requires you to test at high temperatures, do not allow the engine to overheat. This is most important on cars with catalytic converters.

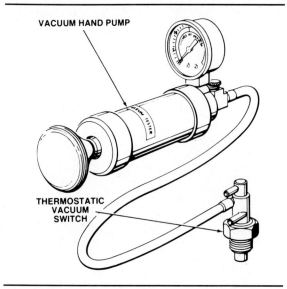

Figure 10-20. Testing a thermostatic vacuum switch.

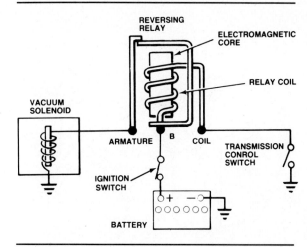

Figure 10-21. When current flows through the coil circuit of this reversing relay, the armature opens and no current flows to the vacuum solenoid.

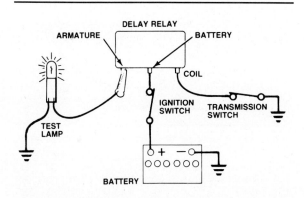

Figure 10-22. Testing a delay relay.

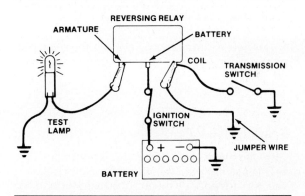

Figure 10-23. Testing a reversing relay.

Apply vacuum to the specified switch port, figure 10-20. Note the gauge reading when the switch is both energized and deenergized. Compare these readings to the manufacturer's specifications to find whether or not the switch is operating correctly.

Relay tests
In spark timing control systems, relays do various jobs. Delaying relays have special circuitry that keeps the contact points from closing for a specific length of time, usually about 20 seconds. Delaying relays are used when the ignition switch is first turned on, to allow vacuum advance for a short time when the car is first started. The vacuum solenoid is not energized to deny vacuum advance until the delaying relay's points have closed.

Reversing relays are used in a few systems where the operation of the speed or transmission control switch does not match the operation of the vacuum solenoid. That is, the transmission control switch is opened when the

vacuum solenoid must be energized. A reversing relay, with normally-closed points that *open* when current flows through the relay coil, can be used in this type of system, figure 10-21.

To test a delay relay, turn the ignition switch on without starting the engine. Count the number of seconds before the vacuum solenoid clicks. If necessary, you can test the relay with a 12-volt test lamp:
1. Refer to figure 10-22.
2. Hook a test lamp between the relay armature terminal and ground.
3. Turn the ignition switch on without starting the engine.
4. Count the number of seconds before the lamp lights. Compare this to the manufacturer's specification; if it does not match, replace the relay.

A reversing relay can also be tested with a 12-volt lamp:
1. Refer to figure 10-23.
2. Connect a test lamp between the relay armature terminal and ground.
3. With the transmission in neutral, turn the ignition switch on. The test lamp should light.

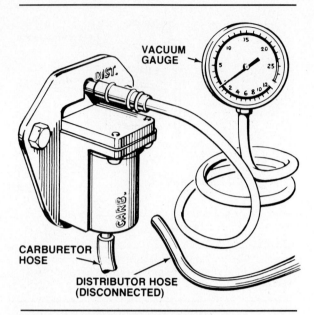

Figure 10-24. Testing an OSAC valve.

4. Connect a jumper wire between the relay coil terminal and ground. The test lamp should go off.
5. If the relay does not work as described, replace it.

Spark Delay Valve Tests

Chrysler OSAC valves and the spark delay valves used by various other carmakers delay vacuum advance by means of a restriction in the vacuum line. They are tested by attaching a vacuum gauge to the distributor side of the valve and applying vacuum to the valve inlet, or carburetor side. The length of time required for the vacuum gauge to rise to a steady reading is noted and compared to the carmaker's specifications.

To test an OSAC valve on the car:
1. Refer to figure 10-24.
2. Connect a vacuum gauge to the distributor port of the valve.
3. Run the engine at 2,200 rpm.
4. Note the time required for the vacuum gauge to rise to a steady reading. Several different OSAC valves are used, providing different delay times for different engines.
5. If the OSAC valve has a temperature override feature, it should permit immediate vacuum advance below 60° F. Heat and cool the temperature sensing portion of the valve to check its operation above and below 60° F.

To test the spark delay valves used by other manufacturers:
1. Refer to figure 10-25.
2. Connect a hand vacuum pump to the black side of the valve, or the side marked CARB.

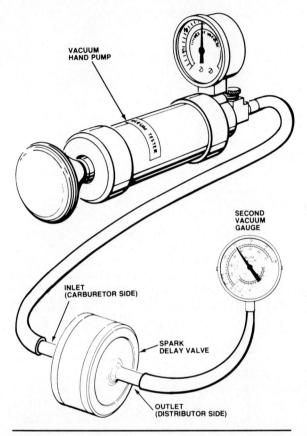

Figure 10-25. The vacuum gauge should show a slow buildup of vacuum.

3. Connect a vacuum gauge to the other side of the valve.
4. Apply 10 to 15 inches of vacuum with the hand pump. The gauge reading should rise slowly to a steady reading. Ford gives specifications for the number of seconds required for various valves to rise to 6 inches of vacuum at the gauge when 10 inches is applied on the carburetor side.
5. To check the valve's release operation, reverse the pump and gauge connections at the valve. When vacuum is applied, the gauge reading should rise immediately.
6. Some GM vacuum delay valves have a cold temperature override feature similar to that of an OSAC valve. When the valve is cooled to below 50° F, there should be no delay in the application of vacuum to the distributor side.
7. For some cars, Ford and some other manufacturers have recommended that spark delay valves be replaced at regular intervals. The valves are usually color coded to indicate different delay times. Always ensure that the correct delay valve is installed and that it is installed in the right direction. Since spark delay valves have been used for jobs other than simple vacuum advance delay, all valves are not installed

in the same way. Doublecheck the installation instructions given by the manufacturer.

CAP, ROTOR, AND CABLE REPLACEMENT

Secondary circuit parts can fail because of physical damage or insulation failure. Physical damage can be found through a visual inspection. Failing insulation can sometimes be seen as carbon tracks, but the most reliable test method is the oscilloscope, as we have explained.

Inspect the distributor cap and replace it if you find:
• A sticking or worn carbon button
• Cracks
• Carbon tracks
• Burned or corroded electrodes
• Corrosion inside cap towers.

Inspect the rotor and replace it if you find:
• A bent or broken contact spring
• A burned or eroded terminal
• A cracked or broken positioning lug
• Carbon tracks or cracks on the body.

Do not try to clean cap electrodes or the rotor terminal by filing, because this will change the rotor air gap.

To replace a set of spark plug cables:
1. Starting at the front of the engine, remove one cable from the distributor cap and the spark plug.
2. Cut the new cable to length and install the terminals.
3. Be sure the cap tower is clean and free of corrosion. Insert the new cable into the cap so that the terminal is firmly seated and the rubber boot seals over the tower. Squeeze the boot to release air trapped in the tower.
4. Install the spark plug end of the cable on the plug. Be sure the connector is firmly seated on the terminal and the boot seals the plug insulator.
5. Repeat the above steps to install the other cables. Be sure all cables are routed as originally placed by the carmaker to avoid crossfiring and cable damage.
6. Secure the cables in their holders and be sure that the cables do not touch hot exhaust manifolds.

SPARK PLUG SERVICE

Spark plug service is an important part of a complete engine tune-up. Vehicle manufacturer's recommendations for plug service intervals vary from as often as every 5,000 miles to as seldom as every 30,000 miles. Spark plug life depends on:
• Engine design
• The kind of driving done
• The type of fuel used
• The kinds of emission control devices used.

Generally, the plugs used in late-model, low-compression engines burning unleaded fuel will last longer than those used in high-compression engines that require premium fuel. Follow the carmaker's recommendation for spark plug service intervals.

Spark plug service on many older engines, and on some late-model inline engines with few accessories, is a fairly straightforward operation. Simply remove the plugs with a spark plug socket and a ratchet handle with a convenient extension. Then install the cleaned or new plugs in the same manner.

Many late-model engines with a maze of air-conditioning and emission control plumbing and several engine-driven accessories are not such a simple matter when it comes to spark plug service. Some plugs may be hidden behind engine accessories, which must be loosened from the mountings and moved for access to the spark plugs. Air conditioning compressors, air pumps, and power steering pumps are frequent candidates for relocation during plug service. Whenever you must move one of these accessories, be careful of its plumbing and wiring. Air conditioning lines are especially bulky and must be handled carefully.

Some spark plugs on some engines are most accessible from below the engine. In these cases, you will have to raise the car on a hoist or with a jack and safety stands and go beneath the engine to remove and replace the plugs.

A variety of special wrench extensions and adapters is available to make spark plug service easier. Regardless of the other special tools you may use, you will need a spark plug socket.

Spark plug sockets come in two sizes:
• A 13/16″ socket for 14-mm gasketed and 18-mm tapered-seat plugs
• A 5/8″ socket for 14-mm tapered-seat plugs.

Most spark plug sockets have a foam rubber insert to grip and cushion the plug insulator during service. Spark plug sockets may be either 3/8- or 1/2-inch drive. Many have an external hex so that they can also be turned with an open-end wrench or a box wrench.

Another item that will make spark plug service easier is a length of rubber or nylon tubing with an inside diameter that fits tightly over the spark plug terminal or insulator. The tubing can be forced over the top of the plug during removal and installation if you cannot reach the plug with your fingers to turn it. The tubing will grip the plug tightly enough to turn it either in or out when the plug is loose.

General spark plug service procedures are given in the following paragraphs.

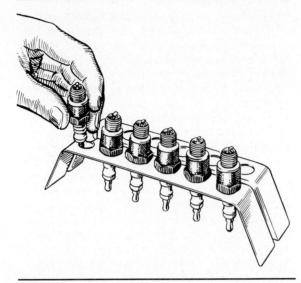

Figure 10-26. A holder like this is handy to keep plugs in order for inspection.

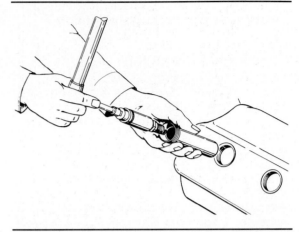

Figure 10-27. Some Chrysler engines have gasket-type spark plugs installed in tubes, using no gaskets.

Figure 10-28. A normal, used spark plug. (Champion)

Figure 10-29. An oil-fouled spark plug. (Champion)

Spark Plug Removal

To remove spark plugs:
1. Remove the cables by grasping the plug boot and twisting gently while pulling. Do not pull on the cables.
2. Loosen each plug one or two turns with a spark plug socket.
3. Blow dirt away from the plugs with compressed air.
4. Remove the plugs and place each one in a tray or holder in cylinder number order for inspection, figure 10-26.
5. On gasketed plugs, be sure the old gasket is removed with the plug. Chrysler sixes and hemispherical V-8's use gasket-type plugs installed in tubes without gaskets, figure 10-27.

Spark Plug Diagnosis

Many spark plug problems can be diagnosed by examining the firing ends of plugs removed from the engine. This is often called "reading" the plugs. Note the amount and kind of deposits and the degree of electrode erosion. The following paragraphs and photographs explain common spark plug conditions.

Normal

The visibly crusty deposits shown in figure 10-28 are present to some degree on used plugs. This is normal, however, and does not affect performance. The insulator nose has a light brown-to-grayish color, and there is very little electrode wear. This indicates the correct plug heat range and a healthy engine. If this plug were to be reinstalled, it should be properly cleaned and the electrodes should be correctly regapped.

Oil fouled

Excessive oil entering the combustion chamber

Figure 10-30. A carbon-fouled spark plug. (Champion)

Figure 10-31. A worn spark plug. (Champion)

Figure 10-32. An ash-fouled spark plug. (Champion)

causes this condition, figure 10-29. In a high-mileage engine, it may be due to piston ring and cylinder wall wear. In a low-mileage or rebuilt engine, normal oil control may not be established. Another cause of oil fouling may be a defective PCV valve. Oil may also seep past worn valve guides, or a ruptured fuel pump diaphragm may draw oil vapor from the crankcase to the carburetor. Clean or replace oil-fouled plugs, and suggest mechanical repair to the car owner.

Carbon fouled
Carbon fouling consists of soft, black, sooty deposits, figure 10-30. First, check plug specifications to make sure the correct heat range is being used. A plug that is too cold will easily foul in this way. If the plug is the recommended heat range, check for an overly rich air-fuel mixture, caused by a stuck choke or clogged air filter. Other possible causes are weak ignition, inoperative manifold heat control valve or thermostatic air cleaner, retarded timing, low com-

pression, faulty plug wires or distributor cap, or, simply, stop-and-start driving.

Worn out
While the color of the insulator nose, figure 10-31, indicates that the heat range is correct and deposits are normal, the rounded and worn electrodes tell you that this plug should be replaced. The voltage required to spark across the gap has doubled and would continue to increase with prolonged use. Misfiring under load is a clue to worn out plugs. Such plugs also contribute to poor gas mileage, loss of power, and increased emissions.

Ash fouled
Ash deposits, figure 10-32, are light brown to white and are caused by burning certain oil or fuel additives during normal combustion. If they are found on the plug, you can be sure that they cover the entire combustion chamber. Normally, ash deposits are nonconductive, but large amounts may mask the spark and cause misfiring.

Splash fouled
Splash fouling, figure 10-33, is caused by deposits breaking loose from pistons and valves and splashing against hot plug insulators. This often occurs after a tune-up, which restores engine power and higher combustion temperatures. Normally, try cleaning and reinstalling splash-fouled plugs before recommending replacement.

Mechanical damage
Spark plug damage, figure 10-34, can be caused by a foreign object in the combustion chamber, by a plug of the wrong reach being hit by a piston or valve, or by careless installation. Be careful to prevent dirt from falling into spark plug holes during service and always handle plugs carefully.

Figure 10-33. A splash-fouled spark plug (Champion)

Figure 10-34. A spark plug that has been mechanically damaged. (Champion)

Figure 10-35. A spark plug with the gap bridged. (Champion)

Figure 10-36. A spark plug with a glazed insulator. (Champion)

Gap bridging

Gap bridging, figure 10-35, is usually due to conditions similar to those described for splash fouling. The difference is one of degree. The deposits form a bridge across the electrodes and cause a short. This condition is common in engines where oil control is poor. Try cleaning and regapping these plugs before recommending replacement.

Insulator glazing

Shiny, yellow or tan deposits, figure 10-36, may be insulator glazing. This is usually caused by frequent hard acceleration with a resulting rise in plug temperature. Normal plug deposits, that would usually flake off, melt and fuse into a conductive coating that can cause misfire. Severe glazing cannot easily be removed by normal cleaning, and the plugs may require replacement. Plugs one range colder than recommended may cure a glazing problem.

Detonation

Detonation is a form of spark knock caused by an explosive burning of part of the air-fuel mixture just after ignition occurs. It is caused by the increased heat and pressure in the combustion chamber and exerts extreme pressure on engine parts. In figure 10-37, it has fractured the plug insulator. Contributing factors are over-advanced timing, lean carburetion, low gasoline octane, or engine lugging.

Preignition

Ignition of the air-fuel charge before the plug fires can cause this kind of severe damage, figure 10-38. Preignition is usually caused by combustion chamber hot spots or deposits, which get hot enough to ignite the air-fuel charge before normal ignition. It can also be caused by crossfiring between plug cables or by a plug heat range much too hot for the engine.

Figure 10-37. A spark plug that has been damaged by detonation. (Champion)

Figure 10-38. A spark plug that has been damaged by preignition. (Champion)

Figure 10-39. An overheated spark plug. (Champion)

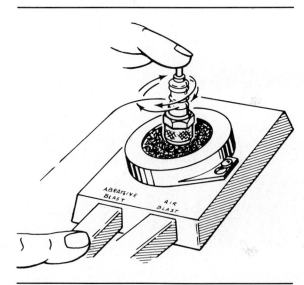

Figure 10-40. Cleaning a spark plug in an abrasive blast.

Overheated

An overheated spark plug, figure 10-39, is often indicated by a clean, white insulator tip or excessive electrode wear, or both. The insulator may also be blistered. The plug may be too hot for the engine, but even the correct plug can be overheated by overadvanced timing, a defective cooling system, or lean air-fuel ratios.

Spark Plug Cleaning and Filing

It is often more economical in terms of labor costs to install new spark plugs than to clean and regap old ones. However, used plugs that are not excessively worn can be cleaned for continued use:

1. Wipe oil and grease from the outside of the plug with a clean cloth. Use a small amount of solvent if necessary. Dry with compressed air.
2. Carefully bend back the ground (side) electrode with thin-nosed pliers for better cleaning.
3. Place the plug in an abrasive-blast machine,

figure 10-40, and rotate plug slowly while sandblasting.
4. Use a compressed air blast to remove cleaning abrasive from the plug. Inspect the plug, particularly inside the shell, to be sure all deposits are removed.
5. Use a hand-held wire brush to clean the plug threads, figure 10-41.
6. File the center electrode until it is flat and the inside surface of the ground electrode until a shiny surface appears, figure 10-42.

Selecting Replacement Plugs

Spark plug manufacturers and carmakers list the proper spark plugs to use in specific engines. If the engine operating conditions require it, you may want to select a plug in a higher or lower heat range than is listed. Whether you are

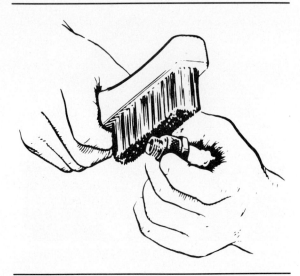

Figure 10-41. Cleaning the spark plug threads with a wire brush.

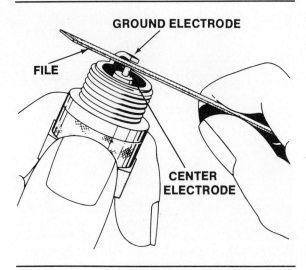

Figure 10-42. Filing the spark plug electrodes.

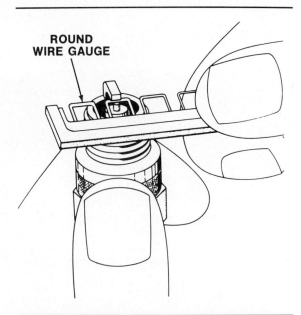

Figure 10-43. Set the plug gap with a round wire feeler gauge.

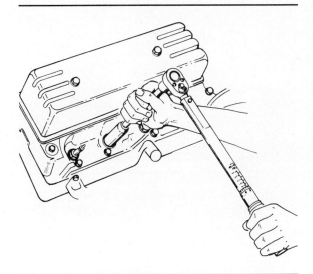

Figure 10-44. Install spark plugs finger tight. Then tighten with a torque wrench to the correct value.

changing heat range or not, be sure to check specifications for the proper spark plug number. Do not assume that the last person working on the car installed the correct plug.

Spark Plug Gapping

Both new and used spark plugs must be gapped to the engine manufacturer's specification. Do not assume that new plugs are correctly pre-gapped. Do not try to set a wide-gap plug (electronic ignition) to a small-gap specification, or the electrodes will be damaged. Use a round

wire feeler gauge, figure 10-43, and a plug gapping tool and carefully bend the ground electrode to the required gap. Do not use a flat feeler gauge, or the measurement will be inaccurate.

Spark Plug Installation

To install new or used spark plugs:
1. Wipe dirt and grease from the engine plug seats with a clean cloth.
2. Be sure the gaskets on gasketed plugs are in good condition and properly placed on the plugs. If possible, install a new gasket on a used plug. Be sure that there is only *one* gasket on the plug.

PLUG TYPE	CAST-IRON HEAD		ALUMINUM HEAD	
	Foot-Pounds	Newton-Meters	Foot-Pounds	Newton-Meters
14-MM GASKETED	25-30	34-40	15-22	20-30
14-MM TAPERED SEAT	7-15	9-20	7-15	9-20
18-MM TAPERED SEAT	15-20	20-27	15-20	20-27

Figure 10-45. Spark plug installation torque values.

3. Install the plugs into the engine and finger tighten. If the plugs cannot be installed easily by hand, the threads in the cylinder head may require cleaning with a thread-chasing tap. Be careful installing plugs or cleaning threads in aluminum heads.

4. Tighten the plugs with a torque wrench, figure 10-44, to the values listed in figure 10-45.
5. If the gasketed plugs have used gaskets, reduce the torque setting. If thread lubricant is used, reduce the torque setting (many spark plug manufacturers do not recommend the use of thread lubricant).

Tapered-seat spark plugs require less torque than gasketed plugs do. If you do not have a torque wrench for plug installation, install the plugs finger tight. Then tighten 14-mm gasketed plugs an additional 1/4 turn with a wrench. Tighten 14-mm and 18-mm tapered-seat plugs an additional 1/16 turn *only*. Do not overtighten.

11

Breaker-Point Distributor Overhaul

This chapter contains removal, disassembly, testing, repair, and installation instructions for Delco-Remy, Motorcraft, and Chrysler breaker-point distributors. Distributor removal, bench testing, adjustment, and installation procedures are presented as general instructions that will help you do these jobs on most domestic cars and light trucks. Overhaul procedures are presented as photographic sequences for four breaker-point distributor models.

DISTRIBUTOR REMOVAL

You may have to remove, or loosen and relocate, other engine accessories, such as the air cleaner, to remove the distributor. It may help to tag all electrical leads disconnected during distributor removal. Observe all electrical safety precautions and shop safety regulations during distributor service.

Before removing the distributor, you must establish a reference point for correct reinstallation. Do this by making a chalk or pencil mark or a light scribe mark on the rim of the distributor housing in line with the rotor tip. Make another pair of marks in line with each other on the base of the housing and the engine block. If you cannot reach the base of the housing, simply note the position of the vacuum advance unit in relation to the engine.

Many mechanics make a habit of always cranking the engine so that the rotor points in the same direction on any engine they are servicing: for example, parallel with the engine centerline and pointing forward. Another way to establish a reference position for distributor reinstallation is to crank the engine until the timing marks are aligned at the initial timing setting for the number 1 cylinder. Then mark the rotor position on the rim of the distributor housing. This takes a bit more time, but it aids static timing when the distributor is reinstalled.

You may have to loosen the distributor housing before it can be removed from the engine. There are several ways to do this after the distributor holddown bolt and the holddown clamp have been removed.

You may try to loosen the distributor housing from the engine by holding it and gently twisting it in a rocking motion. If that does not work, squirt penetrating oil on the housing where it meets the engine. Gently rock the distributor again. You may also attach an oil filter wrench to the distributor housing and *carefully* twist the housing to loosen it for removal. As a last resort, you may attempt to free the distributor from the engine by *gently* tapping the distributor housing with a hammer.

A metal sealing ring is located between the bottom of the distributor housing and the en-

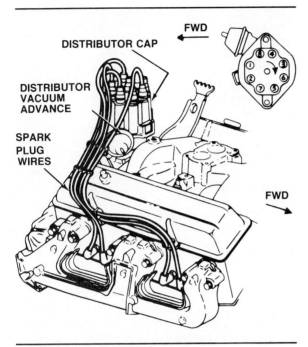

FWD

DISTRIBUTOR CAP

DISTRIBUTOR
VACUUM
ADVANCE

SPARK
PLUG
WIRES

FWD

Figure 11-1. Remove the distributor cap with the spark plug wires attached before removing the distributor. (Chevrolet)

Figure 11-2. Disconnect the primary lead from the distributor side of the coil.

Figure 11-3. Loosen the holddown bolt.

gine on many Chrysler distributors. Do not lose it.

On Ford V-8 engines, the oil pump drive shaft engages the bottom of the distributor drive gear. The bottom end of the shaft rests in the oil pump. The oil pump shaft should stay in the engine when the distributor is removed. However, if the inside of the engine is dirty, the shaft may stick in the distributor drive gear and pull out of the oil pump as the distributor is removed. If the shaft comes all the way out with the distributor, you have no problem because it can be easily reinstalled. But, if it comes part way out and then drops off the distributor into the engine, you have a problem.

If the shaft falls into the oil pan, you may be able to leave it there and install a new one (if you are *sure* it has fallen all the way to the bottom of the pan). However, it usually falls into the timing chain cover, which then requires that the cover be removed to retrieve the shaft.

You can avoid these problems very simply. When you remove a Ford distributor, rock it gently before lifting it from the engine. Then raise it slowly, just enough to reach under the housing to the bottom of the drive gear. If the oil pump shaft is stuck in the distributor, grab hold of it and lift it out with the distributor. It has already pulled out of the oil pump; do not try to push it back into place.

To install a Ford V-8 oil pump shaft, hold the top end with a gripping tool and lower the shaft into the engine. Engage the bottom of the shaft

with the oil pump and release the gripping tool. It is a good habit to remove a distributor from any engine *slowly and carefully*.

These are some general instructions for distributor removal:
1. Be sure the ignition switch is Off. Disconnecting the battery ground cable to prevent the engine from being cranked while the distributor is out is also a good idea.
2. Release the distributor cap clips or holddown screws.
3. Remove the distributor cap, with the spark plug wires intact, figure 11-1. Carefully move the cap and attach wires away from the distributor.
4. Disconnect the primary lead from the distributor side of the coil, figure 11-2.
5. Scribe an alignment mark on the distributor and the engine, in line with the rotor. It is helpful to align all distributor rotors in the same direction as a matter of habit.
6. Disconnect the vacuum line, or lines, from the distributor.
7. Loosen the distributor holddown bolt, figure 11-3. Use an offset distributor wrench or a rat-

Figure 11-4. Remove the holddown clamp and bolt.

Figure 11-5. Remove the distributor, slowly and carefully.

chet with an extension and a universal socket.
8. Remove the distributor holddown bolt and clamp, figure 11-4.
9. Carefully loosen and remove the distributor from the engine, figure 11-5. It may be necessary to rock the distributor gently to loosen it from the engine.
10. Use solvent and a brush to clean oil, grease, dirt, and rust from the distributor shaft and the distributor housing.

BREAKER-POINT DISTRIBUTOR OVERHAUL PROCEDURES

The following pages contain photographic procedures for the disassembly, overhaul, and reassembly of four common domestic breaker-point distributors:
● Delco-Remy 8-cylinder model — Used by GM and AMC until 1975; features external point adjustment.
● Delco-Remy 6-cylinder model — Used by GM and AMC until 1975; features internal point adjustment.
● Motorcraft (Autolite) 8-cylinder model — Used by Ford until 1975; features internal point adjustment. Six-cylinder models are similar.
● Chrysler 6-cylinder model — Used by Chrysler Corporation until 1973; features internal point adjustment. Eight-cylinder models are similar.
   Chapter 15 of your *Classroom Manual* has information and more drawings of these distributors. You may find it helpful to refer to the *Classroom Manual*, also, when overhauling a distributor.

The section of this chapter following the illustrated overhaul procedures contains test procedures using a distributor tester. The distributor tester (also called a synchrograph or synchroscope) is the most useful piece of test equipment for complete distributor service. Many of the distributor test procedures should be done before the distributor is disassembled, in order to find how much overhaul is needed. Other service procedures using the tester (such as point adjustment) are done after the distributor is put back together. Many distributors can be overhauled while mounted in the tester.
   Before overhauling a distributor, read and understand the test and adjustment procedures in the following section. The sequence of steps that you use for distributor test, overhaul, and adjustment should be organized for the best use of your shop facilities and time. If you don't have a distributor tester, you can mount the distributor in a vise for overhaul. Use soft jaw covers on the vise or wrap the distributor housing in a cloth to prevent damage. Read the step-by-step procedure for the distributor that you will be overhauling before you begin work.

DELCO-REMY 8-CYLINDER DISTRIBUTOR OVERHAUL PROCEDURE

1. Mount distributor in vise or tester and remove cap by turning two latch screws with screwdriver. Remove two screws from rotor. Remove rotor.

2. Unhook advance springs from pins on shaft and cam base. Mark springs and pins so that springs are reinstalled in original positions.

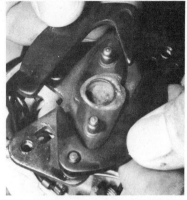

3. Remove advance weights. Mark weights so that they are reinstalled in their original positions.

4. Some distributors have 2-piece RFI shields that must be removed for access to breaker plate. Remove primary lead and condenser lead from breaker-point terminal.

5. Loosen or remove two screws and slide point assembly off breaker plate. In Uniset assembly, condenser is attached to points.

6. Remove screw securing condenser to breaker plate. Remove condenser.

7. Remove screw securing vacuum advance unit inside distributor. Then remove screw securing vacuum unit to rim of housing.

8. Disengage vacuum advance link from breaker plate. Then use screwdriver to release grommet on primary lead from housing. Remove primary lead.

9. To begin reassembly, press grommet of new primary lead into housing from inside. Engage vacuum advance link with breaker plate.

DELCO-REMY 8-CYLINDER DISTRIBUTOR OVERHAUL PROCEDURE

10. Place locator dimple on advance unit in hole in housing.

11. Hold primary lead aside and install screw securing vacuum unit inside distributor.

12. Attach breaker plate ground lead to screw and install screw to secure vacuum unit to rim of distributor.

13. Attach condenser to breaker plate with screw. Engage breaker point assembly with two screws on breaker plate. Tighten screws.

14. Slip primary lead and condenser lead into spring-loaded terminal on breaker points.

15. Apply *one drop* of lubricant to spring pins on distributor shaft and cam base.

16. Assemble weights on cam base and shaft. Be sure they are returned to their original positions.

17. Install springs on pins in their original positions. Align square and round locators on rotor with holes in cam base. Install rotor with two screws.

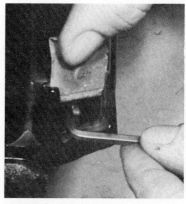

18. With distributor in engine, dwell is adjusted through window in cap. Adjust dwell by turning adjustment screw with allen wrench. Install RFI shield after adjustment.

DELCO-REMY 6-CYLINDER DISTRIBUTOR OVERHAUL PROCEDURE

1. Disconnect primary lead and condenser lead from terminal. Remove screw securing condenser to breaker plate. Remove condenser.

2. Remove screw securing points to breaker plate. Remove points.

3. Carefully pull primary lead grommet from housing, and remove lead.

4. Remove two screws securing vacuum advance. Unhook vacuum advance link from breaker plate and remove vacuum advance.

5. Remove two screws securing breaker plate. Remove breaker plate.

6. Remove two screws securing weight cover. Remove weight cover.

7. Use screwdriver to unhook two weight springs. Remove springs. Mark springs and pins so that springs are reinstalled in original positions.

8. Remove two advance weights. Mark weights so that they are reinstalled in original positions.

9. Pull cam off shaft.

DELCO-REMY 6-CYLINDER DISTRIBUTOR OVERHAUL PROCEDURE

10. Apply silicone grease to shaft sparingly.

11. Install cam on shaft.

12. Apply lubricant *sparingly* to advance weight pivot pins. Install advance weights on pins in their original positions.

13. Install springs on pins in their original positions. Install weight cover with two screws.

14. Apply silicone grease to breaker plate pivot pins *sparingly*. Install primary lead and grommet in breaker plate.

15. Install breaker plate in housing with two screws. Engage vacuum advance link with breaker plate. Attach unit to housing with two screws.

16. Place pivot pin in hole in breaker plate. Attach point assembly to breaker plate with screw.

17. Place rubbing block on high point of cam. Adjust point gap to specifications with feeler gauge and screwdriver.

18. Install condenser to breaker plate with screw. Connect primary and condenser leads to terminal on points. Install rotor.

MOTORCRAFT 8-CYLINDER DISTRIBUTOR OVERHAUL PROCEDURE

1. Remove spring clip securing vacuum advance link. Remove two screws securing vacuum advance. Remove vacuum advance.

2. Disconnect primary lead and condenser lead from terminal.

3. Remove points and condenser from breaker plate. Disconnect one end of ground wire. Remove primary lead from housing.

4. Remove two screws securing breaker plate and ground wire. Remove breaker plate and ground wire.

5. Clean breaker plate and inspect for wear. Lubricate pivot points *sparingly*.

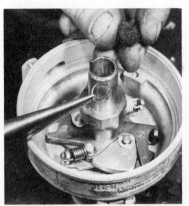

6. Remove lubricating wick and cam retainer from center of cam.

7. Mark one advance weight, its spring, its spring bracket, and its pivot pin. Remove both weight springs.

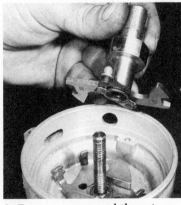

8. Remove cam and thrust washer from shaft.

9. Remove drive gear, if worn, by driving out roll pin securing gear to shaft. To remove shaft, drive out pin securing collar to shaft.

MOTORCRAFT 8-CYLINDER DISTRIBUTOR OVERHAUL PROCEDURE

10. Replace O-ring on housing, if worn. Press worn bushing out of housing. Press in new one.

11. Reassemble shaft and housing. Install drive gear and collar with roll pins. Lubricate shaft. Install thrust washer and cam on shaft.

12. Lubricate weight pivot pins and spring pins *sparingly*. Reinstall springs in their original positions, as marked at disassembly.

13. Apply small amount of distributor cam lubricant to cam. Install cam retainer and lubricating wick. Apply one or two drops of oil to wick.

14. Install breaker plate assembly. Secure plate to distributor with two screws. One end of ground wire goes under screw by primary lead hole.

15. Inspect primary lead for wear. Replace worn lead.

16. Engage vacuum advance link with pin on breaker plate; secure with spring clip. Attach vacuum unit to housing with two screws.

17. Install points and condenser. Secure ground wire to one breaker-point screw. Attach primary and condenser leads to terminal.

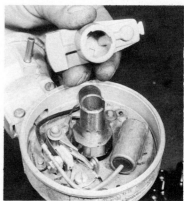

18. Place rubbing block on high point of cam. Adjust point gap to specifications with feeler gauge and screwdriver. Install rotor.

CHRYSLER 6-CYLINDER DISTRIBUTOR OVERHAUL PROCEDURE

1. Disconnect primary lead and condenser lead from terminal.

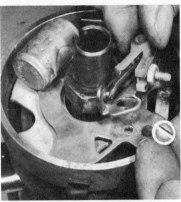

2. Remove screw securing breaker-point assembly. Remove points.

3. Remove screw securing condenser. Remove condenser.

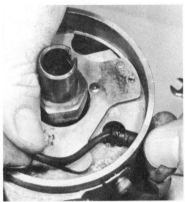

4. Push primary lead grommet inside housing and remove lead.

5. Remove two screws securing vacuum advance. Disengage link from breaker plate and remove vacuum advance.

6. Remove two screws securing breaker plate. Remove breaker plate from housing.

7. Remove lubricating wick and cam retainer from cam sleeve with needlenose pliers.

8. Mark cam base and one pin on advance weight. Then pull cam off shaft.

9. Unhook weight springs from tabs on base plate. Mark springs and tabs so that springs are reinstalled in original positions.

CHRYSLER 6-CYLINDER DISTRIBUTOR OVERHAUL PROCEDURE

10. Remove advance weights. Mark weights so that they are reinstalled in their original positions.

11. Remove, clean, and lubricate cam bushing. Replace it if it is worn.

12. Install weights and springs in their original positions. Be sure weights move freely.

13. Lubricate weight pivot pins, cam pins, and spring pins with *one drop* of oil, each.

14. Install cam in original position on weights. Install cam retainer and wick in cam sleeve. Lubricate wick with one or two drops of oil.

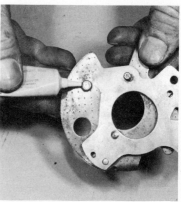

15. Apply silicone grease to breaker-plate pivot pins *sparingly*. Install breaker plate in housing with two screws.

16. Engage vacuum advance link with breaker plate. Install vacuum unit with two screws. Inspect primary lead for wear. Replace worn lead.

17. Align breaker-point pivot with pin on plate. Install points with one screw. Install condenser. Attach condenser and primary leads to terminal on points.

18. Place rubbing block on high point of cam. Adjust point gap with feeler gauge and screwdriver. Tighten point mounting screw.

Figure 11-6. A distributor tester is a valuable piece of equipment for complete distributor service. (Sun)

BREAKER-POINT DISTRIBUTOR TEST AND ADJUSTMENT

The distributor tester, or synchrograph, figure 11-6, is an electronic test machine in which you can mount a distributor for testing and service when it is removed from an engine. Many of the overhaul steps listed in the preceding section of this chapter can be done with the distributor mounted in a tester. Before overhauling a distributor, you should test it for cam, shaft, and bushing wear and for centrifugal and vacuum advance operation to find out how much overhaul you will need to do.

The distributor tester has a fixture for mounting the distributor and a motor to drive it for testing. The motor or drive mechanism is reversible so that the distributor can be rotated clockwise (right-hand drive) or counterclockwise (left-hand drive), as needed. The drive speed is also variable so that the distributor can be rotated at different speeds. Rotation speed is shown on the tester's tachometer.

Electrical test leads from the tester are connected to the breaker-point primary lead and to ground on the distributor housing. These leads provide primary current flow through the points for testing. This primary connection through the breaker points operates the tachometer and the dwell meter that are built into the tester. The circuit also operates the stroboscopic synchronizing scale that surrounds the distributor drive fixture on the tester.

The synchronizing scale is a 360-degree ring, with each degree marked. Each time the breaker points open, the tester circuitry triggers an arrow-shaped neon light. There will be as many light flashes per revolution as there are lobes on

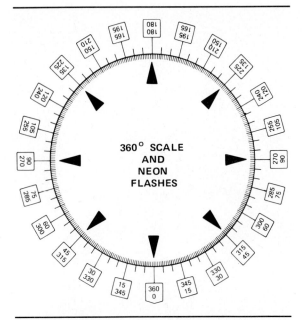

Figure 11-7. The synchronizing scale on the distributor tester is a movable ring, graduated in 1-degree increments. The arrow-shaped flashing lights indicate the distributor firing for each engine cylinder.

the distributor cam, figure 11-7. For most distributors, there are as many cam lobes as there are engine cylinders. Therefore, each flash represents the firing of each cylinder in firing order sequence. Because of the stroboscopic effect of the flashing lights, the arrows appear to stand still as they flash. At medium and high distributor speeds, the arrows for all cylinders appear almost always lighted.

The scale ring on the tester can be moved so that you can align it at the starting points for the number of cylinders in the engine. For an 8-cylinder engine (8-lobe distributor cam), the flashes will appear 45 degrees apart. For an even-firing 6-cylinder engine, the flashes will be 60 degrees apart, and for a 4-cylinder engine, they will be 90 degrees apart. Remember that the degrees and speed of distributor rotation are one-half the degrees and speed of engine rotation.

Because the flashing lights on the synchronizing scale show the distributor firing for each cylinder, variations in dwell and timing among the cylinders can be seen. When the distributor centrifugal and vacuum advance mechanisms are operated, the flashing lights will move around the scale. This enables you to test the exact amount of spark advance at any distributor speed and with any amount of vacuum. Most testers have a built-in vacuum pump to operate the vacuum advance unit. Others also have a condenser tester and an ohmmeter.

Operation of the distributor tester and its use for specific tests and adjustments are explained in the following paragraphs.

Figure 11-8. Installing a distributor in the tester.

Figure 11-9. Tighten the drive chuck on the distributor drive gear or shaft. Do not allow the distributor to bottom in the chuck.

Pretest Inspection

Before testing the distributor, check it for any obvious problem:
1. Look for binding or excessive end play and side play in the shaft. Look for worn or chipped gear teeth. These problems can cause uneven dwell and cylinder timing.
2. Check the cam lobes for obvious wear. This also will affect dwell and timing.
3. Check for a loose breaker plate and worn breaker plate bearings. These problems can cause erratic dwell and vacuum advance operation.
4. Look for signs of improper lubrication. Too little lubrication causes component wear and binding. Too much lubrication may cause breaker-point resistance and burning, crossfiring, and damage to insulation within the distributor.
5. Check the electrical leads and connections. Worn or oil-soaked insulation may cause a short circuit. Loose or dirty connections can cause high resistance and an unwanted primary voltage drop.
6. Inspect the condition of the breaker point contact surfaces. You will probably install a new set of points if you are doing a complete job of reconditioning the distributor. However, if the points are not badly burned or worn and if their alignment is good, you may want to keep them.

Distributor Installation In The Tester

Before mounting the distributor in the tester, clean off any dirt, oil, or grease. Dirt and grime can damage the tester and make distributor service more difficult. Mount the distributor in the tester as follows:
1. Raise the clamp arms so that the distributor will clear the chuck.
2. Place the distributor in the clamp arms so that the arms will grip the largest machined surface of the distributor body, figure 11-8. Use a sleeve adapter to protect any O-rings on the distributor. Some tester manufacturers will specify that the vacuum unit should be pointing in a certain direction.
3. Tighten the clamp arms *lightly*.
4. If necessary, slip rubber tubing over the distributor drive gear to protect it from the chuck.
5. Lower the distributor until the gear or shaft is in the tester chuck. Do not allow the shaft to bottom in the chuck. Use a drive adapter if necessary.
6. Tighten the chuck, figure 11-9, and the clamp arms.
7. Remove the distributor rotor. Turn the distributor shaft by hand to be sure it rotates freely.
8. If required, calibrate the tester dwell meter as follows:
   a. Connect the two tester leads together.
   b. Turn the dwell meter switch to the "Calibrate" position.
   c. Turn the motor switch to the proper direction of rotation.
   d. Turn the dwell meter calibration knob until the meter reads on the "Set" line.

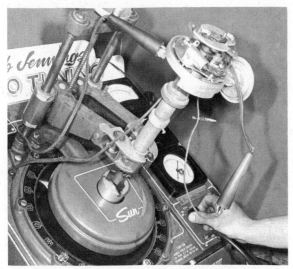

Figure 11-10. Connect the tester leads to the distributor as shown here.

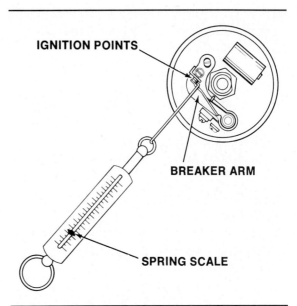

Figure 11-11. Measuring breaker point spring tension.

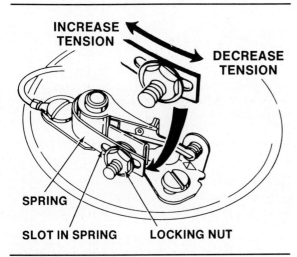

Figure 11-12. Breaker point spring tension adjustment.

e. Before testing, turn the dwell meter switch to the correct position for the number of engine cylinders.

9. Connect the tester's insulated lead (usually red) to the distributor primary lead. Connect the tester's ground lead (usually black) to a grounding stud on the tester or to the distributor housing, figure 11-10.

Point Spring Tension Test

Breaker-point spring tension should be checked if you are going to leave the old points in the distributor. It also should be checked, and adjusted if necessary, after new points are installed. Spring tension is usually in the 15- to 25-ounce range, but check the manufacturer's specifications for the exact setting. You can check spring tension quickly and easily with a

distributor tester. You will also need a spring tension scale.

1. Turn the distributor shaft until the points are closed.

2. Turn the tester "Motor" switch to the correct rotation direction.

3. Hook the spring tension scale over the movable breaker-point arm and slowly pull at a right angle to the point arm, figure 11-11. Do not drag the scale on the distributor housing.

4. Note the reading on the tension scale when the tester arrow flashes or the dwell meter starts to drop to zero.

5. If the spring tension is not within specifications, adjust it by moving the slotted hole in the spring as shown in figure 11-12. If the tension cannot be adjusted within limits, the point set should be replaced.

6. Check for binding at the pivot point by slowly closing the points and noting the spring tension scale reading when the dwell meter starts to rise from zero.

7. If the spring tension is the same when the points open and when they close, there is no binding at the pivot point. If the spring tension varies, there is binding. Binding often can be corrected by lubricating the pivot point with *one drop* of penetrating oil. If this does not cure the problem, replace the point set.

Breaker-Point Alignment

The breaker-point surfaces should be aligned so that they contact each other squarely on the centers of their surfaces, figure 11-13. Misalignment will shorten breaker-point life and

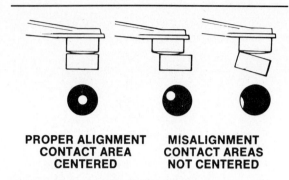

PROPER ALIGNMENT | **MISALIGNMENT**
CONTACT AREA | **CONTACT AREAS**
CENTERED | **NOT CENTERED**

Figure 11-13. Breaker point alignment and misalignment.

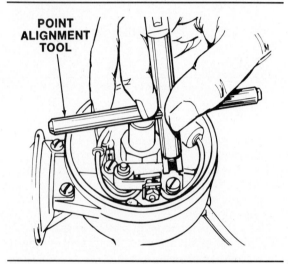

POINT ALIGNMENT TOOL

Figure 11-15. Bend the fixed (ground) breaker point to adjust point alignment. Do not bend the movable point arm.

can cause erratic ignition operation. Align the breaker points as follows:
1. Turn the tester speed control knob to operate the distributor at about 1,000 rpm, figure 11-14.
2. View the breaker points from above and from one side. You should see a small spark near the centers of the contact surfaces.
3. If the spark is near the center of the surfaces, the points are aligned correctly.
4. If the spark is off center, bend the fixed (ground) breaker point with a bending tool, figure 11-15, to correct the alignment. Do not try to bend the movable point arm.

Rubbing Block Alignment

The breaker-point rubbing block must contact the cam squarely to ensure long point life and to prevent dwell change. Check rubbing block alignment as follows:
1. With the distributor operating at 1,000 rpm, look at the rubbing block contact with the cam. It should contact the cam squarely.

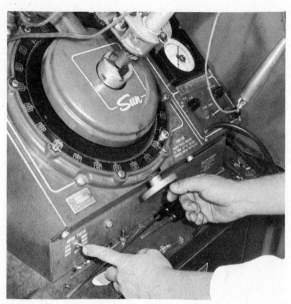

Figure 11-14. Turn the speed control knob to control distributor rotation speed.

2. If the rubbing block does not contact the cam squarely, replace the point set. Do not try to bend the movable point arm.
3. Also check the breaker plate for looseness or misalignment.

Breaker-Point and Distributor Resistance Test

Test the resistance of the breaker-point contact surfaces and of the primary connections within the distributor. High resistance will harm the overall ignition performance. Make these tests after the distributor has been run in the tester for a few minutes to burn any oxidation off the contact surfaces of the points.
1. Stop the distributor with the breaker points closed.
2. Turn the dwell meter switch to the "Calibrate" position.
3. The dwell meter should read within the "Distributor Resistance" area at the end of the scale, figure 11-16. Normal resistance is the same as the 0.2-volt drop that you can measure with a voltmeter when testing the distributor in the car.
4. If the dwell meter does not read within the correct area, take the following steps to find and correct the high resistance:
   a. Repeat the test with the tester insulated (red) lead connected directly to the movable breaker point.
   b. If the results are within limits, replace the distributor primary wire. Be sure the connection to the points is clean and tight.
   c. If the results in step 4a are out of limits, clean the points by drawing a smooth, clean piece of heavy paper between the closed contact surfaces. Do not try to file the points or

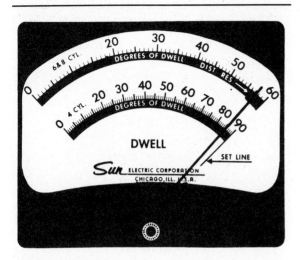

Figure 11-16. The dwell meter should read within the "Points Resistance" area if the distributor resistance is within limits. (Sun)

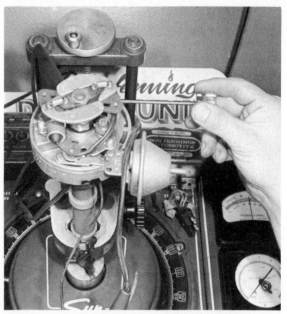

Figure 11-17. Adjusting the dwell on a Delco-Rémy external adjustment distributor.

clean them with emery cloth.

d. If the results are still out of limits, repeat the test with the insulated lead connected to the grounded breaker point. If the results are out of limits, check for a loose or dirty attachment of the breaker plate to the distributor housing.

e. If the distributor resistance is still out of limits after these tests, replace the breaker points and repeat the test sequence.

Dwell Adjustment

Adjusting the distributor dwell with the distributor mounted in the tester is the fastest and most precise way of making this adjustment. If you plan to leave the old breaker points in the distributor, make all of the preceding tests and adjustments described in this section before making the final dwell adjustment. If you have installed new breaker points, you will find it easier to make an initial dwell adjustment before checking spring tension, alignment and the other points we already described. Also, the dwell setting should be rechecked as the final step before removing the distributor from the tester.

Do not lubricate the cam and breaker-point rubbing block before making the final dwell adjustment. Allowing the distributor to operate for a few minutes with no lubricant between the cam and rubbing block will burnish the rubbing block surface and reduce the initial wear of the rubbing block when the distributor is put back in service. This means that your dwell adjustment will not change as quickly or as much between distributor dservice intervals. Lubricate the cam and rubbing block after adjusting the dwell.

You will need the carmaker's specifications for the dwell angle of the particular distributor that you are servicing. These are listed in various specification manuals by distributor part number or by car make, model, engine, and year. The dwell angle will be listed as a range (28° to 32°, for example) or as a nominal setting with a tolerance (30° ± 2°). In either case, adjust the dwell toward the lower end of the specification. In the example above, set the dwell at 28°, 29°, or 30°. This will allow for rubbing block wear and the gradual increase in dwell angle during distributor use.

Adjust the dwell angle in a single-point distributor as follows:

1. Set the dwell meter switch for the correct number of engine cylinders or distributor cam lobes.

2. Be sure the tester leads are correctly connected and that the tester is set for the correct direction of rotation.

3. Turn the tester speed control knob so that the distributor rotates at about 300 rpm.

4. While watching the dwell meter, adjust the dwell angle to specifications as follows:

a. For a Delco-Remy external adjustment distributor, put an allen wrench into the point adjusting screw, figure 11-17. Turn the screw clockwise to increase the dwell angle, counterclockwise to decrease the angle.

b. For an internal adjustment distributor, loosen the point mounting screw if required. Then turn the point adjusting screw, figure 11-18 position A, or move the point base by inserting a screwdriver in the slotted hole, figure 11-18 position B. Tighten the mounting screw after adjustment.

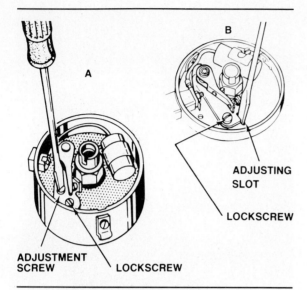

Figure 11-18. Dwell adjustment points for an internal adjustment distributor.

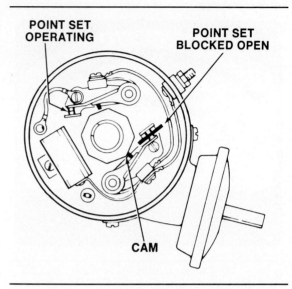

Figure 11-19. Adjusting dual breaker points.

Dual-point distributor dwell adjustment

Some high-performance breaker-point distributors have two sets of breaker points, connected in parallel. One set opens the primary circuit; the other set closes the circuit. The overlapping action of the two point sets produces a larger total dwell angle and longer dwell period for more complete coil saturation at high speed.

Each set of points must be adjusted separately to the specified angle. Then the combined dwell angle must be checked and must be within limits. Adjust dual points as follows:
1. Block one set of points open with a paper match stick or similar insulating spacer, figure 11-19.
2. Perform steps 1, 2, and 3 of the preceding instructions for adjusting a single set of breaker points.
3. Adjust the dwell angle on the set of points that is not blocked open.
4. Stop the distributor rotation. Remove the spacer from the points that were blocked open and place it between the points that you have just adjusted.
5. Adjust the dwell angle on the other set of points.
6. Stop the distributor rotation and remove the spacer from the first set of points that you adjusted.
7. Operate the distributor at 300 rpm and note the dwell meter reading for the combined dwell angle of both sets of points. It must be within the carmaker's specifications.

Dwell Angle Variation Test

Manufacturers allow for a small change in the dwell angle as engine speed increases. This is called dwell variation. The amount of allowable

dwell variation varies for different distributors. Once again, you must know the carmaker's specifications. Generally, the amount of dwell variation is greater for distributors with side-pivot breaker plates than for those with center-pivot breaker plates. Too much dwell variation is usually caused by a worn or loose breaker plate, worn bushings, or a bent distributor shaft. Test for dwell variation as follows:
1. Operate the distributor at 300 rpm or the speed at which you adjusted the dwell angle.
2. While watching the dwell meter, slowly increase the distributor speed to 2,500 rpm.
3. If the dwell changes more than the carmaker's allowable variation, look for a worn shaft, bushing, or breaker plate.
4. Reduce the distributor speed to 200 rpm.
5. Connect the tester vacuum line to the distributor vacuum advance unit.
6. While watching the dwell meter, apply 15 to 20 inches of vacuum.
7. If the dwell changes more than the allowable variation, look for a loose breaker plate or worn breaker-plate bearings.

Point Float Test

The point float test is similar to the dwell variation test. This test will determine whether the points are closing at the proper time. If they remain open longer than they should, the dwell angle will be reduced.
1. Operate the distributor at 300 rpm or the speed at which you adjusted the dwell angle.
2. While observing the dwell meter, increase the distributor speed to 2,500 rpm.
3. Watch for a sudden decrease in the dwell angle.
4. If the dwell angle drops sharply, it means that the points floated, or remained open, for part of the dwell period. This is usually caused by weak

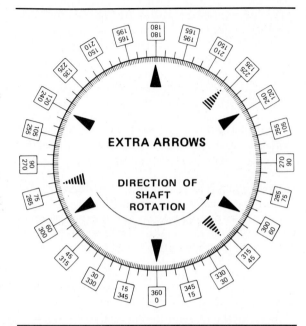

Figure 11-20. Extra arrows, or ghost flashes, on the synchronizing scale indicate point bounce.

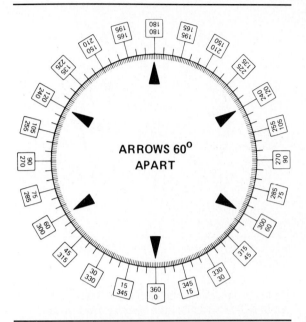

Figure 11-21. The flashing arrows should be evenly spaced around the degree ring. This pattern is for a 6-lobe distributor cam.

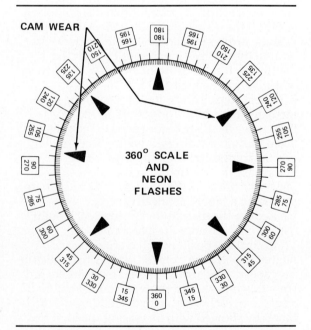

Figure 11-22. If some arrows flash late, while others flash at the correct position, it indicates cam wear.

spring tension or binding at the breaker-point pivot.

Point Bounce Test

Make this test to find out whether the points close, bounce open, and then reclose at the start of the dwell period.

1. Operate the distributor from 300 rpm to 2,500 rpm.

2. Watch the flashing arrows; look for double flashes or ghost arrows, figure 11-20.

3. There should be as many sharp flashing arrows as there are lobes on the distributor cam. Any extra arrows or double (uneven) flashes at any point indicate that the points are bouncing. This is usually caused by incorrect spring tension, misaligned points, or binding at the breaker-point pivot.

Cam Lobe, Bushing, And Shaft Wear Test

Make this test to find out whether all of the cam lobes are an equal distance apart from each other or whether any of them are worn. This test will also show wear in the distributor bushings or shaft.

1. Operate the distributor at 1,000 rpm.

2. Rotate the degree ring on the synchronizing scale until the zero point is aligned with any one of the flashing arrows, figure 11-21.

3. Watch the position on the degree ring of each of the other flashing arrows. They should be evenly spaced, ± 1 degree, as follows:

• 4-lobe cam, every 90 degrees
• 6-lobe cam, every 60 degrees (even firing)
• 8-lobe cam, every 45 degrees.

4. If the flashing arrows are evenly spaced and within 1 degree of their correct positions, figure 11-21, the distributor cam, shaft and bushings are not worn.

5. If the flashing arrows are not in their correct positions, look for these two general conditions:

   a. If any one arrow, or several arrows at random locations are out of position, figure

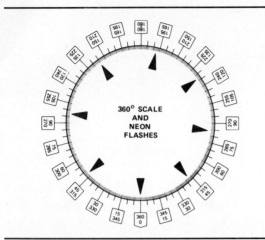

Figure 11-23. If the entire pattern is shifted like this, it indicates shaft or bushing wear.

11-22, it means a worn cam lobe. These arrows will flash later than they should on the degree ring.

b. If the entire pattern of flashing arrows gradually shifts out of position from the zero point on the degree ring, figure 11-23, and the arrow at the 180-degree point is the farthest out of position, look for a bent shaft or worn bushings.

Distributor Spark Advance Tests

The centrifugal and vacuum advance mechanisms of the distributor can both be tested and adjusted in the distributor tester. Distributor advance specifications, called advance curves, are essential for precise testing. Curves are listed for each distributor by the manufacturer's part number. Therefore, before you can test a distributor, you must know its part number. You will find the part number on the side of the distributor housing.

Distributor advance specifications may be given in engine speed and engine degrees or in distributor speed and distributor degrees. To use a distributor tester, you will need specifications in distributor speed and distributor degrees. If the specifications are listed in engine speed and engine degrees, simply divide them by two.

Centrifugal advance curves begin with a starting point that lists zero degrees of advance (sometimes 0 to 1 degree) at a given speed. This means that there should be no advance below this speed and that the advance should start at this speed. Then, one or more intermediate points are listed, giving the number of degrees of advance at higher speeds. Finally, the full centrifugal advance is listed at a specific speed. Above this speed, there should be no more advance.

Vacuum advance curves are listed as the number of degrees of advance with certain amounts of vacuum applied to the diaphragm, such as: 9° at 16 inches of vacuum. Vacuum advance is tested with the distributor operating below the starting speed for the centrifugal advance. This prevents any centrifugal advance from being added to the vacuum advance and giving false test results. Figure 11-24 shows typical centrifugal and vacuum advance specifications for several distributors.

Centrifugal advance test and adjustment
1. Run the distributor at about 200 rpm.
2. Rotate the degree ring so that the zero point is aligned with any one of the flashing arrows.
3. Increase the distributor speed to the specified starting point of the advance curve.
4. Record the position of the arrow on the degree ring. It should remain at zero or show only about 1 degree of advance.
5. Increase the distributor speed to the next specified point in the specifications.
6. Record the position of the arrow on the degree ring. It should indicate the specified amount of spark advance for that distributor speed. If the distributor rotates clockwise, the flashing arrows will advance counterclockwise around the degree ring, figure 11-25. If the distributor rotates counterclockwise, the arrows will advance clockwise.
7. Repeat steps 5 and 6 for the remaining intermediate points in the advance specifications.
8. Increase the distributor speed to the speed listed for full centrifugal advance. Record the position of the arrow on the degree ring.
9. Increase the distributor speed 200 to 400 rpm above the full centrifugal advance speed. There should be no more spark advance.
10. Reduce the distributor speed to each point listed in the advance specifications.
11. Record the position of the arrow on the degree ring at each point as you decrease distributor speed. The arrows should move backward smoothly and should show the same amount of advance at each point with decreasing speed that they showed with increasing speed. If the arrows move unevenly or if they do not show the same amount of advance at each point with decreasing speed, the advance weights are sticking or the springs may be weak or broken.

If the amount of centrifugal advance is out of limits at any point in the specifications, the advance mechanism must be cleaned and lubricated or adjusted, or the springs or weights must be replaced. If the advance is bad at low speeds, but good at high speeds, look for wear, binding, or dirt. If the advance is bad at all speeds, look for broken or binding springs or weights.

DISTRIBUTOR PART NO.	CENTRIFUGAL ADVANCE IN DISTRIBUTOR DEGREES AT DISTRIBUTOR RPM						VACUUM ADVANCE — MAX. DIST. DEGREES AT INCHES OF HG
	START	INTERMEDIATE	INTERMEDIATE	INTERMEDIATE	INTERMEDIATE	MAXIMUM	
1112062 (Delco)	0-2.4 @ 625	7.5-10 @ 950	8-10 @ 960			13-15 @ 2200	10° @ 13-14.75"
1111956 (Delco)	0-3.5 @ 550	1.3-4.8 @ 583	9.5-11.5 @ 1000			15-17 @ 2200	13° @ 16-17.5"
721F-AHA (Ford)	0-1 @ 500	1-3 @ 750	5-7 @ 1000	6-8 @ 1250	7-9 @ 1500	9.5-11.5 @ 2000	4.2°-7.2° @ 10"
D30F-BA (Ford)	0-1.5 @ 500	4-6 @ 750	4.5-6.5 @ 1000	5.2-7.4 @ 1250	6-8.2 @ 1500	7.2-10 @ 2000	6.5°-9.2° @ 10"
3656780 (Chrysler)	1-3.5 @ 500	10-12.5 @ 800		11.2-13.2 @ 1250		13-15 @ 1750	9.5°-12.5° @ 15"
3755365 (Chrysler)	1-4 @ 650	8-10 @ 800	8.7-10.7 @ 1000	7.5-11.5 @ 1250		12-14 @ 2000	9.5°-12.5° @ 15"

Figure 11-24. Typical distributor advance specifications.

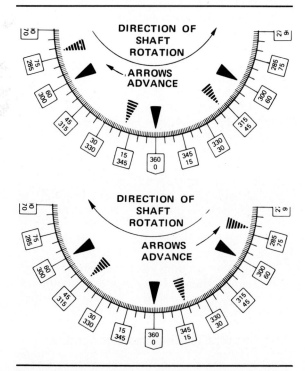

Figure 11-25. The arrows will advance in the direction opposite to shaft rotation. (Sun)

Figure 11-26. Adjusting the centrifugal advance on an internal adjustment distributor.

You can adjust the advance on many internal adjustment distributors by reaching through a slot in the breaker plate with a screwdriver and bending the spring anchors, figure 11-26. Bend the anchors outward to increase spring tension and slow down the advance. Bend the anchors inward to decrease spring tension and speed up or increase the advance. Adjust both the primary and the secondary advance weights. Repeat the tests after adjusting or replacing any parts.

If the advance is out of limits on a Delco-Remy external adjustment distributor, you may be able to correct it by stretching or shortening the ends of the springs. However, this is not a very precise way to adjust the centrifugal ad-

vance. It is better to replace the springs with new ones of the correct part number. You also may need to replace the weights to correct the centrifugal advance.

Vacuum advance test and adjustment
1. Run the distributor at about 200 rpm. Distributor speed must remain constant during this test.
2. Rotate the degree ring so that the zero point is aligned with any one of the flashing arrows.
3. Attach the tester vacuum line to the distributor vacuum advance diaphragm. Adjust the tester for zero inches of vacuum.
4. Slowly increase the vacuum and note the amount of vacuum when the arrow first advances from the zero point.
5. Increase the amount of vacuum to the first test point in the specifications.

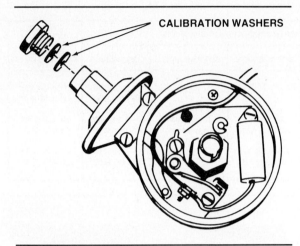

Figure 11-27. Vacuum advance adjustment with calibration washers.

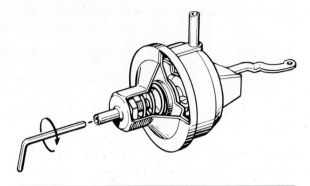

Figure 11-28. Vacuum advance adjustment with an internal screw.

6. Record the position of the arrow on the degree ring.

7. Repeat steps 5 and 6 for the remaining intermediate points in the vacuum advance specifications.

8. Increase the vacuum to the full amount specified. Record the position of the arrow on the degree ring.

9. Reduce the vacuum to zero. The arrow should return to the zero position on the degree ring.

10. Stop the distributor rotation.

If the amount of vacuum advance is out of limits at any point in the specifications, the vacuum unit must be adjusted or replaced. Delco-Remy vacuum advance units must be replaced if they are out of limits. Vacuum advance units on most Ford distributors can be adjusted by two different methods, depending on design.

Autolite and Holley distributors used in 1971 and earlier vehicles are adjusted by changing adjustment washers inside the vacuum advance unit. This type of unit has a removable hex-head plug in the end of the housing, figure 11-27. Some Chrysler and Prestolite distributors can also be adjusted in this way. Autolite and Motorcraft distributors used in 1972 and later vehicles are adjusted by inserting an allen wrench through the vacuum hose nipple in the end of the housing and turning an internal nut, figure 11-28.

On dual-diaphragm distributors, which provide both vacuum advance and retard, the retard diaphragm must be tested before adjusting the advance diaphragm. If the retard diaphragm is not working correctly, the advance diaphragm cannot be adjusted accurately. Retard diaphragms are not adjustable, and the entire vacuum unit must be replaced if it is bad.

To adjust units using adjustment washers,

remove the plug from the end of the housing. Add washers to decrease advance; remove washers to increase advance. Often, removing one washer and replacing it with another of a slightly different thickness will provide a fine degree of adjustment.

To adjust units with an internal adjusting nut, insert a 1/8-inch allen wrench through the hose nipple. Turn the wrench clockwise to increase advance, counterclockwise to decrease it. Make adjustments in small increments and check advance after each change.

After advance is adjusted at one vacuum setting, check the advance points at other specified vacuum settings. Do not change the distributor speed from the original rpm setting while checking the vacuum advance points.

If the other vacuum advance points are not within limits there is leakage in the vacuum unit or line or a defective spring. Bad vacuum units must be replaced.

Distributor Cleaning and Lubrication

Rust, dirt, grease, and varnish tend to collect inside a distributor when it is in operation. Accumulated dirt and grime will affect centrifugal advance operation and can cause crossfiring and short circuits in the electrical connections. You should clean a distributor thoroughly when you service it.

An equally important part of distributor service is distributor lubrication. Proper lubrication is essential for correct operation. However, *you must be very careful not to overlubricate a distributor.* The centrifugal force of distributor rotation will spray excess lubricant around the inside of the distributor, creating more dirt and causing electrical problems such as burned points and short circuits.

The moving parts of a distributor should be cleaned and — with one exception — lubricated *before* the dwell and the advance mechanisms are adjusted. However, lubricate the point rubbing block and cam *after* the dwell is adjusted.

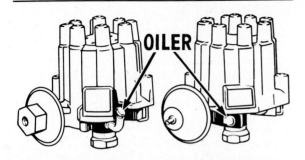

Figure 11-29. If a distributor has an oil or grease cup, apply the recommended lubricant during service.

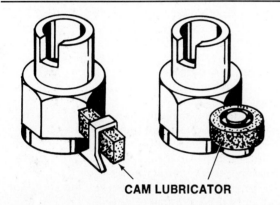

CAM LUBRICATOR

Figure 11-31. These felt lubricators for the cam should be replaced during service.

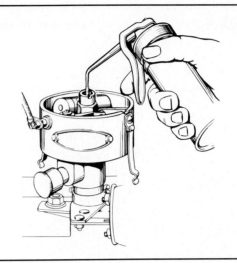

Figure 11-30. If the distributor has a felt wick in the top of the shaft, apply two or three drops of light oil.

Clean the inside of the distributor with solvent and a small brush. Wipe off dirt with a clean, lint-free cloth. Remove the vacuum advance unit before cleaning or be careful not to get solvent on the diaphragm. Be sure that all dirt and solvent residue is removed from all electrical connection points. Dry the inside of the distributor with low-pressure compressed air.

Many older distributors have an oil cup or a grease cup for bushing lubrication, figure 11-29. If one of these is present, apply the oil or grease specified by the carmaker. Some distributors have a felt wick in the top of the shaft, figure 11-30. Apply two or three drops of light motor oil to such a wick. Other distributors have a felt lubricator wick that rubs against the cam during operation, figure 11-31. These lubricators should be replaced during complete distributor service. Do not try to oil them.

Lubricate the contact and pivot points of the centrifugal advance weights and springs with a light coat of distributor cam lubricant or one or two small drops of penetrating oil. Lubricate the breaker plate bearing and pivot point with one or two small drops of penetrating oil. Lubricate the breaker point pivot with *one drop* of penetrat-

ing oil or a light film of distributor cam lubricant when the points are replaced.

If the distributor does not have a grease or oil cup, apply a few drops of motor oil to the shaft through the drive end of the housing and rotate the shaft by hand to ensure adequate lubrication before the distributor is reinstalled. After you make the final dwell adjustment, apply a light film of special distributor cam lubricant to the cam lobes and rubbing block. Remember, during all distributor lubrication, be very careful to keep lubricants off the points, cap, rotor, and all electrical connections.

Before reinstalling the distributor in the engine, install the RFI shield, if needed, and the rotor.

DISTRIBUTOR INSTALLATION

Follow these general instructions for distributor installation:
1. Be sure the ignition switch is off. You may have disconnected the battery ground cable when you removed the distributor.
2. Rotate the distributor shaft so that the rotor is in line with the mark that you made on the housing when you removed it.
3. Align the distributor housing with your reference point on the engine.
4. Insert the distributor into the engine. Be sure the sealing ring is in place on Chrysler distributors.
5. Engage the distributor drive with the camshaft and oil pump drive. If the distributor has a helical drive gear, the rotor may rotate out of position when the distributor is inserted in the engine. If this happens, note the amount that

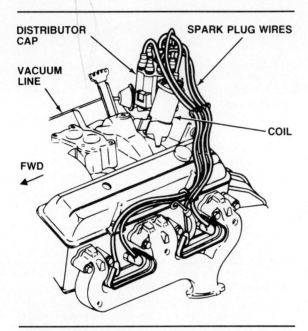

DISTRIBUTOR
CAP

SPARK PLUG WIRES

VACUUM
LINE

COIL

FWD

Figure 11-32. Connect the vacuum line to the distributor and the primary lead to the coil, before securing the distributor cap and attached spark plug wires. (Chevrolet)

the rotor moves. Then raise the distributor up and move the rotor backwards the same amount (usually about 15 to 20 degrees). Then lower the distributor back into place.

6. Be sure the distributor is fully seated in the engine and engaged with the camshaft and oil pump drive. You may have to wiggle the shaft slightly to engage the oil pump or bump the engine with the starter to turn the distributor slightly for shaft engagement.

7. Install the distributor clamp and holddown bolt.

8. Connect the primary lead to the coil.

9. Connect the vacuum line to the vacuum advance unit, figure 11-32.

10. Place the cap and the attached spark plug wires on the distributor and secure it with the clips or holddown screws.

11. Connect the battery ground cable if it was disconnected.

STATIC TIMING

If the engine was not cranked while the distributor was out, it should start and run if the distributor is reinstalled correctly. Initial timing should then be checked and adjusted with a timing light. If the engine was cranked while the distributor was out, you will have to reestablish the basic timing position. This is called static timing. Proceed as follows:

1. Bring the number 1 piston to top dead center on the compression stroke. If the engine is timed on any cylinder other than number 1, use that cylinder for static timing.

2. Align the timing marks at the specified initial timing position.

3. Install the distributor so that the rotor points at the number 1 spark plug terminal in the cap. Make a reference line on the distributor housing to align the rotor with the cap off.

4. Loosen the distributor holddown clamp and bolt.

5. Rotate the distributor housing in the direction of rotor rotation so that the points are closed.

6. Connect one lead of a test lamp to the distributor primary lead terminal on the coil. Connect the other test lead to ground.

7. Turn the ignition on. The test lamp should not light if the points are closed.

8. Slowly rotate the distributor housing opposite to the direction of rotor rotation until the lamp lights. This indicates that the points have just opened.

9. Tighten the holddown bolt. The distributor is now timed well enough for the engine to start and run.

10. Check and adjust the initial timing with a timing light after the engine is started.

To do static timing without a test lamp, do steps 1 through 5 in the preceding procedure. Turn the ignition on with the points closed. Then rotate the distributor housing in the direction opposite to rotor rotation until a small spark jumps between the points. This indicates that the points have just opened. Tighten the holddown bolt.

12

Solid-State Ignition System Testing

As we learned in the *Classroom Manual*, the secondary circuits of breaker-point and solid-state ignition systems are generally the same. The greatest differences lie in the systems' primary circuits. Full testing and servicing instructions for secondary circuits are contained in Chapters 9 and 10; this chapter will explain any exceptions that apply to solid-state systems.

This chapter also contains detailed troubleshooting procedures, using simple test meters and tools, for all major domestic solid-state ignition systems. Manufacturer's special circuit testers are explained, and the oscilloscope patterns typical of solid-state systems are shown.

SECONDARY CIRCUIT TESTING AND SERVICE

Because the secondary circuits of all automotive ignition systems are similar, the testing and servicing instructions given in Chapters 9 and 10 can be used when servicing most solid-state systems. The few exceptions will be explained here and in the specific troubleshooting instructions given later in the chapter.

The caps on some solid-state distributors look different, but they all do the same job in the same way. Delco-Remy Unitized and HEI caps, and all Ford Dura-Spark caps, have male connectors rather than spark plug towers, figures 12-1 and 12-2. When removing a cap from an early-1977 Dura-Spark distributor, remember to unlatch the cap from the adapter ring first. Do not try to lift the cap and the adapter from the body together, because the adapter will jam on the rotor. On later Dura-Spark distributors, the adapter ring is held to the body by two screws inside the ring.

All solid-state distributor rotors perform the same. The only rotor that does not follow the basic description we have given is the rotor used with Ford's electronic engine control (EEC) system. The EEC rotor, figure 12-3, has two pickup arms and two electrode tips. The arms and tips are on different levels, to minimize the chances of crossfiring within the distributor. The distributor cap electrodes are also on two levels, to match the rotor tips. The rotor does not fit into a locating lug on the distributor shaft. Instead, it is held by two mounting screws in slotted holes. When you replace an EEC rotor, you must use a special Ford tool to adjust the rotor position:
1. Refer to figure 12-4.
2. Remove the distributor cap.
3. Turn the crankshaft so that the rotor's upper electrode tip (the tip with a slot in it) is aligned with the locating slot in the distributor body adapter ring.

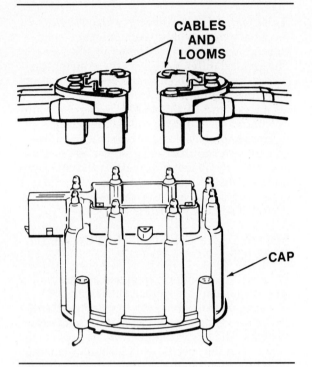

Figure 12-1. Delco-Remy's Unitized and HEI systems have male connectors on the distributor cap for the spark plug cables.

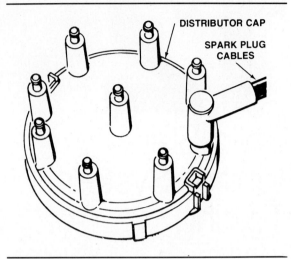

Figure 12-2. Ford's Dura-Spark systems also have male connectors for the spark plug cables.

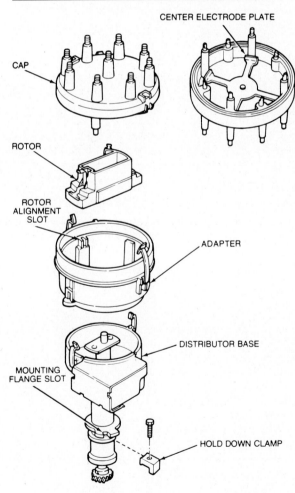

Figure 12-3. Ford's EEC rotor and distributor cap route high voltage on two different levels to reduce the chances of crossfiring within the distributor. (Ford)

4. Take out the two rotor mounting screws and remove the rotor.

CAUTION: Do not turn the crankshaft after the rotor is removed.

5. Put the new rotor on the distributor shaft so that the slot in the upper electrode tip points to the locating slot in the adapter ring.

6. Install, but do not tighten, the two rotor mounting screws.

7. Slide the rotor alignment tool into the adapter ring slot so that the tang on the underside of the tool is in both the adapter ring slot and the rotor electrode slot.

8. Tighten the rotor mounting screws to 15 to 20 inch-pounds or other specified torque.

9. Remove the rotor alignment tool and replace the distributor cap.

Ford and Chrysler solid-state distributor rotors are coated at the factory with a silicone grease. As the silicone ages, it may look like contamination, figure 12-5, but it is not. Do not try to remove or reapply any coating on a used Ford rotor; Chrysler recommends removing any excessive scaling on the tip of their rotor. When a new Ford rotor is installed, put a ⅛-inch thick coating of silicone grease on all sides of the electrode, including the tip. Use Dow Corning number 111, GE number G-627, or equivalent.

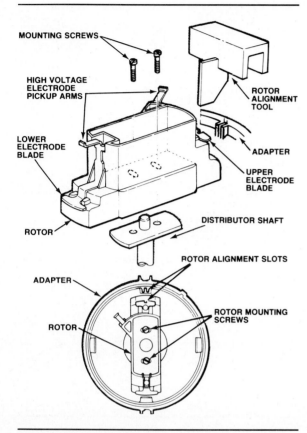

Figure 12-4. The EEC rotor must be aligned whenever it is reinstalled. (Ford)

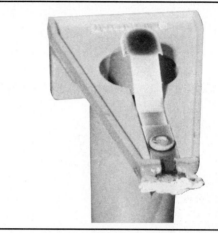

Figure 12-5. What appears to be contamination on the end of this Ford rotor is just silicone grease, and should not be disturbed.

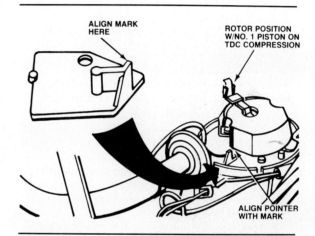

Figure 12-6. The early-model MISAR distributor must be aligned before the crankshaft pickup coil is adjusted.

Most solid-state systems use the same 7-mm TVRS cable as do breaker-point systems. The Delco-Remy HEI and Ford Dura-Spark systems use an 8-mm TVRS cable. *Do not interchange the two sizes.*

INITIAL TIMING TEST AND ADJUSTMENT

The initial timing of most solid-state systems is set by rotating the distributor, as explained in Chapter 10. Many manufacturers also provide brackets for magnetic-probe, or monolithic, timing. This requires special test equipment.

The 1977 version of the Oldsmobile MISAR system is not timed by moving the distributor, but by adjusting the pickup coil at the crankshaft pulley. The later version of MISAR, introduced in 1978, has a standard HEI pickup coil and trigger wheel mounted in the distributor. To time either MISAR system:

1. On early models with the crankshaft sensor, check distributor position and adjust if necessary:
   a. Refer to figure 12-6.
   b. Remove ignition feed wire (black with pink stripe) from distributor, to prevent arcing.

   c. Bump the engine with the starter motor until the rotor points toward the rear of the engine and the timing mark is almost at 0 degrees (tdc).
   d. Use a wrench on the crankshaft bolt head to turn the crankshaft until the timing mark is at tdc.
   e. The white mark on the side of the rotor should be aligned with the white pointer in the distributor. If not, loosen the distributor clamp bolt and turn the distributor to align the mark with the pointer.
   f. Tighten the distributor clamp bolt.
   g. Reassemble the distributor.

2. Connect a jumper wire to the reference timing connector near the controller assembly, figure 12-7. Ground the other end of the jumper wire.

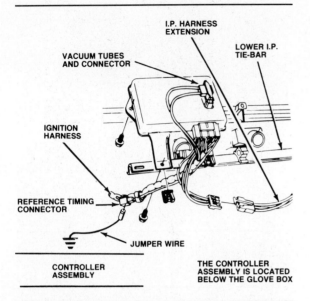

Figure 12-7. A grounded jumper wire is hooked to the reference timing connector at the MISAR controller.

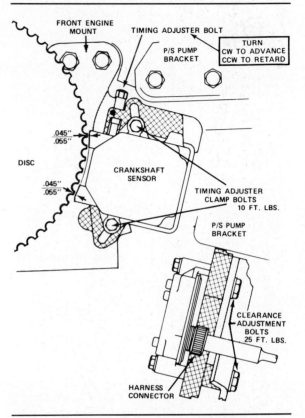

Figure 12-8. The early-model MISAR crankshaft sensor was adjusted to set the ignition timing.

3. With the drive wheels blocked, the parking brake applied, and the transmission in park, start the engine and run it at slow idle or other specified test speed. The "Check Ignition" light on the instrument panel will be lighted because of the jumper wire.

4. With a timing light, compare the position of the timing mark to specifications:

   a. If the mark matches specifications, no adjustment is needed.

   b. If the mark does not match specifications, go to step 5 (early model) or step 6 (late model).

5. To adjust the timing with a crankshaft-mounted pickup coil:

   a. Stop the engine.

   b. Loosen the timing adjuster clamp bolts, figure 12-8.

   c. Turn the timing adjuster bolt clockwise to advance the timing, or counterclockwise to retard the timing.

   d. One complete turn of the bolt equals about 1 degree.

   e. Start the engine, recheck the timing, and repeat steps a through d if necessary.

   f. When the timing mark matches specifications, stop the engine and tighten the timing adjuster clamp bolts.

   g. Remove the jumper wire from the reference timing connector.

6. To adjust the timing with a distributor-mounted pickup coil:

   a. With the engine running, loosen the distributor clamp bolt.

   b. While watching the timing marks, turn the distributor clockwise to advance the timing, or counterclockwise to retard the timing.

   c. When the timing mark matches specifications, tighten the distributor clamp bolt.

   d. Stop the engine and remove the jumper wire from the reference timing connector.

VOLT-OHMMETER TROUBLESHOOTING

Breaker points are the weakest link in an ignition system and the parts that need the most frequent service. By eliminating the points, solid-state ignitions have become almost maintenance free. In most systems, dwell angle, or the period when the primary circuit is complete, is controlled by the solid-state module. There is no dwell period change due to wear of the rubbing block or cam lobes. Dwell angle, or period, is usually a fixed design factor in a solid-state system and cannot be altered. Dwell angle measurements, although they can be made, are not significant for most systems. The dwell period, or angle, on some systems does change with engine speed.

Service of solid-state ignition systems is not the periodic replacement of points and condenser or adjustment of dwell. The new concept in service is that of testing and fault diagnosis.

Figure 12-9. One way to check for adequate reserve voltage is to pull a plug wire off and hold it near the engine block while cranking the engine. If a spark jumps the gap, the ignition is performing well. (Chevrolet)

The control modules, magnetic pickups, and other circuit parts used in solid-state ignitions can fail. Service consists of electronic trouble-shooting followed by part replacement.

Circuits can be tested with oscilloscopes, special circuit testers, or simple volt-ohmmeters. Always check the specifications and follow the procedures of the ignition and test equipment manufacturers.

The following paragraphs contain basic troubleshooting procedures, using simple test equipment, for Delco-Remy, Ford, Chrysler, and AMC-Prestolite solid-state ignitions.

Delco-Remy Unitized Ignition Testing

Before making any circuit checks with test meters, be sure that all primary circuit connectors are properly installed and that spark plug cables are secure at the distributor and at the plugs. Also check that the distributor through-bolts are tight; loose bolts can cause radio interference and poor performance.
1. Connect the voltmeter positive (+) lead to the ignition switch connector at the distributor; connect the voltmeter negative (−) lead to ground.
2. Turn the ignition switch on and observe the voltmeter:
   a. If the reading is zero, trace and repair the circuit between the battery and the distributor; repeat the test.
   b. If the reading is approximately battery voltage, go to step 3.
3. Hold one spark plug cable with insulated pliers about ¼ inch from a clean area on the engine block, figure 12-9, and crank the engine:
   a. If sparking occurs, go to step 4.
   b. If no sparking occurs, test the ignition coil and the pickup coil as explained in the following paragraphs.
4. Check the spark plugs; clean and adjust or replace as necessary. If the engine still does not start, the problem is not in the ignition system.

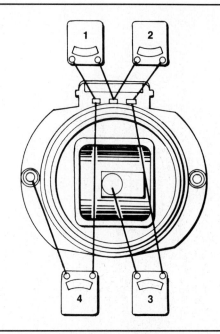

Figure 12-10. Unitized system coil test points.

Unitized coil test
1. Refer to figure 12-10.
2. Remove the coil from the distributor cap by removing the through-bolts.
3. Inspect the cap, rotor, and coil for signs of crossfiring or leakage.
4. Make the ohmmeter connections shown in figure 12-10:
   a. Test points 1 and 2 should both show nearly zero resistance. If not, replace the coil.
   b. Test point 3 should show 6,000 to 9,000 ohms. If not, replace the coil.
   c. Test point 4 should show infinite resistance. If resistance is less than infinite, replace the coil.

Unitized pickup coil test
1. Refer to figure 12-11.
2. Connect a vacuum source to the vacuum advance unit and check the vacuum advance operation. If the vacuum unit is faulty, replace it.
3. Remove the two pickup coil leads from the control module on the side of the distributor.
4. Connect an ohmmeter to test point 1 as shown in figure 12-11 and operate vacuum advance unit through its full range. The ohmmeter should show infinite resistance at all times between the pickup coil lead and the distributor housing:
   a. If the reading is constantly infinite, go to step 5.
   b. If the reading shows continuity, replace the pickup coil.

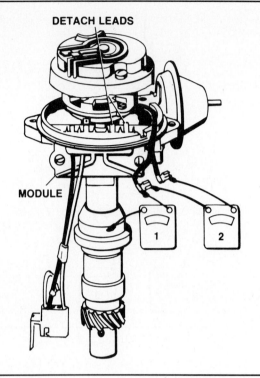

Figure 12-11. Unitized system pickup coil test points.

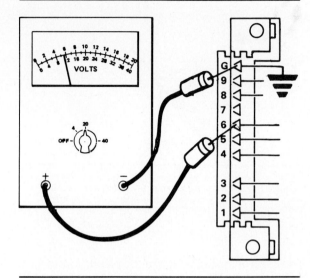

Figure 12-12. GM diagnostic connector test, pin 6. (Oldsmobile)

5. Connect an ohmmeter to test point 2 as shown in figure 12-11 and operate the vacuum advance unit through its full range. Compare the ohmmeter reading to the manufacturer's specifications for pickup coil resistance:

   a. If the reading matches the specification, go to step 6.

   b. If the reading does not meet specifications, replace the pickup coil.

6. If no defects are found in the ignition coil or the pickup coil but the ignition will still not operate, the fault is probably in the electronic control module. Install a new module and retest the system.

GM Diagnostic Connector Tests

If the engine of a late-model full-size GM product or a Chevette cranks properly but will not start, or if the engine starts but stumbles, a few tests can be made at the diagnostic connector. These tests will tell you if the HEI system is at fault or if the problem lies elsewhere. If the HEI system is faulty, or if the car does not have a diagnostic connector, proceed with the volt-ohmmeter troubleshooting instructions in the next section.

1. Using an oscilloscope, check the available voltage, following the manufacturer's recommended procedure, at two separate cylinders:

   a. If either is more than 25,000 volts, go to step 2.

   b. If both are less than 25,000 volts, go to step 3.

2. Check these items, and repair or replace as necessary:

   a. Defective spark plugs

   b. Damaged ignition cables

   c. Cracked or dirty distributor cap

   d. Cracked or dirty distributor rotor.

3. With the engine cranking or idling, connect a voltmeter positive (+) lead to the diagnostic connector terminal 6; connect the voltmeter negative (−) lead to terminal G, figure 12-12:

   a. If the voltage cranking is more than 7 volts, or the voltage idling is more than 9.6 volts, the HEI system is faulty.

   b. If the voltage cranking is less than 7 volts, or the voltage idling is less than 9.6 volts, go to step 4.

4. Move the voltmeter positive (+) lead to terminal 4, figure 12-13:

   a. If the voltage cranking is more than 7 volts, or the voltage idling is more than 9.6 volts, go to step 5.

   b. If the voltage cranking is less than 7 volts, or the voltage idling is less than 9.6 volts, go to step 6.

5. Inspect the wire between the HEI system and connector terminal 6:

   a. If the wire is damaged or grounded, repair it and repeat the test.

   b. If the wire is all right, the HEI system is at fault.

6. Move the voltmeter positive (+) lead to terminal 5, figure 12-14:

   a. If the voltage cranking is more than 7 volts, or the voltage idling is more than 9.6 volts, go to step 7.

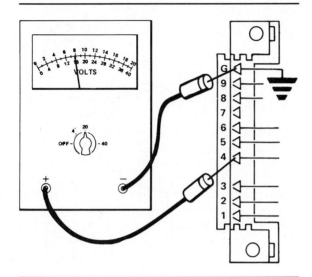

Figure 12-13. GM diagnostic connector test, pin 4. (Oldsmobile)

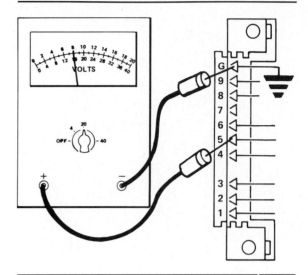

Figure 12-14. GM diagnostic connector test, pin 5. (Oldsmobile)

b. If the voltage cranking is less than 7 volts, or the voltage idling is less than 9.6 volts, replace the ignition switch.

7. Check the bulkhead connector for loose or corroded terminals, and repair or replace as necessary.

Delco-Remy HEI System Testing

Before making any circuit checks with test meters, be sure that all primary circuit connectors are installed properly and that spark plug cables are secure at the distributor and at the plugs. Also check that the four distributor cap latches are tight and the coil and coil cover screws are tight on applicable models.

1. Connect the voltmeter positive (+) lead to the BAT terminal at the distributor; connect the voltmeter negative (−) lead to ground.

2. Turn the ignition switch on and observe the voltmeter:

a. If the reading is zero, the circuit is open between the battery and the distributor and must be repaired.

b. If the reading is approximately battery voltage, go to step 3.

3. Using insulated pliers, hold one spark plug cable about ¼ inch from a clean area on the engine block and crank the engine:

a. If sparking occurs, go to step 4.

b. If no sparking occurs, test the ignition coil and the pickup coil as explained in the following paragraphs.

4. Check the spark plugs; clean and adjust or replace as necessary. If the engine still does not start, the problem is not in the ignition system.

HEI coil tests

To inspect the HEI system coil:

1. Remove the cap and coil from applicable model distributors.

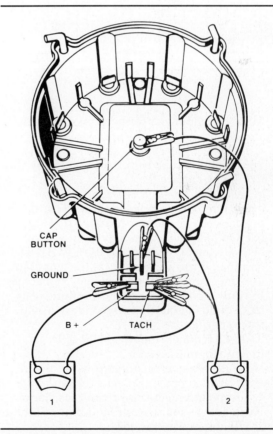

Figure 12-15. HEI integrally mounted coil test points.

2. Inspect the cap, coil, and rotor for signs of crossfiring and leakage.

3. Make the resistance tests described below for the appropriate system.

To test an HEI coil mounted in the distributor cap:

1. Refer to figure 12-15.

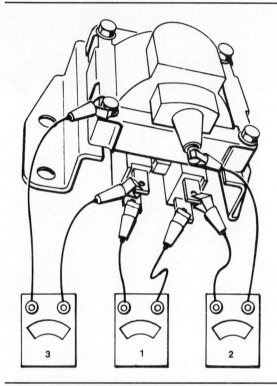

Figure 12-16. HEI remotely mounted coil test points.

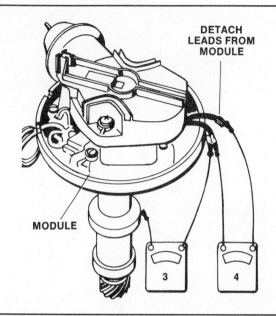

Figure 12-17. HEI pickup coil test points.

2. Make the ohmmeter connections shown in figure 12-15:

   a. Test point 1 measures primary resistance. The reading should be zero to 1 ohm (continuity). If not, replace the coil.

   b. Test point 2 measures secondary resistance. On coils made before May 1975, measure between cap button and the TACH terminal. On coils made after May 1975, measure between the cap button and the GROUND terminal. If you are not sure of the manufacture date, measure at both points. Replace the coil only if both readings show infinite resistance or do not match the secondary resistance specification.

To test a remotely mounted HEI coil:
1. Refer to figure 12-16.
2. Make the ohmmeter connections shown in figure 12-16:

   a. Test point 1 measures primary resistance. The reading should be zero to 1 ohm (continuity). If not, replace the coil.

   b. Test point 2 measures secondary resistance. The reading should be within the carmaker's specifications. If not, replace the coil.

   c. Test point 3 should show infinite resistance. If not, replace the coil.

HEI pickup coil test
1. Refer to figure 12-17.
2. Connect a vacuum source to the vacuum advance unit and check the vacuum advance operation. If the vacuum advance unit is faulty, replace it.
3. Remove the two pickup coil leads from the module inside the distributor.
4. Connect an ohmmeter to test point 1 and operate the vacuum advance unit through its full range.
5. Resistance between either pickup coil lead and the distributor housing must be infinite. If not, replace the pickup coil.
6. Connect the ohmmeter to test point 2. Operate the vacuum advance through its full range. The pickup coil resistance should remain within the manufacturer's specification; if not, replace the pickup coil.
7. If no faults are found in the ignition coil or the pickup coil but the ignition still will not operate, the fault is probably in the module. Install a new module and retest the system.

Motorcraft (Ford) Breakerless And Dura-Spark Ignition Testing

All Motorcraft breakerless ignition systems, except the EEC system, can be tested using the charts presented in figures 12-18, 12-19, 12-20, and 12-21. As we explained in the *Classroom Manual*, color coding is the key to tracing the primary circuit, figure 12-22. Color coding for all Ford systems is:
- White — voltage supply, cranking
- Red — voltage supply, running

1973-74

	Test Voltage Between	Should Be	If Not
Key On	Coil BAT terminal and ground. (Module connected, DEC terminal grounded)	4.9 to 7.9 volts	Low reading - Check primary wiring / High reading - Replace resistance wire
	Socket 3 (Red) and ground	Battery voltage ± 0.1 volt	Repair red wire, check connectors
	Socket 5 (Green) and ground	Battery voltage ± 0.1 volt	Check green wire to coil, check coil
Cranking	Socket 1 (White) and ground	8 to 12 volts	Repair white wire, check connectors
	Socket 5 (Green) and ground	8 to 12 volts	Check green wire to coil, check bypass circuit
	Socket 7 (Purple) and Socket 8 (Orange)	0.5 volt ac or any dc voltage	Replace magnetic pickup (stator)
	Test Resistance Between	**Should Be**	**If Not**
Key Off	Socket 7 (Purple) and Socket 8 (Orange)	400 to 800 ohms	Replace magnetic pickup (stator) or repair ground connection
	Socket 6 (Black) and ground	0 ohms	
	Socket 7 and ground	more than 70,000 ohms	
	Socket 8 and ground	more than 70,000 ohms	
	Socket 3 (Red) and coil tower	7,000 to 13,000 ohms	Replace coil
	Socket 5 (Green) and Socket 4 (Blue)	1.0 to 2.0 ohms	
	Socket 5 (Green) and ground	more than 4.0 ohms	Check for short at coil DEC terminal or in wiring to DEC terminal
	Socket 3 (Red) and Socket 4 (Blue)	1.0 to 2.0 ohms	Replace resistance wire

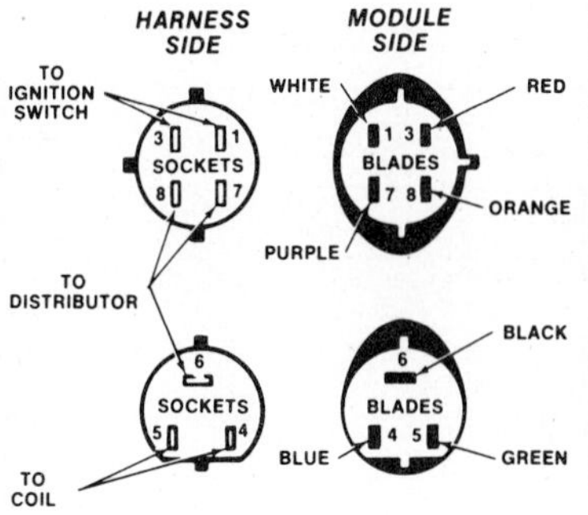

Figure 12-18. Test chart for 1973 through 1974 Ford solid-state ignition systems.

1975

	Test Voltage Between	Should Be	If Not
Key On	Coil BAT terminal and ground (Module connected, DEC terminal grounded)	4.9 to 7.9 volts	Low reading - Check primary wiring / High reading - Replace resistance wire
	Socket 4 (Red) and ground	Battery voltage ± 0.1 volt	Repair red wire, check connectors
	Socket 1 (Green) and ground	Battery voltage ± 0.1 volt	Check green wire to coil, check coil
Cranking	Socket 5 (White) and ground	8 to 12 volts	Repair white wire, check connectors
	Socket 6 (Blue) and ground (Jumper socket 1 to 8)	more than 6 volts	Check coil connections, check bypass circuit
	Socket 3 (Orange) and Socket 7 (Purple)	0.5 volt ac or any dc voltage	Replace magnetic pickup (stator)
	Test Resistance Between	**Should Be**	**If Not**
Key Off	Socket 3 (Orange) and Socket 7 (Purple)	400 to 800 ohms	Replace magnetic pickup (stator) or repair ground connection
	Socket 8 (Black) and ground	0 ohms	
	Socket 3 and ground	more than 70,000 ohms	
	Socket 7 and ground	more than 70,000 ohms	
	Socket 4 (Red) and coil tower	7,000 to 13,000 ohms	Replace coil
	Socket 1 (Green) and Socket 6 (Blue)	1.0 to 2.0 ohms	
	Socket 1 (Green) and ground	more than 4.0 ohms	Check for short at coil DEC terminal or in wiring to DEC terminal
	Socket 4 (Red) and Socket 6 (Blue)	1.0 to 2.0 ohms	Replace resistance wire

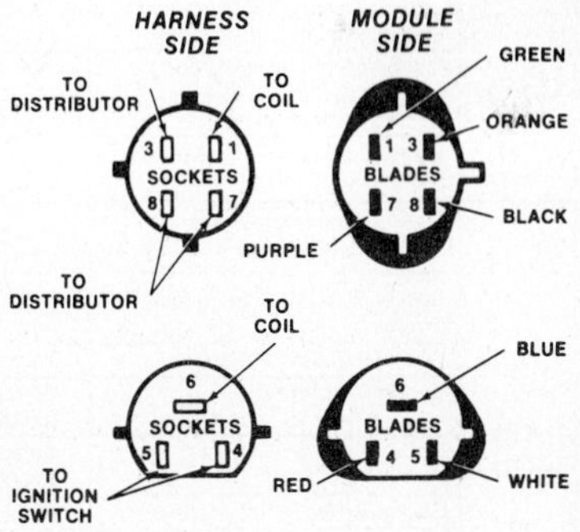

Figure 12-19. Test chart for 1975 Ford solid-state ignition systems.

• Orange and purple — distributor pickup coil signals
• Green — primary current, coil to module
• Black — ground
• Blue — system protection, 1973 through 1975 systems.

Before testing the primary circuit, make these preliminary checks:
1. Be sure that all connections are clean and secure at the coil, the control module, and the distributor. All connectors in the primary circuit

**1976 and 1977-78 Dura-Spark II
1978 American Motors**

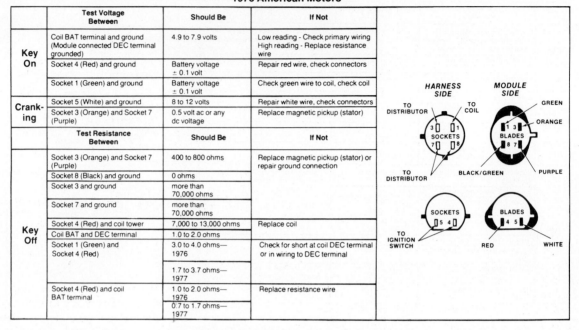

	Test Voltage Between	Should Be	If Not
Key On	Coil BAT terminal and ground (Module connected DEC terminal grounded)	4.9 to 7.9 volts	Low reading - Check primary wiring High reading - Replace resistance wire
	Socket 4 (Red) and ground	Battery voltage ± 0.1 volt	Repair red wire, check connectors
	Socket 1 (Green) and ground	Battery voltage ± 0.1 volt	Check green wire to coil, check coil
Crank-ing	Socket 5 (White) and ground	8 to 12 volts	Repair white wire, check connectors
	Socket 3 (Orange) and Socket 7 (Purple)	0.5 volt ac or any dc voltage	Replace magnetic pickup (stator)
	Test Resistance Between	**Should Be**	**If Not**
Key Off	Socket 3 (Orange) and Socket 7 (Purple)	400 to 800 ohms	Replace magnetic pickup (stator) or repair ground connection
	Socket 8 (Black) and ground	0 ohms	
	Socket 3 and ground	more than 70,000 ohms	
	Socket 7 and ground	more than 70,000 ohms	
	Socket 4 (Red) and coil tower	7,000 to 13,000 ohms	Replace coil
	Coil BAT and DEC terminal	1.0 to 2.0 ohms	
	Socket 1 (Green) and Socket 4 (Red)	3.0 to 4.0 ohms— 1976	Check for short at coil DEC terminal or in wiring to DEC terminal
		1.7 to 3.7 ohms— 1977	
	Socket 4 (Red) and coil BAT terminal	1.0 to 2.0 ohms— 1976	Replace resistance wire
		0.7 to 1.7 ohms— 1977	

Figure 12-20. Test chart for 1976 through 1978 Ford Dura-Spark II and 1978 AMC solid-state ignition systems.

1977-78 Dura-Spark I

	Test Voltage Between	Should be	If Not
Key On	Socket 4 (Red) and ground	Battery voltage ± 0.1 volt	Repair red wire, check connectors
	Socket 1 (Green) and ground	Battery voltage ± 0.1 volt	Check green wire to coil, check coil
Crank-ing	Socket 5 (White) and ground	8 to 12 volts	Repair white wire, check connectors
	Coil BAT terminal and ground (Jumper socket 1 to 8)— less than 30 seconds	more than 6 volts	Check coil connections, check bypass circuit
	Socket 3 (Orange) and Socket 7 (Purple)	0.5 volt ac or any dc voltage	Replace magnetic pickup (stator)
	Test Resistance Between	**Should Be**	**If Not**
Key Off	Socket 3 (Orange) and Socket 7 (Purple)	400 to 800 ohms	Replace magnetic pickup (stator) or repair ground connection
	Socket 8 (Black) and ground	0 ohms	
	Socket 3 and ground	more than 70,000 ohms	
	Socket 7 and ground	more than 70,000 ohms	
	Socket 4 (Red) and coil tower	7,000 to 13,000 ohms	Replace coil
	Coil BAT and DEC terminal	0.5 to 1.5 ohms	
	Socket 1 (Green) and ground (2-wire connector connected)	more than 4 ohms	Check for short at coil DEC terminal or in wiring to DEC terminal

Figure 12-21. Test chart for 1977 and 1978 Ford Dura-Spark I ignition systems.

should be lubricated and protected with a conductive lubricant such as Lubriplate D.S. or its equivalent.

2. Be sure that all secondary cables are secure at the coil, the distributor cap, and the spark plugs.

3. Test the coil output by removing the coil secondary cable from the distributor cap, holding it ¼ inch from a good ground, and cranking the engine. You should see a strong, regular spark.

4. Perform a spark intensity test by removing a spark plug cable, holding it near a ground, and watching for a spark while cranking the engine.

CAUTION: When making a spark intensity test, do not remove the following cables:

- V-8 engines — No. 1 or No. 8
- Inline 6-cylinder engines — No. 3 or No. 5

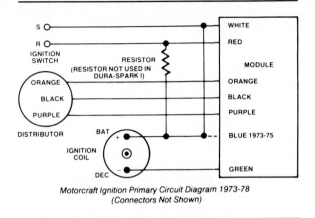

Figure 12-22. Circuit diagram of Ford solid-state ignition primary wiring.

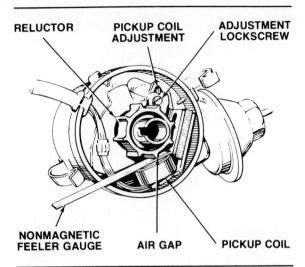

RELUCTOR PICKUP COIL ADJUSTMENT ADJUSTMENT LOCKSCREW

NONMAGNETIC FEELER GAUGE AIR GAP PICKUP COIL

Figure 12-23. Adjusting the reluctor-pickup coil air gap in a Chrysler solid-state distributor.

• V-6 engines — No. 1 or No. 4
• Inline 4-cylinder engines — No. 1 or No. 3
The magnetic pickup coil in the distributor is located directly under these plug terminals in the cap. Opening the circuit to these plugs may allow the rotor to crossfire to the pickup coil and damage the assembly.
5. Also inspect the distributor cap, rotor, coil tower, and ignition cables for cracks, moisture, or other damage.

If these preliminary checks do not locate the ignition problem, test the primary circuit as explained in the charts. All tests at the control module 2- or 3-wire and 4-wire connectors are made on the *harness side (socket side) of the connectors*. All tests at the distributor connector are made on the *distributor side (blade side) of the connector*.

Dura-Spark I stall-shutdown test
The Dura-Spark I module includes a special stall-shutdown feature that turns off the primary current if the engine stalls and keeps it off until the engine is restarted. A voltmeter can be used to check the operation of this part of the module circuitry:
1. Ensure that all ignition connectors are properly mated.
2. Connect the voltmeter positive (+) lead to the coil BAT terminal; connect the voltmeter negative (−) lead to ground.
3. Turn the ignition switch on.
4. The meter should momentarily deflect and then return to zero if the stall-shutdown feature is operating.
5. If the voltmeter continues to read between 4 and 12 volts, the module may be faulty. Before replacing the module, however, perform the troubleshooting tests shown on the Dura-Spark I chart. Also, repeat the stall-shutdown test with a known-good module to verify the correct circuit operation.

Prepare for the chart tests by disconnecting both connectors at the module and connecting the voltmeter negative (−) lead to a good engine ground.

Chrysler Electronic Ignition Testing

Pickup coil air gap adjustment
The air gap between the reluctor and the pole piece of a Chrysler solid-state distributor is adjustable and must be set to a minimum clearance when a new pickup unit is installed. For 1976 and 1977 Lean-Burn systems with two pickup coils, check and adjust each air gap in the same way.

During use, the air gap should not change. However, you should check it and adjust it if necessary before making the volt-ohmmeter troubleshooting tests that follow. A *nonmagnetic* feeler gauge must be used since a steel gauge will be attracted to the permanent magnet, making accurate gap setting impossible.

To check the air gap:
1. Refer to figure 12-23.
2. Align a tooth on the reluctor with the pickup coil.

CAUTION: Do not force the feeler gauges when checking the clearances.

3. Use two feeler gauges of the sizes listed below to check the air gap. The "Go" feeler gauge should just slide between the reluctor tooth and the pickup coil. The "No-Go" feeler gauge should not enter the gap.

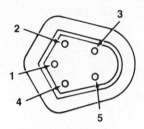

Figure 12-24. Cavity identification for Chrysler solid-state ignition system module connector.

	Go	No-Go
Lean-Burn		
1976 Start pickup	.008	.010
1976-77 Run pickup	.012	.014
All other Lean-Burn pickups	.006	.008
Standard		
1972-76	.008	.010
1977-later	.006	.008

To adjust the gap, if necessary:
1. Align one reluctor blade with the pickup coil.
2. Loosen the pickup coil adjustment lockscrew.
3. Place the "Go" feeler gauge between the reluctor blade and the pickup coil.
4. With a screwdriver blade inserted in the adjustment slot, shift the distributor plate so the feeler gauge contacts the reluctor blade and the pickup coil.
5. Tighten the lockscrew. No force should be required to remove the feeler gauge. The adjustment can be checked by using the specified "No-Go" feeler gauge. Do not force the "No-Go" feeler into the air gap.
6. Apply vacuum to the distributor vacuum advance unit and move the pickup plate through its full range of travel. Watch the pickup coil while applying vacuum to be sure it does not hit the reluctor. Recheck the air gap. If the pickup plate is loose, the distributor should be overhauled.

Before you begin the troubleshooting tests, check these items:
• Battery cranking voltage (9.5 volts or more)
• Primary and secondary wiring (no damage or loose connections)
• Check for spark at one or more spark plugs, engine cranking
• Check reluctor-pickup coil air gap.

CAUTION: Do not touch the switching transistor on the control module when the ignition switch is on. Enough voltage is present to produce a severe shock.

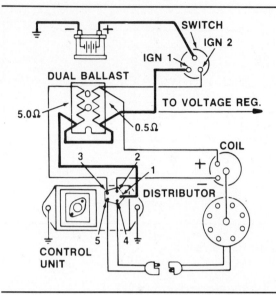

Figure 12-25. Circuit for Chrysler connector cavity number 1.

CAUTION: The ignition switch must be off whenever the connector is removed from, or connected to, the control module.

1. With the ignition switch off, remove the wiring harness connector from the ignition control module.
2. Turn the ignition switch on; connect the voltmeter negative (−) lead to ground.
3. Connect the voltmeter positive (+) lead to the number 1 connector cavity, figure 12-24. With the ignition switch on and all accessories off, the voltmeter reading should be within 1 volt of battery voltage:
   a. If the reading is within specifications, go to step 4.
   b. If the reading is not within specifications, trace and repair the circuit shown in figure 12-25.
4. Connect the voltmeter positive (+) lead to the number 2 connector cavity, figure 12-24. With the ignition switch on and all accessories off, the voltmeter reading should be within 1 volt of battery voltage.
   a. If the reading is within specifications, go to step 5.
   b. If the reading is not within specifications, trace and repair the circuit shown in figure 12-26.
5. Connect the voltmeter positive (+) lead to the number 3 connector cavity, figure 12-24. With the ignition switch on and all accessories off, the voltmeter reading should be within 1 volt of battery voltage:
   a. If the reading is within specifications, go to step 6.

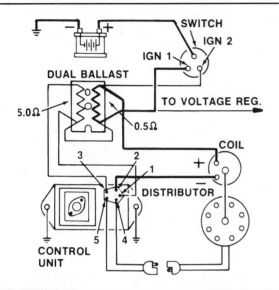

Figure 12-26. Circuit for Chrysler connector cavity number 2.

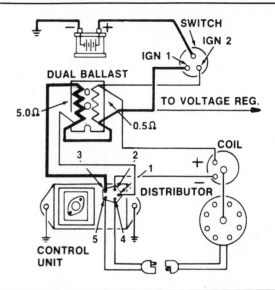

Figure 12-27. Circuit for Chrysler connector cavity number 3.

   b. If the reading is not within specifications, trace and repair the circuit shown in figure 12-27.

6. Turn the ignition switch off.

7. Connect the ohmmeter leads to the number 4 and number 5 connector cavities, figure 12-24. This measures the pickup coil resistance. Resistance should be 150 to 900 ohms:

   a. If the reading is within the manufacturer's specifications, go to step 9.

   b. If the reading is not within specifications, go to step 8.

8. If the pickup coil resistance is out of limits when measured at the connector cavities, disconnect the dual-lead connector at the distributor and check the resistance through the pickup coil leads at the distributor:

   a. If the reading is within specifications, trace and repair the wiring from the control unit to the distributor. Repeat the test at the connector cavities.

   b. If the reading is not within specifications, replace the pickup coil.

9. Connect one ohmmeter lead to ground and touch the other ohmmeter lead alternately to both sides of the pickup coil dual-lead connector at the distributor. The ohmmeter should show infinite resistance at both test points:

   a. If both test points show infinite resistance, go to step 10.

   b. If either test point shows less than infinite resistance the pickup coil is grounded and must be replaced.

10. Connect one ohmmeter lead to ground; connect the other ohmmeter lead to the control unit connector pin number 5, figure 12-28. The ohmmeter should show continuity (zero to 1 ohm) between ground and pin number 5:

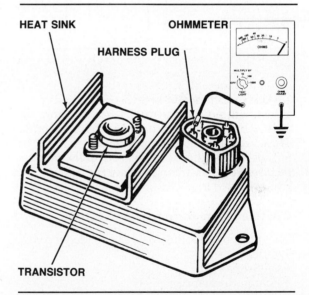

Figure 12-28. Checking the ground circuit at the Chrysler solid-state ignition module.

   a. If the ohmmeter reading is zero to 1 ohm, go to step 12.

   b. If the ohmmeter reading is more than 1 ohm, go to step 11.

11. Tighten the control module mounting bolts and repeat step 10:

   a. If the reading is still more than 1 ohm, replace the control module.

   b. If the reading now shows continuity, go to step 12.

12. With the ignition switch off, use the ohmmeter to measure the coil primary and secondary resistance. If either reading is out of the manufacturer's specifications, replace the coil.

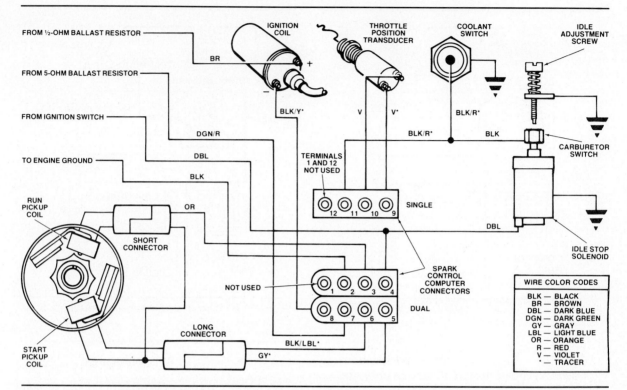

Figure 12-29. Schematic diagram of Chrysler's Lean-Burn system, 1976 and 1977 models (except 1977 318 V-8).

13. Use the ohmmeter to measure the resistance across both sides of the dual ballast resistor. The normal ballast resistor should be 0.5 to 0.6 ohm. The compensating resistor should be 4.75 to 5.75 ohms. If either reading is out of the manufacturer's specifications, replace the ballast resistor.

Chrysler Lean-Burn System Testing

These troubleshooting tests are divided into two symptom tests:
• Failure to start
• Poor performance.
In addition, each symptom test is presented first for the 1976 and 1977 Lean-Burn system (except for the 318 V-8 engine) and then for the 1977 318 V-8 and all 1978 Lean-Burn systems. Be sure to pick the correct symptom test and correct year for the particular car you are testing.

Before you begin the tests, check these items:
• Battery cranking voltage (9.5 volts or more)
• Primary and secondary wiring (no damage or loose connections)
• Check for a spark at one or more spark plug cables and at the coil secondary cable while the engine is cranking
• Check the reluctor-pickup coil air gap (both Start and Run pickups, 1976 and 1977 models)
• Check the coil primary and secondary winding resistances. Replace the coil if the readings are out of limits.

Failure-to-start tests

To test a failure to start on a 1976-77 Lean-Burn system (except the 1977 318 V-8):
1. Refer to figure 12-29.
2. Remove the connector from the coolant temperature sensor.
3. Place a thin insulator between the idle adjustment screw and the carburetor switch, figure 12-30.
4. Connect the voltmeter negative (−) lead to ground.
5. Turn the ignition switch on. Connect the voltmeter positive (+) lead to the carburetor switch terminal. Voltage between the switch terminal and ground should be between 5 and 10 volts:
   a. If the reading is within specifications, go to step 13.
   b. If the reading is more than 10 volts, go to step 6.
   c. If the reading is less than 5 volts, go to step 7.
6. Turn the ignition switch off and disconnect the dual connector from the bottom of the spark control computer. Use an ohmmeter to check for continuity between connector terminal number 2 and ground. If the circuit is open, repair it. Replace the connector and repeat step 5.
7. Turn the ignition switch off. Disconnect the dual connector from the bottom of the spark control computer.

8. Turn the ignition switch on. Connect the voltmeter positive (+) lead to connector terminal number 4. The voltmeter reading should be within 1 volt of battery voltage:

    a. If the reading is within specifications, go to step 10.

    b. If the reading is not within specifications, go to step 9.

9. Turn the ignition switch off. Trace and repair the wiring between terminal 4 and the ignition switch. Repeat step 8.

10. Turn the ignition switch off. Disconnect the single connector from the bottom of the spark control computer.

11. Use the ohmmeter to test for continuity between terminal 11 and the carburetor switch terminal. If there is no continuity, check and repair the wiring.

12. If there is continuity between terminal 11 and the carburetor switch terminal, test continuity between terminal 2 and ground:

    a. If there is no continuity, trace and repair the wiring.

    b. If there is continuity, replace the spark control computer.

13. Turn the ignition switch on. Connect the voltmeter positive (+) lead to terminal 7. The reading should be within 1 volt of battery voltage:

    a. If the reading is within specifications, go to step 15.

    b. If the reading is not within specifications, go to step 14.

14. Trace and repair the wiring between terminal 7 and ground. Repeat step 13:

    a. If the reading is within the specification, go to step 15.

    b. If the reading is not within specifications, check the resistance on the 5-ohm side of the ballast resistor. Replace the resistor if the reading is out of limits (4.75 to 5.75 ohms).

15. Connect the voltmeter positive (+) lead to terminal 8. The voltmeter reading should be within 1 volt of battery voltage:

    a. If the reading is within specifications, go to step 18.

    b. If the reading is not within specifications, go to step 16.

16. Trace and repair the wiring between terminal 8 and ground. Repeat step 15:

    a. If the reading is within specifications, go to step 18.

    b. If the reading is not within specifications, go to step 17.

17. Use the ohmmeter to check the resistance on the ½-ohm side of the ballast resistor. If the reading is out of limits (0.5 to 0.6 ohm), replace the resistor. Also check the resistance of the coil primary winding; if the reading is out of limits, replace the coil.

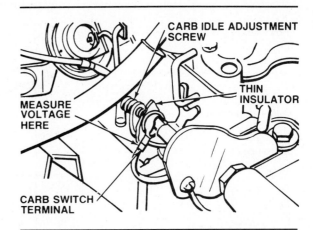

Figure 12-30. Checking voltage at the Lean-Burn carburetor switch terminal.

18. Turn the ignition switch off. Use the ohmmeter to measure the resistance between terminals 5 and 6 of the dual connector. This is the Start pickup coil resistance. Resistance should be 150 to 900 ohms:

    a. If the reading is within specifications, go to step 20.

    b. If the reading is not within specifications, go to step 19.

19. Disconnect the long dual-lead connector at the distributor. Check the Start pickup coil resistance here:

    a. If the reading is within specifications, check the wiring between the distributor and the spark control computer. Repeat step 18.

    b. If the reading is not within specifications, replace the Start pickup coil.

20. Connect one ohmmeter lead to ground. Connect the other lead alternately to both sides of the Start pickup coil lead at the distributor. The ohmmeter should read infinite resistance at both test points. If not, replace the Start pickup coil.

21. If the engine still fails to start after completing steps 1 through 20, replace the spark control computer.

    To test a failure to start on a 1977 318 V-8 and all 1978 and later V-8 Lean-Burn systems:

1. Refer to figure 12-31.

2. Remove the connector from the coolant temperature sensor.

3. Place a thin insulator between the idle adjustment screw and the carburetor switch, figure 12-30.

4. Connect the voltmeter negative (−) lead to ground.

5. Turn the ignition switch on; connect the voltmeter positive (+) lead to the carburetor

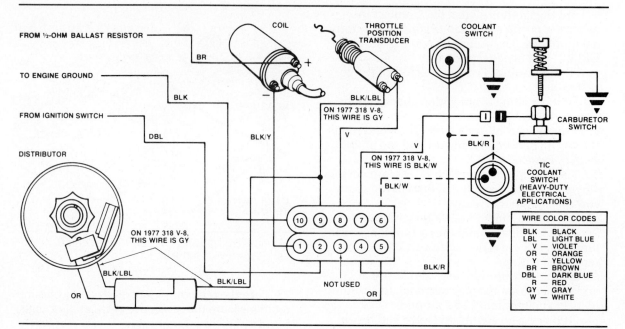

Figure 12-31. Schematic diagram for Chrysler's Lean-Burn system, 1977 318 V-8 and all 1978 models.

switch terminal. Voltage between the switch terminal and ground should be between 5 and 10 volts:

    a. If the reading is within specifications, go to step 13.

    b. If the reading is more than 10 volts, go to step 6.

    c. If the reading is less than 5 volts, go to step 7.

6. Turn the ignition switch off and disconnect the connector from the bottom of the spark control computer. Use an ohmmeter to check for continuity between connector terminal 10 and ground. If the circuit is open, repair it. Replace the connector and repeat step 5.

7. Turn the ignition switch off. Disconnect the connector from the bottom of the spark control computer.

8. Turn the ignition switch on. Connect the voltmeter positive (+) lead to connector terminal 2. The voltmeter reading should be within 1 volt of battery voltage:

    a. If the reading is within specifications, go to step 10.

    b. If the reading is not within specifications, go to step 9.

9. Turn the ignition switch off. Trace and repair the wiring between terminal 2 and the ignition switch. Repeat step 8.

10. Turn the ignition switch off. Disconnect the connector from the bottom of the spark control computer.

11. Use the ohmmeter to test for continuity between terminal 7 and the carburetor switch

terminal. If there is no continuity, check and repair the wiring.

12. If there is continuity between terminal 7 and the carburetor switch terminal, test continuity between terminal 10 and ground:

    a. If there is no continuity, trace and repair the wiring.

    b. If there is continuity, replace the spark control computer.

13. Turn the ignition switch on. Connect the voltmeter positive (+) lead to terminal 1. The reading should be within 1 volt of battery voltage:

    a. If the reading is within specifications, go to step 15.

    b. If the reading is not within specifications, go to step 14.

14. Trace and repair the wiring between terminal 1 and the ignition switch. Repeat step 13:

    a. If the reading is within specifications, go to step 15.

    b. If the reading is not within specifications, check the resistance of the 1/2-ohm ballast resistor. Replace the resistor if the reading is out of limits (0.5 to 0.6 ohm).

15. Turn the ignition switch off; use the ohmmeter to measure the resistance between terminals 5 and 9 of the connector. This is the pickup coil resistance. Resistance should be 150 to 900 ohms:

    a. If the reading is within specifications, go to step 17.

    b. If the reading is not within specifications, go to step 16.

16. Disconnect the dual-lead connector at the distributor; check the pickup coil resistance here:
 a. If the reading is within specifications, check the wiring between the distributor and the spark control computer. Repeat step 15.
 b. If the reading is not within specifications, replace the pickup coil.
17. Connect one ohmmeter lead to ground; connect the other lead alternately to both sides of the pickup coil lead at the distributor. The ohmmeter should read infinite resistance at both test points. If not, replace the pickup coil.
18. If the engine still fails to start after completing steps 1 through 17, replace the spark control computer.

Poor-performance tests, 1976-77
To test the Run pickup in a 1976-77 model (except the 1977 318 V-8):
1. Refer to figure 12-29.
2. Run the engine for 1½ minutes, then disconnect the Start pickup coil lead at the distributor:
 a. If the engine continues to run, the Run pickup is all right. Go to the starting advance test.
 b. If the engine stops, the Run pickup is faulty. Go to step 3.
3. Turn the ignition switch off. Reconnect the Start pickup lead at the distributor. Disconnect the dual connector from the spark control computer.
4. Connect the ohmmeter leads to connector terminals 3 and 5. This measures the Run pickup coil resistance. Resistance should be 150 to 900 ohms:
 a. If the reading is within specifications, go to step 6.
 b. If the reading is not within specifications, go to step 5.
5. Disconnect the short dual-lead connector from the distributor. Use the ohmmeter to measure the Run pickup coil resistance here:
 a. If the reading is within specifications, trace and repair the wiring between the distributor and the computer. Repeat step 4.
 b. If the reading is not within specifications, replace the Run pickup coil.
6. Connect one ohmmeter lead to ground. Connect the other lead alternately to both sides of the Run pickup coil lead at the distributor. The ohmmeter should show an open circuit at both test points. If not, replace the Run pickup coil.
7. If the engine still will not run correctly after completing steps 1 through 6, replace the spark control computer. You may want to complete the starting advance and throttle advance tests before replacing the computer.
 To test the starting advance on a 1976-77 model (except the 1977 318 V-8):

1. Connect an adjustable timing light to the engine.
CAUTION: Be sure that the service brakes are fully applied during steps 2 through 4.
2. Have an assistant start the engine, snap the throttle open and closed, and immediately place the gear shift lever in Drive.
3. Observe the timing marks immediately after the transmission is placed in Drive. Adjust the timing light meter so that the initial timing setting is seen at the timing marks. The timing light meter should show the specified initial advance.
4. Continue to observe the timing marks for 1 minute, while adjusting the timing light so that the initial timing setting is always seen at the timing marks. The initial advance should slowly reduce to the initial timing setting during this 1-minute period:
 a. If the timing did not advance or did not return to the initial timing setting, replace the spark control computer.
 b. If the timing advanced and retarded correctly, go to the throttle advance test.
 To test the throttle advance on a 1976-77 model (except the 1977 318 V-8):
1. Refer to figure 12-29.
2. With the ignition switch off, disconnect the single connector from the spark control computer.
3. Connect the ohmmeter leads to terminals 9 and 10. The reading should be between 50 and 90 ohms:
 a. If the reading is within specifications, go to step 5.
 b. If the reading is not within specifications, go to step 4.
4. Remove the connector from the throttle position transducer. Measure the resistance at the transducer terminals:
 a. If the reading is within the specifications, trace and repair the wiring between the transducer and the computer.
 b. If the reading is not within specifications, replace the throttle transducer.
5. When resistance is established within limits as measured at connector terminals 9 and 10, reconnect all wiring.
6. Turn the ignition switch on. Do not start the engine.
7. Connect the voltmeter positive (+) lead to one terminal of the throttle transducer. Connect the voltmeter negative (−) lead to ground. While observing the voltmeter, fully open and close the throttle linkage.
8. Repeat step 7 at the other transducer terminal. The voltmeter should show a 2-volt fluctuation at either terminal during throttle movement:

a. If the fluctuation occurs, the spark control computer may be faulty. Proceed with the rest of the test before replacing computer.

b. If the fluctuation does not occur, go to step 9.

9. Place the throttle linkage on the fast-idle cam and ground the carburetor switch with a jumper wire.

10. Disconnect the connector from the throttle transducer on the engine. Connect the connector to a known-good transducer.

11. Move the core of the test transducer completely in. Start the engine.

12. Wait 90 seconds and then move the core of the test transducer out about 1 inch.

13. Adjust the timing light so that the initial timing setting is seen at the timing marks. The timing light meter should show the specified amount of advance:

a. If the advance meets specifications, go to step 14.

b. If the advance does not meet specifications, replace the spark control computer.

14. Move the core back into the test transducer. The timing should return to the initial setting:

a. If the timing returns to the initial setting, go to step 15.

b. If the timing does not return to the initial setting, replace the spark control computer.

15. Return the timing light meter to zero. Observe the timing marks while an assistant moves the tranducer core in and out 5 or 6 times quickly. The timing should advance for about 1 second, then return to the initial setting:

a. If the timing does not advance and retard as specified, replace the spark control computer.

b. If the transducer failed the test in step 8, replace it.

Poor-performance tests, 1977-78 and later V-8

To test the starting advance on a 1977 318 V-8 or any 1978 and later V-8 system:

1. Connect an adjustable timing light to the engine.

2. Connect a jumper wire between the carburetor switch and a good ground.

3. Have an assistant start the engine with the vehicle in Park or Neutral.

4. Observe the timing marks immediately after the vehicle is started. Adjust the timing light so that the initial timing setting is seen at the marks. The timing light meter should show the specified initial advance.

5. Continue to observe the timing marks for 1 minute, adjusting the timing light so that the initial setting is seen at the marks. The initial advance should slowly reduce to the initial timing setting during this 1-minute period:

a. If the timing advanced and retarded correctly, go to the throttle advance test.

b. If the timing did not advance and retard

correctly, replace the spark control computer.

To test the throttle advance on a 1977 318 V-8 or any 1978 and later V-8 system:

1. Refer to figure 12-31.

2. With the ignition switch off, disconnect the connector from the spark control computer.

3. Connect the ohmmeter leads to terminals number 8 and number 9. The reading should be between 50 and 90 ohms:

a. If the reading is within specifications, go to step 5.

b. If the reading is not within specifications, go to step 4.

4. Remove the connector from the throttle position transducer. Measure the resistance at the transducer terminals:

a. If the reading is within specifications, trace and repair the wiring between the transducer and the computer.

b. If the reading is not within specifications, replace the throttle transducer.

5. When resistance is established within limits as measured at connector terminals 8 and 9, reconnect all wiring.

6. Turn the ignition switch on. Do not start the engine.

7. Place the throttle linkage on the fast-idle cam and ground the carburetor switch with a jumper wire.

8. Disconnect the connector from the throttle transducer on the engine. Connect the connector to a known-good transducer.

9. Move the core of the test transducer completely in. Start the engine.

10. Wait 90 seconds and then move the core of the test transducer out about 1 inch.

11. Adjust the timing light so that the initial timing setting is seen at the timing marks. The timing light meter should show the specified amount of advance:

a. If the advance meets specifications, go to step 12.

b. If the advance does not meet specifications, replace the spark control computer.

12. Move the core back into the test transducer. The timing should return to the initial setting:

a. If the timing returns to the initial setting, the system is working properly.

b. If the timing does not return to the initial setting, replace the spark control computer.

AMC-Prestolite Ignition Testing, 1975-77

The following test procedures can be used on the Prestolite ignition used by AMC from 1975 through 1977. To test a 1978 and later AMC ignition, refer to the Motorcraft troubleshooting procedures in this chapter. These troubleshooting tests call for a 12-volt test lamp using a No. 57 bulb. Before you begin the tests, check these items:

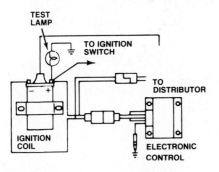

Figure 12-32. Testing available voltage at the AMC-Prestolite coil with a 12-volt test lamp.

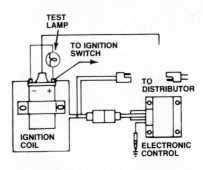

Figure 12-33. Testing the AMC-Prestolite control module with a 12-volt test lamp.

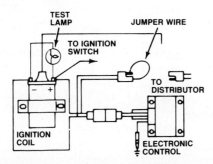

Figure 12-34. Testing the AMC-Prestolite control module with a jumper wire and a 12-volt test lamp.

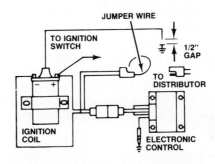

Figure 12-35. Testing the AMC-Prestolite ignition system with a jumper wire.

• Battery voltage during cranking (9.5 volts or more)
• Primary and secondary wiring (no loose or damaged connections)
• Check for a spark at one or more plugs while engine is cranking.
1. Remove the coil secondary cable from the center tower of the distributor cap. Hold it ½ inch from a clean engine block ground while cranking the engine:
　a. If sparking occurs, go to step 2.
　b. If no sparking occurs, go to step 3.
2. Check the spark plugs. Clean and adjust or replace as necessary. If the engine still does not start, then the problem is not in the ignition system.
3. Connect the test lamp leads to the coil positive (+) primary terminal and to ground, figure 12-32.
4. Turn the ignition switch to On and to Start. The test lamp should light in both positions:
　a. If the lamp lights in both positions, go to step 5.
　b. If the lamp does not light, trace and repair the circuit between the battery and the coil. Repeat the test.
5. With the ignition switch off, connect the test lamp leads to the coil positive (+) and negative

(−) primary terminals, figure 12-33.
6. Unplug the distributor sensor leads near the distributor. Turn the ignition switch on. The test lamp should light:
　a. If the lamp lights, go to step 8.
　b. If the lamp does not light, go to step 7.
7. Check the control module ground connection; repair as necessary. If the ground is all right and the test lamp does not light, replace the control module.
8. With the test lamp connected across the coil primary terminals, figure 12-34, connect a jumper wire between the terminals in the sensor lead coming from the control module:
　a. If the lamp goes off, go to step 9.
　b. If the lamp does not go off, replace the control module.
9. Remove the test lamp from the coil primary terminals.
10. Remove the coil secondary cable from the distributor center tower. Hold it ½ inch from a clean engine block ground.
11. Use the jumper wire to make and break connection between the terminals of the sensor lead coming from the control module, figure 12-35. A spark should occur at the coil cable gap each time that the sensor terminals are connected:
　a. If the sparks occur, go to step 14.
　b. If the sparks do not occur, go to step 12.
12. Turn the ignition switch off.

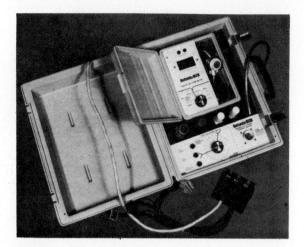

Figure 12-36. Ford's EEC special circuit tester. (Ford)

13. Use an ohmmeter to measure the coil primary and secondary winding resistances. If they do not meet specifications, replace the coil.
14. With the ignition switch off, use an ohmmeter to measure the sensor resistance at the distributor leads. Resistance should be 1.6 to 2.4 ohms:
   a. If the reading matches the specifications, go to step 15.
   b. If the reading does not meet the specifications, replace the sensor unit in the distributor.
15. Connect one ohmmeter lead to either sensor lead. Connect the other ohmmeter lead to ground. The ohmmeter should show an open circuit:
   a. If the ohmmeter does not show an open circuit, replace the sensor in the distributor.
   b. If the ohmmeter shows an open circuit, but the car still will not operate correctly, replace the control module.

SPECIAL SYSTEM TESTERS

Manufacturers often sell special test equipment that has been designed to test their particular product. In a few cases, the special tester is the only equipment that can be used to test a system. The following paragraphs describe the special testers that are built by Ford and Chrysler to test their products. Follow the manufacturer's instructions when using these testers.

Ford

At the time of its introduction, the Ford EEC system can be tested only with the Ford-built tester, marketed by Ford's Rotunda tool division. The tester has a digital-readout volt-ohmmeter and various connectors, figure 12-36, that plug into the EEC system parts. A test

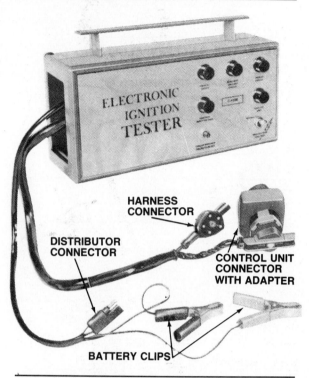

Figure 12-37. Chrysler's standard electronic ignition circuit tester. (Chrysler)

selector switch can be set to 24 different positions. Step-by-step instructions tell you what the meter readout signifies.

Chrysler

Chrysler manufactures a tester for use with their standard electronic ignition system, figure 12-37. The tester can be used for parts testing on and off the car. The battery clips are used only during off-car testing. Red and green lights on the tester face indicate if parts are faulty or all right.

The Lean-Burn system tester not only checks system parts, but also acts as a tachometer and digital-readout timing meter. The digital readout panels show engine rpm, timing setting, and a series of fault codes.

The last two digits of the spark control computer part number are set on numbered knobs to begin the analyzer operation, figure 12-38. The tester also has start, continue, stop, and power-on pushbuttons. The fault code readout shows a 2-digit code that can be matched to a list to determine what is wrong.

OSCILLOSCOPE TESTING

Oscilloscope connections for electronic ignition systems are the same as the connections in a breaker-point system. That is:

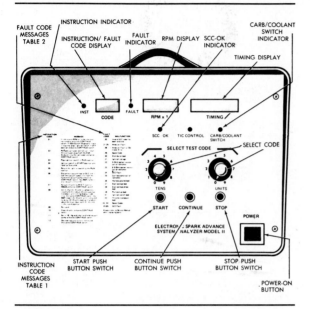

Figure 12-38. Chrysler's Lean-Burn circuit tester. (Chrysler)

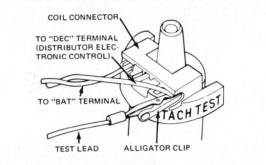

Figure 12-39. Using an adapter with the Ford solid-state coil for a coil primary connection. (Ford)

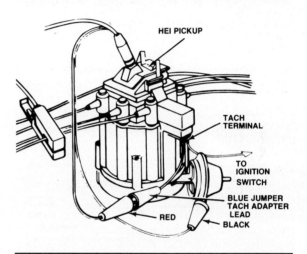

Figure 12-40. Attaching an inductive pickup adapter to the integrally mounted HEI coil. (Sun)

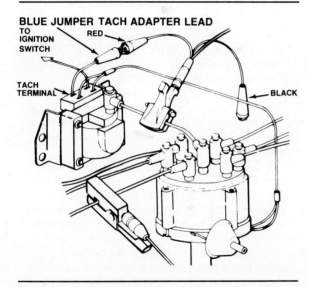

Figure 12-41. Using an adapter with the HEI coil for a coil primary connection. (Sun)

• One lead connects to the distributor (negative) coil terminal.
• One lead connects to the ignition cable between the coil and the distributor.
• One lead connects to the number 1 spark plug cable.
• One lead connects to an engine ground.
Some older scopes that do not have inductive pickups may not be able to test electronic systems. Check the tester manufacturer's recommendations and hookup instructions before beginning any tests.

Two systems require adapters for the coil connections. The Ford solid-state system's coil,

figure 12-39, has a multiple connector on top. An adapter must be inserted at the distributor primary terminal, as shown.

The Delco-Remy Unitized and HEI systems require one or two adapters:
• One adapter is an inductive pickup that fits over the integral coil, figure 12-40. This takes the place of a connection to the coil-to-distributor secondary lead.
• Another adapter plugs into the TACH terminal, providing the coil primary connection, figure 12-41.

The oscilloscope patterns made by solid-state systems vary slightly from manufacturer to manufacturer. Generally, the firing section of the trace can be interpreted in the same way as the firing section from a breaker-point trace, because the same things are happening in both systems. The differences between solid-state and breaker-point systems are most noticeable in the intermediate and dwell sections.

Because there is no ignition condenser, there are no condenser oscillations in the intermediate section. The oscillations are all caused

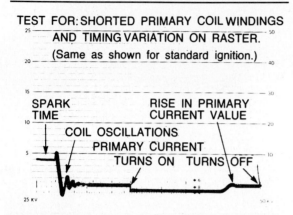

TEST FOR: SHORTED PRIMARY COIL WINDINGS
AND TIMING VARIATION ON RASTER.
(Same as shown for standard ignition.)

SPARK TIME

RISE IN PRIMARY CURRENT VALUE

COIL OSCILLATIONS

PRIMARY CURRENT

TURNS ON   TURNS OFF

25 KV

Figure 12-42. Normal Delco HEI primary superimposed pattern. This is also typical of the AMC-Prestolite and Motorcraft Dura-Spark I systems. (Marquette)

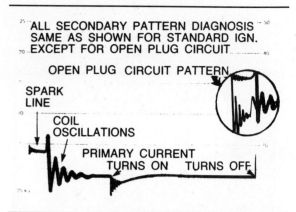

ALL SECONDARY PATTERN DIAGNOSIS SAME AS SHOWN FOR STANDARD IGN. EXCEPT FOR OPEN PLUG CIRCUIT

OPEN PLUG CIRCUIT PATTERN

SPARK LINE

COIL OSCILLATIONS

PRIMARY CURRENT
TURNS ON   TURNS OFF

Figure 12-43. Normal Delco HEI secondary superimposed pattern. This is also typical of the AMC-Prestolite and Motorcraft Dura-Spark I systems. (Marquette)

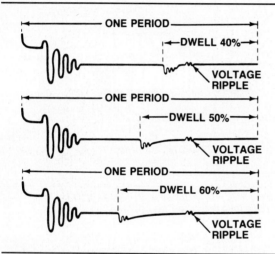

ONE PERIOD
DWELL 40%
VOLTAGE RIPPLE

ONE PERIOD
DWELL 50%
VOLTAGE RIPPLE

ONE PERIOD
DWELL 60%
VOLTAGE RIPPLE

Figure 12-44. The dwell period increases with engine speed in the Delco HEI and Motorcraft Dura-Spark I systems. (Delco-Remy)

Delco-Remy HEI Patterns

Figure 12-42 shows a typical primary super-imposed pattern for the Delco HEI system. Except for the absence of condenser oscillations at the beginning of the trace and the small current hump toward the end of the dwell period, it is quite similar to the pattern for a breaker-point ignition. This pattern is also typical of the AMC-Prestolite ignition and the Motorcraft Dura-Spark I system.

The primary pattern can be used to check for shorted coil primary windings and, in raster display, for timing variation and distributor wear.

Figure 12-43 shows a typical HEI secondary superimposed pattern. The oscillations that occur at the beginning of the dwell period are coil oscillations, not condenser oscillations. Again, the current hump appears in the dwell section of the pattern. This hump, which may also appear as a voltage ripple, is normal. It is caused by the control module circuitry and may occur in the middle or toward the end of the dwell period. This pattern is also typical of the AMC-Prestolite ignition and the Motorcraft Dura-Spark I system.

The dwell period for the HEI system (and the Motorcraft Dura-Spark I system) changes with engine speed, figure 12-44. At idle and low speed, the dwell period may be only 40 percent of the total pattern. As speed increases, the dwell period will increase to as much as 60 percent of the total pattern.

The secondary circuit patterns of the HEI system can be used to check for the same kinds of problems that can occur with a breaker-point ignition. An open plug circuit may appear as shown in figure 12-43.

The oscilloscope patterns for the HEI system used on the 1975-77 uneven-firing Buick V-6 are

by the coil, and can be used to judge coil condition. The beginning of the dwell section in a breaker-point system is the points-close signal. In a solid-state system, it is the transistor-on signal. In either case, it is a sharp drop to zero voltage. The length of the dwell section is not important in most solid-state systems, although some systems are designed to lengthen the dwell at higher engine speeds. During the dwell section, some systems have slight voltage ripples or voltage humps. These are normal, as we will see when we look at specific traces. At the end of dwell in a breaker-point system, the beginning of the firing line should be a sharp upward line. In a solid-state system, there may be a jagged upward-sloping line leading to the firing spike; again, this is normal in many systems.

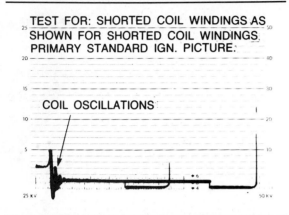

Figure 12-45. Normal primary superimposed HEI pattern for an uneven-firing V-6. (Marquette)

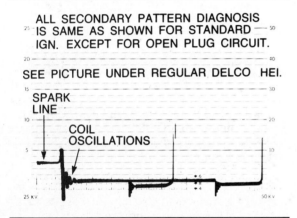

Figure 12-47. Normal secondary superimposed HEI pattern for an uneven-firing V-6. (Marquette)

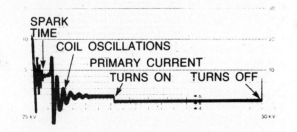

Figure 12-49. Normal Motorcraft breakerless and Dura-Spark II primary superimposed pattern. (Marquette)

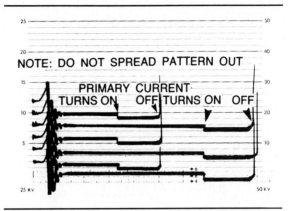

Figure 12-46. Normal primary raster HEI pattern for an uneven-firing V-6. (Marquette)

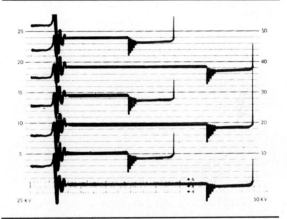

Figure 12-48. Normal secondary HEI raster pattern for an uneven-firing V-6. (Marquette)

shown in figures 12-45, 12-46, 12-47, and 12-48. The scope patterns for an uneven-firing Chevrolet V-6 are similar, but the intervals between alternate cylinders are not as great.

AMC-Prestolite Patterns

The Prestolite electronic ignition used by AMC from 1975 through 1977 has primary and secondary circuit patterns that are quite similar to the Delco HEI patterns, figures 12-42 and 12-43. Troubleshooting criteria are similar to those used for the HEI system.

Motorcraft Ignition Patterns

The Motorcraft breakerless (1973-76) and Dura-Spark II (1977 and later) systems produce primary and secondary patterns, figures 12-49 and 12-50, that are quite similar to breaker-point

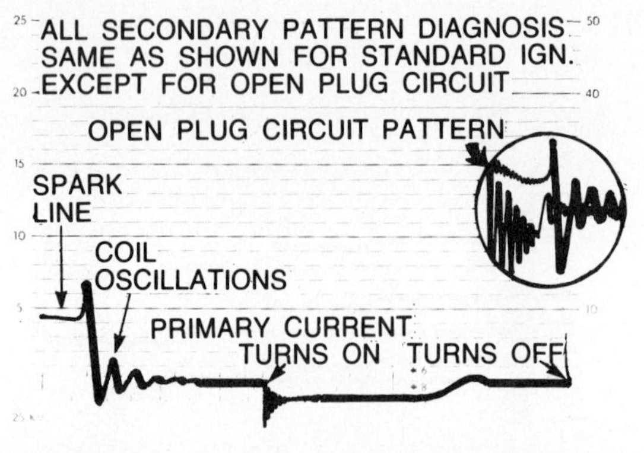

²⁵ ALL SECONDARY PATTERN DIAGNOSIS ⁵⁰
SAME AS SHOWN FOR STANDARD IGN.
²⁰ EXCEPT FOR OPEN PLUG CIRCUIT ___ ₄₀

OPEN PLUG CIRCUIT PATTERN

SPARK
LINE

COIL
OSCILLATIONS

PRIMARY CURRENT
TURNS ON   TURNS OFF

Figure 12-50. Normal Motorcraft breakerless and Dura-Spark II secondary superimposed pattern. (Marquette)

ALL SECONDARY PATTERN DIAGNOSIS
²⁵ SAME AS SHOWN FOR STANDARD IGN.⁵⁰
EXCEPT FOR OPEN PLUG CIRCUIT.
NOTE: SHORTED COIL TURNS WILL AFFECT ₄₀
OSCILLATIONS AS SHOWN IN STANDARD IGN.
PRIMARY PATTERN PICTURE.

SPARK   OPEN PLUG
LINE   CIRCUIT PATTERN

PRIMARY CURRENT TURNS ON

COIL   PRIMARY CURRENT
OSCILLATIONS   TURNS OFF

25 KV   50 KV

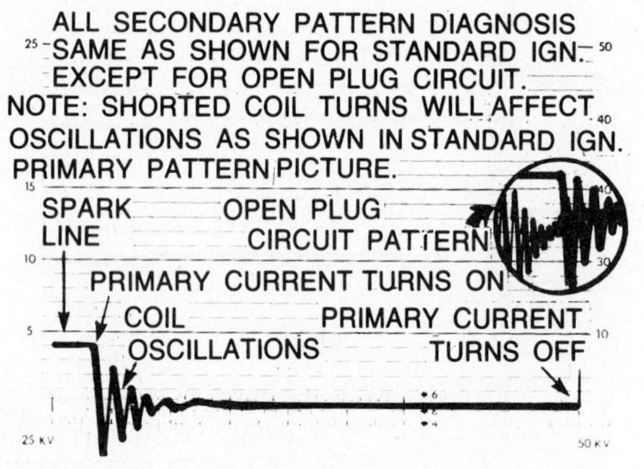

Figure 12-52. Normal Chrysler electronic ignition superimposed secondary pattern. (Marquette)

ignition patterns. The coil oscillations may not be as high as with a breaker-point system, but there should be more of them. The dwell period is longer and, on the secondary pattern, has a gentle curve that decreases toward the end of the dwell period.

The Motorcraft Dura-Spark I system produces primary and secondary patterns that are similar to the Delco HEI patterns, figures 12-42, 12-43, and 12-44. A current hump or voltage ripple will appear in the dwell section, and the dwell period increases with engine speed.

Chrysler Ignition Patterns

A primary superimposed pattern for the standard Chrysler electronic ignition is shown in figure 12-51. A secondary superimposed pattern is shown in figure 12-52. Notice that there

TEST FOR: TIMING VARIATION ON RASTER
(Same as shown for standard ignition.)

ALL OTHER TESTS: Use secondary patterns

SPARK
TIME
          PRIMARY CURRENT
          TURNS ON   TURNS OFF

Figure 12-51. Normal Chrysler electronic ignition superimposed primary pattern. (Marquette)

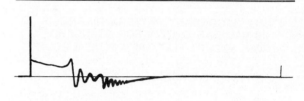

Figure 12-53. A normal secondary trace from Chrysler's Lean-Burn system. (Sun)

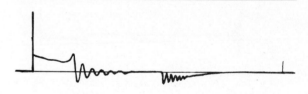

Figure 12-54. A secondary trace from a Chrysler Lean-Burn system running on the Start pickup coil. (Sun)

is no intermediate section as there is in other electronic ignition patterns. The transistor turns on as soon as the spark line stops. There is one set of coil oscillations, caused by the buildup of primary current flow in the coil. The dwell period is a long, straight line, with no humps or ripples.

The Lean-Burn system secondary pattern does have an intermediate section, figure 12-53. The transistor turns on after a short section of coil oscillations. Again, dwell is a long, flat line. When an early-model Lean-Burn engine is running on the Start pickup instead of the Run pickup, the intermediate section is much longer and the dwell period is shorter, figure 12-54.

13

Solid-State Distributor Overhaul

This chapter contains removal, disassembly, testing, repair, and installation instructions for Delco-Remy, Motorcraft, Chrysler, and AMC-Prestolite solid-state electronic distributors. Distributor removal, bench testing, adjustment, and installation procedures are presented as general instructions that will help you do these jobs on most domestic cars and light trucks. Overhaul procedures are presented as photographic sequences for four specific solid-state distributors.

DISTRIBUTOR REMOVAL

Removing a solid-state distributor is about the same as removing a breaker-point distributor. Therefore, review *all* of the instructions given in Chapter 11. In addition to those instructions, observe the following guidelines:
• Be sure the ignition switch is off when disconnecting or connecting any part of an electronic ignition circuit. You may want to disconnect the battery ground cable before removing the distributor. The exposed transistor on the Chrysler ignition module can produce a shock if you touch it when the ignition switch is on.
• Instead of disconnecting the primary lead at the coil, you should unplug the 2- or 3-wire connector at the distributor pickup coil.
• On Delco-Remy High Energy Ignition (HEI) systems, disconnect the ignition feed connector from the distributor cap. This is the outer connector on the cap terminal, figure 13-1. Use a small screwdriver to unlatch it carefully.
• On Delco-Remy HEI systems, remove the spark plug cables and retainers from the distributor cap before removing the distributor, figure 13-2. Remove the distributor, cap, and the coil together.
• On Delco-Remy Unitized ignition systems, remove the spark plug cable harness and the coil from the distributor cap, figure 13-3, before removing the distributor.
• Mark your reference points for distributor reinstallation in the same way that you would for a breaker-point distributor.
• Distributor clamp and holddown bolt arrangements for solid-state distributors are usually the same as they are for breaker-point distributors.
• Follow the same removal methods and precautions that you would for a breaker-point distributor.

SOLID-STATE ELECTRONIC DISTRIBUTOR OVERHAUL PROCEDURES

The following pages contain photographic procedures for the disassembly, overhaul, and reassembly of four common domestic solid-state distributors:

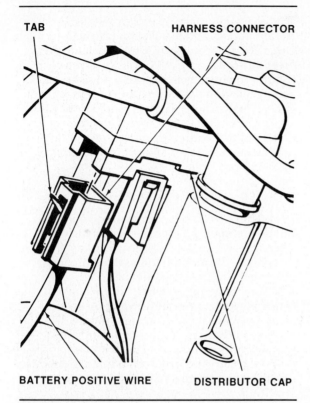

Figure 13-1. Delco-Remy HEI feed wire connection.

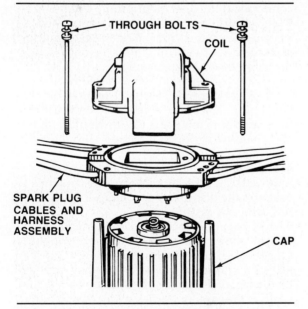

Figure 13-3. Remove the coil and the cable harness assembly from a Delco-Remy Unitized ignition before removing the distributor.

• Delco-Remy 8-cylinder HEI model — Used by GM since 1974.
• Motorcraft 6-cylinder Dura-Spark model — Used by Ford since 1977. This distributor is also typical of earlier Motorcraft breakerless distribu-

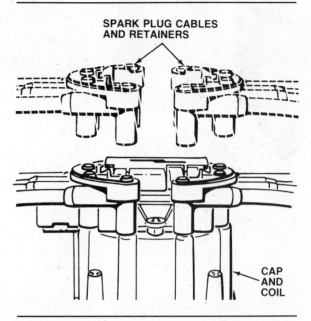

Figure 13-2. Remove cables and retainers from HEI cap before removing the complete distributor.

tors used by Ford since 1974 and by AMC since 1978.
• Chrysler 8-cylinder electronic model — Used by Chrysler since 1972. This distributor is also typical of Chrysler Lean-Burn distributors.
• AMC-Prestolite 6-cylinder model — Used by AMC from 1975 through 1977.

Chapter 16 of your *Classroom Manual* has information and more illustrations of these distributors. You may find it helpful to refer to the *Classroom Manual*, also, when overhauling a distributor.

The section of this chapter following the illustrated overhaul procedures contains test procedures using a distributor tester and other test equipment. The distributor tester is described fully in Chapter 11 of this *Shop Manual*. Many of the test procedures should be done before the distributor is taken apart, in order to find out how much overhaul is needed. Other service procedures using the tester are done after the distributor is reassembled. Many distributors can be overhauled while mounted in the tester.

Before overhauling a distributor, read and understand the test and adjustment procedures in the following section. The sequence of steps that you use for distributor test, overhaul, and adjustment should be organized for the best use of your shop facilities and time. If a distributor tester is unavailable, you can mount the distributor in a vise for overhaul. Use soft jaw covers on the vise or wrap the distributor housing in a cloth to prevent damage. Read the step-by-step procedure for the distributor that you will be overhauling before you begin work.

DELCO-REMY 8-CYLINDER HEI DISTRIBUTOR OVERHAUL PROCEDURE

1. Carefully pry module connector from cap terminal with screwdriver. Release four latches. Remove cap and coil from distributor. Inspect cap for signs of crossfiring.

2. Remove three screws from coil cover. Remove four coil mounting screws. Coil is grounded with lead to one screw and at other screw near screwdriver. Remove coil.

3. Remove rubber seal, carbon button, and spring. Replace seal if brittle. Button and spring are secondary coil lead. Replace if worn or spring is broken.

4. Remove rotor from weight base. Unplug pickup coil leads from module. Test pickup coil resistance with ohmmeter across these leads. If not within limits, replace coil.

5. Unplug connector from B+ and C terminals on module. Remove primary lead grommet from distributor housing.

6. Remove two screws securing module. Remove module. Note silicone grease on module and mounting base. Grease must be applied when module is installed.

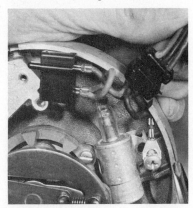

7. Remove screw securing RFI capacitor. Lift capacitor and primary lead harness from distributor.

8. Unplug capacitor from primary lead. Inspect and test capacitor and primary lead for wear, continuity, and short circuits. Replace worn or damaged parts.

9. Remove two springs and weight retainer. Remove weights. Mark springs, pins, and weights so that they are reinstalled in their original positions.

DELCO-REMY 8-CYLINDER HEI DISTRIBUTOR OVERHAUL PROCEDURE

10. Shaft must be removed to remove pickup coil and pole piece. Support gear as shown. Drive roll pin from gear and shaft.

11. Remove gear, shim, and tanged washer. Note positions for reassembly. Dimple toward bottom of gear must align with rotor tip when reassembled.

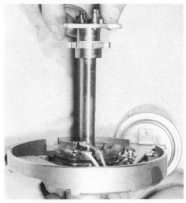

12. Remove shaft, trigger wheel, and weight base from distributor. Do not bump or nick bushings when removing shaft. Trigger wheel can be separated from shaft.

13. Remove three screws securing pole piece to pickup coil. Remove pole piece. Remove rubber gasket beneath pole piece.

14. Remove pickup coil from retainer. During operation, retainer is rotated by vacuum advance mechanism.

15. Carefully pry this small wave-washer from its slot. It holds pickup coil retainer to bushing at top of housing.

16. Remove pickup coil retainer from vacuum advance link. Remove two screws securing vacuum unit. Remove vacuum unit.

17. Lubricate or replace felt washer beneath pickup coil retainer. Apply silicone grease to module mounting base.

18. Install vacuum advance unit. Install pickup coil retainer and its retaining ring. Install pickup coil and gasket.

DELCO-REMY 8-CYLINDER HEI DISTRIBUTOR OVERHAUL PROCEDURE

19. Assemble trigger wheel and weight base to distributor shaft.

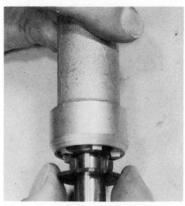

20. Insert shaft into housing. Be careful not to hit bushings. Assemble tanged washer, shim, and gear on shaft.

21. To be sure gear is correctly installed, place rotor on top of weight base. Be sure dimple on gear aligns with rotor tip. Drive roll pin through gear and shaft.

22. Install weights in their original positions on weight base. Place retainer over pins and shaft. Install springs in their original positions.

23. Plug capacitor into primary lead harness. Attach capacitor to distributor with screw. Insert harness grommet into slot in housing.

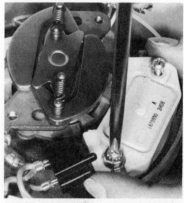

24. Place module on mounting base and secure with two screws. Attach primary connector to one end, pickup coil leads to other end.

25. Thoroughly inspect rotor for signs of carbon tracking and crossfiring. Check the underside for signs of burn-through. Replace rotor if it has any of these signs.

26. Be sure carbon button, spring, and rubber seal are in good condition and correctly installed. Install coil in cap.

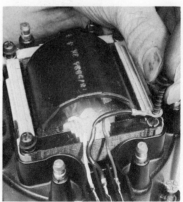

27. Install four coil mounting screws. Install coil cover. Install cap on distributor and secure four holddown latches.

MOTORCRAFT DURA-SPARK DISTRIBUTOR OVERHAUL PROCEDURE

1. Beneath cap, adapter ring, and rotor, Dura-Spark distributor is typical of earlier Motorcraft solid-state units. Remove cap.

2. Remove rotor before removing adapter ring. Early Dura-Spark adapter rings are secured by second pair of clips.

3. Remove two screws and remove adapter ring from housing. This is late-model 6-cylinder unit.

4. Using two screwdrivers, carefully pry trigger wheel (armature) from sleeve.

5. When removing armature, note small roll pin that secures armature to sleeve. Do not lose it.

6. Remove two screws securing pickup coil (stator) and pickup plate to housing. Stator and plate are serviced as assembly.

7. Disengage stator pin from vacuum link. Test stator resistance with ohmmeter. It should be 400 to 800 ohms. Also check for ground to plate. Replace if defective.

8. Remove two screws securing vacuum advance unit. Remove vacuum unit from distributor.

9. Mark advance weights, springs, and pins for correct reassembly. Unhook springs from anchor tabs and pins.

MOTORCRAFT DURA-SPARK DISTRIBUTOR OVERHAUL PROCEDURE

10. Remove felt wick and retaining clip from sleeve. Lift sleeve off shaft and weight base.

11. Tanged washer may stay on weight base or come off with sleeve. Be sure it is installed before reassembly. Lubricate shaft and weight pivot pins sparingly.

12. Install sleeve on shaft. Rubber stop (near screwdriver) must be in place and in good condition or centrifugal advance will be excessive.

13. Reinstall retaining clip and wick in sleeve. Lubricate wick with 2 or 3 drops of lightweight oil.

14. Lubricate spring ends and pins *sparingly* with penetrating oil. Reinstall springs in their original positions marked at disassembly.

15. Install plate and stator assembly on housing. Engage stator pin with vacuum link. Press stator lead grommet into cutout in housing. Tab on grommet is system ground.

16. Attach vacuum unit with two hex-head screws. Secure stator base plate to housing with two screws.

17. Align roll pin slot in armature with slot in sleeve and press armature down onto sleeve.

18. Insert pin into place in armature and sleeve. Tap in with small punch and hammer. Reinstall rotor, adapter, and cap.

CHRYSLER 8-CYLINDER ELECTRONIC DISTRIBUTOR OVERHAUL PROCEDURE

1. Remove cap and rotor. Lean-Burn distributor is similar to this Chrysler conventional electronic distributor, except Lean-Burn has no advance mechanisms.

2. Using two screwdrivers, carefully pry reluctor (trigger wheel) and keeper pin off sleeve.

3. Note two slots inside reluctor and one slot at base of sleeve. Pin must be in reluctor slot by arrow that corresponds to direction of rotation.

4. Pull pickup coil lead grommet from slot in distributor housing. Remove screw securing pickup coil to pickup plate. Remove pickup coil.

5. Remove two screws securing vacuum advance unit to distributor. Disengage vacuum link from pickup plate. Remove vacuum unit.

6. Remove two screws securing pickup plate assembly. Remove plate assembly and inspect pivot point for looseness and wear.

7. Remove felt wick and sleeve retainer from center of sleeve. Early Lean-Burn distributors have advance weights; later ones do not.

8. Remove sleeve from distributor shaft. Inspect for wear or damage.

9. Disengage springs from anchor pins. Remove weights and springs from pivot pins. Mark springs, pins, and weights for reinstallation in original positions.

CHRYSLER 8-CYLINDER ELECTRONIC DISTRIBUTOR OVERHAUL PROCEDURE

10. Clean and reinstall weights and springs. Lubricate pins lightly with distributor lubricant. Remove nylon bushing from shaft. Inspect for wear; replace if worn.

11. Lightly lubricate shaft. Then install sleeve on shaft. Install sleeve retainer and felt wick. Apply 2 or 3 drops of lightweight oil to wick.

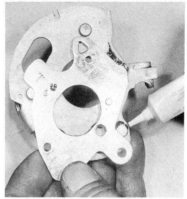

12. Replace pickup plate if pivot is worn. Loose pivot may cause pickup coil to hit reluctor. Lubricate pivot before installing plate.

13. Slide plate assembly into distributor and secure with two screws.

14. Engage vacuum link with movable plate. Secure vacuum unit to distributor with two screws.

15. Test pickup coil resistance with ohmmeter. It should be from 150 to 900 ohms. Install pickup coil and screw. Press lead grommet into slot.

16. On V-8 distributors, place pin in reluctor slot at arrow that matches rotation. If reluctor is installed wrong, timing will be off.

17. Align pin with slot in sleeve and press reluctor carefully into place.

18. Align reluctor tooth with pickup coil. Adjust air gap with nonmagnetic feeler gauge. Loosen screw and move pickup coil with screwdriver in slot. Tighten screw.

AMC-PRESTOLITE ELECTRONIC DISTRIBUTOR OVERHAUL PROCEDURE

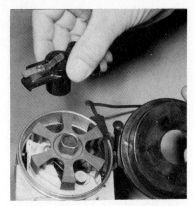

1. Remove rotor and dust shield. Test pickup coil (sensor) resistance with ohmmeter across leads. It should be 1.6 to 2.4 ohms at 77° to 200° F.

2. Remove trigger wheel with battery cable puller. Place washer between top of shaft and puller screw to prevent damage. Be sure jaws grip inner shoulder of trigger wheel.

3. Carefully lift sensor spring up and out of its guide slot to remove tension. Do not let it spring loose.

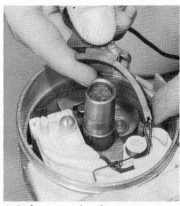

4. Lift sensor lead gormmet from slot in housing. Unwrap sensor twin leads from around spring pivot pin.

5. Original equipment screw has special head. It can be removed only with needlenose pliers. Replacement sensor has screw with slotted head.

6. Small guide will separate from sensor when screw is removed. Foot of guide fits into slot of bracket.

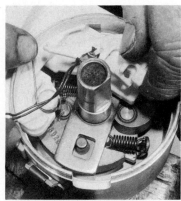

7. Sensor is connected to vacuum advance. Pointed end must fit into slot and under bracket at side of distributor. Check this at reassembly.

8. If further disassembly is required, remove vacuum advance unit. If only sensor replacement is required, go to step 18.

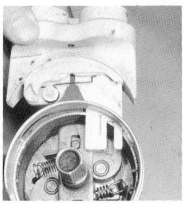

9. Carefully remove vacuum advance unit and sensor bracket from distributor as shown.

AMC-PRESTOLITE ELECTRONIC DISTRIBUTOR OVERHAUL PROCEDURE

10. Remove felt wick and retainer from sleeve. Notice that centrifugal advance is similar to Chrysler and Prestolite breaker-point distributors.

11. Mark sleeve in relation to weights and remove from shaft. Inspect for wear.

12. Unhook weight springs from tabs on base plate. Mark springs and tabs so that springs are reinstalled in original positions.

13. Remove both advance weights. Mark weights and pins so that all parts are reinstalled in their original positions. Inspect for wear.

14. Clean inside of distributor. Apply distributor lubricant sparingly to shaft and pins.

15. Install weights and springs in their original positions. Be sure weights move freely. Lubricate pins sparingly with penetrating oil.

16. Install sleeve, sleeve retainer, and felt wick. Apply 2 or 3 drops of lightweight oil to wick.

17. Reinstall vacuum advance unit. Secure with hex-head screw.

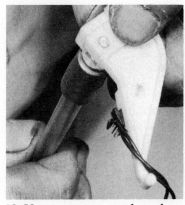

18. Use new screw and washer to assemble sensor and sensor guide. Install screw loosely; do not let it stick through bottom of sensor.

AMC-PRESTOLITE ELECTRONIC DISTRIBUTOR OVERHAUL PROCEDURE

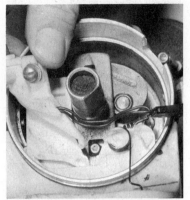

19. Install sensor and guide assembly. Guide foot must be in slot on bracket. Sensor prong must engage vacuum advance.

20. Thread sensor leads behind spring pivot. Press grommet into slot in housing.

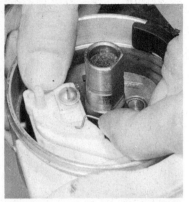

21. Engage sensor screw with bracket. Turn in just enough to hold sensor and guide in place. Install sensor spring into its guide slot.

22. Place adjustment gauge over sensor and shaft sleeve. Adjust sensor position until gauge can be removed and replaced without sensor movement.

23. Tighten sensor retaining screw. Align trigger wheel with sleeve and place over sleeve.

24. Gently tap trigger wheel onto sleeve with 13/16″ socket and hammer. There must be a 0.050″ clearance between legs and base of sensor.

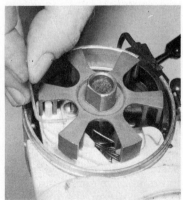

25. Use 0.050″ diameter wire (supplied with sensor) to measure clearance between trigger wheel legs and sensor base. Check all legs.

26. Rotate shaft by hand and check side clearance between sensor and trigger wheel legs. It should be uniform on all legs, as shown here.

27. Replace dust shield and rotor. Overhaul is complete.

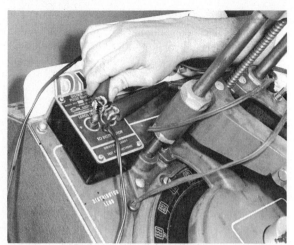

Figure 13-4. Connect distributor tester leads to amplifier module according to equipment maker's instructions.

SOLID-STATE DISTRIBUTOR TEST AND ADJUSTMENT

The distributor tester described in Chapter 11 can be used to test the centrifugal and vacuum advance mechanisms of a solid-state distributor, as well as to check for shaft and bushing wear. Because solid-state distributors have no breaker points, there are no breaker-point tests and adjustments.

Install a solid-state distributor in the tester in the same way that you would a breaker-point distributor. The electrical connections for a solid-state distributor, however, are different from those for a breaker-point distributor. The pickup coil produces a small trigger voltage, which is not strong enough to drive the circuitry of many testers. An additional electronic amplifier module is required for solid-state distributor testing. Many late-model testers have this additional capability built in. An accessory amplifier can be attached to older testers to adapt them for solid-state testing.

Follow the test equipment manufacturer's instructions for circuit connections. Figure 13-4 shows the tester leads connected to an accessory amplifier. The amplifier leads are then connected to the distributor pickup coil leads, figure 13-5. Many late-model testers also have the capability to check out the ignition system control module. They can do about the same tests that are described for on-the-car testing in Chapter 12.

Inspect the distributor before testing as described in Chapter 11.

Bushing and Shaft Wear Tests

Test a solid-state distributor for bushing and shaft wear and alignment as described for a breaker-point distributor in Chapter 11.

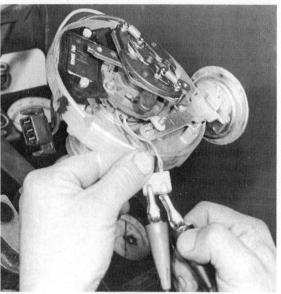

Figure 13-5. Connect amplifier module leads to distributor pickup coil leads.

Centrifugal and Vacuum Advance Test and Adjustment

Except for those used with electronic timing control systems, solid-state distributors have the same kinds of spark advance mechanisms that breaker-point distributors have. They are tested and adjusted in the same way.

You will need the manufacturer's specifications, or advance curve, for the distributor you are testing. Specifications are listed by distributor part number. You will find the part number on the side of the distributor housing.

In a Delco-Remy HEI distributor, the vacuum advance rotates the pickup coil retainer. Connect the tester vacuum line to the vacuum unit and test the vacuum advance as you would for a breaker-point distributor.

Pickup Coil Tests

Many distributor testers have an ohmmeter for testing the pickup coil resistance. Test the resistance by touching the ohmmeter leads to the pickup coil leads. Resistance must be within the manufacturer's specifications. If it is not, replace the pickup coil.

Test for a grounded pickup coil by touching one ohmmeter lead to the distributor housing and the other alternately to each pickup coil lead. The ohmmeter must show infinite resistance. If the ohmmeter shows any continuity, the pickup coil is grounded and must be replaced.

Solid-State Distributor Cleaning and Lubrication

Solid-state distributors should be cleaned and lubricated in the same way as breaker-point distributors. Follow the instructions given in Chapter 11. Because there are no breaker points, no cam or rubbing block lubrication is required. Solid-state distributors do not have provisions to lubricate the shaft and bushings.

Solid-state disibutors should be thoroughly cleaned, and *all* solvent residue must be completely removed. Be extremely careful not to overlubricate any of the locations within a solid-state distributor. Any dirt, solvent residue, or lubricant that gets on a low-voltage connection can disrupt ignition operation.

Many solid-state distributors require that a silicone lubricant be applied to the pickup coil connections or to other specific locations within the distributor. The Delco-Remy HEI distributor requires a silicone lubricant between the module and its mounting base. The Motorcraft Dura-Spark distributor requires a silicone lubricant on the rotor tip and the cap electrodes. Follow the carmaker's specific directions for special solid-state distributor lubrication.

DISTRIBUTOR INSTALLATION

Follow these general instructions for distributor installation:
1. Be sure the ignition switch is off. You may have disconnected the battery ground cable when you removed the distributor.
2. Rotate the distributor shaft so that the rotor is in line with the mark that you made on the housing when you removed it.
3. Align the distributor housing with your reference point on the engine.
4. Insert the distributor into the engine. Be sure the sealing ring is in place on Chrysler distributors.
5. Engage the distributor drive with the camshaft and oil pump drive. If the distributor has a helical drive gear, the rotor may rotate out of position when the distributor is inserted in the engine. If this happens, note the amount that the rotor moves. Then raise the distributor up and move the rotor backwards the same amount (usually about 15 to 20 degrees). Then lower the distributor back into place.
6. Be sure the distributor is fully seated in the engine and engaged with the camshaft and oil pump drive. You may have to wiggle the shaft slightly to engage the oil pump or bump the engine with the starter to turn the distributor slightly for shaft engagement.
7. Install the distributor clamp and holddown bolt.

8. Connect the pickup coil lead and any other wires that were disconnected at removal.
9. Connect the vacuum line to the vacuum advance unit.
10. Place the cap and the attached spark plug wires on the distributor and secure it with the clips or holddown screws.
11. Connect the battery ground cable if it was disconnected.

STATIC TIMING

If the engine was not cranked while the distributor was out, it should start and run if the distributor is reinstalled correctly. Initial timing should then be checked and adjusted with a timing light. If the engine was cranked while the distributor was out, you will have to reestablish the basic timing position. This is called static timing. Proceed as follows:
1. Bring the number 1 piston to top dead center on the compression stroke. If the engine is timed on any cylinder other than number 1, use that cylinder for static timing.
2. Align the timing marks at the specified initial timing position.
3. Install the distributor so that the rotor points at the number 1 spark plug terminal in the cap. Make a reference line on the distributor housing to align the rotor with the cap off.
4. Loosen the distributor holddown clamp and bolt.
5. Rotate the distributor body so that the pickup coil pole piece is exactly aligned with one trigger wheel tooth.
6. Tighten the holddown clamp and bolt.

The distributor should now be timed closely enough for the engine to start and run. If it does not, you can doublecheck the static timing as follows.
1. Be sure that all ignition circuit connections are clean and tight. Turn the ignition switch off.
2. With the distributor rotor and cap in place and all spark plug cables connected, loosen the distributor holddown clamp and bolt.
3. Rotate the distributor housing slightly in the direction of rotor rotation.
4. Connect a timing light to the number 1 spark plug cable. An inductive pickup timing light is preferred.
5. Turn the ignition switch on.
6. Slowly rotate the distributor housing opposite to the direction of rotor rotation until the timing light flashes.
7. Turn the ignition switch off, tighten the holddown clamp and bolt, and disconnect the timing light.

Always check and adjust the initial timing with a timing light at the specified engine speed after the engine is started.

PART FIVE

Lighting and Accessory System Service

14

Lighting System Service

Replacing bulbs is probably the most common lighting system service you'll ever do. Other system services include headlamp aiming and circuit troubleshooting. The following paragraphs give you instructions for replacing and aiming headlamps and replacing other types of bulbs. The rest of the chapter explains circuit troubleshooting. General procedures are given, as well as steps for finding specific problems in the lighting system.

HEADLAMP REPLACEMENT AND AIMING

Headlamps have a great effect on safe driving. If a lamp is burned out or misaimed, the driver's range of vision decreases. A poorly aimed lamp can also momentarily blind pedestrians and other drivers.

Headlamp Replacement

Because sealed-beam headlamp designs are all about the same, the procedures for removal and replacement are similar for all cars:
1. Be sure the headlamp switch is off.
2. Remove any decorative bezel or part of the radiator grille that hides the headlamp mounting.

CAUTION: Do not mistake the headlamp aiming screws for the retaining screws.

3. Loosen the one to six retaining screws.
4. Remove the retaining ring:
   a. For round lamps, turn the ring slightly until it is free of the retaining screws, figure 14-1.
   b. For rectangular lamps, remove the retaining screws, figure 14-2.
5. Pull the headlamp out of its housing and remove the connector from its prongs.
6. Examine the connector for corrosion or damage. Clean or replace if necessary.
7. Plug the new lamp into the connector. Be sure you are installing the correct type of sealed-beam unit for the system.
8. Place the new lamp in the housing and re-install the retaining ring:
   a. For round lamps, push the ring in and turn it slightly until the heads of the retaining screws hold it.
   b. For rectangular lamps, install the retaining screws.
9. Turn the headlamp switch on and check the new lamp's operation.
10. Reinstall any trim or grille parts.
11. Check the aim of all the headlamps. Adjust if necessary, as explained in the following paragraphs.

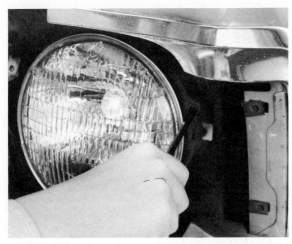

Figure 14-1. Removing the retaining ring from a round headlamp.

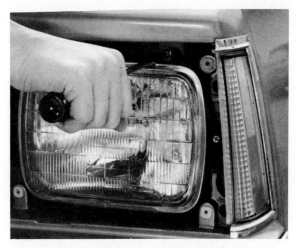

Figure 14-2. Removing the retaining ring from a rectangular headlamp.

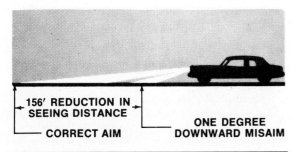

Figure 14-3. A headlamp that is misaimed only one degree downward can reduce the driver's seeing distance by more than 150 feet.

Headlamp Aiming

Three different methods can be used to aim headlamps:
- Aiming screens
- Mechanical aimers
- Photoelectric aimers.

Generally, aiming screens are the least accurate method. Regardless of which method is used, you should prepare the car as follows before aiming the lamps:

1. Remove mud and ice from under the fenders.
2. Inflate the tires to their normal operating pressures.
3. Clean lamp lenses and replace any burned-out units.
4. Place the correct weight load in the car. For example, the manufacturer may specify a full tank of gas and a driver and passenger in the front seat.
5. Use a darkening cloth to cover Type 2 or 2A lamps when aiming Type 1 or 1A lamps in a 4-lamp system with photoelectric and screen aiming methods.
6. Cover any photocell headlamp controls to stop their operation during aiming with a

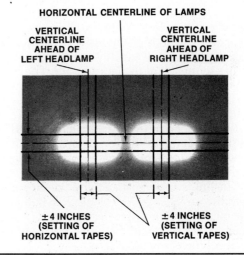

Figure 14-4. The headlamp high beams should show this pattern on the aiming screen.

photoelectric aimer or aiming screen.

Aim limits

Headlamps that are slightly misaimed can greatly reduce a driver's seeing distance, figure 14-3 For this reason, headlamp aiming limits have been established by state and local authorities. The limits may vary from area to area, but the following limits are generally accepted:
- High-beam — Refer to figure 14-4. The center of the lamp high-intensity zone should be horizontally within 4 inches to the right or 4 inches to the left of the lamp center. The center of the lamp high-intensity zone should be vertically within 4 inches above or 4 inches below the horizontal centerline.

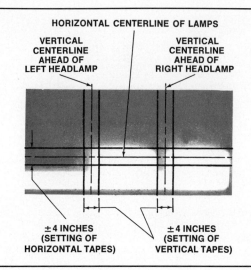

Figure 14-5. The headlamp low beams should show this pattern on the aiming screen.

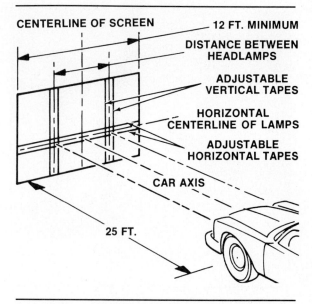

Figure 14-6. Using an aiming screen to adjust headlamps.

• Low-beam — Refer to figure 14-5. The left edge of the lamp high-intensity zone should be horizontally within 4 inches to the right or 4 inches to the left of the lamp center. The top edge of the lamp high-intensity zone should be vertically within 4 inches above or 4 inches below the horizontal centerline.

Remember that these are maximum allowable inspection limits. When adjusting lamp aim, be sure to center the high-intensity zones exactly, both horizontally and vertically.

The limits apply to an aiming screen pattern with the car's lamps 25 feet away. When you use mechanical or photoelectric aiming equipment, check the manufacturer's instructions for establishing equivalent limits.

Aiming screens
An aiming screen is a fixed screen with guidelines on it. The car's lamp beams are projected on the screen and adjusted according to the guidelines.

The screen should be 5 feet high, 12 feet wide, and have a non-gloss white surface. It should be in a large room that can be darkened. The screen must be mounted so that it is perpendicular to the floor, even if the floor slopes. The screen must also be adjustable so that it can be aligned parallel to the car's rear axle.

The guidelines on the screen, figure 14-6, are:
• An adjustable vertical centerline
• At least two adjustable vertical tapes (two tapes must be in front of each lamp during aiming)
• At least two adjustable horizontal tapes.

In addition, a line should be on the floor, parallel to the screen and 25 feet in front of it.

An aiming screen can be used to check and adjust all types of headlamps. To use the screen:
1. Put the car in the test area so that the headlamps are directly over the 25-foot reference line.
2. Adjust the screen so that it is parallel to the car's rear axle.
3. Adjust the vertical centerline tape so that it is in line with the center of the car:
    a. Measure the car's windshield and rear window; mark the centerlines with narrow tape.
    b. Stand behind the car and sight through the windows at the screen.
    c. Have an assistant move the vertical centerline until it is in line with both window centerlines.
4. Adjust high beams first, then low beams, according to these general procedures.
5. Adjust the two vertical tapes so that they are 4 inches to the left and the right of the vertical centerline of the lamp being checked.
6. Adjust the horizontal tapes so that they are 4 inches above and below the horizontal centerline of the lamp being checked.
7. Turn on the lamps and check the aim:
    a. For high beams, refer to figure 14-4.
    b. For low beams, refer to figure 14-5.
8. Adjust the lamps to get the beams within the correct areas.
9. Recheck the vertical and horizontal aim of each lamp before replacing any bezels or trim pieces.
10. If any lamp is out of adjustment, aim all lamps.

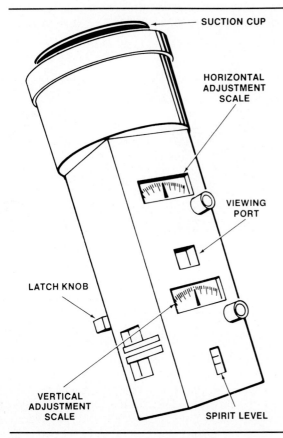

Figure 14-7. A typical mechanical headlamp aimer.

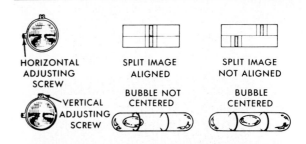

Figure 14-8. The mechanical aimer has adjustments for both horizontal and vertical headlamp aim. (Chrysler)

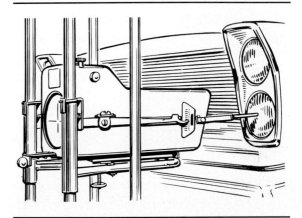

Figure 14-9. A typical photoelectric headlamp aimer.

Mechanical aiming

Mechanical aimers are a pair of portable devices that attach to the headlamp lenses with suction cups, figure 14-7. These aimers can be used on round and rectangular sealed-beams with aiming pads; they cannot be used on bulb-type lamps, lamps without aiming pads, or lamps covered by a fairing.

A set of mechanical aimers usually includes adapter rings for use with various lamp sizes and shapes and a leveling transit to compensate for any slope in the floor. On newer models, the transit may be built into the aimers. Follow the manufacturer's instructions to be sure that the aimers are properly calibrated.

To check or adjust headlamp aim with mechanical aimers:
1. Put the car in the test area.
2. Be sure the headlamps are turned off.
3. Calibrate the aimers.
4. Clamp the aimers in position on the lamp lenses. This may require removing headlamp bezels or trim pieces. Be sure to check 4-lamp systems in matched pairs; that is, both inboard or lower lamps, or both outboard or upper lamps.
5. Check the bubble spirit level or split image on each aimer, figure 14-8. If necessary, use a screwdriver or special tool to turn the headlamp adjusting screws until the bubble is centered or the split image is aligned.
6. After adjusting lamp aim, bounce the car fender to settle the aiming screws. Recheck the bubble spirit level. Remember that adjusting the vertical aim may throw off the horizontal aim, and vice versa. Doublecheck both before replacing the bezels or trim pieces.
7. If any lamp is out of adjustment, aim all lamps.

Photoelectric aiming

Photoelectric, or optical, aimers are mounted on movable frame-type stands, figure 14-9. The stands may be on rollers or tracks on the floor. Because photoelectric aimers contain photocells, they can be used to measure beam intensity as well as lamp aim. They can be used with all headlamps, because they do not mount on the face of the lamp.

To check or adjust headlamp aim with a photoelectric aimer:
1. Position the car in the test area.
2. Turn on the headlamps.
3. Place the aimer in front of the lamps, figure 14-10, as described in the manufacturer's instructions.
4. Check the location of the high-intensity zone on each headlamp. Check Type 1 lamps on high

Figure 14-10. A photoelectric aimer must be properly positioned in front of the headlamp.

Figure 14-11. Many automotive bulb sockets can be removed from the rear of the lamp assembly.

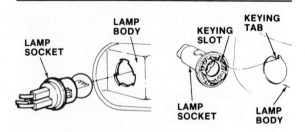

Figure 14-12. The sockets have indexing, or keying, tabs to hold them in the lamp. (Ford)

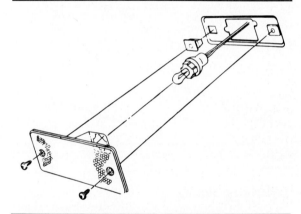

Figure 14-13. This lamp lens is removed by taking screws out from the front of the lamp. (GM)

beam; check Type 2 lamps on low beam.
5. If necessary, turn the lamp adjusting screws while watching the aiming screen.
6. If any lamp is out of adjustment, aim all lamps.

SMALL BULB REPLACEMENT

Most small bulbs used in exterior lighting systems can be removed and replaced from the rear of the lamp assembly. The lens does not have to be removed. You turn the socket base and pull it out of the rear of the lamp assembly, figure 14-11. Some sockets are indexed in different ways, figure 14-12. Be sure that you are removing a socket correctly to avoid damaging it. Other sockets simply snap out of the rear of the lamp housing.

Nonindexed-base bulbs can be pulled from the socket and a replacement bulb pushed in. Indexed bulbs must be pushed into the socket and turned until the bulb is free. The replacement indexed bulb is pushed into the socket and turned until it is secure.

If the rear of the lamp assembly cannot be reached, the lamp lens must be removed before the bulb can be replaced. Lamp lenses must also

be removed for cleaning or replacement. Lenses are attached either with screws on the outside of the car, figure 14-13, or with nuts on the inside of the car, figure 14-14. You may have to remove other trim parts to reach the screws or nuts. When reinstalling the lens, be sure that all gaskets and washers are placed correctly. These protect the lamp assembly from dirt and water, which could damage the bulb and socket.

Some interior lamps, especially those on the instrument panel, can also be replaced from the rear of the lamp assembly. In other cases, you will have to remove the lens to reach the bulb. The lenses can be held by screws or they can be pried loose, figure 14-15.

GENERAL TROUBLESHOOTING PROCEDURES

Some lighting faults can affect all types of circuits. The following paragraphs contain troubleshooting instructions that can be used in many

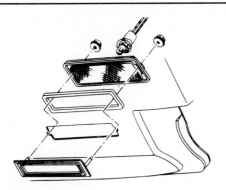

Figure 14-14. This lamp lens is removed by taking nuts off the back of the lamp. (GM)

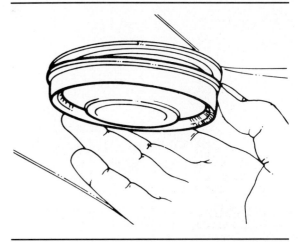

Figure 14-15. Some interior lamp lenses can be pried loose. (AMC)

different cases. The problems examined are:
• One small bulb does not light
• Circuit protector opens repeatedly (fuse or circuit breaker).
    These tests can be made with:
• A voltmeter or a 12-volt test lamp
• An ohmmeter or a self-powered test lamp
• A jumper wire.
Meters will give more accurate results in some tests, such as finding a high-resistance connection that allows enough current flow to light the test lamp but not enough to light the normal bulb.

CAUTION: When working with a jumper wire around a lamp socket, be careful not to connect the jumper wire from the insulated (hot) terminal to ground. This would bypass the bulb, which is the circuit load, and can blow a fuse or burn up a socket connection.

    In most cases, when only one bulb in a circuit will not light, the bulb is at fault. However, there are other problems that will make a single bulb fail. Here is a guide to troubleshooting these cases:
1. Substitute a known-good bulb of the proper type and base; if it will not light, continue the test.
2. Remove the bulb from the socket.
3. Turn on the switch or switches that control current flow to this bulb.
4. Test for battery voltage at the bulb socket by connecting either the voltmeter or the 12-volt test lamp in series between ground and the insulated terminal on the inside of the bulb socket:
    a. If voltage is present, go to step 7.
    b. If voltage is not present, go to step 5.
5. Turn off the switches that control current flow.
6. Use the ohmmeter or the self-powered test lamp to check continuity through the socket insulated terminal (if the socket terminals are

completely encased in plastic, test from the inside of the socket to the nearest connector):
    a. If there is continuity, trace and repair the wiring between the socket and the next common circuit point.
    b. If there is no continuity, replace the socket and any wiring that was included in the test.
7. Reinstall the bulb in the socket.
8. Connect a jumper wire between the socket base and ground.
9. Turn on the switches that control current flow to the bulb:
    a. If the bulb lights, go to step 10.
    b. If the bulb does not light, retest the socket's insulated terminal and the bulb condition.
10. Repair the socket ground connection by cleaning and tightening the socket mounting or by checking continuity through the separate ground wire and connection.

    A short or a ground in a lighting circuit will bypass all or part of the circuit's resistance (bulbs). If too much current flows through the circuit, the circuit protector (fuse or breaker) opens. It is usually easy to recognize this problem, but it can be very hard to find the damaged part of the circuit.

    One way to locate the damage is with a special piece of equipment called a short finder. It consists of a compass and a jumper wire with a circuit breaker in it. The circuit breaker is connected into the problem circuit in place of the original circuit protector. Current will flow through the circuit in short spurts as the circuit breaker opens and closes. When the compass is held near the circuit wiring, its needle is affected by the magnetic field of the conductor. The circuit wiring does not have to be exposed — it can be within a harness or under a carpet and the compass will still be affected. The

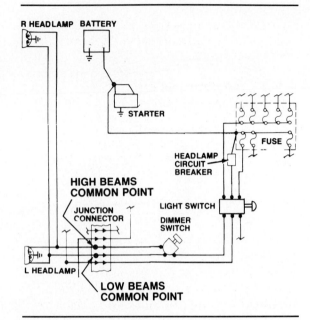

Figure 14-16. A typical grounded-lamp headlamp circuit.

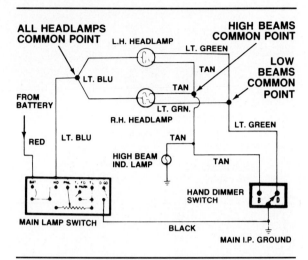

Figure 14-17. A typical insulated-lamp headlamp circuit. (Oldsmobile)

needle will swing back and forth with the spurts of current flow. Move the compass along the circuit wiring until the needle stops swinging. That is the point where the circuit is shorted or grounded to another conductor.

If you do not have a short finder, there is another way to locate the damage:
1. Disconnect all of the connectors in the problem circuit.
2. Put in a new fuse, or let the circuit breaker cool and close.
3. Close the switch or switches in the circuit.
4. Reconnect the circuit sections one by one, starting at the fuse or breaker and working towards ground.
5. When you reconnect a section and the circuit protector opens, you know that the damage is within that section of wiring.

SPECIFIC CIRCUIT TROUBLESHOOTING

The following instructions cover problems within specific lighting circuits. Because wiring is often hard to reach for testing, you may want to start each test by substituting a known-good bulb for the ones that will not light. If the problem still exists, you must continue with the tests described below.

Headlamp Circuit Troubleshooting

Where it applies, these instructions are divided into those for grounded-lamp circuits, figure 14-16, and those for insulated-lamp circuits, figure 14-17. The instructions apply to either

2-lamp or 4-lamp systems.

Some of our tests are affected by the design of the car. For example, we will have you test the dimmer switch before testing the main headlamp switch. This is because, in most systems, the dimmer switch is easier to reach for testing. A floor-mounted dimmer switch is also more likely to fail because of its exposure to dirt and rough handling.

All headlamps do not light — both high- and low-beams
To test a grounded-lamp system:
1. Clean and tighten the bulbs' ground connections.
2. Turn on the main headlamp switch.
3. Test for battery voltage at both terminals on the headlamp side of the dimmer switch, moving the dimmer switch from low-beam to high-beam and back:
   a. If battery voltage is present at each terminal when the dimmer switch is in the appropriate position, test the individual lamp circuit branches as described in the test "One lamp does not light — both high- and low-beams."
   b. If battery voltage is not present, go to step 4.
4. Test for battery voltage at the headlamp switch side of the dimmer switch:
   a. If voltage is present, replace the dimmer switch.
   b. If voltage is not present, go to step 5.
5. Test for battery voltage at the headlamp terminal on the dimmer switch side of the main headlamp switch:
   a. If voltage is present, trace and repair the wiring between the dimmer switch and the main headlamp switch.
   b. If voltage is not present, go to step 6.

6. Test for battery voltage at the battery side of the main headlamp switch:

    a. If voltage is present, replace the main head-iamp switch.

    b. If voltage is not present, trace and repair the wiring between the battery and the main headlamp switch.

    To test an insulated-lamp system:

1. Clean and tighten the ground connection at the dimmer switch.

2. Turn on the main headlamp switch.

3. Test for battery voltage at the ground side of the dimmer switch, moving the switch from low-beam to high-beam and back:

    a. If battery voltage is present at both positions, recheck the dimmer switch ground connection.

    b. If voltage is present at one switch position but not at the other, test the faulty circuit branches as described in the test "All headlamps do not light — low-beam or high-beam only."

    c. If voltage is not present at either switch position, go to step 4.

4. Test for battery voltage at both terminals on the headlamp side of the dimmer switch:

    a. If voltage is present at both terminals, replace the dimmer switch.

    b. If voltage is present at one of the terminals but not at the other, test the faulty circuit branches as described in the test "All headlamps do not light — low-beam or high-beam only."

    c. If voltage is not present at either terminal, go to step 5.

5. Test for battery voltage at the last common circuit point between the headlamps and the main headlamp switch:

    a. If voltage is present, test the individual circuit branches as described in the test "One headlamp does not light — both high- and low-beam."

    b. If voltage is not present, go to step 6.

6. Test for battery voltage at the headlamp terminal on the battery side of the bulkhead disconnect:

    a. If voltage is present, trace and repair the wiring between the last common circuit point and the bulkhead disconnect.

    b. If voltage is not present, go to step 7.

7. Test for battery voltage at the headlamp terminal on the headlamp side of the main headlamp switch:

    a. If voltage is present, trace and repair the wiring between the bulkhead disconnect and the main headlamp switch.

    b. If voltage is not present, go to step 8.

8. Test for battery voltage at the battery side of the main headlamp switch:

    a. If voltage is present, replace the main head-lamp switch.

    b. If voltage is not present, trace and repair the wiring between the battery and the main headlamp switch.

All headlamps do not light — low-beam or high-beam only

To test a grounded-lamp system:

1. Turn on the main headlamp switch.

2. Test for battery voltage at the appropriate terminal on the headlamp side of the dimmer switch, with the dimmer switch in the correct position:

    a. If voltage is present, go to step 3.

    b. If voltage is not present, replace the dimmer switch.

3. Test for battery voltage at the last common circuit point between the appropriate dimmer switch terminal and the headlamps:

    a. If voltage is present, test the individual circuit branches as described in the test "One headlamp does not light — low-beam or high-beam only."

    b. If voltage is not present, trace and repair the wiring between the dimmer switch and the circuit common point.

    To test an insulated-lamp system:

1. Turn on the main headlamp switch.

2. Test for battery voltage at the appropriate terminal on the headlamp side of the dimmer switch, with the switch in the correct position:

    a. If voltage is present, replace the dimmer switch.

    b. If voltage is not present, go to step 3.

3. Test for battery voltage at the last common circuit point between the dimmer switch terminal and the headlamps:

    a. If voltage is present, trace and repair the wiring between the dimmer switch and the common circuit point.

    b. If voltage is not present, test the individual circuit branches as described in the test "One headlamp does not light — low-beam or high-beam only."

One headlamp does not light — both high- and low-beams

To test a grounded-lamp system:

1. Clean and tighten the faulty lamp's ground connection.

2. Turn on the main headlamp switch.

3. Test for battery voltage at both the high- and low-beam terminals on the headlamp side of the headlamp connector, moving the dimmer switch from low-beam to high-beam and back:

    a. If voltage is present at both terminals when the dimmer switch is in the correct position, replace the lamp.

b. If voltage is present at one terminal but not at the other, test the faulty circuit branch as described in the test "One headlamp does not light — low-beam or high-beam only."

c. If voltage is not present at either terminal, go to step 4.

4. Test for battery voltage at both the high- and low-beam wires on the battery side of the connector:

a. If voltage is present at both terminals, replace the connector.

b. If voltage is not present, go to step 5.

5. Test for battery voltage at the last common circuit point between the lamps in both the high-beam and the low-beam circuit branches:

a. If voltage is present, trace and repair the wiring between the headlamp connector and the common point.

b. If voltage is not present, test the system as described in the test "All headlamps do not light — both low- and high-beams."

To test an insulated-lamp system:

1. Turn on the main headlamp switch.

2. Test for battery voltage at the battery terminal on the headlamp side of the headlamp connector:

a. If voltage is present, go to step 5.

b. If voltage is not present, go to step 3.

3. Test for voltage at the battery terminal on the battery side of the connector:

a. If voltage is present, replace the connector.

b. If voltage is not present, go to step 4.

4. Test for battery voltage at the last common point between the main headlamp switch and the lamps:

a. If voltage is present, trace and repair the wiring between the common point and the headlamp connector.

b. If voltage is not present, test the system as described in the test "All headlamps do not light — both low- and high-beams."

5. Substitute a known-good lamp in the circuit:

a. If the lamp lights, the old lamp must be replaced.

b. If the known-good lamp does not light, go to step 6.

6. Test for battery voltage at the high- and low-beam wires on the dimmer switch side of the headlamp connector, moving the dimmer switch from high-beam to low-beam and back:

a. If voltage is present, go to step 7.

b. If voltage is not present, replace the connector.

7. Test for battery voltage at both circuit branch common points between the lamps and the dimmer switch, moving the dimmer switch from low-beam to high-beam and back:

a. If voltage is present, trace and repair the wiring between the common points and the dimmer switch.

b. If voltage is not present, trace and repair

the wiring between the common points and the headlamp connectors.

One headlamp does not light — low-beam or high-beam only

To test a grounded-lamp system:

1. Turn on the main headlamp switch.

2. Test for battery voltage at the appropriate terminal on the headlamp side of the headlamp connector, with the dimmer switch in the correct position:

a. If voltage is present, replace the sealed-beam unit.

b. If voltage is not present, go to step 3.

3. Test for battery voltage at the appropriate wire on the battery side of the headlamp connector:

a. If voltage is present, replace the connector.

b. If voltage is not present, go to step 4.

4. Test for battery voltage at the last common circuit point between the lamps in the appropriate circuit branch:

a. If voltage is present, trace and repair the wiring between the common point and the headlamp connector.

b. If voltage is not present, test the system as described in the test "All headlamps do not light — high-beam or low-beam only."

To test an insulated-lamp system:

1. Turn on the main headlamp switch.

2. Test for battery voltage at the appropriate wire on the ground side of the headlamp connector:

a. If voltage is present, go to step 4.

b. If voltage is not present, go to step 3.

3. Test for continuity through the appropriate terminal of the connector:

a. If there is continuity, replace the sealed-beam unit.

b. If there is no continuity, replace the connector.

4. Test for battery voltage just before the first common point in the appropriate circuit between the lamps:

a. If voltage is present, test the circuit between this point and ground as described in the test "All headlamps do not light — both high- and low-beams."

b. If voltage is not present, trace and repair the wiring between the common point and the connector.

All headlamps dim at idle

Some dimming may be normal when many accessories are used at the same time. If only the headlamps are being used, and they are dim, check the following items:

1. Test the battery for state-of-charge.

2. With the main headlamp switch on, test for full battery voltage at the headlamp connector:

a. If full battery voltage is present, check for

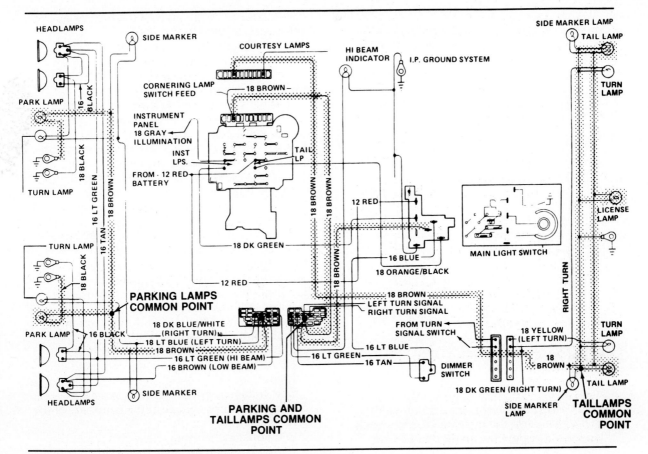

Figure 14-18. A typical parking and taillamp circuit. (Buick)

too much resistance in the circuit between the lamps and ground.

b. If full battery voltage is not present, check for too much resistance in the circuit between the battery and the lamps.

Headlamp dimming at idle can also result from low charging system voltage.

Taillamp, License Plate Lamp, Parking Lamp, Side Marker Lamp, And Clearance Lamp Circuit Troubleshooting

All lamps in one circuit do not light

1. Refer to figures 14-18, 14-19, and 14-20.
2. Check the circuit fuse; replace if necessary.
3. Turn on the main headlamp switch.
4. Test for battery voltage at the last common circuit point between the main headlamp switch and the lamps:

   a. If voltage is present, test the individual circuit branches as if only one lamp did not light.

   b. If voltage is not present, go to step 5.

5. Test for battery voltage at the appropriate terminals on the lamp side of the main headlamp switch:

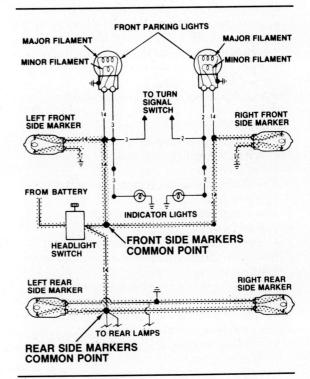

Figure 14-19. A typical side marker circuit, with grounded bulbs. (Ford)

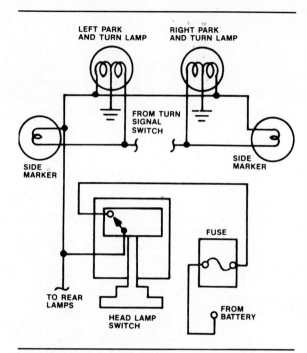

Figure 14-20. A typical side marker circuit, with the bulbs grounded through the turn signal lamps.

a. If voltage is present, trace and repair the wiring between the main headlamp switch and the last common circuit point of the lamps.
b. If voltage is not present, but the headlamps light, replace the main headlamp switch.
c. If voltage is not present, and the headlamps do not light, trace and repair the wiring between the battery and the main headlamp switch; replace the switch if necessary.

Stop Lamp Circuit Troubleshooting

All lamps do not light
If the circuit passes stop lamp current through the turn signal switch, use this test procedure:
1. Refer to figure 14-21, position B.
2. Check the circuit fuse; replace if necessary.
3. Close the brake switch.
4. Test for battery voltage at the last common circuit point of the lamps:
    a. If voltage is present, test the individual circuit branches as if only one lamp did not light.
    b. If voltage is not present, go to step 5.
5. Test for battery voltage on the lamp side of the switch nearest the lamps (either the turn signal switch or the brake switch):
    a. If voltage is present, trace and repair the wiring between the switch and the last common circuit point of the lamps.
    b. If voltage is not present, go to step 6.

6. Test for battery voltage on the battery side of the switch nearest the lamps:
    a. If voltage is present, replace the switch.
    b. If voltage is not present, go to step 7.
7. Test for battery voltage at the lamp side of the switch farthest from the lamps:
    a. If voltage is present, trace and repair the wiring between the two switches.
    b. If voltage is not present, go to step 8.
8. Test for battery voltage at the battery side of the switch farthest from the lamps:
    a. If voltage is present, replace the switch.
    b. If voltage is not present, trace and repair the wiring between the battery and the switch.
    If the circuit does not pass stop lamp current through the turn signal switch, use this test procedure:
1. Refer to figure 14-21, position A.
2. Check the circuit fuse; replace if necessary.
3. Close the brake switch.
4. Test for battery voltage at the last common circuit point of the lamps:
    a. If voltage is present, test the individual circuit branches as if only one lamp did not light.
    b. If voltage is not present, go to step 5.
5. Test for battery voltage at the lamp side of the brake switch:
    a. If voltage is present, trace and repair the wiring between the switch and circuit common point.
    b. If voltage is not present, go to step 6.
6. Test for battery voltage at the battery side of the brake switch:
    a. If voltage is present, replace the switch.
    b. If voltage is not present, trace and repair the wiring between the battery and the switch.

All lamps stay on with brake pedal released
1. Replace brake switch.

Turn Signal And Hazard Flasher Circuit Troubleshooting

All lamps in one circuit do not light
1. Refer to figure 14-21.
2. For turn signal circuit troubleshooting, make all voltage tests with the ignition switch on.
3. Check the circuit fuse.
4. Test for battery voltage at the last common circuit point between the appropriate switch and the bulbs:
    a. If voltage is present, test the individual circuit branches as if only one lamp did not light.
    b. If voltage is not present, go to step 5.

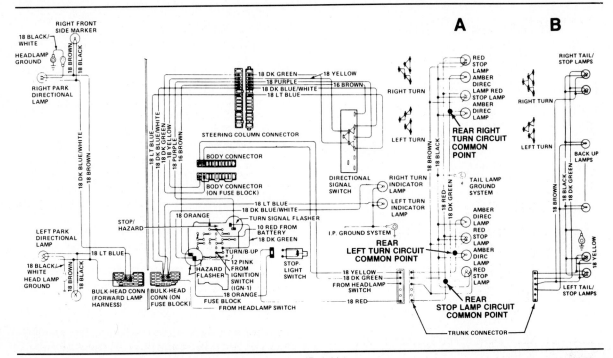

Figure 14-21. Typical stop and turn signal lamp circuits. (Buick)

5. Test for battery voltage at the lamp side of the appropriate switch, with the switch closed. Test the turn signal circuit at the turn signal switch and the hazard flasher circuit at the hazard flasher switch:

    a. If voltage is present, trace and repair the wiring between the switch and the last common circuit point of the lamps.

    b. If voltage is not present, go to step 6.

6. Test for battery voltage at the battery side of the appropriate switch:

    a. If voltage is present, replace the switch.

    b. If voltage is not present, trace and repair the wiring between the battery and the switch.

Flashing rate too fast

1. Check the rating of the flasher unit; replace if necessary.
2. Check the size and type of bulbs in the circuit; replace if necessary.
3. Test the charging system for too much voltage.

No flashing, or flashing rate too slow

1. Check the rating of the flasher unit; replace if necessary.
2. Check the size and type of bulbs in the circuit; replace if necessary.
3. Make voltage drop tests of the circuit wiring to pinpoint any areas of very high resistance; correct as necessary. Be sure to check for high-resistance ground connections.
4. Test the charging system for low voltage.

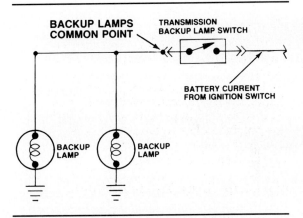

Figure 14-22. A typical backup lamp circuit. (Chrysler)

Backup Lamp Circuit Troubleshooting

All lamps do not light

1. Refer to figure 14-22.
2. Check the circuit fuse; replace if necessary.
3. Turn the ignition switch on.
4. Shift the transmission into Reverse.
5. Test for battery voltage at the last common circuit point of the lamps:

    a. If voltage is present, test the individual circuit branches as if only one lamp did not light.

    b. If voltage is not present, go to step 6.

6. Test for battery voltage at the lamp side of the backup lamp switch:

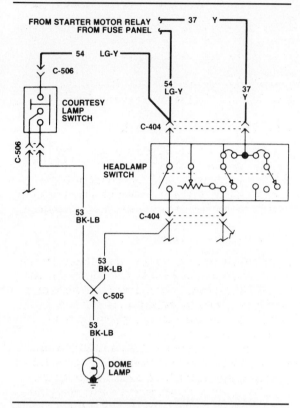

Figure 14-23.   A typical dome lamp circuit. (Ford)

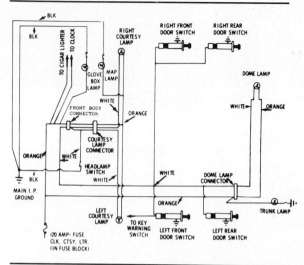

Figure 14-24.   A typical interior lamp circuit. (Oldsmobile)

a. If voltage is present, trace and repair the wiring between the switch and the last common circuit point.

b. If voltage is not present, go to step 7.

7. Test for battery voltage at the battery side of the backup lamp switch:

a. If voltage is present, replace or adjust the switch. Many backup lamp switches are combined with starting safety switches. Adjustment instructions are in Chapter 7.

b. If voltage is not present, trace and repair the wiring between the backup lamp switch and the ignition switch.

Panel And Interior Lamp Circuit Troubleshooting

Panel and interior lamp circuits that are controlled by contacts within the main headlamp switch can be tested using the procedures given for taillamps. If the circuit is controlled by a separate switch or combination of switches, the procedure will be different. Also, if the bulb is insulated and the switch grounded, the testing procedure will be different than if the bulb is

grounded and the switch insulated. The printed circuitry used with some panel lamps cannot be repaired, but must be replaced.

To test a typical panel or interior lamp circuit:

1. Refer to figures 14-23 and 14-24.

2. Check the circuit fuse; replace if necessary.

3. Close the switch or switches in the circuit that should make the lamps light.

4. Clean and tighten the grounded part's ground connection.

5. Test for battery voltage at the battery side of the grounded part:

a. If voltage is present, replace the part.

b. If voltage is not present, go to step 6.

6. Test for battery voltage at the ground side of the insulated part:

a. If voltage is present, trace and repair the wiring between the insulated part and the grounded part.

b. If voltage is not present, go to step 7.

7. Check for continuity through the insulated part:

a. If there is continuity, go to step 8.

b. If there is no continuity, replace the part.

8. Test for battery voltage at the first common circuit point of the lamp:

a. If voltage is present, trace and repair the wiring between the insulated part and the common circuit point.

b. If voltage is not present, trace and repair the wiring between the common circuit point and the ignition switch or fuse panel.

15

Horn, Windshield Wiper and Washer, and Instrument Service

These common accessory circuits do not require frequent service. When they do, the following troubleshooting instructions will help you solve the problem. In many cases, you will need to have the manufacturer's specifications and circuit diagrams for the system you are testing.

HORN SYSTEM SERVICE

If a horn will sound but the tone is not right, it can be adjusted. If a horn does not sound at all, or if it cannot be shut off, the circuit must be tested. Testing instructions for different types of horn systems follow the adjustment procedure.

Adjusting Horn Tone

If the adjuster nut can be reached, figure 15-1, a horn can be adjusted while it is mounted in the car. If the nut cannot be reached, the horn must be removed and adjusted on a test bench. In either case, be sure the horn's ground connection is secure.

Horns are adjusted to draw a specified amperage, usually between 3 and 8 amperes. Do not try to muffle the horn's sound during testing. This affects the amperage draw, and your test will be inaccurate. In multiple-horn systems, disconnect the wire from one horn while you adjust the other.
1. Refer to figures 15-2 and 15-3.
2. Remove the wire from the horn being adjusted.
3. Connect the ammeter positive (+) lead to the wire. Connect the ammeter negative (−) lead to the terminal on the horn.
4. Sound the horn and observe the ammeter reading. Compare it to the manufacturer's specifications:
   a. If the reading is within specifications but the horn tone is bad, replace the horn.
   b. If the reading is not within specifications, go to step 5.

CAUTION: Do not turn the horn adjustment nut while the horn is sounding, or the horn will be damaged.

5. Turn the horn adjustment nut 1/10-turn at a time. Repeat step 4 between each 1/10-turn until the ammeter reading is within specifications.

Horn Circuit Troubleshooting

If the horn will not sound, or if it cannot be shut off, use these instructions to pinpoint the problem. Where it applies, the tests are divided into those for single- or multiple-horn systems, with and without a horn relay.

Figure 15-1. If the adjuster nut is within reach, the horn does not have to be removed from the car for adjustment. (Chrysler)

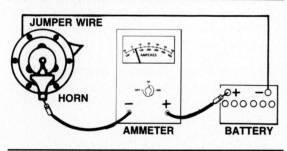

Figure 15-3. Testing and adjusting the horn out of the car. (AMC)

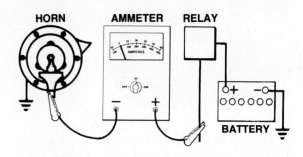

Figure 15-2. Testing and adjusting the horn while it is installed in the car. (AMC)

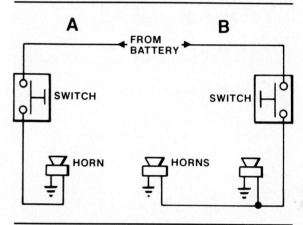

Figure 15-4. Horn systems without relays: position A, one horn; position B, two horns.

Horn will not sound — single-horn system

If the system has no horn relay:
1. Refer to figure 15-4, position A.
2. Check the circuit fuse or fusible link.
3. Clean and tighten the horn ground connection.
4. Close the horn switch.
5. Test for battery voltage at the terminal on the horn:
    a. If voltage is present, replace the horn.
    b. If voltage is not present, go to step 6.
6. Test for battery voltage at the horn side of the horn switch:
    a. If voltage is present, trace and repair the wiring between the switch and the horn.
    b. If voltage is not present, go to step 7.
7. Test for battery voltage at the battery side of the horn switch:
    a. If voltage is present, replace the horn switch.

    b. If voltage is not present, trace and repair the wiring between the battery and the switch.
    If the system has a horn relay:
1. Refer to figure 15-5.
2. Check the circuit's fuse or fusible link.
3. Clean and tighten the horn's ground connection.
4. Close the horn switch.
5. Test for battery voltage at the terminal on the horn:
    a. If voltage is present, replace the horn.
    b. If voltage is not present, go to step 6.
6. Test for battery voltage at the armature terminal on the horn side of the horn relay (terminal 3 in figure 15-5):
    a. If voltage is present, trace and repair the wiring between the relay and the horn.
    b. If voltage is not present, go to step 7.
7. Test for battery voltage at the battery feed terminal of the horn relay (terminal 1 in figure 15-5):
    a. If voltage is present, go to step 8.
    b. If voltage is not present, trace and repair the wiring between the battery and the relay.

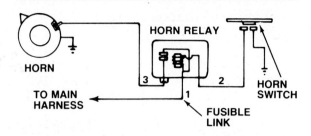

Figure 15-5. A single-horn system with a horn relay. (AMC)

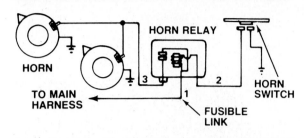

Figure 15-6. A multiple-horn system with a horn relay. (AMC)

8. Test for battery voltage at the horn switch terminal on the horn relay (terminal 2 in figure 15-5):
   a. If voltage is present, go to step 9.
   b. If voltage is not present, replace the horn relay.
9. Test for battery voltage on the battery side of the horn switch:
   a. If voltage is present, go to step 10.
   b. If voltage is not present, trace and repair the wiring between the relay and the horn switch.
10. Test for battery voltage on the ground side of the horn switch:
   a. If voltage is present, go to step 11.
   b. If voltage is not present, replace the horn switch.
11. Clean and tighten the horn switch ground connection; if the horn still does not sound, replace the horn relay.

Horns will not sound — multiple-horn system
If the system has no horn relay:
1. Refer to figure 15-4, position B.
2. Check the circuit's fuse or fusible link.
3. Close the horn switch.
4. Test for battery voltage at the last common circuit point between the horns and the horn switch:
   a. If voltage is present, test each horn's circuit branch as described in the test "Horn will not sound — single-horn system," steps 2 through 5.
   b. If voltage is not present, go to step 5.
5. Test for battery voltage on the horn side of the horn switch:
   a. If voltage is present, trace and repair the wiring between the horn switch and the common circuit point.
   b. If voltage is not present, go to step 6.
6. Test for battery voltage on the battery side of the horn switch:
   a. If voltage is present, replace the horn switch.
   b. If voltage is not present, trace and repair the wiring between the horn switch and the battery.

If the system has a horn relay:
1. Refer to figure 15-6.
2. Check the circuit's for fuse or fusible link.
3. Close the horn switch.
4. Test for battery voltage at the last common circuit point between the horns and the horn relay:
   a. If voltage is present, test each horn's individual circuit branch as described in the test "Horn will not sound — single-horn system," steps 3 through 6.
   b. If voltage is not present, test the horn relay and horn switch circuitry as described in the test "Horn will not sound — single-horn system," steps 6 through 10.

One horn will not sound — multiple-horn system
1. Test the horn's individual circuit branch as described in the test "Horn will not sound — single-horn system," steps 3 through 6 of the with-relay or without-relay test.

Horn will not shut off — system with no horn relay
In either a single-horn or a multiple-horn system with no relay, a continuously sounding horn must be caused by the horn switch contacts sticking closed. Check for continuity through the horn switch. If there is continuity through the switch when it should be open, replace it.

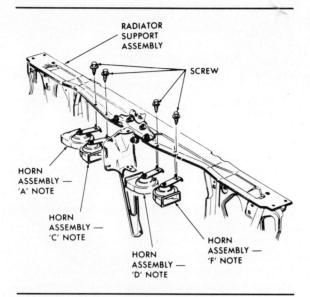

Figure 15-7. A typical horn installation. This automobile has four different horns tuned F^6. (Cadillac)

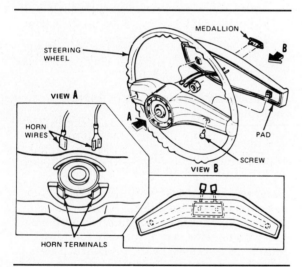

Figure 15-9. This Ford horn switch has two leads and terminals because it is used in a system that has no horn relay — all of the current that flows to the horns must pass through this switch. (Ford)

Horn will not shut off — system with horn relay

In either a single-horn or a multiple-horn system with a horn relay, a continuously sounding horn could be caused by sticking contact in the horn switch or the relay. Check for continuity through the horn switch and the relay armature circuit. If there is continuity when there should be none, replace the part.

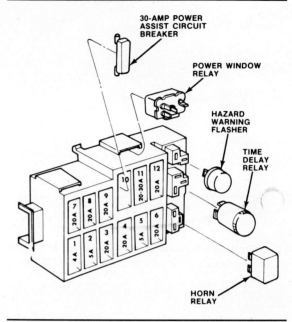

Figure 15-8. The horn relay can plug into the fuse panel. (Chrysler)

Replacing Horn System Parts

To replace a horn, screw or bolt the new part into the mounting holes of the old part, figure 15-7. Some manufacturers use a specially plated, corrosion-resistant screw for the ground connection. Be sure that this is used with the new horn.

If the horn relay is mounted in the engine compartment, the new part can be bolted or screwed into the mounting holes of the old part. The relay may be mounted on the fuse panel, figure 15-8. The new part is plugged into the proper terminals on the panel.

Horn switches are mounted in the center of the steering column. All or part of the steering wheel may have to be removed to expose the switch. Some typical switch installations are shown in figures 15-9, 15-10, and 15-11.

WINDSHIELD WIPER AND WASHER SERVICE

Windshield wiper and washer systems vary greatly from manufacturer to manufacturer, but some basic troubleshooting instructions can be applied to all electrical parts of the systems. In some cases, you must have the manufacturer's specifications and diagrams for the system you are testing.

Windshield Wiper System Testing — On-Car

The windshield wipers can stop working because of an electrical problem or a mechanical

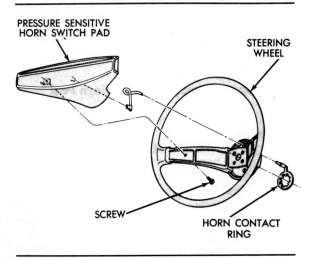

Figure 15-10. This Chrysler horn switch can be closed by pressure on any part of the central pad. It is a grounding switch, and so has only one lead and terminal. (Chrysler)

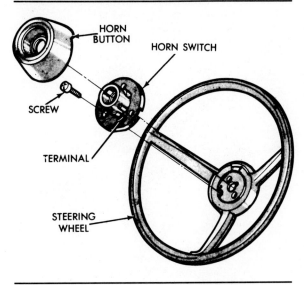

Figure 15-11. A simple horn switch installation. (Chrysler)

bind in the wiper arm linkage. Generally, if the wipers will work in one speed but not another, the problem will be electrical. An exception to this would be in a depressed-park system. If the wipers will not depress properly, it could be a mechanical or an electrical problem.

To tell the difference in these cases, disconnect the wiper arm linkage from the motor. If the motor now works in all speeds, a mechanical bind is causing the problem. If the motor still will not work, the problem is electrical.

Make a preliminary check of the system to see that:
- The fuse or circuit breaker is not open.
- The wiper motor ground connection is clean and tight.
- The connectors at the wiper motor, wiper switch, and any system relays or governors are tight.

If the problem is still not evident:
1. Turn on the ignition switch.
2. Turn the wiper switch to low speed, or to the speed at which the motor will not work.
3. Test for battery voltage at the appropriate terminal on the wiper motor:
   a. If voltage is present, the motor must be removed for further testing or replacement.
   b. If voltage is not present, go to step 4.
4. Test for battery voltage at the appropriate terminal on the motor side of the wiper switch:
   a. If voltage is present, trace and repair the wiring between the switch and the motor.
   b. If voltage is not present, go to step 5.
5. Test for battery voltage at the battery side of the wiper switch:

   a. If voltage is present, replace the switch.
   b. If voltage is not present, trace and repair the wiring between the battery and the switch. Be sure to check the ignition switch teminals and the fuse panel.

Windshield Washer System Testing

If no fluid is sprayed when the washer is turned on, the problem could be in the pump or in the delivery system of hoses and nozzles. To tell the difference between these cases, disconnect the main hose from the washer pump. Turn on the washer switch. If the pump sprays fluid, then the problem is in the delivery system. If the pump does not spray, it is defecitve and must be replaced.

Windshield Wiper And Washer System Part Replacement

Some parts of windshield wiper motors can be rebuilt, but they are often simply replaced if faulty. They are mounted at the base of the windshield, usually on the engine compartment side. Some typical wiper motor installations are shown in figures 15-12, 15-13, and 15-14.

Windshield washer pumps are replaced if faulty. Some GM systems have pumps mounted in the wiper motor, figure 15-15. Most others are mounted in or near the washer fluid reservoir. Typical installations are shown in figures 15-16 and 15-17.

Control switches can be mounted on the instrument panel, figure 15-18, or on a lever (stalk) on the steering column, figure 15-19.

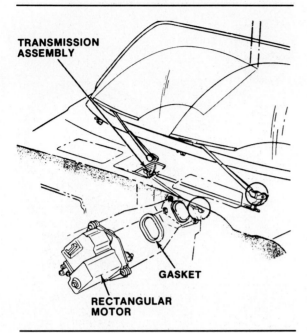

Figure 15-12. A typical GM windshield wiper motor installation. (GM)

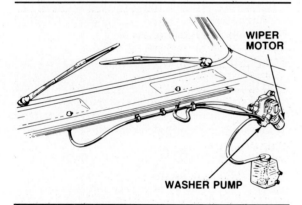

Figure 15-15. Some GM washer pumps are mounted on the windshield wiper motor.

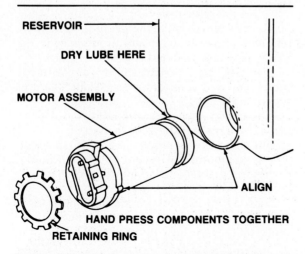

Figure 15-16. The Ford windshield washer pump. (Ford)

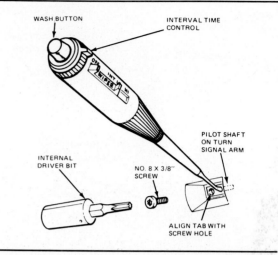

Figure 15-13. A typical Ford windshield wiper motor installation.

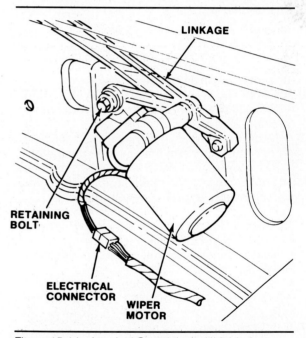

Figure 15-14. A typical Chrysler windshield wiper motor installation.

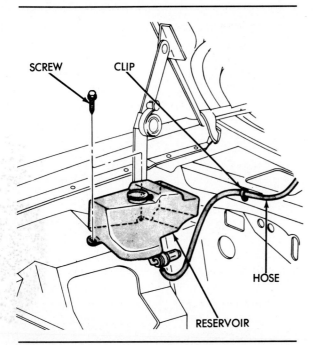

Figure 15-17. The Chrysler windshield washer pump. (Chrysler)

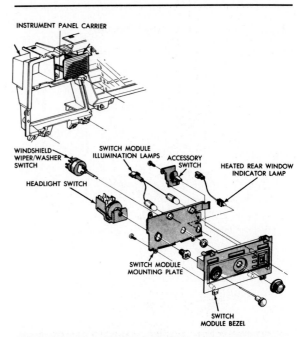

Figure 15-18. Many windshield wiper switches are mounted on the instrument panel. (Chrysler)

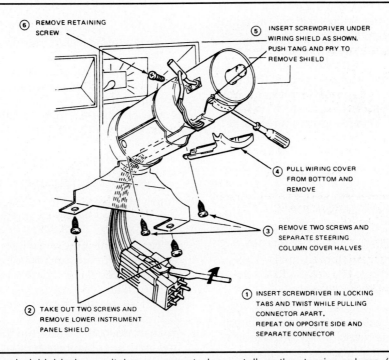

Figure 15-19. Some windshield wiper switches are mounted on a stalk on the steering column. (Ford)

INSTRUMENT SERVICE

The following paragraphs contain troubleshooting instructions for the most common gauges, warning lamps, and buzzers. Many manufacturers use printed circuitry in the instrument panel. If the printed circuitry opens or shorts, the entire piece must be replaced.

Before testing any instrument that seems to be faulty, make sure that the engine condition it monitors is truly normal. For example, if a coolant temperature gauge or warning lamp indicator indicates an overheated engine, test the engine cooling system before assuming that the instrument is wrong.

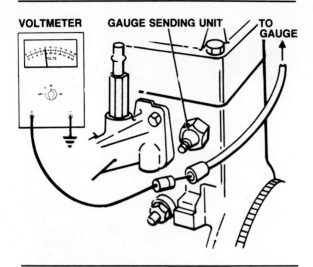

Figure 15-20. Testing the instrument voltage regulator at one of the gauge sending units. (Ford)

Instrument Voltage Regulator Testing And Replacement

An important part of many gauge systems is the instrument voltage regulator. If it is not working properly, none of the gauges will give accurate readings. The gauges could even be damaged by excessive voltage if the regulator fails. In some systems, the regulator only serves a few of the gauges. The rest work on unregulated system voltage. Be sure you know which gauges work on regulated voltage and which do not.

The intrument voltage regulator is often at fault when:
• All regulated-voltage gauges fail at once.
• All regulated-voltage gauges give inaccurate readings.
• All regulated-voltage gauge needles vibrate by more than the needle's width.

CAUTION: When testing the regulator while it is connected to battery voltage, do not ground or short any of the regulator terminals. This could damage both the regulator and the instrument panel wiring harness.

You should use a voltmeter to test the regulator. A 12-volt test lamp can be used, but it will not show you if the regulator is working to the manufacturer's specifications.

If the regulator is hard to reach for testing, you can make a quick test at one of the gauge sending units in the engine compartment. If the test results show a faulty regulator, you must continue to test the regulator itself:
• If the regulator can be reached, and if the instrument panel has multistrand wiring, the regulator can be tested at its mounting.
• If the regulator cannot be reached with test leads, or if the instrument panel has printed circuitry, the regulator must be removed for testing.

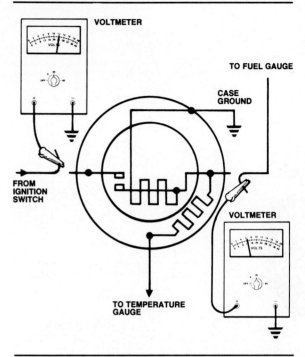

Figure 15-21. Testing the instrument voltage regulator at the instrument panel. (AMC)

To begin the test in the engine compartment:
1. Refer to figure 15-20.
2. Check the circuit fuse; replace if necessary.
3. Disconnect the wire from one of the gauge sending units.
4. Connect the voltmeter positive (+) lead to the wire. Connect the voltmeter negative (−) lead to ground.
5. Turn on the ignition switch and observe the voltmeter:
   a. If the needle is rapidly pulsating from zero to a positive voltage, the regulator is working.
   b. If the needle does not pulsate as described, go to step 6.
6. Turn off the ignition switch, reconnect the sending unit wire, and continue the test:
   a. If the regulator can be tested at its mounting, go to step 7.
   b. If the regulator must be removed for testing, go to step 11.
7. Disconnect the wire from the gauge side of the instrument voltage regulator, figure 15-21.
8. Connect the voltmeter positive (+) lead to the exposed regulator terminal. Connect the voltmeter negative (−) lead to ground.
9. Turn on the ignition switch and observe the voltmeter:
   a. If the needle pulsates as described in step 5a, the regulator is working.
   b. If the needle does not pulsate as described, go to step 10.
10. Test for battery voltage at the battery side of the regulator:
   a. If voltage is present, replace the regulator.

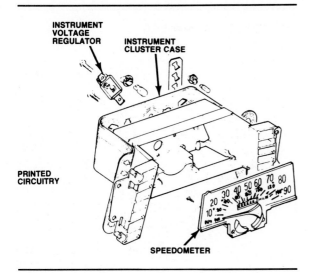

Figure 15-22. A typical instrument voltage regulator mounting. (AMC)

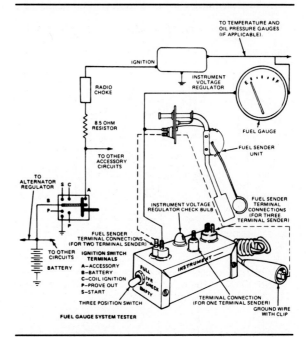

Figure 15-23. Ford's special tester for the fuel gauge system. (Ford)

b. If voltage is not present, trace and repair the wiring between the battery and the regulator. Repeat steps 7 through 10.
11. Remove the instrument voltage regulator from its mounting.
12. Connect the voltmeter positive (+) lead to the terminal on the gauge side of the regulator. Connect the voltmeter negative (−) lead to ground.
13. Connect a jumper wire between the terminal on the battery side of the regulator and the battery positive (+) terminal.
14. Observe the voltmeter:
   a. If the needle is pulsating as described in step 5a, the regulator is working.
   b. If the needle is not pulsating as described in step 5a, replace the regulator.

Most instrument voltage regulators are separate units, figure 15-22, held to the back of the instrument panel by screws or nuts or plugged into a printed circuit board. You may have to remove some instrument panel trim or part of the panel to reach it. If the regulator is built into a gauge, the entire gauge must be replaced if the regulator is faulty.

Testing Gauges And Sending Units

The most common electrical gauges are either bimetallic or electromagnetic. Both types depend on a variable-resistance sending unit to control the amount of current flow through the gauge. The ammeter is an exception to this, and will be covered in a separate test later in this chapter.

If only one gauge fails or shows an inaccurate reading, the problem is probably in that gauge's circuit branch. If all of the gauges fail or show inaccurate readings, the problem is probably in

their shared circuitry. These tests can be made using:
• A voltmeter or a 12-volt test lamp
• A field rheostat or a known-good sending unit.
You will need the manufacturer's specifications for sending-unit resistance if you use a field rheostat. Some manufacturers have special testers that can be used instead of a known-good sending unit, such as the Ford fuel gauge tester shown in figure 15-23.

Single gauge failure
To test a single faulty gauge:
1. Check the circuit fuse; replace if necessary.
2. Disconnect the wire from the gauge sending unit.
3. Turn on the ignition switch.
4. Use the voltmeter or 12-volt test lamp to test for battery or regulated voltage at the gauge sending unit, figure 15-20:
   a. If the proper voltage is present, go to step 5.
   b. If voltage is present but it is not properly regulated, test the instrument voltage regulator.
   c. If voltage is not present, go to step 8.
5. Connect the sending unit wire to:
   a. The field rheostat lead; connect the second rheostat lead to ground.
   b. A known-good sending unit; connect a jumper wire between the sending unit and ground. For oil-pressure sending units or in cases in which the wire cannot reach the new unit, install the known-good sending unit in the proper mounting.

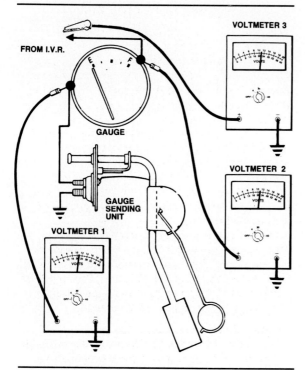

Figure 15-24. Testing an individual gauge's circuit branch. (Ford)

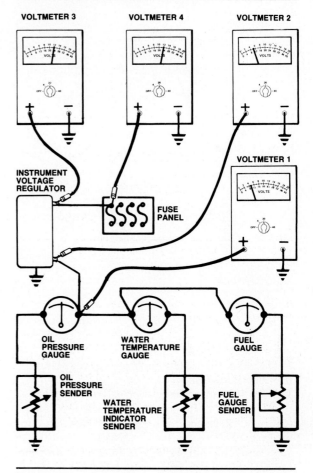

Figure 15-25. Testing the gauge system's shared circuitry.

c. The manufacturer's special tester.

6. Vary the resistance of the test sender by:
   a. Adjusting the field rheostat to varying resistances as specified by the manufacturer.
   b. Operating the known-good sending unit by moving its float, heating it, or running the engine as required.
   c. Following the instructions for the manufacturer's special tester.

7. Observe the gauge:
   a. If the gauge now operates properly, replace the sending unit.
   b. If the gauge still does not operate properly, replace the gauge.

8. Reconnect the wire to the sending unit.

9. Use the voltmeter or the 12-volt test lamp to test for battery or regulated voltage at the sending unit side of the gauge, figure 15-24:
   a. If voltage is not present, go to step 10.
   b. If voltage is present, trace and repair the wiring between the gauge and the sending unit.

10. Test for battery or regulated voltage at the battery side of the gauge:
    a. If the voltage is present, replace the gauge.
    b. If voltage is not present, go to step 11.

11. Test for battery or regulated voltage at the gauge system common circuit point:
    a. If voltage is present, trace and repair the wiring between the common circuit point and the gauge.
    b. If voltage is not present, trace and repair

the gauge system shared circuitry as explained in the following test.

Multiple gauge failure

If all of the gauges in a circuit fail or show inaccurate readings:

1. Refer to figure 15-25.
2. Check the circuit fuse; replace if necessary.
3. Turn on the ignition switch.
4. Use the voltmeter or the 12-volt test lamp to test for battery or regulated voltage at the gauge system's last common circuit point:
   a. If the proper voltage is present, test the individual gauge circuit branches as explained in the first test.
   b. If voltage is present but it is not properly regulated, test the instrument voltage regulator.
   c. If voltage is not present, go to step 5.
5. Test for regulated voltage at the gauge side of the voltage regulator, if present:
   a. If voltage is present, trace and repair the wiring between the regulator and the gauge common circuit point.
   b. If voltage is not present, go to step 6.

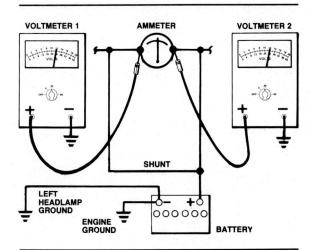

Figure 15-26. Testing the ammeter circuitry. (Chrysler)

6. Test for battery voltage at the battery side of the regulator, if present:
    a. If voltage is present, replace the regulator.
    b. If voltage is not present, go to step 7.
7. Test for battery voltage at the appropriate terminal on the gauge side of the fuse panel:
    a. If voltage is present, trace and repair the wiring between the fuse panel and the regulator, if present, or the last common gauge circuit point.
    b. If voltage is not present, recheck the fuse. Trace and repair the wiring between the fuse panel and the battery.

Ammeter testing

To test an ammeter's circuit branch:
1. Refer to figure 15-26.
2. Turn on the ignition switch but do not start the engine.
3. Turn on the headlamps and other accessories.
4. Observe the ammeter needle:
    a. If the needle moves to the discharge side of the scale, the gauge is working correctly.
    b. If the needle moves to the charge side of the scale, the ammeter connections are reversed.
    c. If the needle does not move, go to step 5.
5. With a voltmeter or a 12-volt test lamp, test for battery voltage at the alternator side of the ammeter:
    a. If voltage is present, trace and repair the wiring between the ammeter and the alternator.
    b. If voltage is not present, go to step 6.
6. Test for battery voltage at the battery side of the ammeter:
    a. If voltage is present, replace the ammeter.
    b. If voltage is not present, trace and repair the wiring between the ammeter and the battery.

Testing Warning Lamps and Buzzers

Warning lamps and buzzers are controlled by one or more switches. The exception to this is the charging system warning lamp, which is controlled by current flow into and out of the battery. Tests of the charging system warning lamps are covered separately, manufacturer by manufacturer.

The rest of the warning lamps and buzzers are either grounded units controlled by insulated switches or insulated units controlled by grounded switches. Seatbelt warning systems often include a timed circuit breaker so that the lamp and buzzer work for a short period of time and then shut off.

You may want to start each test by substituting a known-good lamp or buzzer in the circuit, especially if only that one unit has failed. If this does not solve the problem, the circuit can be tested in the same way as the interior lamp circuits we tested in Chapter 14.

Testing alternator warning lamps

Always test the charging system as explained in Chapter 5 to be sure it is in proper operating condition before troubleshooting the warning lamp circuit.

Tests of the warning lamp used with a Delco-Remy 10-SI are grouped under three conditions:
• The lamp stays on when the ignition switch is off.
• The lamp is off while the ignition switch is on and the engine is stopped.
• The lamp stays on while the engine is running.

Be sure that the battery and the charging system are in good condition before testing the lamp.

If the lamp stays on with the ignition switch off:
1. Disconnect the leads from the number 1 and the number 2 terminals at the alternator:
    a. If the lamp goes out, the alternator diode bridge is faulty.
    b. If the lamp stays on, there is a short between the leads to the number 1 and number 2 terminals.

If the lamp is off when the ignition switch is on and the engine is stopped:
1. Repeat step 1 of the previous test.
2. Check for an open in the warning lamp circuit, such as:
    a. A blown fuse
    b. A burned-out bulb
    c. A defective bulb socket
    d. An open in the number 1 lead between the alternator and the ignition switch.

If the lamp stays on when the engine is running:
1. Check for a blown 20-ampere air conditioning fuse between the warning lamp and the ignition switch.

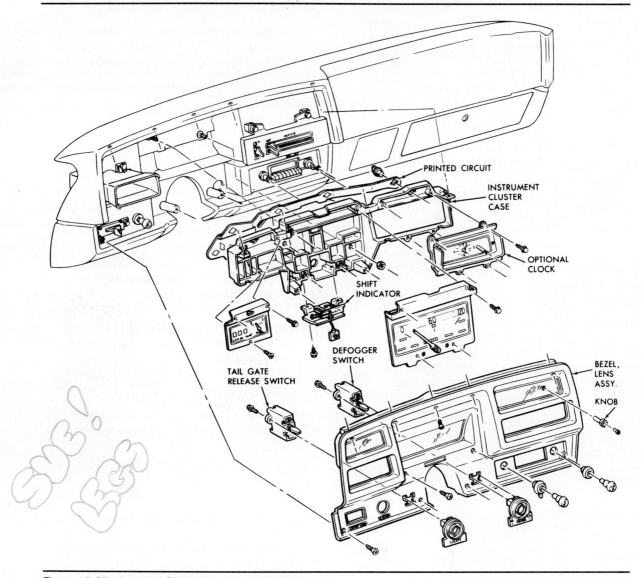

Figure 15-27. A typical GM instrument panel. (Chevrolet)

If the warning lamp used with a Delco-Remy 10-DN system will not go out when the engine is running, check for:
• A problem with the charging system
• A defective bulb socket
• An open in the regulator, the field, or the charging system wiring.

If the warning lamp in a Ford system does not come on when it should, check for:
• A burned-out bulb
• A defective bulb socket
• An open in the warning lamp circuitry.

If the lamp stays on when it should go off:

1. With the ignition switch off, disconnect the multiple-plug connector from the voltage regulator.
2. Turn the ignition switch on.
3. Connect a 12-volt test lamp (using a No. 67 or 1155 bulb) between the base of the regulator and the I terminal on the regulator:
   a. If the test lamp lights, the circuit is all right.
   b. If the test lamp does not light but the warning lamp does, there is an open in either the warning lamp circuit or the resistor that is connected in parallel with the lamp.

   To test LED warning on a Chrysler ammeter face:

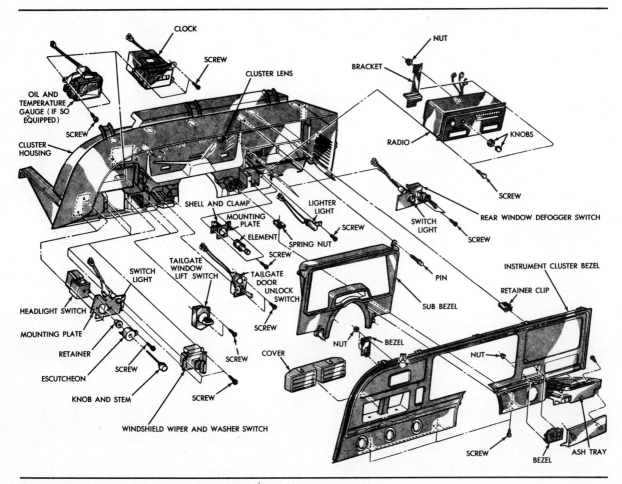

Figure 15-28. A typical Chrysler instrument panel. (Chrysler)

1. If the battery and charging systems are all right but the LED stays lighted, replace the gauge.
2. If the LED does not light, turn on the ignition switch but do not start the engine.
3. Turn on the headlamps and other accessories and observe the LED:
    a. If it does not light within one minute, replace the gauge.
    b. If it lights, go to step 4.
4. Start and run the engine at a fast idle. If the LED does not go off, replace the gauge.

    To test the warning lamp in a Motorola alternator system, check all system fuses. If the bulb lights when the engine is running, check for:
- An open in the instrument panel printed circuitry

- A short in the wiring between the bulb and the regulator.

If the bulb flashes while the engine is running, check the yellow feed wire to the printed circuitry. If the bulb does not light when the ignition switch is on and the engine is stopped, check for:
- A defective bulb
- An open in the printed circuitry
- An open between the regulator and the printed circuitry.

Instrument Replacement

You will have to disassemble all or part of the instrument panel to replace a gauge, lamp, or buzzer. Figures 15-27 and 15-28 show some typical instrument panel assemblies.

Index

Ig. Sw.

B S

Solenoid

S

starter
motor

Batt
12v